Managers of Global Cha

Managers of Global Change

The Influence of International Environmental Bureaucracies

edited by Frank Biermann and Bernd Siebenhüner

Institutional Dimensions of Global Environmental Change
A Core Research Project of the International Human Dimensions
Programme on Global Environmental Change (IHDP)

The MIT Press
Cambridge, Massachusetts
London, England

This book was set in Sabon by SNP Best-set Typesetter Ltd., Hong Kong. Printed and bound in the United States of America.

Library of Congress Cataloging-in-Publication Data

Managers of global change : the influence of international environmental bureaucracies / edited by Frank Biermann and Bernd Siebenhüner.
  p. cm.
Includes bibliographical references and index.
ISBN 978-0-262-01274-4 (hardcover : alk. paper)—ISBN 978-0-262-51236-7 (pbk. : alk. paper)
1. International officials and employees. 2. Environmental agencies—Officials and employees. 3. Environmental policy. I. Biermann, Frank. II. Siebenhüner, Bernd.
JZ4850.M35   2009
341.4—dc22

                                                                    2008042142

Printed on Recycled Paper.

In memoriam
Gerhard Petschel-Held

Contents

Preface

This book is the result of a journey that brought together more than a dozen researchers with a shared interest in the role of international organizations and, more specifically, of international bureaucracies in world politics.

The first idea for this project was developed in 2000 by a group of three researchers at the Potsdam Institute for Climate Impact Research in Germany. It was a combination of three academic concerns: Frank Biermann had a long-standing interest in the reform of the United Nations, in particular, in the field of the environment. In 1997, he published a proposal on the establishment of a world environment organization that would replace the United Nations Environment Programme, and has since participated in several policy networks on this issue. Whatever the benefits of a new agency, it became obvious that the theory of international relations lacked detailed understanding of the role of international bureaucracies in world politics. Bernd Siebenhüner had developed at the same time an interest in social learning and the role of knowledge in organizational change. Much research in this area focused on private organizations or national bureaucracies, and it appeared interesting to apply these theories and hypotheses to international bureaucracies. Combining international relations theory with management theory to study the behavior of international bureaucracies became thus a fruitful avenue for a joint research project.

Gerhard Petschel-Held was the third colleague involved in developing this research idea. Gerhard at the time specialized in computer-based modeling of social processes. His first research projects in this field focused on local questions, such as land degradation or fisheries. This project on international bureaucracies provided a unique opportunity to pioneer new analytical methods at a higher scale of social organization, and in a different context. Gerhard was a great source of inspiration in the early stages of this project, and his analytical rigor as a physicist, combined with a deep interest in social issues and in environmental policy and social justice, had a major impact on the final product of this research. Gerhard passed away in September 2005. We miss his ideas, his brilliance, his enthusiasm, and his humor. We dedicate this volume to his memory.

The project—which became known as the "MANUS (Managers of Global Change)" Project—has subsequently involved a large number of researchers, most of whom participated in this book as authors of the conceptual or empirical chapters. In addition, the project has drawn on the support and constructive criticism of Philipp H. Pattberg, Kunihiko Shimada, and Hans-Dieter Sohn. In particular, we wish to thank the student researchers and interns associated with this project: Romy Dudek, Johannes Ebeling, Anna Schreyögg, Mathijs Seegers, Bonne van der Veen, David Wabnitz, and Carolin Zerger. Many thanks also to Marc Heinitz, who compiled the index.

The book builds on interviews and surveys of almost three hundred international civil servants and experts involved with international bureaucracies. We wish to thank all of them for their time and insights, without which this book would not have been possible. All case studies have been reviewed by a number of experts in the respective fields, whom the case authors acknowledge in their chapters. In addition, we thank those colleagues who provided comments, suggestions, empirical data, and encouragement for the overall project during the last years: our thanks to Steinar Andresen, Richard E. Benedick, William C. Clark, Daniel Compagnon, Tom Dedeurwaerdere, Bharat Desai, Hansjörg Elshorst, Aarti Gupta, Peter M. Haas, Klaus Jacob, Martin Jänicke, Sheila Jasanoff, Norichika Kanie, Marc A. Levy, Ronald B. Mitchell, Udo E. Simonis, Klaus Töpfer, and Michael Zürn.

A special thank to John Schellnhuber, the director of the Potsdam Institute for Climate Impact Research, who not only provided intellectual stimulation for this project but also enabled a stimulating environment at the Potsdam Institute that made work on this project a pleasant experience. In addition, we wish to thank the other institutions that have hosted and supported researchers involved in this project: the Environmental Policy Research Centre at the Freie Universität Berlin, the Carl von Ossietzky Universität Oldenburg, and the Institute for Environmental Studies at the Vrije Universiteit Amsterdam.

Throughout its duration, the project has enjoyed the endorsement and moral and material support of the core project "Institutional Dimensions of Global Environmental Change" of the International Human Dimensions Programme on Global Environmental Change. We wish to thank in particular Oran R. Young, chair of these programs, for his continuous support and encouragement.

Funding for this project was ensured through a four-year grant from the Volkswagen Foundation of Germany, which supported this research from January 2002 through December 2005. We owe our gratitude in particular to Professor Hagen Hof of the Volkswagen Foundation, who was responsible for this project throughout its duration and at several times went the extra mile to increase flexibility in project management and finances. Additional funding was provided by Caixa d'Estalvis i Pensions de Barcelona Foundation, Spain (Mireia Tarradell); Caja Madrid Foundation, Spain (Mireia Tarradell); Carlo Schmid Foundation, Germany (Robert Marschinski); German Academic Exchange Service (Mireia Tarradell); and the German National Merit Foundation (Klaus Dingwerth).

Finally, we are grateful to the MIT Press for a speedy and professional process in turning this manuscript into a book. We thank in particular our editor at the press, Clay Morgan, for instant valuable feedback, and three anonymous reviewers, who provided us, in addition to their generally positive assessment, with nine pages of detailed comments and much "food for thought." Last but not least, we are grateful to manuscript editor Kathleen A. Caruso and copyeditor Nancy Kotary for help copyediting this lengthy manuscript that was written exclusively by non-native speakers.

This book has been an intense learning process for all involved. As such, it has been both inspiring and enjoyable. Whatever the detailed results of this project, as laid out in the thirteen chapters of this book, nothing has changed the generally optimistic and normatively positive attitude that all project researchers shared. There are pathologies and problems in the work of many international bureaucracies. Yet without these bureaucracies and their dedicated staff, global policies for environmental protection and sustainable development would likely be less effective, efficient, and equitable.

On behalf of all project team members:

Frank Biermann and Bernd Siebenhüner
Amsterdam and Oldenburg, May 2008

List of Acronyms

AFS Convention	Convention to Control Harmful Antifouling Systems on Ships
CBD	Convention on Biological Diversity
CDM	Clean Development Mechanism
CITES	Convention on International Trade in Endangered Species of Wild Fauna and Flora
ENB	Earth Negotiations Bulletin
FAO	United Nations Food and Agriculture Organization
G-77	Group of 77
GDP	Gross Domestic Product
GEF	Global Environment Facility
GESAMP	Joint Group of Experts on the Scientific Aspects of Marine Environmental Protection
IBRD	International Bank for Reconstruction and Development
IHDP	International Human Dimensions Programme on Global Environmental Change
IISD	International Institute for Sustainable Development
IMO	International Maritime Organization
ITCP	Integrated Technical Cooperation Programme
MANUS	Managers of Global Change Project
MARPOL 73/78	International Convention for the Prevention of Pollution from Ships, 1973, as modified by the Protocol of 1978 Relating Thereto
OECD	Organisation for Economic Co-operation and Development
OILPOL	International Convention for the Prevention of Pollution of the Sea by Oil

SBSTTA	Subsidiary Body for Scientific, Technical and Technological Advice
SCBD	Secretariat of the Convention on Biological Diversity
UN	United Nations
UNCCD	United Nations Convention to Combat Desertification in those Countries Experiencing Serious Drought and/or Desertification, Particularly in Africa
UNCED	United Nations Conference on Environment and Development
UNCTAD	United Nations Conference on Trade and Development
UNDP	United Nations Development Programme
UNEP	United Nations Environment Programme
UNESCO	United Nations Educational, Scientific and Cultural Organization
UNFCCC	United Nations Framework Convention on Climate Change
USD	United States Dollar
WMO	World Meteorological Organization
WWF	World Wide Fund for Nature

1

The Role and Relevance of International Bureaucracies: Setting the Stage

Frank Biermann and Bernd Siebenhüner

What is the role and relevance of international bureaucracies in world politics? In public perception and political debate, they often play a noticeable part. The election of the new United Nations (UN) secretary-general in January 2007 has generated wide media attention. In many countries and capitals, the offices and officers of the world organization and its many specialized agencies and programs are highly visible. From telecommunication to shipping, trade, science, environment, technology transfer, air transportation, tourism, financing—all of these areas of economic production and daily life are at some stage affected by the activities of international bureaucracies and influenced by international civil servants. For example, in 2006 when health scientist David de Ferranti wrote about an election of "what is potentially the most important position in global health," he meant not the representative of any government or foundation, but the director general of the leading international bureaucracy in this field—the World Health Organization.[1]

And yet, international bureaucracies enjoy a mixed reputation. Although some observers deride the UN and its subcommittees and sister bodies as an assembly of ineffective, inefficient, and unresponsive bureaucrats, the recruitment officers of these agencies cannot complain about a lack of talented people from all walks of life who seek to serve international bureaucracies. Whereas one U.S. ambassador to the UN famously quipped that one could take away the top floors of the UN secretariat building without anybody noticing, others still see a crucial and often powerful influence of international bureaucracies in world politics.

Given these conflicting perspectives, it is remarkable that the scholarly study of the influence of international bureaucracies has been a rather peripheral research object for most of the post-1945 period. In the academic field of international relations, most research has focused on states as actors of world politics and on international institutions and regimes as constraints that place limits on state action. Within the recent discourse on global governance, students of international relations have reached beyond this traditional focus on state-to-state relations and included non-state actors in the analysis. One example is studies on transnational nongovernmental groups in fields such as environmental policy or human rights or on the privatization of global politics. Yet the myriad international bureaucracies from the specialized agencies and programs of the UN to the minuscule secretariat of the convention for the protection of European bats have stayed outside the mainstream state-centric international relations research programs.

The same holds for contributions of other disciplines. International lawyers offered extensive surveys of the setup, mandate, diplomatic history, and functions of international organizations. The increasing political relevance of international organizations is reflected, for example, in recent debates in the International Law Commission on the applicable law for treaties between international organizations and between international organizations and states,[2] or on the legal responsibility of international organizations for wrongful acts.[3] Yet legal science provides no convincing comparative assessments of the influence that bureaucracies within organizations have, or comprehensive explanations for possible variations in this influence.[4] Management studies have brought forth a vast literature on the influence of private businesses as well as non-profit organizations that includes analyses of institutional dynamics, organizational learning, principal-agent problems, and structural constraints.[5] Insights generated from this research, however, have rarely been applied to public administrations, particularly international bureaucracies (Dijkzeul 1997; Siebenhüner 2003). Likewise, findings from the analysis of policy diffusion that identify international bureaucracies as key agents in the transnational transfer of technologies and policies (Busch and Jörgens 2005) have hardly been taken up.

This gap in the literature is problematic. First, the limited understanding of the influence of international bureaucracies is likely to mislead conclusions about the state of world politics, and to result in an overemphasis on state power and on a perception of international institutions as mere structures devised by states with no role of other actors. Policy outcomes that may have been strongly influenced by international bureaucracies are thus likely to be overlooked.

Second, a better understanding of the role of international bureaucracies might assist in addressing democratic deficits of the current global governance system that have been intensely debated in recent years.[6] Given the need to find new ways for the democratic legitimization of global decision making, several authors have pointed to the democratizing influence of involving non-state actors, such as environmentalists or human rights groups, in international negotiations. Others, however, are more cautious regarding the role of private actors. They point to problems of selection bias, as only parts of "global civil society" have the means to voice their views in global fora (Dingwerth 2005, 2007).

Although some view international bureaucracies as the embodiment of an undemocratic liberalism at the global level (Barnett and Finnemore 2004, 15), these agencies could as well be seen as proponents of global legitimacy. Often, their policies support the interests of weaker actors against more powerful ones, as well as collective international interests (e.g., environment, food, or security) as opposed to the particular interests of powerful states.[7]

Third, a better understanding of the influence of international bureaucracies will help resolve policy debates about the reform of the United Nations and other bodies. The "effectiveness" of the UN and its specialized agencies—often judged against economic notions of efficiency by national policy makers—has been subject to public debate for decades, with little response from scholars of international relations (see also De Senarclens 2001). For example, there is a vivid policy controversy over whether to create a new specialized UN agency on environmental issues, a "world environment organization" (Biermann and Bauer 2005b). This debate has largely remained within the public policy community and has benefited little from substantiated findings from international relations research on the influence of international bureaucracies or on the optimal design for a world environment organization, if it were deemed necessary. As politicians and practitioners push for organizational reform, academics remain unable to specify how international bureaucracies affect the outcomes and impacts of global governance (Biermann and Bauer 2005a).

Taken together, the state of knowledge on the influence and dynamics of international bureaucracies in world politics is unsatisfactory. This is the central motivation of this book.

In particular, this research is motivated by a puzzling disparity between two observations about international bureaucracies: on one hand, most international bureaucracies are similar in their institutional and legal setting. A large number of bureaucracies resemble each other in their mandate, the number and type of countries they are reporting to, and the general functions that they are expected to perform in specific policy domains. On the other hand, there is a notable variation in the role and influence of these international bureaucracies that is difficult to explain through their mandate, resources, and function—factors that dominate the debates in international relations theory.

For example, many international environmental treaties in force have a secretariat to support the implementation of the treaty and to facilitate negotiations on further action. Most of these secretariats are similar in mandate, means, and general function. Yet their reputation varies, often substantially: some are described as a "lean shark," such as the secretariat of the Convention on Biological Diversity (Siebenhüner, this volume, chapter 11); others as "living in a straitjacket" designed by governments as their powerful masters, such as the secretariat to the UN Framework Convention on Climate Change (Busch, this volume, chapter 10). Others again have generated substantial controversy and requests for substantial overhaul, such as the secretariat of the UN Convention to Combat Desertification (Bauer, this volume, chapter 12). Yet these three bureaucracies are largely similar in mandate, size, financial means, and principals.

How can one explain this disparity between institutionally comparable bureaucracies and their apparently different actual roles? This book addresses this question. It reports on the core findings of a four-year research program that brought together a team of thirteen researchers and collaborating scholars: the Managers of Global Change (MANUS) project. The project first investigated the type and degree of autonomous influence of international bureaucracies. Second, we looked for possible factors to explain any differences in this influence. We wanted to know what accounts for variation: is it the complex web of external factors that cause differences in degree and type of influence—in other words, the structure of the political problem to be addressed? Or is it the specific institutional design that defines the relationship between international bureaucracies and governments and that regulates the embedding of the bureaucracies in a larger regime? Or is it rather the softer internal factors of people and procedures—the type of its leadership and the way its business is organized—that account for sizable variation in the influence of a bureaucracy?

With few exceptions (which we review in chapter 2), the international relations literature is surprisingly silent regarding the explanation of variation in the influence of bureaucracies. Partially, this reflects a general neglect of international bureaucracies in international relations theory after 1945. The few studies of the early post-1945 period were more descriptive and have been described as "idiographic institutional analysis" (Martin and Simmons 1998, 729). Some comparative studies were undertaken in the early 1970s, but all of them had a different focus, looking at—for example—decision making in international organizations or at the attitudes of delegates to international organizations. In the last decade, international bureaucracies have become a more common study object in international relations research. Yet as we lay out in chapter 2, the main research focus is not the question that interests us here. Instead, recent studies have concentrated on functional theories of why states create and support international organizations, on the stability and membership patterns of international bureaucracies, or on organizational change, along with a growing number of edited volumes with a more generalist analytical framework.

Our project goes beyond this work by an explicit focus on explaining variation in the autonomous influence of international bureaucracies as actors in world politics. In this respect, our research has some similarities with two strands of theory on international bureaucracies: principal-agent theory and sociological institutionalism. Our research differs, however, from these theories in a number of fundamental points.

First, although we draw on key aspects of principal-agent theory, we go beyond this approach by looking at factors that leave behind the dichotomic relationship between governments as principals and international bureaucracies as their agents. Principal-agent theory has contributed important work that explains the relationships between international bureaucracies and governments, and provides a solid explanatory basis for autonomous influence of international bureaucracies. Yet most of its core hypotheses assume variation in the type, number, or interest of the *principals* to an international bureaucracy (Hawkins et al. 2006; Vaubel 2006). For example, principal-agent theory offers explanations of autonomous activity of international bureaucracies that rely on situations of common agency, that is, either a collectivity of principals or a multiplicity of principals. Yet many international bureaucracies are constant regarding this variable. The same holds for the interest of principal-agent theory in the chain of delegation as a potential source of agency slack

(Pollack 1997; Nielson and Tierney 2003; Vaubel 2006). Again, most international bureaucracies have comparable chains of delegation, so this factor cannot account for different degrees or types of influence of international bureaucracies. Principal-agent theory thus offers theoretical models to elucidate the general influence of bureaucracies as well as variation of influence of bureaucracies with *different institutional embedding, mandate, or principals*. Variation of influence of bureaucracies that are similar with regard to these key variables of principal-agent theory cannot be assessed based on principal-agent theory.

Second, our work is related to—but goes beyond—the recent work in sociological institutionalism on international bureaucracies (Bauer et al., this volume, chapter 2). We share with sociological institutionalism a key interest in international bureaucracies as autonomous actors in world politics, and are interested in explaining their influence in particular. We thus do not assume—as realism and some strands of rational institutionalism would argue—that international bureaucracies are mere structures that function purely in accordance with the interest of states. Instead, we assume that international bureaucracies regularly have autonomous influence in world politics, and much of the empirical work in this book in fact attests to this claim.

Yet we also diverge from sociological institutionalism in a number of respects. For one, we employ a narrower definition of international bureaucracies. Barnett and Finnemore, for example, equate international organizations with international bureaucracies and use both terms interchangeably. For them, international organizations *are* international bureaucracies (Barnett and Finnemore 2004, 3). This approach serves them well in the three empirical cases that they choose. Yet a systematic comparative research effort that includes a large number of international bureaucracies as actors requires, we argue, a more precise conceptualization. We therefore distinguish between "international organizations," on the one hand, and "international bureaucracies" on the other (see Biermann et al., this volume, chapter 3, for more details).

We define international bureaucracies as agencies that have been set up by governments or other public actors with some degree of permanence and coherence and beyond formal direct control of single national governments (notwithstanding control by multilateral mechanisms through the collective of governments) and that act in the international arena to pursue a policy. In many cases, such bureaucracies will be part of international organizations. The concept of international "organization" is thus broader: we define an international organization as an institutional arrangement that combines bureaucracies with a normative framework that is set by and is effective on states (and sometimes on non-state actors). The International Maritime Organization (IMO) may serve as an example: The IMO agrees through decision of its general assembly and subsequent ratification by member states on the creation of new international rules in its area of activity. States can join the organization, they can participate in rule making, and they are then expected to accept and implement the collectively agreed rules. Here, the IMO does not differ much from an intergovernmental regime. In addition, the IMO comprises a hierarchically organized group of civil servants who are expected to act following the mandate of the organization and the decisions of the assembly of member states. This is what we call an international bureaucracy. We hence differentiate between the IMO—as an institutional arrangement that brings together a normative framework, member states, and the IMO secretariat as the organization's bureaucracy—from this bureaucracy itself.

As we lay out in chapter 3, this definition of international bureaucracies also differs from the narrow concept of international organizations in international law and the broad concepts of organizations in management theory. It also differs from the concept of "institutions," which usually denotes systems of rules and decision-making procedures (IHDP 1999; Young 2002; Young, King, and Schroeder 2008; Simmons and Martin 2002, 192–194), but is in nonscholarly writing also sometimes used for international bureaucracies (such as in "the Bretton Woods institutions," when in fact the bureaucracies are meant).

Our definition solves a variety of problems in recent research. It allows work in the lines of both sociological institutionalism and principal-agency theory to differentiate between states as actors within international organizations and the international bureaucracies as semi-autonomous actors within these organizations. It is more parsimonious than other attempts at solving the conceptual problem of international organizations being at the same time normative frameworks and bureaucratic actors (see Biermann et al., this volume, chapter 3, for a more detailed discussion). The differentiation between international bureaucracies and international organizations helps to keep apart international bureaucracies as actors and the collectivity of member states of an international organization, both of which are referred to as "international organizations" in most writing on international relations.

In addition, our approach departs from sociological institutionalism in drawing less from research in the field of sociology than from organizational theory and management studies. Barnett and Finnemore (1999, 2004), for example, build their work essentially on a Weberian notion of bureaucracy and of a bureaucratic functional rationale and culture that pervades international bureaucracies. This sociological concept of a bureaucratic culture explains certain elements of their autonomous influence as actors in international relations similar to Weber's explanation of the role of Prussian bureaucracy in his time. However, concerning most modern international bureaucracies, this bureaucratic culture is a constant—most UN agencies, programs, and secretariats are likely to function according to similar rational-legal bureaucratic patterns. The bureaucratic rationale thus explains elements of their *overall* influence and authority, but less so *variation* in this influence. Our project therefore rather draws on organizational theory and its *empirical* notions of organizational cultures and internal procedures. We thus analyze international bureaucracies as social processes and collective entities constituted by their distinct organizational cultures, structures, and behaviors (e.g., March and Simon 1958; Thompson 1967; Mintzberg 1979; Schein 1985; Morgan 1986; Nonaka 1994). As we argue in this book, much variation in the autonomous influence of international bureaucracies can be traced back to differences in these organizational cultures, the "software" within bureaucracies that are otherwise similar in their legal mandate, resources, and general function.

Finally, our approach differs from both sociological institutionalism and principal-agent theory in the normative motivation of our research. Sociological institutionalism and principal-agent theory often assume a self-centered interest of bureaucracies, which leads, in their view, to "pathological" bureaucratic behavior. Bureaucracies are assumed to strive predominantly to maximize their mandate, funding, staff, and power, and to fend off interference from governments and other actors. In this view, international bureaucracies are a problem for democracies, as some sort of leviathan that has been created by democratically elected governments but that managed to loosen control from their creators to advance an independent agenda. Our approach differs inasmuch as it is empirically based rather than theoretically derived. We find international bureaucracies more often interested in resolving political problems than increasing their power as such. For us, autonomous influence of international bureaucracies indeed requires some monitoring and control to ensure their legitimacy—yet we do not see autonomous influence as a problem or pathology per se.

Empirically, the research for this book covers nine international bureaucracies (although comparable studies on other bureaucracies have been reviewed as well). As we describe later (see Biermann et al., this volume, chapter 3), all case studies are based on the examination of primary sources, such as internal and published documents of the bureaucracies; secondary sources, such as academic studies and written assessments of diplomats; a series of interviews and participatory observation gained through field visits to all headquarters of the bureaucracies studied; as well as an expert survey to collect data from external stakeholders. Altogether, more than one hundred civil servants were interviewed for this study. Because of the number of cases and researchers, we took special care with the methodological and practical preparation of field visits to guarantee the validity and comparability of data from different bureaucracies.

To keep this comparative research effort focused, we restrict our empirical analysis to global governance in the area of environmental protection. This field is of particular interest for the guiding question of this book, because it is one of the institutionally most dynamic areas in world politics regarding the number of international institutions and actors that emerged over the past three decades. More than seven hundred multilateral environmental agreements are in force (Mitchell 2003)—this makes global environmental policy a fertile ground for larger comparative efforts, unlike many other institutionally more centralized areas of world politics.

Within this domain, this book covers two types of bureaucracies that have so far rarely been systematically included in comparative research programs: *secretariats* of international environmental treaties, and *environmental departments* of the secretariats of intergovernmental organizations that cover more than merely environmental policy. The selection of cases within these two groups has been based on the comparability of the studied bureaucracies regarding core function and size, but also on prima facie variation regarding possible explanatory variables of problem structures, institutional settings, and policies. Within the group of environmental departments, we analyzed the environmental department and other subdivisions of the World Bank, the environmental department of the secretariat of the IMO, the environment directorate of the Organisation for Economic Cooperation and Development

(OECD) secretariat, the secretariat of the United Nations Environment Programme (UNEP), and the secretariat of the Global Environment Facility (GEF). Within the group of treaty secretariats, we studied the secretariat of the 1985 Vienna Convention for the Protection of the Ozone Layer and its 1987 Montreal Protocol on Substances that Deplete the Ozone Layer ("ozone secretariat"); the secretariat of the 1992 Convention on Biological Diversity ("biodiversity secretariat"); the secretariat of the 1992 United Nations Framework Convention on Climate Change ("climate secretariat"), and the secretariat of the 1994 United Nations Convention to Combat Desertification in Countries Experiencing Serious Drought and/or Desertification, Particularly in Africa ("desertification secretariat").

The research documented in this book has yielded two core findings that could not be explained by previous work. First, international bureaucracies with similar legal mandates, financial and staff resources, and institutional functions vary in their autonomous influence. In other words, factors that are often seen as key variables in institutional theory—such as mandate or resources—matter less in explaining the outcome of bureaucratic activity than might have been expected. Second, we explain this variation by extending the analysis through including the macro level of politics—the problem structure—as well as the micro level, that is, the people in the bureaucracies and the particular organizational procedures, cultures, and leadership styles that they develop.

This book is organized as follows. Chapter 2 reviews the state of the art in the academic disciplines of international relations and organizational and management studies and places our research in the larger theoretical context. Chapter 3 presents the research design that underlies this project and all case studies and a description of our empirical research methodology. Chapters 4 through 12 present the nine in-depth case studies that have been at the center of this project. Finally, chapter 13 draws the overall conclusions of this four-year research project and outlines its general findings.

Notes

1. *International Herald Tribune*, 4–5 November 2006, 4.

2. See the Vienna Convention on the Law of Treaties between States and International Organizations or between International Organizations of 21 March 1986, UN Doc. A/CONF.129/15.

3. In 2000, the International Law Commission decided to include the topic "Responsibility of International Organizations" in its long-term work program, with the eventual goal of a legal agreement on this subject. See International Law Commission 2003, para. 41–54.

4. On international organizations and the law of international organizations and institutions, see Aldrich 1979; Amerasinghe 1996; Bennett 1991; Dupuy 1998; Kirgis 1993; Schermers and Blokker 1995; and White 1996, among others.

5. Key publications include Argyris 1990; Argyris and Schön 1996; Denton 1998; Argote 1999; Carnall 1999; Schwandt and Marquard 2000.

6. See, in particular, Barnett and Finnemore's chapter on the legitimacy of an expanding global bureaucracy (2004, 156–173). On the democratic deficit of inter- and transnational politics more generally, and on different attempts to conceptualize democratic governance on the transnational level, see, for instance, Archibugi and Held 1995; Archibugi, Held, and Köhler 1998; Bohman 1999; Dahl 1994; Dingwerth 2007; Held 1995, 1997, 2000; Rosow 2000; Scholte 2002; Wolf 1999; Zürn 2000; as well as the reports of the Commission on Global Governance 1995 and the South Centre 1996.

7. As in the case of the International Labor Organization, which includes unions and industry representatives in its decision making, international bureaucracies could also provide models for the institutionalized and balanced involvement of stakeholders and civil society at the global level. See Biermann 2002 for a discussion of stakeholder involvement in international environmental organizations.

References

Aldrich, Howard E. 1979. *Organizations and Environments*. Englewood Cliffs, NJ: Prentice Hall.

Amerasinghe, Chittharanjan F. 1996. *Principles of the Institutional Law of International Organizations*. Cambridge, UK: Cambridge University Press.

Archibugi, Daniele, and David Held, editors. 1995. *Cosmopolitan Democracy: An Agenda for a New World Order*. Cambridge: Polity Press.

Archibugi, Daniele, David Held, and Martin Köhler, editors. 1998. *Re-imagining Political Community: Studies in Cosmopolitan Democracy*. Stanford: Stanford University Press.

Argote, Linda. 1999. *Organizational Learning: Creating, Retaining, and Transferring Knowledge*. Boston: Kluwer.

Argyris, Chris. 1990. *Overcoming Organizational Defenses: Facilitating Organizational Learning*. Boston: Allyn and Bacon.

Argyris, Chris, and Donald A. Schön. 1996. *Organizational Learning II. Theory, Method and Practice*. Reading, MA: Addison-Wesley.

Barnett, Michael N., and Martha Finnemore. 1999. "The Politics, Power, and Pathologies of International Organizations." *International Organization* 53 (4): 699–732.

Barnett, Michael N., and Martha Finnemore. 2004. *Rules for the World: International Organizations in Global Politics.* Ithaca, NY: Cornell University Press.

Bennett, Alvin LeRoy. 1991. *International Organizations: Principles and Issues.* 5th edition. Englewood Cliffs, NJ: Prentice Hall.

Biermann, Frank. 2002. "Strengthening Green Global Governance in a Disparate World Society: Would a World Environment Organization Benefit the South?" *International Environmental Agreements: Politics, Law, and Economics* 2:297–315.

Biermann, Frank, and Steffen Bauer. 2005a. "Conclusion." In *A World Environment Organization: Solution or Threat for Effective International Environmental Governance?*, edited by Frank Biermann and Steffen Bauer, 257–269. Aldershot, UK: Ashgate.

Biermann, Frank, and Steffen Bauer, editors. 2005b. *A World Environment Organization: Solution or Threat for Effective International Environmental Governance?* Aldershot, UK: Ashgate.

Bohman, James. 1999. "International Regimes and Democratic Governance: Equal Access to Influence Over Global Institutionalization." *International Affairs* 75 (3): 499–514.

Busch, Per-Olof, and Helge Jörgens. 2005. "International Patterns of Environmental Policy Change and Convergence." *European Environment* 15 (2): 80–101.

Carnall, Colin A. 1999. *Managing Change in Organizations.* 3rd edition. Harlow: Financial Times/Prentice Hall.

Commission on Global Governance. 1995. *Our Global Neighbourhood: The Report of the Commission on Global Governance.* Oxford: Oxford University Press.

Dahl, Robert A. 1994. "A Democratic Dilemma: System Effectiveness Versus Citizen Participation." *Political Science Quarterly* 109 (1): 23–34.

De Senarclens, Pierre. 2001. "International Organizations and the Challenges of Globalization." *International Social Science Journal* 170:509–522.

Denton, John. 1998. *Organizational Learning and Effectiveness.* London: Routledge.

Dijkzeul, Dennis. 1997. *The Management of Multilateral Organizations.* The Hague: Kluwer Law International.

Dingwerth, Klaus. 2005. "The Democratic Legitimacy of Public-Private Rule-Making: What Can We Learn from the World Commission on Dams?" *Global Governance* 11 (1): 65–83.

Dingwerth, Klaus. 2007. *The New Transnationalism: Transnational Governance and Democratic Legitimacy.* Basingstoke, UK: Palgrave Macmillan.

Dupuy, René Jean, editor. 1998. *Manuel sur les Organizations Internationales. A Handbook on International Organizations.* 2nd edition. The Hague: Martinus Nijhoff Publishers.

Hawkins, Darren G., David A. Lake, Daniel L. Nielson, and Michael J. Tierney, editors. 2006. *Delegation and Agency in International Organizations*. Cambridge, UK: Cambridge University Press.

Held, David. 1995. *Democracy and the Global Order: From the Modern State to Cosmopolitan Governance*. Cambridge, UK: Cambridge University Press.

Held, David. 1997. "Democracy and Globalization." *Global Governance* 3 (3): 251–267.

Held, David. 2000. "Regulating Globalization? The Reinvention of Politics." *International Sociology* 15 (2): 394–408.

IHDP, International Human Dimensions Programme on Global Environmental Change. 1999. *Institutional Dimensions of Global Environmental Change: Science Plan*. IHDP Report 9. Bonn: IHDP.

International Law Commission. 2003. Report of the 55th Session of the International Law Commission (5 May–6 June and 7 July–8 August). Official Records of the 58th Session of the United Nations General Assembly, Supplement 10, UN Doc. A/58/10. New York: United Nations.

Kirgis, Frederic L. 1993. *International Organizations in their Legal Setting*. 2nd edition. Saint Paul, MN: West Wadsworth.

March, James G., and Herbert A. Simon. 1958. *Organization*. New York: Wiley.

Martin, Lisa L., and Beth A. Simmons. 1998. "Theories and Empirical Studies of International Institutions." *International Organization* 52 (4): 729–757.

Mintzberg, Henry. 1979. *The Structure of Organizations: A Synthesis of Research*. Upper Saddle River, NJ: Prentice Hall.

Mitchell, Ronald B. 2003. "International Environmental Agreements. A Survey of Their Features, Formation, and Effects." *Annual Review of Environment and Resources* 48:429–461.

Morgan, Gareth. 1986. *Images of Organization*. Newbury Park, CA: Sage.

Nielson, Daniel L., and Michael J. Tierney. 2003. "Delegation to International Organizations: Agency Theory and World Bank Environmental Reform." *International Organization* 57 (2): 241–276.

Nonaka, Ikujiro. 1994. "A Dynamic Theory of Organizational Knowledge Creation." *Organization Science* 5:14–37.

Pollack, Mark A. 1997. "Delegation, Agency, and Agenda Setting in the European Community." *International Organization* 51 (1): 99–134.

Rosow, Stephen J. 2000. "Globalization as Democratic Theory." *Millennium: Journal of International Studies* 29 (1): 27–45.

Schein, Edgar H. 1985. *Organizational Culture and Leadership*. San Francisco: Jossey-Bass.

Schermers, Henry G., and Niels M. Blokker. 1995. *International Institutional Law*. 3rd rev. edition. The Hague: Martinus Nijhoff Publishers.

Scholte, Jan Aart. 2002. "Civil Society and Democracy in Global Governance." *Global Governance* 8 (3): 281–304.

Schwandt, David R., and Michael J. Marquard. 2000. *Organizational Learning: From World-class Theories to Global Best Practices*. Boca Raton: CRC Press/St. Lucie Press.

Siebenhüner, Bernd. 2003. *International Organisations as Learning Agents in the Emerging System of Global Governance. A Conceptual Framework*. Global Governance Working Paper no 8. Amsterdam and others: The Global Governance Project. Available at www.glogov.org (accessed 10 January 2009).

Simmons, Beth A., and Lisa L. Martin. 2002. "International Organizations and Institutions." In *Handbook of International Relations*, edited by Walter Carlsnaes, Thomas Risse, and Beth A. Simmons, 192–211. London: Sage.

South Centre. 1996. *For a Strong and Democratic United Nations. A South Perspective on UN Reform*. Geneva: South Centre.

Thompson, James D. 1967. *Organizations in Action*. New York: McGraw-Hill Book Company.

Vaubel, Roland. 2006. "Principal-Agent Problems in International Organizations." *Review of International Organizations* 1 (2): 125–138.

White, Nigel D. 1996. *The Law of International Organizations*. Manchester: Manchester University Press.

Wolf, Klaus D. 1999. "The New Raison d'État as a Problem for Democracy in World Society." *European Journal of International Relations* 5 (3): 333–363.

Young, Oran R., Leslie A. King and Heike Schroeder, editors. 2008. *Institutions and Environmental Change: Principal Findings, Applications, and Research Frontiers*. Cambridge, MA: MIT Press.

Zürn, Michael. 2000. "Democratic Governance beyond the Nation-State: The EU and Other International Institutions." *European Journal of International Relations* 6 (2): 183–221.

2

Understanding International Bureaucracies: Taking Stock

Steffen Bauer, Frank Biermann, Klaus Dingwerth, and Bernd Siebenhüner

With few exceptions—which we discuss in this chapter—the international relations literature is surprisingly silent regarding the explanation of variation in the influence of international bureaucracies. There have been a number of peaks of scholarly interest in international organizations and their bureaucracies, and there are several clusters of research around specific questions in this field. Yet by and large—and in particular, if compared with international institutions and regimes—the study of international bureaucracies has been rather a fringe issue in the social sciences. Also, students of public administration have for the most part been occupied with the study of domestic agencies.

International Organizations and Bureaucracies in International Relations Research

Admittedly, there are exceptions to the relative neglect of international bureaucracies in international relations theory. In fact, the study of international organizations and their bureaucracies stood at the very beginning of the discipline in the 1920s. The creation of the League of Nations sparked much interest in international organizations and their bureaucracies, fueled by debates on world peace through law and on world federalism. Yet this research remained rather descriptive and idealistic, and it ended with the demise of the League and the post-1945 hegemony of political realism. The early post-1945 period was marked by critical studies of new bodies such as the United Nations, the World Bank, and the International Monetary Fund. Yet these studies suffered from a lack of theory and comparative research designs. As Lisa Martin and Beth Simmons observed, "There was no conceptual framework that could tie these insights together; nor was there a systematic comparative enterprise to check for their regularity" (1998, 732–733). Instead, the early years of research on international bureaucracies can best be characterized as "idiographic institutional analysis" (729).

In the 1950s, functionalism developed some interest in the emergence of international organizations and international bureaucracies. This was, however, largely a by-product of the overall functionalist interest in interstate integration, and empirically focused on European integration (e.g., Haas 1958). This regional bias reduced the value of the functionalist school for a more general assessment of the influence of international bureaucracies (critically, see De Senarclens 1993, 454; Ness and Brechin 1988).

Some interest in international bureaucracies emerged again in the 1960s and 1970s. A 1970 survey of fourteen journals and eleven edited volumes identified more than three hundred academic articles on international organizations between 1960 and 1969 (Alger 1970b). A closer examination of sixty-one of these works showed that as with previous research, most articles were single-case studies and comparative research was an exception. Although many of these studies made use of quantitative data analysis—out of a total of sixty-one studies, Alger identified forty-three that use descriptive statistics, fifteen that use bivariate statistics, and eight that use multivariate statistics—and included substantial field research, the analysis was focused on the United Nations (1970b, 432–433). Voting patterns and delegate attitudes in the General Assembly constituted a main area of research, much in line with the study of domestic politics and voting behavior. Alger concluded, "Considering the exciting advances being made in comparative methods of political analysis, the slight effect this has had on research on international organizations is surprising" (1970b, 444) and "There is reason for some concern about both the limited amount of comparative research on international organizations and the small number of the total population of organizations that receive the attention of researchers" (1970a, 220).

In the 1970s, research on international bureaucracies became more diverse, and comparative empirical studies were accompanied by theoretical attempts to grasp the functioning of international organizations and their interaction with states and societies (e.g., Keohane and Nye 1974). A first attempt to measure the effectiveness of international organizations in the area of peace and security was made by David Singer and Michael Wallace (1970), who sought to understand whether governments believed that creating international organizations would decrease the likelihood of war and whether this belief was empirically warranted.[1]

Other authors were more sensitive to differences among international organizations and explored these in more detail. Robert Cox and Harold Jacobson's *The Anatomy of Influence* (1973b) included detailed case studies of eight international bureaucracies tied together by a single theoretical framework. The authors' main interest was to examine who wields influence in international organizations—their study aimed at answering questions such as to what extent the decisions of international organizations are made by governmental delegates, what the relative powers are of the members of international secretariats, and which factors influence the relative decision-making power of national delegates versus international bureaucrats. Comparing decision-making processes of eight organizations, the authors drew a comprehensive picture of the internal dynamics of international bureaucracies. Among other things, they discerned a trend toward increased bureaucratization of decision making in all organizations and concluded that although decision making in organizations whose work had little salience for (powerful) states tends to be driven by "participant subsystems"—that is, delegates, international officials, and associated independent experts—other organizations are dominated by "representative subsystems," that is, by member states (Cox and Jacobson 1973a, 424–428).

Methodologically, Cox and Jacobson disaggregated influence into several indicators, such as the structure of formal authority, the reputation for influence, and the success in initiating proposals, in order to allow for meaningful measurement. The measurements were made comparable through the application of a unified theoretical framework and the use of similar methods of data collection for all case studies (Cox 1973, 129; Nye 1973, 361; Scheinman 1973, 252).

Using a similar approach, Weiss (1975) explored the attitudes of staff members of and delegates to international organizations and the prospects for a "global perspective" on some of the world's most pressing problems. Weiss analyzed the rhetoric of universal secretariats and compared six organizations regarding their commitment to welfare cooperation. His study thus followed on Cox and Jacobson's attempt to determine the degree of autonomy of international secretariats from the organizations' member states.

First articles on the relation between international bureaucracies and environmental protection appeared in a special issue of *International*

Organization, published in the context of the 1972 United Nations Conference on the Human Environment (Kay and Skolnikoff 1972). This issue contained several articles on international institutions and the environment. In general, contributions discussed proposals for institutional reform, yet without building on sound empirical knowledge about the functioning of international organizations and their bureaucracies.[2] With the rise of the regime concept in the study of international relations in the second half of the 1970s, research mostly "turned away from the study of formal IOs [international organizations] to the study of regimes and institutions, informal as well as formal" (Simmons and Martin 2002, 204).

As a result, a promising research program initiated in the first half of the 1970s was largely abandoned, and international organizations and their bureaucracies became again "subjected to academic disregard" (Stevis and Wilson 1995, 122).[3] Keohane and Nye's (1977) concept of complex interdependence could have offered a framework to address international bureaucracies as actors (Verbeek 1998, 12–13), yet the proponents of complex interdependence rather turned, as De Senarclens writes (2001, 510), to the analysis of regimes and dealt with bureaucracies only "superficially, attaching no great importance to their internal functioning, decision-making processes, and political role."[4]

The few later systematic studies of international bureaucracies include a comparative study of the effectiveness of international environmental organizations by David A. Kay and Harold K. Jacobson (1983, treated in more detail shortly); a quantitative analysis of the stability and membership patterns of international organizations (Shanks et al. 1996); several edited volumes with relatively loose analytical frameworks (Bartlett et al. 1995; Dijkzeul and Beigbeder 2003), and the emergence of a sociological approach to international bureaucracies (see following).

The objective of the comparative study edited by Kay and Jacobson (1983) appears closest to the one taken in this book. They examined why some international organizations do a better job than others in performing particular functions (Jacobson and Kay 1983a, 323–324). Their work included case studies of eleven international environmental issues. In each study, the roles of intergovernmental organizations were analyzed and their performance evaluated. To allow for a meaningful comparison, they developed a theoretical framework that distinguished between ten functions of international organizations, defined five criteria for measuring effectiveness, and identified five groups of factors to explain relative successes or failures of international organizations in protecting the environment (Jacobson and Kay 1983b). Although this framework may have served as a good starting point for a comparison of the performance of different international bureaucracies, the case study chapters are, however, inconsistent in their application of this framework. Thus, with few exceptions, case study authors make only occasional and implicit references to the functions performed by the bureaucracies of the international organizations they analyze, the criteria for measuring the effectiveness with which these functions are performed, and the factors that could explain this effectiveness.[5] In addition, the case studies tend to treat a relatively large number of organizations involved in addressing each environmental problem at the cost of an in-depth analysis of each organization's activities and performance. Data are in most cases derived from official documents, secondary sources, or personal experience. Interviews seem exceptional. Consequently, we learn less from the study than we could have learned if the editors' framework had been applied more fully, as the editors themselves pointed out in their concluding chapter.[6] The study nonetheless closes with a number of interesting findings about the effectiveness with which different international environmental bureaucracies perform different functions and a list of hypotheses about "background variables" and "organizational variables" that may have contributed to the successes and failures.

Ernst and Peter Haas furthermore tried to reconceptualize international bureaucracies as creators and administrators of knowledge. Ernst Haas (1990) focused on ways through which organizational change may occur ("managed interdependence learning," "adaptation through incremental growth," and "adaptation through turbulent non-growth"), and Peter Haas and Ernst Haas (1995) attributed to these actors a potential role as "agents for the redefinition" of the international agenda through the development of "road maps for governance." More recently, Joachim, Reinalda, and Verbeek reassessed Cox and Jacobson's *Anatomy of Influence* by looking into autonomous policy making by and decision making within international organizations as well as their roles in policy implementation (Joachim, Reinalda, and Verbeek 2008; Reinalda and Verbeek 1998, 2004b).

In sum, although the study of international organizations and their bureaucracies has enjoyed a relatively peripheral role in the field of international relations over the course of the last half-century, there are a fair number of insightful studies. Yet many of them lack a coherent and convincing analytical framework, or simply ask questions different from those analyzed in this volume.

Theoretical Approaches from International Relations Research

One factor to account for this is the state-centric perspective that has dominated the discipline of international relations for much of the post-1945 period. In this perspective, international organizations—let alone their bureaucracies—have no significant autonomous influence in world politics. This denial is evident for political realism, which views international bureaucracies merely as structural epiphenomena of interstate competition that reflect the sum of individual national interests (Waltz 1979, 18). In the realist paradigm, international bureaucracies mirror existing power structures and support the influence of hegemonic states. Because neorealism views relative gains concerns as ultimate determinant of state behavior, mutual benefits through international cooperation and the delegation of substantive competencies to international bureaucracies are unlikely (e.g., Grieco 1988; Mearsheimer 1995; Strange 1987; Waltz 1979). Consequently, realism denies any autonomy and influence of international bureaucracies beyond the will and power of individual state members, notably hegemonic powers.

Likewise, scholars in the tradition of critical theory conceptualize international organizations and their bureaucracies as contingent on dominant material and ideological structures and with only modest autonomous agency. Critical theorists view international organizations as mediators between the centers and their peripheries in the international system. By ideologically legitimating the norms of the world order, co-opting the elites from peripheral countries and absorbing counterhegemonic ideas, international organizations are seen as a "mechanism through which the universal norms of a world hegemony are expressed" (Cox 1983, 172). This quotation illustrates that critical theory is at least marginally interested in international organizations, but also the failure of critical theorists to clearly distinguish between organizations and bureaucracies. In the end, both neorealism and critical theories have thus neglected the study of international bureaucracies. Instead, they conceptualize international bureaucracies as dependent or intermediary variables determined by variant constellations of state power, state interests, or ideological structures, but with no significant autonomous role as actors in international relations.

State-centrism has also dominated much research in the rationalist strand of institutionalism in international relations research. The rational institutionalist understanding of international bureaucracies differs from realism inasmuch as it expects states to be able to cooperate through international institutions, which may rely on bureaucracies. Realism and rational institutionalism come close, however, in their state-centric understanding of international bureaucracies as outcomes of interstate cooperation, not as active participants in world politics. Rational institutionalists see the nation-state with fixed interests at the center of global institution building. They conceptualize international bureaucracies therefore either as result of interstate negotiation, created by states to further collective goals, or as intervening variables with a limited degree of agency resulting from interstate negotiations.

As a consequence, to the extent that rational institutionalists provide theoretical propositions or empirical findings on international bureaucracies, it is generally a by-product of the study of international institutions, insofar as international bureaucracies help states to set up institutions or serve as elements of institutional design. This holds in particular for research on regime effectiveness (Hasenclever, Mayer, and Rittberger 1997), notably in the field of environmental policy.[7] In many of these studies, international bureaucracies have been identified as influential for overall regime effectiveness, and it has repeatedly been pointed out that these agencies must not be ignored (e.g., Young 1994, 28). Jørgen Wettestad, for example, identified variation in the role of treaty secretariats as one of six factors that influences regime effectiveness, along with the organization of the science-policy interface and the verification and compliance mechanisms, both of which often also relate to the work of secretariats (2001, 319–320). Edward Miles and colleagues (2001) tested the hypothesis that actor capacity of international organizations and its subordinate bodies and officials enhances regime effectiveness, and found this to be supported by case studies and statistical analysis. Also, Brown Weiss and Jacobson (1998) and Sandford (1994) found that officials of treaty secretariats played important roles in furthering the implementation of treaties.

Overall, however, the basic heuristic concept that underlies most rational institutionalist research remains state-centric. Rational institutionalists are interested in the conditions under which states will delegate administrative tasks to international or supranational bureaucracies, in particular in the case of the European Union.[8] The focus is less on the bureaucracies themselves.[9]

This is different for sociological institutionalism. Sociological institutionalism shares many facets of rational institutionalism, but differs inasmuch as it draws more on the older institutionalism of sociology and the constructivist critique of mainstream international relations theories. Sociological institutionalism remains committed to the general cause of institutionalist research on international relations and to a firm grounding in empirical work as central research methodology. Yet sociological institutionalism also highlights the limits of rationality and questions the instrumentalist view of international institutions. In the distinction of March and Olsen, sociological institutionalism differs from rational institutionalism by replacing the rationalist interest-based "logic of consequentiality" of the *homo oeconomicus* with the normative "logic of appropriateness" of the *homo sociologicus* (1989, 23).[10] Sociological institutionalism challenges rationalism for its failure to convincingly account for the persistence and emergence of ever more institutions "in a world already replete with institutions" (Hall and Taylor 1996, 953). Sociological institutionalism also differs from the more radical strands of constructivism in that it seeks to supplement rather than to replace established explanatory categories of interest and power through norms and information, and to integrate the analysis of norms and ideas in a positivist epistemology (Finnemore and Sikkink 1998, 888; Schmidt 2002, 16; Wendt 2000). Taking such a pragmatic stance enables scholars to benefit from the compatibility of rationalist and constructivist arguments, rather than insisting on their incompatibility (Reinalda and Verbeek 2004a, 11–12).

Increased attention for normative considerations requires considering actors other than states, especially actors that lack traditional material "power resources" such as military might or economic assets. Once one sees normative structures as causal factors in world politics that shape cooperation processes, then all actors that create, shape, and maintain such normative structures must be part of the analysis. This includes actors that have not material but largely ideational resources such as legitimacy, credibility, knowledge, and information.

International bureaucracies may have such soft power resources. If state interests can be changed through normative influence and interaction with global discourses and normative frameworks, then non-state actors that focus on normative development become more relevant. All this puts the study of non-state actors, ranging from private advocacy groups to international bureaucracies, at the center of sociological institutionalism.

Consequently, in the 1990s several studies added empirical substance to the assumptions of sociological institutionalism about international bureaucracies and their relevance in international norm dynamics. One attempt to reconsider the role of international bureaucracies has been a series of studies by Michael Barnett and Martha Finnemore (1999, 2004). They draw on Max Weber's concept of organizations and his concept of rational-legal authority to propose a redefinition of international bureaucracies in international relations research. In their discussion of the politics, power, and pathologies that they observe in international bureaucracies, they see "a basis for understanding organizational autonomy" (Barnett and Finnemore 1999, 703) that has so far been neglected in international relations research. In a sense, they continue where Cox and Jacobson (1973b), Keohane and Nye (1974), and Weiss (1975) left off in the early 1970s before the discipline shifted its attention to the study of regimes and informal institutions.

The research reported in this book shares many tenets of sociological institutionalism, in particular its proposition that international bureaucracies are autonomous actors in world politics that may influence norm-building processes. Yet as we laid out in the introductory chapter (Biermann and Siebenhüner, this volume, chapter 1), we also differ from mainstream sociological institutionalism in three respects. First, we employ a narrower concept of international bureaucracies, which we clearly separate from international organizations. Second, we start from a different normative perspective that is less concerned with pathologies of bureaucracies than with their potential to contribute to problem solving. Third and finally, we rely more on management theory and organizational studies than on Weberian notions of rational-legal actors.

Theoretical Approaches from Management Studies

Like international relations theory, management studies have largely neglected international bureaucracies. Yet with the more recent discourse on new public management, management studies have opened up to more general problems of organizations, be they commercial or non-profit, private or public, small or large. New public management builds on the understanding of public authorities as service units that can improve their efficiency and their effectiveness through the implementation of modern management techniques (Reschenthaler and Thompson 1997; Jones and Thomson 1999; Schedler and Proeller 2003; Geri 2001). Most new public management concepts address national and local government agencies.[11] Thus the frameworks and focus of the approach remain limited to the conditions of smaller-scale administrations.

International bureaucracies have largely stayed outside of this debate (one exception is Geri 2001), and only few studies have applied insights from management studies to international bureaucracies. One of the first examples was Allison (1971), who drew on insights in organizational processes in his seminal study of the Cuban missile crisis. The concept of organizational learning was employed by Jervis (1976) for his analysis of how perceptions and misperceptions shape international politics. But it was not until the late 1980s that Ness and Brechin (1988) took up an organizational perspective on international bureaucracies. Later Dijkzeul (1997) applied a management perspective to three UN bureaucracies. He found the most striking differences between international bureaucracies and business organizations in the different opportunities of internal evaluation and assessment, deficiencies of human resource management in international bureaucracies, and their limited autonomy. Jordan (2001) analyzed international cooperation within and through international bureaucracies, but evades an explicit management perspective. The lack of mutual exchange between management studies and international relations theory has also been criticized by LaPalombara (2001b), who complains about the absence of fruitful contributions from political science to the organizational learning literature.

In management theory, different forms of organizations share similar problems concerning the internal structuring, principal-agent problems, the interaction between different individuals working together for a common goal, the exchanges between the inside and outside of the organization, and problems of changing processes of the whole organization. Therefore, significant insights and analytic tools from the study of commercial organizations can deliver fruitful knowledge for the analysis of international bureaucracies (exemplary studies are Beigbeder 1997; Dijkzeul and Beigbeder 2003; Jordan 2001; and LaPalombara 2001a, 2001b).

Yet there are also important differences between private for-profit organizations and public non-profit bureaucracies. This is more the case for international bureaucracies, which are based on international treaties with a clear mandate and are thus not subject to constant changes in political priorities of governments, as national bureaucracies are. One striking difference between private and public organizations is the target structure and the related evaluation criteria. Whereas commercial organizations have to focus on profit and economic survival in the market, public sector organizations have to pursue a multitude of qualitative targets, such as environmental protection, poverty reduction, or capacity building, as determined by their political constituencies. Therefore, they will be evaluated in the first place in terms of effectiveness in achieving their objectives.

Second, commercial organizations and bureaucracies differ with respect to the groups and institutions to which they are accountable. Private corporations are accountable in the first place to their shareholders, but also to their stakeholders who have an interest in the organization's success or in some activities of the organization (Freeman 1984). Public-sector bureaucracies in the international arena are mostly accountable to states and other international bureaucracies.

Third, because international bureaucracies are exposed to multiple political targets and heterogeneous interests by key constituents, they generally have less autonomy than private organizations. Private companies are granted a number of fundamental rights by most national constitutions so that they can decide independently about their own goals. Public organizations, by contrast, must often implement decisions from superior units and are integrated in a system of other agencies, which limits their freedom to act (LaPalombara 2001a). In particular, their goals are given from the outside; in the case of intergovernmental bureaucracies, it is their mandates that regulate most of their tasks.

Fourth, private corporations directly depend on markets and thus have to adapt to changes in the markets. Therefore, private-sector organizations can be assumed to have a greater ability to change than public sector organizations that are not exposed to these pressures. Most students of public bureaucracies found a structural conservatism in these organizations, due to their internal processes of bureaucratization and the external political influence they gain over time (Powell and DiMaggio 1991).

Given the characteristics of the different types of organization, any management analysis has to acknowledge these differences in the research design. In particular, as we lay out in chapter 3, the predominant focus on effectiveness rather than efficiency in international public sector organizations will have to play a key role in the analysis of autonomous influence of these organizations.

Principal-Agent Approaches

A second contribution from the study of firms for the study of international bureaucracies is principal-agent theory, which originates from new institutional economics. New institutional economics underscores the role of institutional frames and explicit or implicit contracts for the behavior of individual and collective actors. It builds on the assumption of the dominance of the self-interested and opportunistic motivations of all actors (Williamson 1985). Principal-agent theory was first applied to large corporations. Here, managers are conceptualized as agents who pursue individual interests that differ from the interests of the company's principals; namely, the shareholders. Although the managers can benefit from information asymmetries due to their better knowledge of the firm and the markets, the shareholders retain the final decision about the usage of their financial resources and can thus bestow and revoke authority from their agents. New institutional economic research has addressed the various dimensions of this relationship and potential institutional arrangements to overcome disparities between the principals' fundamental interests and the agents' information advantage.

When applied to international bureaucracies, principal-agent theory highlights the fundamental differences in individual interests of national governments as the principals and the bureaucracies as the agents.[12] It maintains that international bureaucracies are able to develop autonomy from its principals and thereby need to be conceptualized as actors in their own right. In this view, international bureaucracies are seen as self-interested bodies that are predominantly interested in increasing their individual resources and competences.[13] As for international bureaucracies, national governments can only partly control the behavior of the agents whom they entrusted with particular tasks in international politics. Within this framework, the activities of international bureaucracies need to be explained on the basis of their relationship to national governments that delegate authority to international bureaucracies. As Pollack (1997) points out, states act in situations of uncertainty and information asymmetries. Therefore, they create international bureaucracies to garner information about states and to disseminate this information to all other states. International bureaucracies can also help overcome uncertainties due to the inevitable incompleteness of contracts as a means of conflict resolution or help resolve social dilemma situations (Hawkins et al. 2006b). Within this framework of principal-agent theory, their autonomous influence results from the formation of preferences of national governments, from the imposed sanctions and voting schemes and from the uncertainty of the particular international policy field. According to Nielson and Tierney's model (2003), autonomous activities of international bureaucracies can be explained by the degree of homogeneity of national governments' interests and the coalitions they form vis-à-vis international bureaucracies and the international policies they address. What is more, international bureaucracies act within a chain of principal-agent relations that goes from national electorates to national governments, international organizations, and international bureaucracies. Their case study of the World Bank's environmental policies provides explanatory avenues to the understanding of several strategic choices of this international bureaucracy.

Though the principal-agent approach provides a strong set of arguments for the *existence* of autonomous influence of international bureaucracies, it has its limitations with regard to its *explanation*. First, principal-agent theories to a large part neglect the internal dynamics and formation of autonomous interests of international bureaucracies. These approaches emphasize the opportunistic behavior of bureaucracies and assume often the dominance of self-interested behavior with little empirical foundation. Hence, principal-agency theories have difficulties in capturing differences in the formation of preferences in international bureaucracies. The internal dynamics within bureaucracies and the emergence of organization-wide sets of preferences largely remain a black box.

Second, although the approach has proven fruitful for explaining behavioral choices of international bureaucracies through variation in principal-agent relations, it fails to explain variation in the behavior of international bureaucracies in cases of comparable principal-agent relations—which is rather frequent in the study program of this book. Principal-agent theory can thus be of only complementary use for this study program.

Summary

To sum up, despite a number of studies in international relations research and management studies that have been brought forward over the last decades, we still know little about the overall influence of international bureaucracies, and our knowledge is particularly poor when it comes to the *comparative* appraisal of the influence of *different* bureaucracies. Only few studies have dealt so far with international bureaucracies in a comparative way. This dearth is both surprising and unfortunate, given the general acknowledgment in political science that comparative research is well suited to provide insights that can hardly be expected from the isolated study of individual cases. Although our stock-taking exercise shows that the study of international relations has over the past decades learned some lessons about the roles and dynamics of international bureaucracies, we believe that a comparative approach that follows a coherent theoretical framework and a clear empirical methodology has great potential to advance our knowledge on international bureaucracies and, thereby, international organizations.

This is what we attempt in this book. Following this review of the literature, we now elaborate in chapter 3 on our research design, methodology, and empirical research procedures.

Notes

1. Dividing the period from 1816 to 1964 into thirty five-year periods, Wallace and Singer were able to answer the first question in the affirmative by discovering a positive correlation between the number of wars ended in one period and the number of international bureaucracies created in the following two periods. To answer the second question, the authors examined the reverse causal relation, that is, the correlation between the number of international bureaucracies created in one period and the frequency, magnitude, and severity of war in the following periods. As they found no significant correlation between these two variables, they concluded that international organizations were largely ineffective in preserving peace. The article triggered an intense debate about the limitations of Wallace and Singer's approach; see the comment by Bleicher (1971) and the reply by Wallace and Singer (1971).

2. The debate that preceded the foundation of the United Nations Environment Programme shares many similarities with the current debate about the need for a world environment organization. See Biermann and Bauer 2005.

3. For more detailed accounts of intergovernmental organizations and bureaucracies in the history of international relations theories, see Rochester 1986; Malik 1995; and Verbeek 1998.

4. See also Strange 1998, 214; De Senarclens 1993, 454–455; Kratochwil and Ruggie 1986; Martin and Simmons 1998.

5. Although none of the eleven case studies explicitly refers to the complete theoretical framework developed in the first chapter of the study, some chapters selectively apply parts of the framework, which, however, impedes a systematic comparison of their results (see Cain 1983; McJunkin 1983a, 1983b; Miller 1983).

6. In particular, Jacobson and Kay state that the selection of case study authors based on their expertise related to the specific problem areas implied that "the authors of the case studies were inevitably more interested in, and skilled at . . . assessing the state of progress of international action in each area" rather than in measuring and theoretically explaining the effectiveness of international organizations involved in addressing the respective problems (1983a, 314).

7. See Haas, Keohane, and Levy 1993; Keohane and Levy 1996; Miles et al. 2001; Mitchell 2002; Victor, Raustiala, and Skolnikoff 1998; Young 1997, 1999; Zürn 1998.

8. For illustrations, see Caporaso 1999; Moravcsik 1997, 1999; and Pollack 1997, 2003. We return to the "principal-agent problem" in more detail in the following. But see Verbeek 1998 and Reinalda and Verbeek 2004a for critical appraisals of the potential of public choice and rationalist approaches in discussing international organizations as autonomous actors. See also Stevis and Wilson (1995, 135–137) for a neofunctionalist critique of an epiphenomalist view of international bureaucracies.

9. Principal-agent approaches to the study of international organizations have recently begun to address this gap. For a discussion of their works, see the respective following section.

10. For details on the theoretical foundations of sociological institutionalism, see Finnemore 1996; Hall and Taylor 1996; and especially March and Olsen 1989, 1996, 1998.

11. See Araújo 2002; Boston et al. 1996; Jones et al. 2004; Kettl 2000; McLaughlin et al. 2002; and Pollitt and Bouckaert 2004.

12. Political science research that applied principal-agent theory started out from the study of domestic politics, as in Kiewiet and McCubbins 1991. Recent applications to international bureaucracies are Hawkins et al. 2006a; Nielson and Tierney 2003; Pollack 1997.

13. Hawkins et al. claim that principal-agent theory is principally open for different assumptions on the actors' preferences: "The approach is equally consistent with theories that posit rational, egoistic, wealth-maximizing actors and those that assume bounded-rational altruistic actors" (2006b, 7). However, the general thrust of this field addresses problems of (potential) opportunistic behavior of actors and thereby treats the latter as its basic assumption about the actors' preferences.

References

Alger, Chadwick F. 1970a. "Methodological Innovation in Research on International Organizations." In *Political Science Annual: An International Review,* edited by James A. Robinson, 209–240. Indianapolis and New York: Bobbs-Merrill.

Alger, Chadwick F. 1970b. "Research on Research: A Decade of Quantitative and Field Research on International Organizations." *International Organization* 24 (3): 414–450.

Allison, Graham T. 1971. *Essence of Decision Making: Explaining the Cuban Missile Crisis.* New York: HarperCollins.

Araújo, Joaquim. 2002. "NPM and the Change in Portuguese Central Government." *International Public Management Journal* 5 (3): 223–36.

Barnett, Michael N., and Martha Finnemore. 1999. "The Politics, Power, and Pathologies of International Organizations." *International Organization* 53 (4): 699–732.

Barnett, Michael N., and Martha Finnemore. 2004. *Rules for the World: International Organizations in Global Politics.* Ithaca, NY: Cornell University Press.

Bartlett, Robert V., Priya A. Kurian, and Madhu Malik, editors. 1995. *International Organizations and Environmental Policy.* Westport and London: Greenwood Press.

Beigbeder, Yves. 1997. *The Internal Management of United Nations Organizations: The Long Quest for Reform.* New York: St. Martin's Press.

Biermann, Frank, and Steffen Bauer, editors. 2005. *A World Environment Organization: Solution or Threat for Effective International Environmental Governance?* Aldershot, UK: Ashgate.

Bleicher, Samuel A. 1971. "Intergovernmental Organization and the Preservation of Peace: A Comment on the Abuse of Methodology." *International Organization* 25:298–305.

Boston, Jonathan, John Martin, June Pallot, and Pat Walsh. 1996. *Public Management: The New Zealand Model.* Oxford: Oxford University Press.

Brown Weiss, Edith, and Harold K. Jacobson, editors. 1998. *Engaging Countries. Strengthening Compliance with International Environmental Accords.* Cambridge, MA: MIT Press.

Cain, Melinda L. 1983. "Carbon Dioxide and the Climate: Monitoring and a Search for Understanding." In *Environmental Protection: The International Dimension,* edited by David A. Kay and Harold K. Jacobson, 75–100. Totowa, NJ: Allanheld, Osmun, and Co.

Caporaso, James A. 1999. "Toward a Normal Science of Regional Integration." *Journal of European Public Policy* 6 (1): 160–164.

Cox, Robert W. 1973. "ILO: Limited Monarchy." In *The Anatomy of Influence: Decision-Making in International Organization,* edited by Robert W. Cox and Harold K. Jacobson, 102–138. New Haven: Yale University Press.

Cox, Robert W., and Harold K. Jacobson. 1973a. "The Anatomy of Influence." In *The Anatomy of Influence: Decision-Making in International Organization,* edited by Robert W. Cox and Harold K. Jacobson, 371–436. New Haven: Yale University Press.

Cox, Robert W., and Harold K. Jacobson, editors. 1973b. *The Anatomy of Influence: Decision Making in International Organization.* New Haven and London: Yale University Press.

Cox, Robert W. 1983. "Gramsci, Hegemony, and International Relations: An Essay in Method." *Millennium: Journal of International Studies* 12 (2): 162–175.

De Senarclens, Pierre. 1993. "Regime Theory and the Study of International Organizations." *International Social Science Journal* 138:453–462.

De Senarclens, Pierre. 2001. "International Organizations and the Challenges of Globalization." *International Social Science Journal* 170:509–522.

Dijkzeul, Dennis. 1997. *The Management of Multilateral Organizations.* The Hague: Kluwer.

Dijkzeul, Dennis, and Yves Beigbeder, editors. 2003. *Rethinking International Organizations: Pathology and Promise.* New York and Oxford: Berghahn Books.

Finnemore, Martha. 1996. "Norms, Culture, and World Politics: Insights from Sociology's Institutionalism." *International Organization* 50 (2): 325–347.

Finnemore, Martha, and Kathryn Sikkink. 1998. "International Norm Dynamics and Political Change." *International Organization* 52 (4): 887–917.

Freeman, R. Edward. 1984. *Strategic Management: A Stakeholder Approach.* Boston: Pitman.

Geri, Laurance R. 2001. "New Public Management and the Reform of International Organizations." *International Review of Administrative Sciences* 67:445–460.

Grieco, Joseph M. 1988. "Anarchy and the Limits of Cooperation: A Realist Critique of the Newest Liberal Institutionalism." *International Organization* 42 (3): 485–507.

Haas, Ernst B. 1958. *The Uniting of Europe. Political, Social and Economical Forces 1950–1957.* London: Stevens.

Haas, Ernst B. 1990. *Where Knowledge is Power: Three Models of Change in International Organizations.* Berkeley: University of California Press.

Haas, Peter M., and Ernst B. Haas. 1995. "Learning to Learn: Improving International Governance." *Global Governance* 1:255–285.

Haas, Peter M., Robert O. Keohane, and Marc A. Levy, editors. 1993. *Institutions for the Earth: Sources of Effective International Environmental Protection.* Cambridge, MA: MIT Press.

Hall, Peter A., and Rosemary C. R. Taylor. 1996. "Political Science and the Three New Institutionalisms." *Political Studies* 44:936–957.

Hasenclever, Andreas, Peter Mayer, and Volker Rittberger. 1997. *Theories of International Regimes*. Cambridge, UK: Cambridge University Press.

Hawkins, Darren G., David A. Lake, Daniel L. Nielson, and Michael J. Tierney, editors. 2006a. *Delegation and Agency in International Organizations*. Cambridge, UK: Cambridge University Press.

Hawkins, Darren G., David A. Lake, Daniel L. Nielson, and Michael J. Tierney. 2006b. "Delegation Under Anarchy: States, International Organizations, and Principal-Agent Theory." In *Delegation and Agency in International Organizations*, edited by Darren G. Hawkins, David A. Lake, Daniel L. Nielson and Michael J. Tierney, 3–38. Cambridge, UK: Cambridge University Press.

Jacobson, Harold K., and David A. Kay. 1983a. "Conclusions and Policy." In *Environmental Protection: The International Dimension*, edited by David A. Kay and Harold K. Jacobson, 310–332. Totowa, NJ: Allanheld, Osmun, and Co.

Jacobson, Harold K., and David A. Kay. 1983b. "A Framework for Analysis." In *Environmental Protection: The International Dimension*, edited by David A. Kay and Harold K. Jacobson, 1–21. Totowa, NJ: Allanheld, Osmun, and Co.

Jervis, Robert. 1976. *Perception and Misperception in International Politics*. Princeton: Princeton University Press.

Joachim, Jutta, Bob Reinalda, and Bertjan Verbeek, editors. 2008. *International Organizations and Implementation: Enforcers, Managers, Authorities?* London: Routledge.

Jones, Lawrence R., and Fred Thomson. 1999. *Public Management: Institutional Renewal for the Twenty-First Century*. Stamford, CT: JAI Press.

Jones, Lawrence R., Kuno Schedler, and Ricardo Mussari, editors. 2004. *Strategies for Public Management Reform*. Amsterdam: Elsevier.

Jordan, Robert S. 2001. *International Organizations: A Comparative Approach to the Management of Cooperation*. Westport, CT: Praeger.

Kay, David A., and Harold K. Jacobson, editors. 1983. *Environmental Protection: The International Dimension*. Totowa, NJ: Allanheld, Osmun, and Co.

Kay, David A., and Eugene B. Skolnikoff, editors. 1972. *International Institutions and the Environmental Crisis*. Special issue of *International Organization* 26 (2).

Keohane, Robert O., and Marc A. Levy, editors. 1996. *Institutions for Environmental Aid: Pitfalls and Promise*. Cambridge, MA: MIT Press.

Keohane, Robert O., and Joseph S. Nye. 1974. "Transgovernmental Relations and International Organizations." *World Politics* 27 (1): 39–62.

Keohane, Robert O., and Joseph S. Nye. 1977. *Power and Interdependence. World Politics in Transition*. Boston: Little Brown.

Kettl, Donald F. 2000. *The Global Public Management Revolution. A Report on the Transformation of Governance*. Washington, DC: Brookings.

Kiewiet, D. Roderick, and Matthew D. McCubbins. 1991. *The Logic of Delegation: Congressional Parties and the Appropriation Process*. Chicago: University of Chicago Press.

Kratochwil, Friedrich, and John Gerard Ruggie. 1986. "International Organization: A State of the Art on an Art of the State." *International Organization* 40 (4): 753–775.

LaPalombara, Joseph. 2001a. "Power and Politics in Organizations: Public and Private Sector Comparisons," In *Handbook of Organizational Learning and Knowledge*, edited by Meinolf Dierkes, Ariane Berthoin Antal, John Child, and Ikujiro Nonaka, 557–581. Oxford: Oxford University Press.

LaPalombara, Joseph. 2001b. "The Underestimated Contributions of Political Science to Organizational Learning." In *Handbook of Organizational Learning and Knowledge*, edited by Meinolf Dierkes, Ariane Berthoin Antal, John Child, and Ikujiro Nonaka, 137–161. Oxford: Oxford University Press.

Malik, Madhu. 1995. "Do We Need a New Theory of International Organizations?" In *International Organizations and Environmental Policy*, edited by Robert V. Bartlett, Priya A. Kurian, and Madhu Malik, 223–237. Westport, CT: Greenwood Press.

March, James G., and Johan P. Olsen. 1989. *Rediscovering Institutions. The Organizational Basics of Politics*. New York: Free Press.

March, James G., and Johan P. Olsen. 1996. "Institutional Perspectives on Political Institutions." *Governance. An International Journal of Policy and Administration* 9 (3): 247–264.

March, James G., and Johan P. Olsen. 1998. "The Institutional Dynamics of International Political Orders." *International Organization* 52 (4): 943–969.

Martin, Lisa L., and Beth A. Simmons. 1998. "Theories and Empirical Studies of International Institutions." *International Organization* 52 (4): 729–757.

McJunkin, F. Eugene. 1983a. "Schistosomiasis: Limiting Adverse Health Consequences of Development Projects." In *Environmental Protection: The International Dimension*, edited by David A. Kay and Harold K. Jacobson, 200–216. Totowa, NJ: Allanheld, Osmun, and Co.

McJunkin, F. Eugene. 1983b. "Water Supply and Sanitation: Improving Life for the Rural Majority." In *Environmental Protection: The International Dimension*, edited by David A. Kay and Harold K. Jacobson, 119–139. Totowa, NJ: Allanheld, Osmun, and Co.

McLaughlin, Kate, Stephen Osborne, and Ewan Ferlie, editors. 2002. *New Public Management: Current Trends and Future Prospects*. London: Routledge.

Mearsheimer, John J. 1995. "The False Promise of International Institutions." *International Security* 19 (3): 5–49.

Miles, Edward L., Arild Underdal, Steinar Andresen, Jørgen Wettestad, Jon Birger Skjærseth, and Elaine M. Carlin, editors. 2001. *Environmental Regime Effectiveness. Confronting Theory with Evidence*. Cambridge, MA: MIT Press.

Miller, Kenton R. 1983. "The Earth's Living Terrestrial Resources: Managing their Conservation." In *Environmental Protection: The International Dimension*, edited by David A. Kay and Harold K. Jacobson, 240–266. Totowa, NJ: Allanheld, Osmun, and Co.

Mitchell, Ronald B. 2002. "International Environment." In *Handbook of International Relations*, edited by Walter Carlsnaes, Thomas Risse, and Beth A. Simmons, 500–516. London: Sage.

Moravcsik, Andrew. 1997. "Taking Preferences Seriously: A Liberal Theory of International Politics." *International Organization* 51 (4): 513–533.

Moravcsik, Andrew. 1999. "A New Statecraft? Supranational Entrepreneurs and International Cooperation." *International Organization* 53 (2): 267–306.

Ness, Gayl D., and Steven Brechin. 1988. "Bridging the Gap: International Organizations as Organizations." *International Organization* 42 (2): 245–273.

Nielson, Daniel L., and Michael J. Tierney. 2003. "Delegation to International Organizations: Agency Theory and World Bank Environmental Reform." *International Organization* 57 (2): 241–276.

Nye, Joseph S. 1973. "UNCTAD: Poor Nations' Pressure Group." In *The Anatomy of Influence: Decision-Making in International Organization*, edited by Robert W. Cox and Harold K. Jacobson, 334–370. New Haven: Yale University Press.

Pollack, Mark A. 1997. "Delegation, Agency, and Agenda Setting in the European Community." *International Organization* 51 (1): 99–134.

Pollack, Mark A. 2003. *The Engines of European Integration: Delegation, Agency and Agenda Setting in the EU*. Oxford: Oxford University Press.

Pollitt, Christopher, and Geert Bouckaert. 2004. *Public Management Reform. A Comparative Analysis*. Oxford: Oxford University Press.

Powell, Walter W., and Paul J. DiMaggio, editors. 1991. *The New Institutionalism in Organizational Analysis*. Chicago: Chicago University Press.

Reinalda, Bob, and Bertjan Verbeek, editors. 1998. *Autonomous Policy Making by International Organizations*. London: Routledge.

Reinalda, Bob, and Bertjan Verbeek. 2004a. "The Issue of Decision Making within International Organizations." In *Decision Making within International Organizations*, edited by Bob Reinalda and Bertjan Verbeek, 9–41. London: Routledge.

Reinalda, Bob, and Bertjan Verbeek, editors. 2004b. *Decision Making Within International Organizations*. London: Routledge.

Reschenthaler, G. B., and Fred Thompson. 1997. "The Learning Organization Framework and the New Public Management." In *International Perspectives on the New Public Management*, edited by Lawrence R. Jones, Kuno Schedler and Stephen W. Wade, 297–327. Greenwich, CT: JAI Press.

Rochester, Martin J. 1986. "The Rise and Fall of International Organizations as a Field of Study." *International Organization* 40 (4): 777–813.

Sandford, Rosemary. 1994. "International Environmental Treaty Secretariats: Stage-Hands or Actors?" In *Green Globe Yearbook of International Co-operation on Environment and Development 1994*, edited by Helge Ole Bergesen and Georg Parmann, 17–29. Oxford: Oxford University Press.

Schedler, Kuno, and Isabella Proeller. 2003. *New Public Management.* Bern, Suttgart, and Wien: Paul Haupt.

Scheinman, Lawrence. 1973. "IAEA: Atomic Condominium?" In *The Anatomy of Influence: Decision-Making in International Organization*, edited by Robert W. Cox and Harold K. Jacobson, 216–262. New Haven: Yale University Press.

Schmidt, Brian C. 2002. "On the History and Historiography of International Relations." In *Handbook of International Relations*, edited by Walter Carlsnaes, Thomas Risse, and Beth A. Simmons, 3–22. London: Sage.

Shanks, Cheryl, Harold K. Jacobson, and Jeffrey H. Kaplan. 1996. "Inertia and Change in the Constellation of International Governmental Organizations, 1981–1992." *International Organization* 50 (4): 593–627.

Simmons, Beth A., and Lisa L. Martin. 2002. "International Organizations and Institutions." In *Handbook of International Relations*, edited by Walter Carlsnaes, Thomas Risse, and Beth A. Simmons, 192–211. London: Sage.

Singer, J. David, and Michael Wallace. 1970. "Intergovernmental Organization and the Preservation of Peace, 1816–1964." *International Organization* 24 (3): 520–547.

Stevis, Dimitris, and Clifton Wilson. 1995. "The Institutionalization of International Environmental Policy: International Law and International Organizations." In *International Organizations and Environmental Policy*, edited by Robert V. Bartlett, Priya A. Kurian, and Madhu Madlik, 121–138. Westport, CT: Greenwood Publishing.

Strange, Susan. 1987. "The Persistent Myth of Lost Hegemony." *International Organization* 41 (4): 551–574.

Strange, Susan. 1998. "Why Do International Organizations Never Die?" In *Autonomous Policy Making by International Organizations*, edited by Bob Reinalda and Bertjan Verbeek, 213–220. London: Routledge.

Verbeek, Bertjan. 1998. "International Organizations: The Ugly Duckling of International Relations Theory?" In *Autonomous Policy Making by International Organizations*, edited by Bob Reinalda and Bertjan Verbeek, 11–26. London: Routledge.

Victor, David G., Kal Raustiala, and Eugene B. Skolnikoff. 1998. *The Implementation and Effectiveness of International Environmental Commitments. Theory and Practice.* Cambridge, MA: MIT Press.

Wallace, Michael D., and J. David Singer. 1971. "The Use and Abuse of Imagination." *International Organization* 25 (4): 953–957.

Waltz, Kenneth. 1979. *Theory of International Politics*. Reading, MA: McGraw-Hill.

Weiss, Thomas G., editor. 1975. *International Bureaucracy*. Lexington, MA: Lexington Books.

Wendt, Alexander. 2000. "On the Via Media: A Response to Critics." *Review of International Studies* 26 (1): 165–180.

Wettestad, Jørgen. 2001. "Designing Effective Environmental Regimes: The Conditional Keys." *Global Governance* 7 (3): 317–341.

Williamson, Oliver E. 1985. *The Economic Institutions of Capitalism: Firms, Markets, Regional Contracting*. New York: Free Press.

Young, Oran R. 1994. *International Environmental Governance: Protecting the Environment in a Stateless Society*. Ithaca, NY: Cornell University Press.

Young, Oran R., editor. 1997. *Global Governance: Drawing Insights from the Environmental Experience*. Cambridge, MA: MIT Press.

Young, Oran R., editor. 1999. *The Effectiveness of International Environmental Regimes: Causal Connections and Behavioral Mechanisms*. Cambridge, MA: MIT Press.

Zürn, Michael. 1998. "The Rise of International Environmental Politics." *World Politics* 50 (4): 617–649.

3

Studying the Influence of International Bureaucracies: A Conceptual Framework

Frank Biermann, Bernd Siebenhüner, Steffen Bauer, Per-Olof Busch, Sabine Campe, Klaus Dingwerth, Torsten Grothmann, Robert Marschinski, and Mireia Tarradell

This chapter develops the conceptual framework used in this book to assess and explain the influence of international bureaucracies. We conceptualize, first, the object of our studies: international bureaucracies. The next section elaborates our dependent variables and the concept of "influence" as we have employed it in our research. The third main section focuses on three clusters of explanatory factors that may explain variation in the degree and type of influence of international bureaucracies, and that we have analyzed in this book. The final section expounds our empirical research procedures, including our case selection, field research and interview methodology, and the expert survey.

Conceptualization of International Bureaucracies

We define international bureaucracies as agencies that have been set up by governments or other public actors with some degree of permanence and coherence and beyond formal direct control of single national governments (notwithstanding control by multilateral mechanisms through the collective of governments) and that act in the international arena to pursue a policy. In other words, international bureaucracies are a hierarchically organized group of international civil servants with a given mandate, resources, identifiable boundaries, and a set of formal rules of procedures within the context of a policy area.[1]

We thus distinguish international bureaucracies from ad hoc agencies, such as temporary conference secretariats or expert commissions; from loose networks of public or private actors that lack central control mechanisms; from purely national agencies, such as national development banks or environmental agencies; from transnational non-state actors ranging from Greenpeace International to the Catholic Church; and from profit-seeking corporations, such as Monsanto or Royal Dutch Shell. Our definition thus includes a wide array of actors, ranging from the United Nations Organization and its specialized agencies to its many semi-autonomous sub-bodies, such as treaty secretariats or specific programs.

Our concept of international bureaucracies, however, differs from terminology used in other bodies of literature; in particular, from international law, management studies, and parts of international relations research, in the following ways.

First, our definition of international bureaucracies is independent from their status under international law. International law accepts intergovernmental organizations as actors, that is, as entities "established by a treaty or other instrument governed by international law and possessing its own international legal personality."[2] Yet this legal conceptualization is of little use for a comparative political science analysis on the influence of international bureaucracies, some of which—such as the United Nations Development Programme—are important actors in international relations without having "personality" under international law. In the context of this book, the legal concept would render it impossible, for example, to compare the role of international bureaucracies in the international regimes on the protection of the high seas, on the ozone layer, and on the climate, which are covered by the mandates of the International Maritime Organization (legally an organization), the United Nations Environment Programme (legally a program of an organization), and the secretariat to the UN Framework Convention on Climate Change (legally a treaty sub-body). Our broader definition of international bureaucracies allows analyzing and comparing all of these entities notwithstanding their different legal status.

Second, our understanding of international bureaucracies is narrower than the concept of "organization" used in management studies. Here, organizations are often broadly conceptualized as "social device for efficiently accomplishing through group means some stated purpose" (Katz and Kahn 1966, 16), as formally established systems of social interactions to achieve certain goals (Blau and Scott 1962), or as "systems of coordinated and controlled activities that arise when work is embedded in complex networks of technical relations and boundary-spanning exchanges" (Meyer and Rowan 1991, 41). These definitions include almost any organized group. In particular, they include—and empirically in fact focus on—private commercial organizations, which are excluded in our study.

Third, we differentiate between international "bureaucracies" and "institutions." We recognize that it is not uncommon in broader policy debates to refer, for example, to the World Bank as part of the "Bretton Woods institutions." This usage, however, differs from the one that we use in this book and that is common in most social science writing. We define institutions as systems of norms, rules and decision-making procedures that give rise to social practices, that assign roles to participants in these practices, and that guide interactions among participants.[3] International bureaucracies have a normative structure—such as the basic legal framework that governs the work of the civil servants—but are essentially defined through their actor properties, including their physical existence in the form of buildings, personnel, letterheads, or seals. Institutions and regimes, on the other hand, remain abstract sets of principles, norms, rules, and procedures that do not possess a material entity of their own.

Fourth, as a consequence, we differentiate between international "organizations" and international "bureaucracies." We see an international organization as an institutional arrangement that combines a normative framework, member states, and a bureaucracy. For example, the International Labour Organization agrees through decision of its general assembly and subsequent ratification by member states on the creation of new international rules in its area of activity. States can join the organization, can participate in the rule-making process, and are then expected to accept and implement the collectively agreed-upon rules. In addition, the International Labour Organization comprises a hierarchical organized group of civil servants that acts within the mandate of the organization and within the decisions of the assembly of member states. This is what we call the international bureaucracy—in the case of the International Labour Organization, it even has a different name, the "International Labour Office."[4]

This more precise terminology increases the analytical rigor of this study. Reinalda and Verbeek, for example, employ three different definitions of "international organizations" in the same volume. As they write, *"When in this volume we discuss an international organization's policy description*, we imply the acts of the international secretariat, including its substructures of committees, commissions, and departments (*unless stated otherwise*). *When we employ the term decision-making within international organizations, we usually* refer to the entire policy process as defined by the international legal framework of an intergovernmental organization, in which member states, the international secretariat and various other actors participate. *Occasionally, however, decision-making within international organizations explicitly refers to* the policy process within the international secretariat" (Reinalda and Verbeek 2004, 14, emphasis added). Cortell and Peterson (2004) have been analytically more rigorous in delineating a "supportive administrative apparatus" within international organizations. We believe that our use of the term "bureaucracy" is similar to their concept of a supportive administrative apparatus, yet also less cumbersome.

In sum, our approach of differentiating between international bureaucracies and international organizations helps to keep analytically apart the international bureaucracies as actors and the collectivity of member states of an international organization, both of which are referred to as international organizations in much writing in the mainstream international relations literature.

Measuring the Influence of International Bureaucracies

Conceptualization of Influence
In this book, we assess the influence of international bureaucracies in world politics. We prefer the concept of "influence" to other terms used to assess the consequences of the behavior of actors. The concept of "power" denotes a degree of involuntary, forced action by the addressee of an international bureaucracy, which is at odds with the "soft" character of the influence that most international bureaucracies can bestow. *Webster's Dictionary* defines "influence" as "the bringing about of an effect . . . by a gradual process; controlling power quietly exerted; agency . . . of any kind which affects, modifies, or sways."

The term "effectiveness" is widely used in the analysis of regimes, where scholars attempt to study and to compare the effectiveness of regimes. Yet when applied not to normative settings such as regimes but to bureaucratic actors, "effectiveness" would gain a narrow managerial and normatively loaded connotation in the sense of assessing relative differences in the outcome of an actor's behavior. Antonyms then were ineffectiveness or ineffectualness, which *Webster's Dictionary* defines as "lacking the power to be effective." In our view, political science is better advised to concentrate on understanding the overall influence that international bureaucracies have, as opposed to determining which organization is effective or more or less ineffective. On the other hand, we are interested in understanding the "effects" of the actions of international bureaucracies, that is—according to *Webster's Dictionary*—something that is "produced by an agent or cause; the event which follows immediately from an antecedent, called the cause; the result, consequence, or outcome." Hence, the sum of all effects observable for, and attributable to, an international bureaucracy is what we understand as its "influence."

The influence of international bureaucracies can be assessed at three levels: the *output*, which is the actual activity of the bureaucracy; the *outcome*, which is the observable changes in the behavior of actors targeted by the bureaucracies' output (including unintended consequences); and the *impact*, which is the changes in economic, social or ecological parameters that result from the change in actors' behavior. The distinction between output, outcome, and impact is common, though often with varying terminology, in the field of policy analysis. It is also the main distinction in the international relations literature on the effectiveness of international regimes. This distinction has several advantages (Young 2001, 114–115): it allows linking the study of regime effectiveness to the literature in policy analysis dealing with similar analytical problems. It encourages a systematic consideration of substantive regulations and procedural efforts where the length of the causal chain linking regimes and their potential effects is short. For the same reasons, we use output, outcome, and impact as starting points for the analysis of the influence of international bureaucracies.

The differentiation of output, outcome and impact is also consistent with most regime studies that adopt different terminology, which allows for general comparisons of empirical findings. For example, Edith Brown Weiss and Harold Jacobson's edited volume (1998) analyzes as dependent variables regime "implementation"—defined as "measures that states take to make international accords effective in domestic law"—and "compliance"—whether countries adhere to the provisions of an accord and implement corresponding measures. Both terms fall under our notion of outcome (Jacobson and Brown Weiss 1998, 4). Jacobson and Brown Weiss define "effectiveness" as attaining the objectives of regimes with a view to both achieving the stated objectives of the treaty and addressing the underlying problem (5). This again falls under our category of (organizational) impact.

In sum, output, outcome, and impact are useful to categorize different dimensions of the influence of international bureaucracies. They also allow linking the analysis of this influence with the much larger literature on regime effectiveness.

Within this conceptual framework, the eventual *impact* of bureaucracies on targeted policy objectives in the economic, social or ecological sphere is the broadest notion of the influence of international bureaucracies. Yet, it is also the most difficult indicator. Regarding environmental bureaucracies such as the secretariat of the UN Environment Programme, for example, one could try to assess the "environmental influence" of the bureaucracy. On the one hand, such an approach is warranted because any organizational activity will be fruitless if no real changes in final target indicators of a policy can be identified, be they improvements in the natural environment, in health indicators, or in economic wealth. In practice, however, this link is highly difficult to make. Regarding international environmental policy, the state of most ecological systems has deteriorated despite all efforts. In those areas where improvements are observable, it is difficult to identify the influence of an international regime, let alone the influence of an international bureaucracy in the regime. Most regime analysts in this field have thus discarded the possibility of measuring the ecological impact of the regime that they study,[5] notwithstanding some exceptions that argue for the inclusion of, or even for focusing on, ecological indicators for the analysis of regime influence.

A less demanding approach—and the other extreme on a continuum of influence indicators—is measuring organizational influence based on the *output* of the international bureaucracy, that is, its actual activity and productivity such as laws and standards enacted, publications and scientific findings disseminated, money spent, or advisors dispatched.[6] An advantage of output indicators is the ease by which they can be measured. Data are generally available and can be collected from the archives or Web sites of the agencies. International lawyers heavily focus on output indicators, particularly in studies on the effectiveness of international treaties. For political scientists, however, studying output indicators alone is hardly satisfactory. This is because they do not inform about whether governments have complied with laws and standards; whether publications and scientific findings have been noticed, considered, or accepted; whether money spent has had any real impact or has instead been wasted; or whether advisors who have been sent out could muster any influence with their addressees.

Therefore, all case studies in this book focus on measuring the *outcome* of the policies enacted by international bureaucracies. Outcome is a more informative variable than purely studying organizational output, and a more feasible variable than studying the environmental or economic impact of a bureaucracy.[7] Policy outcome comprises the (anticipated and unanticipated) changes in the behavior of other actors—such as governments, nongovernmental lobbyist groups, scientists, the mass media, or individual actors—induced by the bureaucracy. We do not make a distinction here between targeted actor and nontargeted actors, thus casting the net wider and allowing for the identification of broader unintended effects of activities of international bureaucracies.

Point of Reference

A key methodological problem in assessing the influence of international bureaucracies is the point of reference against which variation in the influence of international bureaucracies is measured. We discuss here two options—the concept of compliance with internal or external goals and the concept of relative change—and then elaborate on the relationship between the influence of international bureaucracies and regime effectiveness.

Compliance with Internal or External Goals   One option is to measure influence against the backdrop of internal or external goals, that is, the absolute influence of a bureaucracy in terms of goal attainment. Degrees in influence would be assessed in relation to the *bureaucracy's own goals*, either as autonomously developed by the bureaucracy's leadership and published, for example, in mission statements, or as given by member states. This would be in parallel to the notion of compliance with the norms and rules of a regime as known from international law and some strands of regime analysis. For example, Chayes, Handler Chayes, and Mitchell argue that an actor complies with a treaty if its "behavior conforms to an explicit rule of a treaty" (1998, 40). According to this essentially legalistic conceptualization, it is analyzed to what degree the observed behavior conforms to the behavior required by a treaty provision.

Regarding international bureaucracies, compliance would indicate their influence as long as they have the mandate to set standards and regulations. One would then measure governments' compliance with different sets of regulations of the bureaucracy, for example with the World Bank's standards on "good governance." Likewise, many secretariats of environmental treaties may request reports on environmental policies of treaty members, which could also be analyzed in terms of governmental compliance with the goals set by the secretariat. Then, compliance could be parsed out in weak, moderate, and strong compliance, which would—if variation between different bureaucracies were observable—allow for an examination of the causes of such variation. However, in general international bureaucracies have only limited legislative competencies, and "compliance" will thus be of little help for larger comparative studies, such as the one in this book. Compliance with organizational standards can be only an additional indicator for measuring the influence of international bureaucracies.

Furthermore, use of compliance indicators that refer to the bureaucracy's own goals for comparision can cause an endogeneity problem: bureaucracies that set only modest goals would be seen as highly effective if these goals were met, whereas more ambitious agencies would be easily seen as lacking influence, although their actual influence on the behavior of actors may be comparable or even larger. This problem would also pertain to the method of externally setting goals by the analyst, for example, developing a baseline of influence for different bureaucracies. In short, although compliance may help as an indicator for measuring the outcome of the activity of international bureaucracies with a legislative mandate, we prefer in this book to focus on functional indicators, that is, on changes in actors' behavior that can be traced back to activities of a bureaucracy.

Theoretically, another alternative would have been to draw on economic concepts of optimal solutions, such as the regime effectiveness scale from 0 to 1 advanced by Helm and Sprinz (2000). They employ, based on economic theory, a concept of collective optimum for regime effectiveness that resulted in effectiveness scores for international regimes calculated as "actual regime performance" minus "no-regime counterfactual" divided by "collective optimum" minus "no-regime counterfactual." Helm and Sprinz argue that this measurement procedure would be superior to qualitative studies on effectiveness, because both method and underlying assumptions have been clearly described and because their standardized method lends itself to the comparison of the effect of different regimes. This approach, however, suffers from the definition of collective optimum. It is based on the extrapolation of the pre-regime situation and economic equilibrium models rather than on empirical observation. This makes it difficult to assess the optimal level of environmental policy, which Helm and Sprinz see at the point at which marginal social benefits associated with the last unit of abatement equal the marginal social costs of achieving that unit.[8] These problems multiply if one uses economic methods for assessing the influence of international bureaucracies. Such concepts are thus inapplicable for the study of the influence of international bureaucracies within regimes, which is a more daunting task.

Relative Change   For these reasons, we employ in this book the concept of *relative change* in the behavior of actors. We compare actor behavior before and after an organizational activity has been enacted without referring to some form of absolute standard, either the regime goals and objectives or a collective optimum.

A central methodological element— in particular regarding changes in behavior of actors—is therefore the assessment against the *counterfactual situation*: how would the behavior of an actor have evolved if the international bureaucracy in question would not have been involved or if it would not have enacted the policy the outcome of which is studied?[9] The general idea thus is to assess an improvement in relation to the hypothetical state of affairs that would most likely not have occurred in the absence of activity of the bureaucracy in question. Methodologically, we have addressed this issue by, for example, interviews with senior experts and decision makers in which we elicited their assessment of the no-bureaucracy counterfactual. Although this method of counterfactual reasoning is problematic and has been controversial in political science for decades, it remains a highly useful tool to assess the outcome of activities of international bureaucracies. To avoid the fallacies of counterfactual reasoning, our case study authors have tried to identify and subsequently to focus on key actors in crucial situations of decision making as well as to be precise in the description of an assumed counterfactual development (see also Underdal 2001a, 53).

Bureaucratic Influence versus Regime Effectiveness   Finally, a special problem for measuring the influence of international bureaucracies is the separation of the influence of policies of an international bureaucracy from the background noise of general political developments, which may range from the activities of other international bureaucracies or of governments to other, more generic factors that influence changes in the behavior of actors, such as changes in the economic situation, elections, or some form of crisis. In particular, the assessment of the outcomes of activities of international bureaucracies is often compounded by the problem of assessing first the outcomes of the international regime (or regimes) that may influence the particular issue area, and second to separate the outcomes of the activities of the bureaucracy from the outcome of the regime.[10] This is a widespread analytical problem, because issue-specific international bureaucracies are usually established by multilateral treaties for a range of functions. For instance, the regime on substances that deplete the ozone layer is commonly found to be effective (see Bauer, this volume, chapter 9). Would it still have been (as) effective without its secretariat that has been set up through the 1987 Montreal Protocol? Which indicators could plausibly help us to assess the distinct effect of the ozone secretariat in successfully implementing the policies of this regime?

It is therefore necessary to separate the outcome of a treaty-based regime as a normative framework that governs the behavior of states and other actors, and the outcome of the policies enacted by the treaty secretariat, that is, the international bureaucracy active in this area.

One could argue that such separation would be superfluous, as what really matters is the change of behavior of actors, no matter whether this has been brought about by the regime as a normative framework or by the international bureaucracy as an actor in its own right. Yet such separation is necessary for the comparative analysis of different international bureaucracies in different regime settings, in which the regimes may all have similar degrees of effectiveness with similar regime characteristics, but in which the setup of the international bureaucracy significantly differs. Hence, the analysis of the outcome of the activities of international bureaucracies will remain inherently interlinked with the study of regime effectiveness.

In addition to the difficulty of separating regime effectiveness from the influence of the bureaucracy itself, a dynamic perspective needs to analyze the bureaucracy and its influence over time. Ideally, this would require a long-term study with data collections at several points in time over a number of years. Moreover, one would have to strive for comparable data and data collection processes in each field of study in order to be able to identify inherent changes in the research object. In general, this empirical research design is hardly economical and practically feasible. Research funds often do not allow for several data collection rounds and only very few research projects can be extended to periods of about ten years. This book is no different. Therefore, the case study authors in this volume had to satisfy themselves with one or a few data collection processes. Under these circumstances, a retrospective research design was employed. It poses retrospective questions to interviewees and analyzes available data from different periods in time. In doing so, information on past dynamics could be gathered even though—as in the case of interview data—it might be biased through the present views and perceptions of the interviewees.

Areas of Influence

In this book, we have organized the empirical analysis of the influence of international bureaucracies through looking at three areas. We describe them as their cognitive, normative, and executive influence: in other words, we look at bureaucracies as knowledge-brokers, as negotiation-facilitators, and as capacity-builders.

Cognitive Influence First, we analyze whether international bureaucracies influence the behavior of political actors by changing their knowledge and belief systems. It is a robust finding in the literature that knowledge brokers have a significant influence on the creation and effectiveness of regimes. Miles and colleagues (2001), for example, hypothesized that the existence of informal networks of experts contributes to regime effectiveness by strengthening the knowledge base on which regimes can be designed and can operate. Also, the more integrated an epistemic community is and the deeper it penetrates national decision making, the more effective Miles and colleagues expect a regime to be. This is also supported by the comparative study program by Brown Weiss and Jacobson (1998), who concluded that the greater the size, strength, and activism of epistemic communities, the greater the probability of both implementation and compliance. They found that implementation and compliance became more likely with increases in the flow of scientific and technical information about targeted activities, if the information is in a form that is understood by governments and public pressure groups.

All case studies in this book analyzed in detail the extent to which international bureaucracies have an autonomous influence on knowledge production and consumption. Indicators for such cognitive influence that were analyzed include: uptake of information from the bureaucracy (e.g., press declarations, annual reports, thematic studies, databases, scientific publications, or official strategy papers) in public debate and general media coverage; use of information through decision makers; impact of such information on the generation or synthesis of scientific or technical knowledge.

Normative Influence   Second, the case studies in this book analyze how international bureaucracies influence global environmental governance through the creation, support and shaping of norm-building processes for issue-specific international cooperation. We look at how bureaucracies influence international norm setting both in the early stages—for example, through the initiation of diplomatic conferences at which international treaties are negotiated and signed—and in the later phase of treaty implementation and treaty revision (e.g., Young 1994; Sandford 1996; Beach 2004). Oran Young, for instance, observes that international bureaucrats can exercise considerable influence in international negotiations "even when they are not key players during the negotiation stage" (1994, 170). We thus analyzed to what extent international bureaucracies shape procedures and provide arenas for issue-specific negotiations, frame inter- and transnational processes of bargaining and arguing, advance the inclusion or exclusion of actors in international policy processes, and advance the codification and development of international law.

Executive Influence   Third, we analyze the influence of international bureaucracies on global environmental governance through the direct assistance to countries in their effort to implement international agreements, which might reshape national interests. Research on regime effectiveness has shown that administrative capacity at the national level is a crucial factor in explaining variance among the performances of countries in implementing international agreements.[11] Countries with stronger administrative capacities are in a better position to implement international environmental standards. Here, again, it is particularly international bureaucracies that help raise the administrative capacity in many countries, especially in the developing world.[12]

Capacity building is more than a technical endeavor. International bureaucracies shape through their outreach programs in the capitals of member states the policies of their host countries, through, for example, training programs for mid-level civil servants that are influenced by ideas, concepts and policies that international bureaucracies propagate. This is, for example, one main conclusion of the United Nations Educational, Scientific, and Cultural Organization (UNESCO) study by Finnemore

(1993). Bureaucracies are also important diffusion agents of national policies or technologies. Once policies in one country, for example, have been identified as useful to reach certain policy targets, they could be spread to other countries through an international bureaucracy (Busch and Jörgens 2005).

In this area, all case study authors searched for the effects of actions of the bureaucracies on the exchange of information at the national level; for the influence of workshops, skills-oriented training programs, and demonstration projects provided for by the international bureaucracy; for the influence of national and transnational partnerships generated or supported by the bureaucracy; for the effects of the financial support or technology transfer provided for or supported by the international bureaucracy; as well as for the adoption or reformulation by governments of new laws and programs, new agencies (e.g., research institutions, environmental ministries, or advisory councils), or new instruments and practices to protect the environment.

The empirical findings in these three areas are presented in the case study chapters in this book independently. In practice, the three areas are often interlinked, and areas of influence may overlap. Within the framework of larger institutions, bureaucracies assist in generating the knowledge base for regime creation and development, provide facilities for continued negotiations, and assist in regime implementation by building up capacities in member states.

Explaining Variation in the Influence of International Bureaucracies

If international bureaucracies vary in their influence, the question arises of how to explain this variation. Understanding such variation might help devise reform strategies to assist them to learn and to adjust their influence and, with a view to decision makers in national governments, to make international bureaucracies more efficient and effective by altering their design. There is hardly any literature that offers convincing and tested hypotheses on explaining variation in output, outcome, and impact of international bureaucracies. In this book, we therefore analyze a set of potential explanatory variables that are derived from different strands of research, including international relations theory, management studies, and policy science.

We distinguish between three clusters of explanatory variables: the external *problem structure*; the *polity* set by the bureaucracies' principals within which the bureaucrats need to function; and the *activities and procedures* that the staff of the bureaucracies develops and implements within the constraints of problem structure and polity framework. The following section summarizes the main hypotheses that we developed at the start of the project. Chapter 13 presents in detail our findings.

Problem Structure

First, all case studies have analyzed how the influence of international bureaucracies has been affected by the type of problem they are faced with. The relevance of problem structures is a robust finding of the regime literature, and it is plausible to also hold for the influence of international bureaucracies. Miles and colleagues (2001), for example, point to the character of the problem as a potential influence on regime effectiveness. According to Arild Underdal's conceptualization (2001a, 2001b), the character of a problem can be benign (characterized by problems of coordination, symmetry or indeterminate distribution and crosscutting cleavages) or malign, that is, characterized by incongruity, asymmetry, and cumulative cleavages. Likewise, they emphasize the relevance of the problem-solving capacity in an issue area to account for observable variation in regime effectiveness, with problem-solving capacity being a function of the institutional setting (the rules of the game), the distribution of power among the actors involved, and the skill and energy available for the political engineering of cooperative solutions. In a similar vein, the "international environment" and the "characteristics of the activity" are conceptualized as key factors to explain regime effectiveness by Jacobson and Brown Weiss, in addition to regime-specific factors (Jacobson and Brown Weiss 1998, 6–7). Problem structures may explain variation in influence between bureaucracies that have otherwise identical characteristics.

Problems are differentially structured, first, in different policy areas: international bureaucracies may be less likely to be influential in questions of security and war and peace than in the international regulation of telecommunication. Second, problems are differentially structured within a policy area: the regulation of the emission of ozone-depleting substances is easier than that of the emission of greenhouse gases, and the influence of international bureaucracies may be greater when easy problems are at stake. Third, problems are differentially structured over time in the policy cycle, which may grant bureaucracies different degrees and types of influence during the stages of agenda setting, regime negotiation, or policy implementation. Some bureaucracies are more focused on, and influential in, standard setting and policy implementation than in influencing the agenda of world politics.

We have hypothesized that in environmental policy, two factors make a problem less conducive for the influence of an international bureaucracy: the cost of public action and regulation, and the international and national salience of a problem. First, we have hypothesized that the higher the costs of international regulation, the more likely it is that governments try to retain control over the political process and to withhold influence and authority from international bureaucracies (or any other actors, for that matter). Second, we have hypothesized that the higher the saliency of a problem in a country, the more likely it is that governments withhold influence from international bureaucracies (see also Cox and Jacobson 1973). By saliency, we mean the perceived relevance of a problem to a national government, including the visibility of the problem, its perceived urgency, and the level of affectedness of a country. Chapter 13 reports on our results.

Polity

In addition, all case studies have explored the extent to which the influence of bureaucracies has been determined by their legal, institutional, and financial framework that has been set—and continuously altered and affected—by states as their principals. We conceptualize this framework as the *polity* within which the members of bureaucracies are forced to act. In the domestic context, the principals are parts of the government of a country—often the legislative bodies that enact new laws, policies, and programs and that allocate resources, both of which determine the degree of freedom of the bureaucratic actors. For international bureaucracies, the principals are usually governments. Governments keep some control in different forms. In the case of full-fledged international organizations, governments will be formally members of the organization and set the polity through their participation in the general assembly of the organization or in its governing council, executive boards, or commissions. In the case of subordinate programs, such as the UN Development Programme, final control rests with the collective of governments represented in the UN General Assembly, delegated to a governing council of the program that comprises fewer governments. Finally, in the case of treaty secretariats, governments set their polity framework through participation in the conference of the parties of the treaty.

This principal-agent relationship creates particular problems for the analysis of international bureaucracies. One is the problem of attribution discussed previously, that is, the question whether a change in actor behavior is attributable to the overall effectiveness of a regime—understood as a set of principles, rules, norms and decision-making procedures—or to a particular bureaucracy in this field. The result of the work of the World Bank, for example, is determined by the overall legal and political regime created by governments and the financial resources made available, as well as by the policies enacted by the Bank's leadership and staff. We look, in particular, at three factors of the institutional and legal framework: competences, resources, and embeddedness.

Competences   The polity framework that governments create for an international bureaucracy is characterized by the degree of competences that they grant to the bureaucracy, including the formal rights of the leadership and staff of the bureaucracy. The degree of competences that governments concede to an international bureaucracy varies and could help explain variation in its subsequent influence. Hence, we have hypothesized that a bureaucracy equipped with many and far-reaching competencies vis-à-vis member states is likely to have more autonomous influence than a bureaucracy with little or no such competencies.

The question of the formal mandate given by governments to a bureaucracy relates to the question of its setting within the framework of an international regime. For example, many international bureaucracies are formally secretariats of multilateral treaties and may differ with regard to the formal competences they have been granted by treaty parties. As for the larger international bureaucracies, such as the secretariats of specialized UN agencies or of the United Nations Organization as such, all are usually embedded in some normative framework that is governed by states, ranging from human rights regimes to economic and environmental regimes. Moreover, governments may limit the freedom of an organization to decide on its internal rules of procedure through, for example, restrictions regarding staff recruitment and selection of the organization's leadership. It seems plausible that bureaucracies are more influential the more weakly they are regulated within a regime. Wettestad (2001), for example, argues that regimes with secretariats that have a financially strong and relatively autonomous position tend to be more effective. One potential factor is the form of voting within the collective assembly of principals (such as the general assembly of an organization or the conference of the parties). Unanimity could grant a bureaucracy a higher degree of autonomy, as it needs only one principal as support to block regulation through the community of principals (Reinalda and Verbeek 2004, 23). Another factor could be the degree of discretion that governments grant a bureaucracy in fulfilling its mandate (Cortell and Peterson 2004). In sum, we have hypothesized that the more autonomously a bureaucracy may act within a given institution, the more influential its actions will be vis-à-vis other actors operating within the same regime.

Related to this is the hypothesis drawn from regime analysis that regimes with few and homogeneous participants tend to be more effective than regimes with many and heterogeneous participants. Many regional regimes in the industrialized world, for example, appear to have high degrees of effectiveness. As argued by Wettestad (2001), however, in the longer term it is doubtful whether regimes that do not cover all contributors to a problem can remain effective. It has been shown, for example, that the influence of global institutions for scientific advice, such as the Intergovernmental Panel on Climate Change, is limited if not all constituencies are included (Biermann 2002). In line with principal-agent theory (Hawkins et al. 2006; Nielson and Tierney 2003), however, we believe that international bureaucracies are likely to be able to increase their autonomy the more principals they have. More and heterogeneous principals create opportunities for international bureaucracies to utilize disagreement and complex negotiation situations to their advantage and to gain influence in negotiations through offering their services as neutral mediator and broker in a contested bargaining situation (see Reinalda and Verbeek 2004, 23). Therefore, we have hypothesized that bureaucracies tend to have more autonomous influence the more principals they have and the more members the underlying regime or overall organization has.

Resources Governments regulate the scope of activities of an international bureaucracy through the allocation of resources regarding their staff and finances. This includes the absolute amount of resources as well as the reliability of funding (which could be based on assessed contributions or made dependent on regular pledging conferences) and the freedom to spend the resources, which could be, for example, earmarked or transferred to trust funds. In public discourse, it is generally maintained that organizational influence increases with more resources.

Within management studies, however, several studies have shown that a more generous allocation of resources does not necessarily correlate with increases in organizational influence. On the other hand, in the case of international bureaucracies, financial and human resources could well translate into influence in world politics. We have thus hypothesized that size grants larger degrees of autonomy from governments and that it tends to increase the autonomous influence of bureaucracies.

Embeddedness   Third, the polity framework set by governments is characterized by both degree of fit between the bureaucracy's mandate and the respective problem, and by the embedding of a particular bureaucracy in a larger organizational setting. Especially in the field of environmental policy, probably the area most diverse and fragmented in its institutional setting, the "problem of fit" is increasingly discussed with a view to possible limits in the influence of policies due to a mismatch between the problem and the institutional and organizational response to it.[13] This does not imply that multi-issue agencies covering a wide range of issues are always less influential than single-issue bureaucracies. Multi-issue bureaucracies can have advantages because they can use inter-issue linkages and learning processes more effectively. We have hypothesized that multi-issue bureaucracies are less likely to succeed when the different issues they deal with have highly different problem structures and relate to different organizational fields. On the contrary, if multi-issue organizations are well connected to other institutions and actors in *all* different policy fields and do not prioritize one over another, the more likely it is that they use issue linkages and learning processes, thereby increasing their influence.

People and Procedures
Finally, all case studies have investigated in detail the role of leadership and staff of an international bureaucracy that shape its policies, programs, and activities, and eventually its influence. The relation between organizational setup in terms of people and procedures and its influence has been studied in depth in the management literature, from which we derive a number of hypotheses regarding international bureaucracies. We distinguish four variables: organizational expertise, organizational structure, organizational culture, and organizational leadership. All are determined by the bureaucracy within the framework of the polity and can potentially explain variation in its influence.

Organizational Expertise First, international bureaucracies may have influence through their expertise, that is, their ability to generate and process knowledge. Given significant scientific and political uncertainties in global environmental governance, knowledge and adequate methods to process knowledge inside international bureaucracies seems important. International bureaucracies therefore require well-functioning systems of collecting, generating, selecting, processing, and distributing knowledge on various issues.[14] Therefore, we have hypothesized that the better an international bureaucracy is at generating and processing knowledge, the more influential it is.

In our empirical studies, we focused on internal mechanisms to build and maintain expertise. Empirical research hence investigated the mechanisms of how and how often the bureaucracy and its members draw on external expertise from scientific sources, conferences, or nongovernmental sources. We also studied how international bureaucracies build their own expertise, for instance through internal seminars, study programs, own research, or external consultants. Because it is the individuals who carry the knowledge, we included the professional backgrounds and trainings of the workforce in our study. Also, the technical devices to maintain expertise such as data bases, libraries, or research facilities were of interest to us. Factors such as the scientific credibility and political neutrality of the documents and the work of the bureaucracy were treated as mediating factors between the internal features and the external influence.

Organizational Structure Second, the formal structures of bureaucracies—that is, the formalized internal rules and procedures that assign tasks and positions in the hierarchy—may influence behavior of individuals and processes of change and development. Several factors relate to the ability of an international bureaucracy to achieve its goals and to learn (March and Simon 1958, Blau and Scott 1962, Mintzberg 1979). For example, bureaucracies may vary regarding the definition and assignment of tasks and responsibilities that regulate the division and coordination of work between staff. Poor management may lead to conflicts, redundancies, inefficiencies, delays, and reduced or lacking outputs. Therefore, the clear structuring of tasks and responsibilities seems key for an effective performance of international bureaucracies. Likewise, bureaucracies may have different degrees of formalization of internal routines and decision-making procedures. To act as a collective body, some formalized rules for decision making will be mandatory and efficient organization of work requires some standardization and formalization. However, many studies show the emerging problems and inefficiencies arising from formalization (see, e.g., Argyris 1996; Dierkes et al. 2001). On the other hand, the structures must provide sufficient flexibility and freedom for learning on the individual as well as collective level. Therefore, a balance between openness and formalization is needed (Schwandt and Marquard 2000).

Furthermore, all case study authors looked at internal "learning mechanisms" of bureaucracies (Popper and Lipshitz 1995). These are structural arrangements to use experiences by reflecting on them and to turn them into action.[15] Learning mechanisms can be informal, like focused personal communication among participants, or formalized, in the form of evaluation workshops or institutionalized review committees with a distinct set of rules of procedure. Another mechanism can be the deliberate exchange of individuals among different units or departments. This has often triggered changes and fast distribution of new knowledge throughout an organization (Marquardt 1996). As far as international bureaucracies are concerned, we assumed that a transfer of procedural knowledge from one organizational unit to another or from one organization to another can best be carried out through real people who carry this knowledge. Without such mechanisms, we expected few learning processes within an organization and thereby limited influence. Based on these considerations, we have hypothesized that organizational structures within international bureaucracies need to have clear responsibilities and, at the same time, to be open for change and to provide opportunities to reflect and to learn in order to enable the bureaucracy to be influential.

Organizational Culture   Third, bureaucracies differ regarding their organizational culture. In contrast to a formalized structure, the culture of an organization is largely informal and highlights hidden and soft factors that are more difficult to analyze and measure. We define organizational culture as the set of commonly shared basic assumptions in the organization that result from previous organizational learning processes and include the professional cultures and backgrounds of the staff members.[16] In general, these basic assumptions are value-laden ways to view the world that include certain solutions to known problems. Among the numerous factors that are of relevance for the culture of international bureaucracies, we focus on professional cultures.[17] Professional cultures are relevant for the external influence and the exchange of knowledge among staff members. If an international bureaucracy is for instance dominated by economists, one can expect a focus on market-based solutions. The same bureaucracy dominated by other professionals—say, biologists—might generate different influence and possibly favor state intervention to save ecological systems. Also, organizations with a mix of individuals from different professions who need to collaborate might be better equipped to exchange knowledge between different fields of expertise than organizations dominated by one profession. A mix of professions can thus be assumed to promote the exchange of knowledge.

Organizational Leadership Finally, we assume that the influence of bureaucracies differs with the specific behavior of staff members. Within the framework of a specific organizational context, individuals and groups have different choices in how to behave and how to fill their given positions. This applies in particular to executive personnel.[18] Here, the management literature distinguishes different types of leadership: a hierarchical style of leadership, where executives decide by themselves without involving their employees; a consultative style of leadership, in which executives ask for the opinion of their employees and decide by themselves; cooperative leadership, in which directors together with employees search for new solutions but directors decide by themselves; and participatory leadership, in which employees are granted far-reaching participation in decision making, for instance through voting. Whereas hierarchical styles are expected to allow for efficient and expeditious decision making, participatory styles increase employees' commitment to find new solutions and to implement and communicate them internally and externally.

Within this framework, leaders of bureaucracies can be popular, charismatic and effective, or the opposite. According to Young (1991), leaders will be able to have influence in bargaining and shaping international regimes when they exhibit structural, entrepreneurial, or intellectual leadership. This distinction refers to the material and intellectual means to influence negotiations as well as the skills to use negotiations for one's own interests. Moreover, the commitment and work ethics of the rank and file—indeed, a bureaucracy's corporate identity—correlates with leadership inasmuch as staff members "are not passive receptables but *imaginative consumers* of leaders visions" (Bryman 1996, 286, original emphasis; see also Witt 1998). Furthermore, leadership also includes the leader's flexibility and openness to change. We view it as a particular strength of the leader and the international bureaucracy as such to be able to adapt their goals, internal processes, and the organizational structure to perceived external challenges. If internal or external reviews give rise to learning processes that result in executive decisions to revise internal structures and procedures, leadership qualities are essential.

Building on these considerations on leadership in international bureaucracies, we conceptualize "strong leadership" as the behavior of a leader of an international bureaucracy that follows a style of leadership that is charismatic, visionary, and popular, as well as flexible and reflexive. Strong leadership thus includes the ability to rapidly gain acceptance and acknowledgment by employees and externals, to develop, communicate, and implement visions, and to learn and change routines. On this basis, we have hypothesized that strong leadership positively correlates with organizational performance and will thus increase bureaucratic influence in the development and implementation of international policy. Chapter 13 reports on the findings.

The Empirical Research Methodology

Finally, this section discusses the operationalization, methods, and research techniques that were used to implement this research program. We present this more detailed elaboration in the framework of this book because hardly any methods on systematically studying the influence of international bureaucracies are available in the literature, which makes this study a largely pioneering work. In particular the relatively small number of comparable international bureaucracies and the variety of potential organizational influence exacerbate the general problem in qualitative social science of "comparing apples with oranges," and thus require special methodological attention.

Case Selection
Most previous studies on international bureaucracies have focused on a small set of bureaucracies. Thus, although the UN and some of its specialized agencies have been the subject of numerous studies, the activities of a large number of other bureaucracies—one data set counts as many as 1,147 international organizations that had been active in 1992 (Shanks

et al. 1996)—have with few exceptions not yet empirically been assessed. This study is no different, inasmuch as intense qualitative analysis was possible for only nine international bureaucracies.

All of these nine bureaucracies are active in the field of environmental policy. Because this study program aims at identifying key variables that explain variation in the influence of international bureaucracies, the selection of cases has been based, to the extent possible, on the comparability of the bureaucracies regarding their core function, but on *prima facie* variation regarding the independent variables of this study, problem structure, polity, and people and procedures. This study hence includes two different types of international bureaucracies (see table 3.1).

First, we have analyzed five international bureaucracies that are secretariats of intergovernmental agencies; some with an environmental mandate, others with a rather broad, not issue-specific mandate that includes environmental issues only as one concern among many others. Within the larger multi-issue bureaucracies, we have focused the analysis on the respective environmental departments or subdivisions, while keeping in mind their larger organizational setting. This type of bureaucracy is represented here through the environmental department and other subdivisions of the International Bank for Reconstruction and Development (the "World Bank"); the environmental division within the secretariat of the IMO, the environment directorate of the OECD; the secretariat of UNEP; and the secretariat of the GEF.

The latter two are idiosyncratic to some extent. UNEP is a program of the UN that was set up as the environmental "conscience and catalyst" within the world organization. This makes the program quite special, yet also an indispensable case study in this research program. The GEF is institutionally complex; it is a financial mechanism to fund the incremental costs of developing countries under a number of international environmental agreements with a global dimension. The facility is overseen by its own executive body, yet its projects are jointly implemented through three other international agencies: the World Bank, UNEP, and the UN Development Programme (UNDP). The GEF secretariat is hosted on the premises of the World Bank (on the GEF's legal structure, see Silard 1995). This complex institutional structure makes it an interesting case, especially regarding key variables such as autonomy from member states and other bureaucracies.

Second, this research program includes four secretariats of international treaties. We have chosen here four major environmental conven-

Table 3.1
Description of case studies

	OECD environment directorate	World Bank	IMO secretariat	UNEP secretariat
Official term	Environment Directorate within the Secretariat of the Organisation for Economic Co-operation and Development	International Bank for Reconstruction and Development (focus on Environment Department and other environmental activities)	Marine Environment Division within the Secretariat of the International Maritime Organization	Secretariat of the United Nations Environment Programme
Year of foundation	1961 (for the organization)	1944 (environmental protection as policy objective in 1987)	1958	1973
Location	Paris	Washington, DC	London	Nairobi
Policy area	Environmental protection within economic development processes in industrialized countries	Environmental protection and stewardship within economic development processes in developing countries	Mitigation of environmental impact of shipping; maritime safety	Environmental policy
Core function	Information and advice Preparation of standards and guidelines	Lending for development projects	Preparation and implementation of legal agreements and decisions	Information, advice, preparation, and facilitation of policy processes

GEF secretariat	Ozone secretariat	Climate secretariat	Biodiversity secretariat	Desertification secretariat
Secretariat of the Global Environment Facility	Secretariat of the Vienna Convention on the Ozone Layer and its Montreal Protocol	Secretariat of the United Nations Framework Convention on Climate Change	Secretariat of the Convention on Biological Diversity	Secretariat of the United Nations Convention to Combat Desertification in those Countries Experiencing Serious Drought and/or Desertification, Particularly in Africa
1991/1994	1987	1991/1996	1993	1998
Washington, DC	Nairobi	Bonn	Montréal	Bonn
Financial support of policies of developing countries on a number of "global environmental problems"	Protection of the stratospheric ozone layer	Prevention of dangerous human-made climate change	Protection of biodiversity	Prevention of land degradation in arid, semi-arid and dry sub-humid regions
Grant financing of incremental costs of developing countries	Implementation and further development of international treaty	Implementation and further development of international treaty	Implementation and further development of international treaty	Implementation and further development of international treaty

tions, which makes potential influence levels more comparable as when some minor regional treaty would have been included. In addition, all four secretariats are old enough to make some influence possible. However, the four secretariats chosen vary regarding their size (the ozone secretariat is the smallest); regarding their problem area; and regarding their embedding in larger regimes and organizational structures. We have thus included as case studies the secretariat of the 1985 Vienna Convention for the Protection of the Ozone Layer and its 1987 Montreal Protocol ("ozone secretariat"); the secretariat of the Convention on Biological Diversity ("biodiversity secretariat"); the secretariat of the United Nations Framework Convention on Climate Change ("climate secretariat"), and the secretariat of the United Nations Convention to Combat Desertification in Countries Experiencing Serious Drought and/or Desertification, Particularly in Africa ("desertification secretariat").

Data Collection
The qualitative analysis of the nine international bureaucracies was based on the examination of primary sources, including internal and published documents of the bureaucracies and the bureaucracies' Web sites; secondary sources, such as academic studies and written assessments of diplomats; a series of interviews and participatory observation, mainly gained through field visits to the headquarters of the respective bureaucracies; as well as a senior expert questionnaire that has been distributed to experts in two developing countries and two industrialized countries.

Field Research and Interviews   More than one hundred international civil servants—in addition to a number of external experts, such as government delegates—have been interviewed for this research program. Interviews with international civil servants whose influence is the main research interest pose a special methodological challenge. Particular care has therefore been taken with the methodological and practical preparation of the field visits in order to guarantee both the validity and comparability of data from different international bureaucracies. To improve the comparability of case studies while retaining openness to the respondents' views, all case studies employed half-standardized interviews (see Merton and Kendall 1946; Meuser and Nagel 1991; Scheele and Groeben 1988). This interview method allows for data collection that is both restrictive (deductive) and open (inductive) and enables both general and specific conclusions about different cases. In particular, researchers have employed the expert interview technique developed by Meuser and Nagel (1991). The expert interview restricts the information that is expected from respondents more than other interview techniques, but it is sufficiently open to identify case-specific factors and to generate new ideas about a research topic.

Special care has also been taken to guarantee the validity of interview data. Naturally, if civil servants agree on participating in an interview that they perceive as evaluation of their work, they are likely to present their work more positively. This bias problem with expert interviews has been a major concern before and during the field visits. For example, most interviews were conducted personally in the office of the interviewee. To minimize influence from other staff members and superiors, interviewees were questioned separately whenever possible. In most cases, only one person was interviewed at a time.

The selection of the interviewees within a bureaucracy was done by the researchers of the case study, because most researchers worked for several days or weeks in the bureaucracies and gained in-depth knowledge about the expertise of employees. Due to reasons of anonymity, names of interviewees are not mentioned in this book (except for heads of bureaucracies). To the extent that the involvement of researchers in the bureaucracy's everyday business gave them valuable background knowledge to understand and contextualize interview data, this study is also based on ethnographic research techniques like participant observation and ethnographic interviews (Spradley 1979, 1980). The written interview guideline included core questions complemented by specific interview modules, which were used for only a subset of interviews. The core questions were structured along five broader themes that had been communicated to interviewees when fixing the interview appointment through a one-page preparatory leaflet.[19]

In addition, complementary data was sought from specialized experts such as financial officers or human resources managers. To guarantee comparability and validity of interview data, interviewers were extensively trained in a series of workshops, where different interviewee behavior was simulated and reactions by interviewers were evaluated in the project team (based on Merton and Kendall 1946; Fowler and Mangione 1990; and Meuser and Nagel 1991). Finally, to complement the data assessment from inside of the bureaucracies and to obtain information on as many indicators as possible, most interviewees were asked to complete a brief complementary questionnaire on internal decision-making procedures with ten questions in close-ended answer format, including questions of decision making and leadership and the processing of information inside the bureaucracies. The turnout was satisfactory, and the questionnaire served as an efficient tool to address indicators less suitable for an open-answer interview format and to avoid bloating the interview with too many questions. Given that only one researcher visited each bureaucracy, reliability of data was a methodological problem that required special attention. To guarantee comparability and reliability of data analysis among different raters, an intensive rater training was conducted before the data analysis and later supplemented by an extensive interrater reliability check to assess reliability of an interview analysis through comparing independent assessments by different raters.

The Expert Survey   Field visits to the headquarters of international bureaucracies can be only one source of data to assess their influence. A second source of data (in addition to primary documents and secondary sources) was hence a senior expert survey in four countries that covered a range of indicators of influence of bureaucracies (published independently as Tarradell 2007). By asking the "stakeholders" of international bureaucracies for their perception of the quality of the work of international bureaucracies, it was possible to include crucial data on indicators of dependent variables that are presumably less affected by the "optimistic bias" that is likely included in data gathered from interviews with the bureaucracies' staff members.

The senior expert survey was based on questionnaire methods developed by Simsek and Veiga for Internet organizational surveys (2001). It consisted of an online questionnaire with largely closed questions.[20] The electronic format allowed for a computerized treatment of the data. Another advantage of using a standardized survey was that the same questions were asked to all experts, which generated directly comparable data for the analysis. This was done, however, at the expense of having a single standardized questionnaire for experts on all nine bureaucracies.

To gain a broad range of expert perspectives, the survey targeted four types of experts—government officials, representatives of non-profit and for-profit nongovernmental organizations, and researchers—from two developing and two industrialized countries, namely, Germany, India, Mexico, and the United States. Experts for the survey were identified through Web sites of international bureaucracies that contain published online data with details of organizations involved in the bureaucracy's activities; direct inquiry for additional experts during interviews; electronic mail communication; written requests; and Internet search engines.

From a total number of 600 experts addressed, 145 answered the survey, representing a roughly 25 percent response rate. The respondent rates for each bureaucracy studied were 35 percent for the UNEP secretariat, 29 percent for the climate secretariat, 22 percent for the biodiversity secretariat, 20 percent for the World Bank, 16 percent for the secretariat of the GEF, 10 percent for the desertification secretariat, 5 percent for the environment directorate of the OECD, and 4 percent each for the secretariat of the IMO and the ozone secretariat.

Statistical Analysis   In addition to intense qualitative research, some case study data has also been used in a statistical analysis that helped shed light on the relationship between variables. It is widely assumed that small samples prohibit statistical tests. Although most statistical tests are parametric and often require as a rule normal distributions of the characteristics to be tested—an assumption that is often not fulfilled for small samples—nonparametric tests have been developed in the last years that do not have such strict premises (for an overview, see Bortz and Lienert 1998). Therefore, we applied also limited statistical tests to the data generated from the nine environmental international bureaucracies we studied. The main purposes of these tests were, first, to identify statistically significant differences between different bureaucracies with regard to their influence (that is, differences on the dependent variables); second, to detect on which independent variables the more influential bureaucracies differed from the less influential ones; and third, to check the interconnectedness of independent variables.

To this end, some indicators for independent and dependent variables have been quantified depending on the level of detail of available data. Most indicators were defined as ordinal variables, that is, variables with nominal properties and values that signal order from low to high without assuming identical intervals between different numeric values (e.g., the interval from 1 = low to 2 = medium might be bigger than from 2 = medium to 3 = high).[21] The validity of all indicators has been examined regarding face or content validity, mainly through evaluation based on external expert knowledge, which resulted in further refinement of the analytical framework. In addition, the validity of indicators has been checked based on exemplary interview data.

The statistical analysis served as an important heuristic tool to sharpen the argument based on the qualitative study. However, given the difficulties in quantifying most conceptual variables that have been analyzed in this project, we have in the end refrained from drawing theoretical conclusions based on the statistical outcome as such. The conclusions presented in this book are thus essentially based on the qualitative methods described in this chapter, even though the statistical exercises have shed some insights on the hypotheses and relationships that were analyzed.

Notes

1. For similar concepts, see Arild Underdal (2001b, 27), who derives actor status for international organizations through the degree of their internal coherence, autonomy, organizational activity and resources, and Barnett and Finnemore (2004, 16–20).

2. See article 2 of the draft articles on responsibility of international organizations of the International Law Commission (reprinted in International Law Commission 2003).

3. IHDP 1999; Young, King, and Schroeder 2008; see also Simmons and Martin 2002, 192–194. Likewise, we use the term "international regimes" more specifically as denoting—in Krasner's (1983, 2) standard definition—"sets of implicit or explicit principles, norms, rules, and decision-making procedures around which actors' expectations converge in a given area of international relations."

4. According to the mission statement of the organization, the International Labour Office is the permanent secretariat of the International Labour Organization. It is the focal point for the ILO's overall activities, which it prepares under the scrutiny of the governing body and under the leadership of a director-general. The Office employs about 1900 officials at the Geneva headquarters and in 40 field offices around the world.

5. Keohane, Haas, and Levy (1993, 11) argued that the best avenue to address institutional effectiveness is to "focus on observable political effects of institutions rather than directly on environmental impact." Most subsequent research followed this reasoning. Arild Underdal, for instance, views the "biophysical impact" as the ultimate goal of an environmental regime, which, however, would need to be accomplished through changes in human behavior (2001b, 6).

6. More generally, the conceptualization of output in social science dates back to David Easton's systems analysis (1965).

7. See, for example, the conceptualization in Victor, Raustiala, and Skolnikoff 1998b, 1, where effectiveness is defined as the "degree to which international environmental accords lead to changes in behavior [of targeted actors] that help solve environmental problems." They do not assess the effectiveness of an environmental accord with its ability to eliminate the environmental threat or the effectiveness by the extent to which behavior conforms to international treaties,

that is, compliance. Instead, they argue that one finds many examples where environmental law has seen high compliance but prompted only limited influence on behavior (Victor, Raustiala, and Skolnikoff 1998b, 39n13). Hence, compliance is not an end in itself but rather a means to achieve effectiveness, which is in turn a means to manage environmental stresses.

8. See Young 2001 for a critique of quantitative approaches to regime effectiveness. See also Underdal 2001a, 2001b on methodological discussions of regime effectiveness.

9. A set of case studies convincingly employing counterfactual thought experiments is provided in the volume on regime effectiveness edited by Young (1999). For standard literature on counterfactual methods, see Fearon 1991; on causal inference in qualitative research, see King, Keohane, and Verba 1994 with further references.

10. On regime effectiveness, see for example Haas, Keohane, and Levy 1993; Bernauer 1995; Keohane and Levy 1996; Young 1997; Victor, Raustiala, and Skolnikoff 1998a; Zürn 1998; Young 1999, 2001; Miles et al. 2001.

11. See also Economy and Schreurs 1997, 8, who emphasize the importance of capacities at the national level as they highlight how institutional effectiveness "is strongly mitigated by domestic political and economic structures and institutions."

12. See Grindle 1997 and Lusthaus, Adrien, and Morgan 2000, as well as Underdal 1997 for analytical criteria to assess capacity building in international environmental governance.

13. See in particular Oran Young's (2002, 55–82) discussion on how to match ecosystem properties with the attributes of international institutions (see also IHDP 1999).

14. On the role of knowledge in international relations, see Sabatier 1987; Haas 1990, 1992; Social Learning Group 2001; Siebenhüner 2003; Geller and Vasquez 2004; Mitchell et al. 2006. For related studies and insights in management studies, see Kogut and Zander 1992; Nonaka 1994; Pisano 1994; Spender 1996; Argote 1999; Kieser et al. 2001.

15. This approach draws on the concept of "organization learning mechanisms" as defined by Armstrong and Foley (2003, 75), building on Popper and Lipshitz (1995), who distinguish between cultural facets and structural facets of organization learning mechanisms. The structural part resembles the notion of reflexive mechanisms as presented here when being defined as "the institutionalized structural and procedural arrangements that allow organizations to systematically collect, analyze, store, disseminate, and use information that is relevant to the effectiveness of the organization."

16. This definition builds on the notion of organizational culture as defined by Schein (1985, 8). In this view, the culture of a group is "a pattern of shared basic assumptions that the group learned as it solved its problems of external adaptation and internal integration, that has worked well enough to be considered valid and therefore, to be taught to new members as the correct way to perceive, think,

and feel in relation to those problems." For related concepts see also Frost et al. 1991.

17. Other factors and indicators to assess an organization's culture, such as prevalent discourses, the use of symbols, or dress codes have been left out of this study due to practical reasons; their empirical examination is generally highly complicated and hard to measure at all.

18. International relations scholars have largely limited themselves to analyzing the role of leaders in international negotiations and regime creation. Notable contributions include Oran Young's (1991) typology of political leadership in regime formation, in which he distinguishes structural, entrepreneurial and intellectual leadership, and the "intergovernmental conference leadership model" developed by Derek Beach (2004). From a principal-agent perspective, Bart Kerremans (2004) and Jill Lovecy (2004) have provided empirical case studies of leadership of international organizations in an European Union context.

19. These five themes in the core questions were: (1) The personal background of the interviewee (career background and history inside and outside the organization); (2) successes, challenges, and effects of the bureaucracy, including questions on what interviewees perceived as main achievements of their bureaucracy, difficulties encountered, instruments used in pursuing the bureaucracy's objective, or factors outside of the bureaucracy's reach that might have shaped eventual outcomes of its activities; (3) relationship of the bureaucracy vis-à-vis member states, including whether interviewees pursued initiatives that arise out of the processes inside the bureaucracy rather than being covered by official mandates and terms of reference, and whether conflicts between the bureaucracy and member states exist; (4) the role of bureaucratic behavior and procedures within the bureaucracy, covering questions such as the interviewees' perception of "red tape" and the handling of divergent interests inside the bureaucracy; and finally (5) organizational learning—for example, whether the interviewee sees the bureaucracy as responsive to critical reviews. Interviewees were also asked whether they wished to add something they felt was important but not covered by interview questions.

20. The questionnaire was structured as follows. The respondent first rated the perceived relevance of the nine listed international bureaucracies, with the possibility of listing other relevant bureaucracies. The respondents then chose from the list of nine international bureaucracies the bureaucracy that they perceived as most relevant for their work. They were then requested to answer further questions on this bureaucracy, and to provide information on their own background, including country of origin and professional affiliation (government, environmental nongovernmental organization, research institution, or business corporation). The experts were contacted mainly through electronic mailing, and anonymity was guaranteed. We avoided answers from nontargeted respondents by making the survey "invisible" to Internet search engines and by asking experts to first contact our research team to only then be invited to fill in our survey. Furthermore, the survey system did not allow the filling in of the survey more than once by the same person.

21. The independent variables were operationalized by indicators rated mostly on three-level scales (1 = low, 2 = medium, 3 = high). Many dependent variables were operationalized by indicators rated on two-level scales (0 = no change, 1 = change because of the bureaucracy's influence). The indicators of the other dependent variables were rated on three-level scales (−1 = change for worse, 0 = no change, 1 = change for better because of the bureaucracy's influence).

References

Argote, Linda. 1999. *Organizational Learning. Creating, Retaining, and Transferring Knowledge.* Boston: Kluwer.

Argyris, Chris. 1996. "Skilled Incompetence." In *How Organizations Learn,* edited by Ken Starkey, 82–92. London: International Thomson Business Press.

Armstrong, Anona, and Patrick Foley. 2003. "Foundations for a Learning Organization: Organization Learning Mechanisms." *The Learning Organization* 10 (2): 74–82.

Barnett, Michael N., and Martha Finnemore. 2004. *Rules for the World: International Organizations in Global Politics.* Ithaca, NY: Cornell University Press.

Beach, Derek. 2004. "The Unseen Hand in Treaty Reform Negotiations: The Role and Influence of the Council Secretariat." *Journal of European Public Policy* 11 (3): 408–439.

Bernauer, Thomas. 1995. "The Effect of International Institutions: How We Might Learn More." *International Organization* 49 (2): 351–377.

Biermann, Frank. 2002. "Institutions for Scientific Advice. Global Environmental Assessments and Their Influence in Developing Countries." *Global Governance* 8 (2): 195–219.

Blau, Peter M., and W. Richard Scott. 1962. *Formal Organization: A Comparative Approach.* San Francisco: Chandler.

Bortz, Jürgen, and Gustav A. Lienert. 1998. *Kurzgefasste Statistik für die Klinische Forschung.* Berlin: Springer.

Brown Weiss, Edith, and Harold K. Jacobson, editors. 1998. *Engaging Countries. Strengthening Compliance with International Environmental Accords.* Cambridge, MA: MIT Press.

Bryman, Alan. 1996. "Leadership in Organizations." In *Handbook of Organization Studies,* edited by Walter R. Nord, 276–292. London: Sage.

Busch, Per-Olof, and Helge Jörgens. 2005. "International Patterns of Environmental Policy Change and Convergence." *European Environment* 15 (2): 80–101.

Chayes, Abram, Antonia Handler Chayes, and Ronald B. Mitchell. 1998. "Managing Compliance: A Comparative Perspective." In *Engaging Countries. Strengthening Compliance with International Environmental Accords,* edited by Edith Brown Weiss and Harold K. Jacobson, 39–62. Cambridge, MA: MIT Press.

Cortell, Andrew P., and Susan Peterson. 2004. "The Independence of International Organizations: Unpacking the Member State-IO Relationship." Paper presented at the *45th Annual Convention of the International Studies Association*, 17–20 March, Montreal (Quebec), Canada.

Cox, Robert W., and Harold K. Jacobson, editors. 1973. *The Anatomy of Influence. Decision-Making in International Organization*. New Haven: Yale University Press.

Dierkes, Meinolf, Ariane Berthoin Antal, John Child, and Ikujiro Nonaka, editors. 2001. *Handbook of Organizational Learning and Knowledge*. Oxford: Oxford University Press.

Easton, David. 1965. *A Systems Analysis of Political Life*. New York: Wiley.

Economy, Elizabeth, and Miranda A. Schreurs. 1997. "Domestic Institutions and International Linkages in Environmental Politics." In *The Internationalization of Environmental Protection*, edited by Miranda A. Schreurs and Elizabeth Economy, 1–18. Cambridge, UK: Cambridge University Press.

Fearon, James. 1991. "Counterfactuals and Hypothesis Testing in Political Science." *World Politics* 43 (2): 169–195.

Finnemore, Martha. 1993. "International Organizations as Teachers of Norms: The United Nations Educational, Scientific and Cultural Organization and Science Policy." *International Organization* 47 (4): 565–598.

Fowler, Floyd J., and Thomas W. Mangione. 1990. *Standardized Survey Interviewing. Minimizing Interviewer-Related Error*. Newbury Park, CA: Sage.

Frost, Peter J., Larry F. Moore, Meryl R. Louis, Craig C. Lundberg, and Joanne Martin. 1991. *Reframing Organizational Cultures*. Newbury Park, CA: Sage.

Geller, Daniel S., and John A. Vasquez. 2004. "The Construction and Cumulation of Knowledge in International Relations: Introduction." *International Studies Review* 6 (4): 1–6.

Grindle, Merilee S., editor. 1997. *Getting Good Government: Capacity Building in the Public Sectors of Developing Countries*. Cambridge, MA: Harvard University Press.

Haas, Ernst B. 1990. *When Knowledge Is Power: Three Models of Change in International Organizations*. Berkeley: University of California Press.

Haas, Peter M. 1992. "Introduction: Epistemic Communities and International Policy Coordination." *International Organization* 46 (1): 1–35.

Haas, Peter M., Robert O. Keohane, and Marc A. Levy, editors. 1993. *Institutions for the Earth: Sources of Effective International Environmental Protection*. Cambridge, MA: MIT Press.

Hawkins, Darren G., David A. Lake, Daniel L. Nielson, and Michael J. Tierney, editors. 2006. *Delegation and Agency in International Organizations*. Cambridge, UK: Cambridge University Press.

Helm, Carsten, and Detlef Sprinz. 2000. "Measuring the Effectiveness of International Environmental Regimes." *Journal of Conflict Resolution* 44 (5): 630–652.

IHDP, International Human Dimensions Programme on Global Environmental Change. 1999. *Institutional Dimensions of Global Environmental Change. Science Plan.* IHDP Report 9. Bonn: IHDP.

International Law Commission. 2003. Report of the 55th Session of the International Law Commission (5 May–6 June and 7 July–8 August). Official Records of the 58th Session of the United Nations General Assembly, Supplement 10, UN Doc. A/58/10. New York: United Nations.

Jacobson, Harold K., and Edith Brown Weiss. 1998. "A Framework for Analysis." In *Engaging Countries. Strengthening Compliance with International Environmental Accords,* edited by Edith Brown Weiss and Harald K. Jacobson, 1–18. Cambridge, MA: MIT Press.

Katz, Daniel, and Robert Kahn. 1966. *The Social Psychology of Organizations.* New York: Wiley.

Keohane, Robert O., Peter M. Haas, and Marc A. Levy. 1993. "The Effectiveness of International Environmental Institutions. In *Institutions for the Earth: Sources of Effective International Environmental Protection,* edited by Peter M. Haas, Marc A. Levy, and Robert O. Keohane, 3–24. Cambridge, MA: MIT Press.

Keohane, Robert O., and Marc A. Levy, editors. 1996. *Institutions for Environmental Aid: Pitfalls and Promise.* Cambridge, MA: MIT Press.

Kerremans, Bart. 2004. "The European Commission and the EU Member States as Actors in the WTO Negotiating Process. Decision Making between Scylla and Charibdis?" In *Decision Making within International Organizations,* edited by Bob Reinalda and Bertjan Verbeek, 45–58. London: Routledge.

Kieser, Alfred, Nikolaus Beck, and Risto Tainio. 2001. "Rules and Organizational Learning: The Behavioral Theory Approach. In *Handbook of Organizational Learning and Knowledge,* edited by Meinolf Dierkes, Ariane Berthoin Antal, John Child, and Ikujiro Nonaka, 598–623. London: Oxford University Press.

King, Gary, Robert O. Keohane, and Sidney Verba. 1994. *Designing Social Inquiry: Scientific Inference in Qualitative Research.* Princeton, NJ: Princeton University Press.

Kogut, Bruce, and Udor Zander. 1992. "Knowledge of the Firm and the Replication of Technology." *Organization Science* 3:383–397.

Krasner, Stephen D. 1983. "Structural Causes and Regime Consequences: Regimes as Intervening Variables." In *International Regimes,* edited by Stephen D. Krasner, 1–21. Ithaca, NY: Cornell University Press.

Lovecy, Jill. 2004. "Framing Decisions in the Council of Europe. An Institutionalist Analysis." In *Decision Making within International Organizations,* edited by Bob Reinalda and Bertjan Verbeek, 59–73. London: Routledge.

Lusthaus, Charles, Marie-Hèlene Adrien, and Peter Morgan. 2000. *Integrating Capacity Development into Project Design and Evaluation.* Washington, DC: GEF.

March, James G., and Herbert A. Simon. 1958. *Organization.* New York: Wiley.

Marquardt, Michael J. 1996. *Building the Learning Organization*. New York: McGraw-Hill.

Merton, Robert K., and Patricia L. Kendall. 1946. "The Focused Interview." *American Journal of Sociology* 51:541–557 (reprinted in 1979).

Meuser, Michael, and Ulrike Nagel. 1991. "ExpertInneninterviews—Vielfach erprobt, wenig bedacht. Ein Beitrag zur qualitativen Methodendiskussion." In *Qualitativ-empirische Sozialforschung*, edited by Detlev Garz and Klaus Kraimer, 441–468. Opladen: Westdeutscher Verlag.

Meyer, John W., and Brian Rowan. 1991. "Institutionalized Organizations: Formal Structure as Myth and Ceremony." In *The New Institutionalism in Organizational Analysis*, edited by Walter W. Powell and Paul J. DiMaggio, 41–66. Chicago: University of Chicago Press.

Miles, Edward L., Arild Underdal, Steinar Andresen, Jørgen Wettestad, Jon Birger Skjærseth, and Elaine M. Carlin, editors. 2001. *Environmental Regime Effectiveness. Confronting Theory with Evidence*. Cambridge, MA: MIT Press.

Mintzberg, Henry. 1979. *The Structure of Organizations: A Synthesis of Research*. Upper Saddle River, NJ: Prentice Hall.

Mitchell, Ronald B., William C. Clark, David W. Cash, and Nancy M. Dickson. 2006. "Information as Influence: How Institutions Mediate the Impact of Scientific Assessments on International Environmental Affairs." In *Global Environmental Assessments: Information and Influence*, edited by Ronald B. Mitchell, William C. Clark, David W. Cash, and Nancy M. Dickson, 307–338. Cambridge, MA: MIT Press.

Nielson, Daniel L., and Michael J. J. Tierney. 2003. "Delegation to International Organizations: Agency Theory and World Bank Environmental Reform." *International Organization* 57 (2): 241–276.

Nonaka, Ikujiro. 1994. "A Dynamic Theory of Organizational Knowledge Creation." *Organization Science* 5:14–37.

Pisano, Gary P. 1994. "Knowledge Integration and the Locus of Learning: An Empirical Analysis of Process Development." *Strategic Management Journal* 15:85–100.

Popper, Micha, and Raanan Lipshitz. 1995. *Organizational Learning Mechanisms: A Structural/Cultural Approach to Organizational Learning*. Haifa: University of Haifa.

Reinalda, Bob, and Bertjan Verbeek. 2004. "The Issue of Decision Making Within International Organizations." In *Decision Making within International Organizations*, edited by Bob Reinalda and Bertjan Verbeek, 9–41. London: Routledge.

Sabatier, Paul. 1987. "Knowledge, Policy-Oriented Learning and Policy Change." *Science Communication* 8 (4): 649–692.

Sandford, Rosemary. 1996. "International Environmental Treaty Secretariats: A Case of Neglected Potential?" *Environmental Impact Assessment Review* 16:3–12.

Scheele, Brigitte, and Groeben, Norbert. 1988. *Dialog-Konsens-Methoden zur Rekonstruktion subjektiver Theorien*. Tübingen: Francke.

Schein, Edgar H. 1985. *Organizational Culture and Leadership*. San Francisco: Jossey-Bass.

Schwandt, David R. and Michael J. Marquard. 2000. *Organizational Learning. From World-Class Theories to Global Best Practices*. Boca Raton, FL: St. Lucie Press.

Shanks, Cheryl, Harold K. Jacobson, and Jeffrey H. Kaplan. 1996. "Inertia and Change in the Constellation of International Governmental Organizations, 1981–1992." *International Organization* 50 (4): 593–627.

Siebenhüner, Bernd. 2003. "The Changing Role of Nation States in International Environmental Assessments: The Case of the IPCC." *Global Environmental Change* 13 (2): 113–123.

Silard, Stephen. 1995. "The Global Environment Facility: A New Development in International Law and Organization." *The George Washington Journal of International Law and Economics* 28 (3): 607–654.

Simmons, Beth A., and Lisa L. Martin. 2002. "International Organizations and Institutions." In *Handbook of International Relations*, edited by Walter Carlsnaes, Thomas Risse, and Beth A. Simmons, 192–211. London: Sage.

Simsek, Zeki, and John F. Veiga. 2001. "A Primer on Internet Organizational Surveys." *Organizational Research Methods* 4 (3): 218–235.

Social Learning Group. 2001. *Learning to Manage Global Environmental Risks: Vol. 1—A Comparative History of Social Responses to Climate Change, Ozone Depletion, and Acid Rain; Vol. 2—A Functional Analysis of Social Responses to Climate Change, Ozone Depletion, and Acid Rain*. Cambridge, MA: MIT Press.

Spender, J.-C. 1996. "Making Knowledge the Basis of a Dynamic Theory of the Firm." *Strategic Management Journal* 17 (Winter Special Issue): 45–62.

Spradley, James P. 1979. *The Ethnographic Interview*. New York: Holt, Rinehart and Winston.

Spradley, James P. 1980. *Participant Observation*. New York: Holt, Rinehart and Winston.

Tarradell, Mireia. 2007. *The Influence of International Bureaucracies in Global Environmental Politics: Results from an Expert Survey*. Global Governance Working Paper 26. Amsterdam and others: The Global Governance Project.

Underdal, Arild. 1997. "Capacity for International Environmental Governance." In *Umweltpolitik und Staatsversagen. Perspektiven und Grenzen der Umweltpolitikanalyse. Festschrift für Martin Jänicke zum 60. Geburtstag [Environmental Policy and State Failure]*, edited by Helmut Weidner, 252–257. Berlin: Edition Sigma.

Underdal, Arild. 2001a. "Methods of Analysis." In *Environmental Regime Effectiveness. Confronting Theory with Evidence*, edited by Edward L. Miles, Arild Underdal, Steinar Andresen, Jørgen Wettestad, Jon Birger Skjærseth, and Elaine M. Carlin, 47–62. Cambridge, MA: MIT Press.

Underdal, Arild. 2001b. "One Question, Two Answers." In *Environmental Regime Effectiveness. Confronting Theory with Evidence*, edited by Edward L. Miles, Arild Underdal, Steinar Andresen, Jørgen Wettestad, Jon Birger Skjærseth, and Elaine M. Carlin, 3–45. Cambridge, MA: MIT Press.

Victor, David G., Kal Raustiala, and Eugene B. Skolnikoff, editors. 1998a. *The Implementation and Effectiveness of International Environmental Commitments. Theory and Practice*. Cambridge, MA: MIT Press.

Victor, David G., Kal Raustiala, and Eugene B. Skolnikoff. 1998b. "Introduction and Overview." In *The Implementation and Effectiveness of International Environmental Commitments. Theory and Practice*, edited by David G. Victor, Kal Raustiala, and Eugene B. Skolnikoff, 1–46. Cambridge, MA: MIT Press.

Wettestad, Jørgen. 2001. "Designing Effective Environmental Regimes: The Conditional Keys." *Global Governance* 7 (3): 317–341.

Witt, Ulrich. 1998. "Imagination and Leadership: The Neglected Dimension of an Evolutionary Theory of the Firm." *Journal of Economic Behavior and Organization* 35:161–177.

Young, Oran R. 1991. "Political Leadership and Regime Formation: On the Development of Institutions in International Society." *International Organization* 45 (3): 281–308.

Young, Oran R. 1994. *International Environmental Governance. Protecting the Environment in a Stateless Society*. Ithaca, NY: Cornell University Press.

Young, Oran R., editor. 1997. *Global Governance. Drawing Insights from the Environmental Experience*. Cambridge, MA: MIT Press.

Young, Oran R., editor. 1999. *The Effectiveness of International Environmental Regimes: Causal Connections and Behavioral Mechanisms*. Cambridge, MA: MIT Press.

Young, Oran R. 2001. "Inferences and Indices: Evaluating the Effectiveness of International Environmental Regimes." *Global Environmental Politics* 1 (1): 99–121.

Young, Oran R. 2002. *The Institutional Dimensions of Environmental Change. Fit, Interplay, and Scale*. Cambridge, MA: MIT Press.

Young, Oran R., Leslie A. King, and Heike Schroeder, editors. 2008. *Institutions and Environmental Change: Principal Findings, Applications, and Research Frontiers*. Cambridge, MA: MIT Press.

Zürn, Michael. 1998. "The Rise of International Environmental Politics." *World Politics* 50 (4): 617–649.

4

The OECD Environment Directorate: The Art of Persuasion and Its Limitations

Per-Olof Busch

Introduction

The intergovernmental bureaucracy that supports the countries in the Organization for Economic Cooperation and Development (OECD), the OECD secretariat, was the first with a separate environmental division: the environment directorate (Sullivan 1997, 50). In 1971, when the environment directorate started its operations, no other intergovernmental organization had institutionally responded to environmental challenges. Since the creation of the organization in 1961, the OECD secretariat and its subdivisions have supported the thirty mostly developed member countries[1] of the organization in the development of policies that sustain economic growth and prosperity. It assists member countries in the promotion of trade and competition, but also helps them improve their development, education, and agriculture policies.

In this chapter, I assess and explain the autonomous influence of the environment directorate in environmental governance. This study is one of the first to analyze this question. Only Bill Long, former director of the environment directorate, has given a historical account of the role of the OECD and its intergovernmental bureaucracy in environmental governance (Long 2000). In general, the intergovernmental bureaucracy of the OECD has so far been the subject of no more than a handful of studies (see Marcussen 2004a, 2004b, 2004c on the influence of the secretariat on the diffusion of ideas; and Trondal, Marcussen, and Veggeland 2004 on the roles and behavior of civil servants in the secretariat).

Structure and Activities

Like any other directorate in the OECD, the environment directorate services intergovernmental committees, namely, the environmental policy and chemicals committees and their subsidiary bodies. The main task of the environment directorate is to provide knowledge, ideas, concepts, and arguments, which it generates through research, introduces into discussions in both committees, and publishes in reports or official documents. In the category "Environment and Sustainable Development," the online library "SourceOECD" lists more than 350 books for the period between 1997 and 2005. The environment directorate's Web site grants access to over one thousand publications that the environment directorate prepared. Between 1995 and 2005, staff of the OECD secretariat have contributed to fifty-five articles on environmental issues in academic journals, of which staff in the environment directorate authored eight (according to the SCOPUS database at www .scopus.com).

All research addresses policy questions and political, economic, or societal dimensions of environmental challenges and emphasizes practical issues. The output of the environment directorate spreads across three distinct categories: informatory, conceptual, and analytical. The informatory output comprises all publications in which the environment directorate presents information about past, present, and future environmental conditions or policies. The conceptual output includes all publications in which the environment directorate develops indicators or methods for designing, testing, and assessing environmental policies and conditions. The analytical output covers all publications in which the environment directorate assesses policies and instruments, evaluates and reviews environmental performance, analyzes implementation processes, and identifies environmental challenges and trends.

In these activities, the environment directorate has addressed almost all environmental policy and environmental problems. Its main focus has been on two areas: the use of economic instruments and the integration of environmental policies with other policies, notably economic, trade, and energy policies; and the reduction of environmental impacts of chemicals, energy production and consumption, transport, waste, and agriculture, as well as the protection of biodiversity and the global climate (OECD 2001b, 2002a). Since its creation, the organizational structure of the environment directorate has been oriented toward the most important thematic areas and consequently, has changed frequently.

In addition, the environment directorate supports the intergovernmental bodies in the OECD in preparing their main outputs. In one instance, the environment directorate helps the environmental policy committee and the chemicals committee to organize forums for consultation, exchange, and discussion, which is generally the most important but less visible output of the OECD intergovernmental bodies. Every year more than 40,000 government officials, national civil servants, and independent experts get together at meetings of the intergovernmental bodies, conferences, workshops, and seminars (OECD 2004c). The environment directorate's Web site lists more than 140 conferences, workshops, and meetings that took place under its auspices between 1998 and 2005. The environment directorate also facilitates the preparation of council decisions, council decision recommendations, council recommendations, and other legal instruments, which are the most visible but less important output of the OECD governing bodies. In 2005, six council decisions, eight council decision recommendations, forty-nine council recommendations, and four other legal instruments related to environmental issues were in force (OECD 2005b).

The Influence of the OECD Environment Directorate

Cognitive Influence

Scholars often describe the OECD and its secretariat as a "think tank" or "laboratory of policy concepts" (e.g., Dostal 2004; Sullivan 1997). These attributes suggest that the organization and its bureaucracy influenced other actors in generating and disseminating new knowledge, ideas, concepts, and arguments. Indeed, the environment directorate has cognitive influence on four dimensions, comparable to the secretariat of UNEP (see Bauer, this volume, chapter 7).

First, the environment directorate has defined concepts that other actors later used. For example, in evaluating environmental policies, many intergovernmental bureaucracies have copied the concept of "pressure-state-response," which goes back to the first report of the environment directorate on the state of the environment in OECD countries (Comolet 1990). Likewise, when the Statistical Office of the European Communities and the United Nations Statistics Division collect environmental data, they apply a questionnaire that the environment directorate had first developed. Comolet (1990) characterized the OECD secretariat as the "leader in this field." Lehtonen (2005) even labels the concept of "pressure-state-response" as the "OECD model."

Second, the environment directorate has framed discourses, diffused ideas, and changed problem perceptions. Representatives from governments and nongovernmental organizations commended the environment related work of the OECD secretariat and referred to it as a source of new reference frameworks (Lehtonen 2005, 178). Through participation in the OECD, government officials often develop a common language or even worldviews, identify common concerns, and establish professional networks (Lehtonen 2005; see also Dostal 2004, 447; Porter and Webb 2004, 9; and Marcussen 2004a). More generally, the secretariat is "playing the idea game through which it collects and manipulates data, visions, and ideas and diffuses them to its member countries" (Marcussen 2004b, 91). In many policy areas, the secretariat and its subdivisions have operated as an "ideational artist," creating and diffusing ideas; as an "ideational agent," picking up ideas from OECD member countries and transferring them to other members; and as an "ideational arbitrator," teaching ideas to national civil servants and socializing them (Marcussen 2004b; see also Dostal 2004). The environment directorate drove such socialization processes (Lehtonen 2005, 178) and often "played a leading role in defining and promoting particular policy responses ahead of the policy transition in member states" (Bernstein 2000, 495).

The environment directorate has, for instance, changed perspectives of government officials and other intergovernmental organizations, such as the European Communities or the World Trade Organization, in the integration of environmental policies with other policies. Its pioneering work in this area is "unsurpassed in the international community" (Long 2000, 128). Delegates participating in these discussions reported learning processes and appreciated the debates (Bernstein 2000, 496).[2] Through the organization of high-level meetings, the directorate could change the views of policy makers on the relationship between environment and economy (Bernstein 2000, 496). It changed domestic discourses about the impacts of environmental regulation on economic growth by helping "to demystify some of the perceived wisdoms about environmental rules being bad for competitiveness"[3] and providing delegates with arguments against the allegation of business that environmental policy reduces economic growth. It "played a pivotal role in reframing the problem of environment and development" (Bernstein 2000, 495). In sum, the environment directorate raised the awareness of governments and other intergovernmental organizations about the necessity of pursuing inter-disciplinary and interinstitutional approaches in environmental policy (Long 2000, 128).

Third, the environment directorate has set agendas, thereby raising the awareness among OECD member countries. It convinced OECD member countries to include topics that it considered as important in the official two-year work program (see, e.g., Long 2000, 42–50 and 60–65).[4] In 1989, the then–environment director defined nine goals for sustainable development, which the environmental policy committee endorsed and which spread across the organization. They "were treated as the 'gospel' on sustainable development for the next decade" (Long 2000, 73). Throughout the 1970s, the OECD secretary-general, Emile van Lennep, together with the environment directorate, succeeded in setting specific issues on the agendas of the committees, such as the relationship between environmental and economic policies or trade and environment, environ-mental indicators, and the economics of transboundary pollution. In sum, the secretary-general aided by the environment directorate "was extremely prescient, or influential, or both in his formulation of the key issues for the organization" (Long 2000, 40; see also 49).

Fourth, the output of the environment directorate has influenced sci-entific debates. Between 1995 and 2005, more than 2,700 academic articles on environmental issues quoted OECD publications (according to the SCOPUS database at www.scopus.com). Most frequently, these articles quoted the OECD environmental data compendiums, publica-tions on the use of economic instruments, assessments of national envi-ronmental performance, and environmental indicators. Moreover, OECD member countries asked the environment directorate for assistance in developing policy options to counter environmental degradation (e.g., Long 2000, 60). Overall, "a lot of countries really look to the OECD for the latest information and sharing of experiences on how they might actually put policies in place."[5] That the OECD environmental outlook received the 2001 award for notable government documents of the American Library Association indicates furthermore the relevance of the output of the environment directorate.

Publications of the environment directorate influenced public debates, most prominently the OECD environmental performance reviews. In the reviewed countries, governments feel they have to react publicly to the recommendations of the reviews (Lehtonen 2005). Often, domestic environmental institutions use the recommendations to advance the domestic debate about environmental policies (Lehtonen 2005). In Canada, the environment minister used the findings of the 1995 review to demand more government action in climate change mitigation (Environment Canada 1995). The German government used the 2001 review to counter criticism of the ecological tax reform.[6] In the same year, the German environment minister concluded that the "OECD performance reviews have proved to be useful and helpful for promoting national debate about the environment" (Bundesministerium für Umwelt 2001). Often, public and private actors used the reviews to strengthen the legitimacy of environmental policies (Lehtonen 2005, 179). Above all, the performance reviews unfolded effects in particular through the argumentation processes following their publication (Lehtonen 2005, 179), but one should not overestimate their cognitive influence. Often the debates on their recommendations ended quickly (Lehtonen 2005) and, only occasionally, the performance reviews resulted in policy changes.

Normative Influence

The environment directorate has neither initiated negotiations nor tried to direct negotiations. Tolba and colleagues nevertheless conclude that the "OECD has also been an important forum for international policy development" (1995, 770). Like most other intergovernmental bureaucracies studied in this book, the environment directorate supported and occasionally shaped international negotiations. Moreover, it provided guidance in the implementation of international agreements, which is comparable to the "implementation engineer" description that likewise characterized the normative influence of the multi-issue bureaucracies studied in this book.[7]

Often quoted as its major achievement, the environment directorate defined the "polluter-pays" principle, which has guided national and international environmental policies alike since its conception in the environment directorate (Bernstein 2000, 472–473 and 495–496; Lönngren 1992).[8] For example, in the 1972 Declaration of the United Nations Conference on the Human Environment, the action plan for the human environment and the 1992 Rio Declaration on Environment and Development, governments included the polluter-pays principle. Bernstein shows that the definition and promotion of the principle through the environment directorate has been the first step in institutionalizing sustainable development as an international norm (2000, 495–496).

Moreover, the environment directorate has been influential in elaborating and monitoring the implementation of the principles of national treatment (that is, identical treatment for imported and similar domestic products) and the principle of nondiscrimination (that is, identical treatment for imported products regardless of their origin). It "has placed the OECD in the centre of international efforts to define environmental goals, strategies, and programme priorities for governments" (Long 2000, 124).

The important role of the organization and its secretariat in the international control of chemicals is also highlighted in the literature (e.g., Lönngren 1992; Tolba et al. 1995). By 2005, eleven council decisions, fifteen council recommendations, two other legal instruments, and more than one hundred guidelines were in force in this field (OECD 2004a, 2004b). Referred to as landmarks in the history of chemicals control (Lönngren 1992, 301), some have evolved into global standards and were incorporated into international agreements (OECD 2004b). For example, the 1999 Guidelines for the Identification of Polychlorinated Biphenyls of the United Nations Environment Programme, the International Code of Conduct on the Distribution and Use of Pesticides of the Food and Agriculture Organization, and the Rotterdam Convention on the Prior Informed Consent Procedure for Certain Hazardous Chemicals and Pesticides in International Trade all refer to OECD council decisions and recommendations.

Together with two other intergovernmental organizations, the OECD operates as basis for international cooperation on chemicals policy (Lönngren 1992, 167 and 201; Tolba et al. 1995, 252). As the environment directorate provided analytical support to the formulation of international chemicals policy at the OECD,[9] "great credit for the success of this pioneering work should be paid to the OECD secretariat" (Lönngren 1992, 194, see also 201–204 and 246–247). Notwithstanding these merits, the environment directorate encountered difficulties, for example, when attempting to convince OECD member countries to adopt legal instruments for improved risk management in the chemicals policy.[10]

In other environmental policy areas and comparable to the secretariat of the United Nations Environment Programme (see Bauer, this volume, chapter 7), the research of the environment directorate was often the vantage point of international negotiations. In this sense, the normative influence partially rests upon the previously discussed cognitive influence.

In the 1989 Basel Convention on the Control of Transboundary Movements of Hazardous Wastes and Their Disposal, governments resorted to the environment directorate's preparatory work (Tolba et al. 1995, 273). The OECD and its secretariat was one of three important actors driving the adoption of the 1979 Framework Convention on Long-Range Transboundary Air Pollution (Haas and McCabe 2001). Through an international project on long-range transport of air pollutants, the environment directorate, together with its partners, had sensitized countries for the nature and seriousness of the problem (Jäger et al. 2001; Hanf 2000; Tolba et al. 1995). Likewise, governments drew on the environment directorate's research on chlorofluorocarbons when they adopted the 1987 Vienna Convention for the Protection of the Ozone Layer and the related 1989 Montreal Protocol (Long 2000, 55). When the environment directorate later started developing a set of legal rules targeting transboundary air pollution, OECD member countries however stopped its work.[11] In the area of environmental taxation, too, the environment directorate faced resistance. Although it urged member countries to coordinate environmental taxation measures starting in the early 1990s, by 2005 these had still to take concrete steps.[12]

Once governments had concluded international agreements, the environment directorate has often influenced implementation by providing guidance to the parties. For example, it has contributed to the implementation of the United Nations Framework Convention on Climate Change by developing methodologies for greenhouse gas emissions inventories. With some modifications, the Intergovernmental Panel on Climate Change and the implementing bodies of the climate convention continue using these (UNFCCC 2002, 92 and 127). In the implementation of international biodiversity policies, the European Union recommends that governments use relevant OECD guidelines. The Protocol on Biosafety to the Convention on Biological Diversity (CBD 2004) as well as statements of convention bodies advise parties to draw on OECD guidance documents of the environment directorate when they implement the convention and its protocols (CBD 2001, 2002).

Executive Influence

In comparison to its cognitive and normative influence, the executive influence of the environment directorate has been weak. The literature lacks concrete examples for executive influence, for example, on the creation of new institutions or the adoption of new policies. Neither did enquiries in the interviews unveil such cases. In his analysis of the OECD involvement in environmental governance, Long mentions one single example where activities of the environment directorate contributed to the creation of a new institution: when the government of New Zealand established an environment agency in response to the 1996 environmental performance review (2000, 67).

Instead, in many areas where the environment directorate has been advocating new approaches, OECD member countries show little effort toward following the advice. For example, the environment directorate has criticized the exemptions that governments concede to energy intensive economic sectors in the taxation of energy (e.g., OECD 2001a). Even though it had formulated detailed recommendations on how to remove these exemptions without harming the international competitiveness, the exemptions continue to exist. Likewise, the environment directorate has tried to convince OECD member countries to abolish environmentally harmful subsidies (e.g., OECD 2003a). Yet, progress has been rather modest (e.g., OECD 2005a). In policy integration, into the promotion of which the environment directorate has put considerable efforts, the overall implementation has remained poor: "Countries always support the idea of policy integration verbally, but they do not spend enough resources to actually implement it."[13]

At best, executive influence has been indirect.[14] The environment directorate has supported governments in designing and implementing policies once they make the political decision independent from it. Even if the environment directorate prepared policies like during the accession processes of Mexico, the Czech Republic, Poland, Hungary, and the Republic of Korea or the implementation of the environmental action program in Central and Eastern Europe, it did not have executive influence on the actual decision to introduce new policies.

Explaining the Influence

In sum, the cognitive and normative influence of the environment directorate was strong, compared to its executive influence. The strengths of the environment directorate are its abilities: (1) to define principles and concepts; (2) to frame discourses, diffuse ideas, and change perceptions; (3) to set agendas and raise awareness among OECD member countries; (4) to generate output that is relevant for public and scientific debates; (5) to supply analytical support on which governments drew in international negotiations; and (6) to provide guidance for the implementation of international agreements. Its obvious weakness is its poor record in "turning talk into action." The environment directorate faced difficulties in changing the behavior of governments and other political actors. It has neither triggered the start of international negotiations nor provoked any measures implementing international agreements. Governments and other actors made fundamental political decisions *whether* to take action often independently from the environment directorate, whereas when they decided *how* to design and implement policies, they drew on the environment directorate's work.

Against this background, two questions guide the following explanation of the environment directorate's influence: how the environment directorate achieved the cognitive and normative influence, and why similar strong executive influence is missing. I argue that the polity—namely, the resources at the command of the environment directorate as well as its status and role in the organization—is crucial in understanding the differences in the three spheres of influence. They both constrain and enable the environment directorate to influence actors by defining boundaries within which parties expect the directorate to operate. However, they do not elucidate the question of *how* it has realized its influence. The environment directorate's embeddedness and expertise and the organizational culture are the most important sources of its influence.

Polity

Resources   The lack of any legal or financial resources to influence other actors constrained the executive and normative influence of the secretariat. As all other intergovernmental bureaucracies studied in this book (except for the environmental department of the World Bank; see Marschinski and Behrle, this volume, chapter 5), they cannot legally compel other actors to adopt measures or lure them by offering funds. Occasionally and on the request of parties, the secretariat monitors implementation, but peer pressure remains the only compliance mechanism, because the secretariat is not entitled to enforce sanctions (OECD 2004a; Marcussen 2004b; Pagani 2002).

Even the OECD as intergovernmental organization and its intergovernmental bodies lack financial or legal resources. The OECD does not issue grants or loans, or dispense money for the implementation of projects. The budget of the OECD and its secretariat funds the generation of knowledge and the organization of conferences, workshops, and meetings. Hence, the OECD cannot offer financial rewards in exchange for behavior complying with the organization's rules or expectations. Moreover, the council lacks formal means to enforce the implementation of its legally binding acts (that is, council decisions and council decision recommendations). Therefore—and because OECD member countries can avoid any of these legal obligations by abstaining from the council meeting where their peers adopt the decision—none of the decisions qualifies as an international treaty in a legal sense (Bonuci 2004; OECD 2004a).

Thus, knowledge, ideas, concepts, and arguments are essentially the only resources of the secretariat and the environment directorate. These resources, however, quickly meet limitations when the environment directorate attempts to have executive influence. It has no direct control over implementation (Dostal 2004, 454), and often governments lack political will to follow the knowledge, ideas, concepts, and arguments. Even when governments agreed to act, domestic political opposition often prevents governments from adhering to suggestions of the environment directorate.[15] In the case of environmental taxes and environmental harmful subsidies, the environment directorate excelled in criticism of the policies in OECD member countries, but staff reported that although "we are doing what we can; there are elements that are out of our reach in terms of implementing policies."[16] These limitations also applied to the normative influence within the OECD.[17] Often the problem at hand increased or decreased the willingness of OECD member countries to agree on the adoption of legal instruments. In general, the likelihood that actors agreed on legal instruments increased when larger number of actors shared the costs. Moreover, OECD member countries welcomed anything that helped save costs to the governments as well as to the regulated actors. The relative success of the environment directorate in chemicals policy partly goes back to the fact that many measures in this area helped governments and industry to save expenses (OECD 2004b, 5). In comparison, cognitive influence is easier to achieve by providing knowledge, ideas, concepts, and arguments. Unless they do not result in any concrete measures, changes in the knowledge and belief systems of actors are unlikely to provoke the same powerful opposition like the adoption and implementation of new international or domestic policies, as they do not necessarily have noticeable consequences on the interests and behavior of actors.

In sum, that the secretariat and the environment directorate command the output of knowledge, ideas, concepts, and arguments only as resources helps to understand the limitations in its executive and normative influence as well as its achievements in cognitive influence. Yet this limitation in resources cannot elucidate how the environment directorate actually realized its influences. In the next section, I argue that the competences and the embeddedness in the organizational setting enable the environment directorate to have influence, namely the explicit and implicit rules that govern the work at the OECD and that determine the constraints and the opportunities in the relationship and interaction between principal and agent.

Competences   OECD member countries grant the secretariat and its subdivisions greater autonomy than, for example, the treaty secretariats studied in this book or the secretariat of the IMO have (see Campe, this volume, chapter 6). Four observations illustrate the relative large autonomy of the environment directorate.

First, the OECD secretariat and its subdivisions lack any formal mandate. The founding convention of the OECD does not spell out the secretariat's assignments. The only convention articles that deal with the secretariat contain vague definitions (articles 10 and 11). Neither do the mandates of the organization, of the environmental policy committee, or of the chemicals committee specify the environment directorate's responsibilities. Instead, they outline major functions of the intergovernmental organization and committees as well as the thematic priorities. Like all other intergovernmental bureaucracies studied in this book, the OECD secretariat is however not entitled to take any formal decisions. The council holds all decision-making power and applies the consensus rule for all decisions.

The two-year work programs contain the only formal limitation to the activities of the environment directorate. The programs, which require the formal approval by the council, broadly define what thematic priorities the environment directorate should address. While the environment directorate "cannot burgeon in all directions"[18] and is "far from able to act as a self-governed epistemic community" (Marcussen 2004b, 99), they enjoy "quite a bit freedom and flexibility on *how* to do the work"[19] (see, e.g., Lönngren 1992, 410–411; Henry et al. 2001). In fact, OECD member countries expect the environment directorate "to come up with ideas in an anticipatory and not reactive mode."[20] The self-descriptions of the OECD secretariat and its subdivisions mirror these statements: Here, the secretariat "carries out research and analysis at the request of the OECD's 30 member countries" (OECD 2005a, 121) and works "to support the activities of the committees" (OECD 2004e). The self-description of the environment directorate states: "Working closely with member country delegates the staff researches and analyses the underlying issues. The findings and recommendations of this work are discussed at meetings of the EPOC [Environmental Policy Committee], its subsidiary and collaborating bodies, or with groups of experts" (OECD 2002b, 12; 2004c, 6).

Second, when OECD member countries disagree, they do not necessarily stop the analysis, as long as the environment directorate does not present its findings as consensus position.[21] Even if OECD member countries object to endorse a publication on behalf of the OECD, the secretary-general can still publish the study as work of the secretariat.

Third, the environment directorate does not spare criticism of OECD member countries. In the evaluation of the progress in implementing the OECD environment strategy, the environment directorate concluded: "Much more ambitious measures will be needed if the strategy is to be fully implemented by 2010. Current policies are insufficient to adequately protect biodiversity or address climate change, and the decoupling of environmental pressures from economic growth in key sectors is proceeding too slowly" (OECD 2004d; see also Lorentsen 2004).

Fourth, the studies of the environment directorate occasionally meet opposition. In 2003, for example, OECD member countries criticized a publication on the use of voluntary approaches in environmental policy that had questioned the effectiveness of these instruments (OECD 2003b).[22]

Embeddedness The organizational positioning in the OECD working process enables the secretariat and its subdivisions to translate this autonomy into influence (for related arguments, see Marcussen 2004b; Porter and Webb 2004). Dostal describes the position of secretariat staff as "gate keepers" (2004, 454). Exchanges in the organization's intergovernmental bodies typically "flow from information and analysis provided by [the] secretariat" (OECD 2004e). The working process starts with data collection and continues with the preparation of analyses by the secretariat. The delegates in the intergovernmental committees then discuss the resulting output. Apart from publications, the working process may culminate in formal council decisions (OECD 2004e). Likewise, first proposals for organizational action often originate from the secretariat and its subdivisions (Bonuci 2004; Marcussen 2004b). Hence, the secretariat's output often constitutes the vantage point from which discussions among government officials evolve. Staff members control the chain of expertise and prepare political issues for discussion or decision making in the intergovernmental bodies. This position empowers staff members to define problems and solutions (Dostal 2004, 454), but the "closer it gets to legal acts, the more difficult it gets."[23] The consensus rule for formal decisions constrains the ability of the secretariat and its subdivision to have normative influence. Any government that feels essential interests threatened can veto legal instruments.

Besides this "internal embeddedness," its close links to stakeholders often facilitated the autonomous influence of the environment directorate. It maintains formal cooperation agreements with other intergovernmental and nongovernmental business and environmental organizations that have a stake in environmental governance. These organizations participate in the regular meetings of the environmental policy and chemicals committee. On one hand, this cooperation often ensured that the output of the environment directorate finds acceptance and support among stakeholders.[24] On the other hand, it provided the environment directorate with alternative indirect channels of communication with OECD member countries when these stakeholders and experts supported its recommendations. "Non-governmental organizations are more likely to succeed in getting a door opened for us than we are. They can act as political champions who see a political necessity, can make public pressure and convince politicians that they shall have an environmental component in this or that activity."[25] Even in the controversial issue of environmental harmful subsidies, the environment directorate succeeded to convince OECD member countries to abolish some of these, once it involved stakeholders in decision making.[26]

People and Procedures
In this section, I argue that in addition to the competences and the embeddedness of the environment directorate, it is its expertise and organizational culture that have enabled it to generate, process, and disseminate an output that has been influential. I start with a brief characterization of the perception and reputation of the environment directorate's output and its relevance for the environment directorate's achievements.

Subsequently, I highlight those characteristics of the environment directorate that have enabled it to produce such an output.

Organizational Expertise   Lacking any legal or financial competencies, the key to the achievements of the environment directorate must be its informatory, conceptual, and analytical output.[27] The environment directorate "depends solely on the quality of its advice and expertise as it is perceived by its member states" (Dostal 2004, 446) and must rely on the intellectual persuasiveness of its arguments (OECD 1985, 3; Beyeler 2004, 1). "You have to put enough arguments on the table and to provide very strong analytical support."[28]

Indeed, several indications suggest that the knowledge, ideas, concepts, and arguments that the secretariat and its subdivisions generate, process and disseminate fulfill these qualities (Henry et al. 2001, 48) and thus are important sources of its influence. Marcussen characterizes the organization and its bureaucracy as a "mythical, neutral, scientific, and objective soothsayer that one cannot afford to ignore" (2004a). When authors of academic articles quote OECD publications, they often see no need to justify the authoritative character of the knowledge beyond the mere use of the OECD label (Porter and Webb 2004). Their publications have gained a reputation of "authoritative statements of knowledge in many policy areas" (Porter and Webb 2004, 7). Albeit occasionally criticized, OECD statistical data "are among the most reputable available" (Porter and Webb 2004, 7). Long concluded that "high-quality work has been a hallmark of the Organization's environmental work" (2000, 132; see also 88 and 131). The high quality and credibility of its output explain the environment directorate's cognitive influence and the resort to its input in international negotiations and the implementation of international agreements.[29] "Our safeguard is the quality of work and our credibility. We have the reputation to make good quality work."[30]

On several occasions, external experts commended the environment directorate's work. In 1996, fourteen independent experts who assessed the environment directorate's future role in international environmental affairs honored the unique ability of the environment directorate to provide systematic analysis (OECD 1997). With regard to the use of economic instruments in environmental policy, the environment directorate has achieved expert status (Tolba et al. 1995, 366–367). In general, the reputation of the OECD as a legitimate and engaged expert in economic matters helped the secretariat and the environment directorate to get noticed by policy makers in environmental matters, too (Bernstein 2000, 497). Likewise, it "could provide an unsurpassed quality of analytical work" in the support of the integration of trade and environmental policies (Long 2000, 88). The influence of the performance reviews but also other influences of the environment directorate depend to a high degree on its reputation as an unbiased expert source of knowledge that is independent from governments under review and from its peers (Pagani 2002; Lehtonen 2005; Henry et al. 2001; Marcussen 2004a).

However, how did the environment directorate establish the good reputation of its output?

The secretariat and its subdivisions control unique expertise that confers staff members a comparative advantages vis-à-vis other actors (Dostal 2004, 446). This almost monopolistic control helps to explain the frequent references to the secretariat's output in public debates as well as in scientific discourses and publications. The secretariat has pioneered the collection and processing of comprehensive statistical data on environmental conditions in OECD member countries (Trondal, Marcussen, and Veggeland 2004; Dostal 2004). In the harmonization of data, for example, the secretariat has established a quasi monopoly on comparable statistical data for developed countries in almost any conceivable policy area, including environmental protection. At the same time, the abundant number of analytical studies that the environment directorate has conducted since its creation add up to an unmatched body of specialized knowledge that the environment directorate has at its command.

Comparable to the environmental department of the World Bank (see Marschinski and Behrle, this volume, chapter 5), the privileged and regular access of staff to inside knowledge of governments further increases the uniqueness of the expertise and provides a major source for the persuasiveness and authority of the environment directorate's output (Henry et al. 2001; Porter and Webb 2004). The meetings, conferences, and workshops the directorate organizes offer staff members the opportunity to establish personal contacts to government officials, thereby facilitating the access to inside knowledge.

The practice of the environment directorate to utilize external resources often enhanced the credibility and authority of its output. Throughout its history, the environment directorate has identified new issues and devised innovative solutions by inviting external experts or stakeholders to conferences, workshops or seminars with the aim to learn about the latest state of knowledge on an issue. For example, the conceptual background of the successful definition and promotion of the polluter-pays principle through the environment directorate was a series of subsequent seminars that brought together the most advanced researchers with public and administrative stakeholders (Long 2000, 44, including additional examples). In addition, the environment directorate successfully utilized these meetings between experts and stakeholders to convince participants of its views and proposals and to frame discourses (see, e.g., Bernstein 2000, 496).

Organizational Culture   The organizational culture is another source for the persuasiveness and authority of the output of the environment directorate. First, the skills and status of staff members who are responsible for research and analysis enable the secretariat to generate authoritative and persuasive knowledge. The secretariat continuously attracted qualified and competent staff (Marcussen 2004a). The majority of professional staff has an academic background and/or professional experience in public administrations of OECD member countries or other intergovernmental bureaucracies.[31] They have several years of professional experiences within their discipline (Marcussen 2004b). The dominant peer groups are economists followed by lawyers, scientists, and regulatory experts (Dostal 2004, 446). This high share of economists in the secretariat and the environment directorate constitutes the background for the importance of the economic dimension in environmental governance in the overall quality of the directorate's cognitive influence.

Second, the environment directorate's practice and ability to stay as close as possible to real-world problems and the practical experiences of its principals ensured that its output was conceived as relevant and useful. "Our clients are governments and they do not want theoretical or academic work."[32] All publications start from the experiences in OECD member countries, emphasize practical issues and challenges, and address policy questions as well as political, economic, or societal dimensions of environmental pollution. The environment directorate picks up new ideas and policies from the countries and then develops their potential for implementation. This ensures that government officials in OECD member countries can relate the results to their reality (Papadopoulos 1994, 203).

Third, the environment directorate's culture of presenting findings, recommendations, or proposals in a diplomatic, depoliticized, and nonconfrontational style further adds to the acceptance of its output (Dostal 2004; Henry et al. 2001). For example, when a proposal by the environment directorate met opposition by OECD member countries staff often tried to "circumvent the positions by making the work more technical and less political."[33] Staff attempts to depoliticize issues and transform these into questions of expertise (Dostal 2004, 446). Often the language and formulations in the secretariat's publications are open for a number of interpretations, so that almost everybody can agree with one or another interpretation (Dostal 2004). In doing so, the secretariat maintains its perceived neutrality (Dostal 2004, 447; see also Lehtonen 2005), which is essential for its ability to influence other actors (Marcussen 2004a). In sum, playing the game within the boundaries that the OECD member countries define helps the environment directorate to gain credibility among member states (Marcussen 2004b; Armingeon 2004).

Organizational Structure   The acceptance of the boundaries that the OECD member countries define is also reflected in the flexibility of the environment directorate in adapting the organizational structure to the needs of its principals. The environment directorate has frequently and successfully adapted its internal structures and shifted its activities to new thematic priorities in response to new demands by OECD member countries or events external to the organization (see, e.g., Long 2000). Through this openness for change, the environment directorate enhanced the acceptance of its output, because member countries feel better serviced by the directorate.

In addition, the environment directorate has internal structures and procedures in place that ensure the authority and persuasiveness of its output. The rules governing the recruitment procedure and the responsibilities strengthen the credibility as well as independence of staff from the principals and attach great importance to qualification. The OECD convention even guarantees staff their independency: staff "shall neither seek nor receive instructions from any of the Members or from any Government or authority external to the Organization" (paragraph 2, article 11). Staff is recruited because of professional or academic merits and experiences instead of country of origin. The recruitment is the sole responsibility of the secretary-general without any participation of the member countries.[34] Although formal learning mechanisms at the level of the directorate are missing, staff is encouraged to continually improve their expertise and reputation, for example, by attending international academic conferences and publishing in academic outlets (Trondal, Marcussen, and Veggeland 2004).

Organizational Leadership   Evidence that indicates a noticeable explanatory power of organizational leadership for the influence of the environment directorate hardly exists. Nevertheless, two observations suggest that at least external leadership contributed to the influence of the environment directorate. Bernstein attributes the success of the environment directorate in promoting the polluter-pays principle to the ability of a number of individual staff members in mobilizing and spreading the idea (2000, 495–496). Likewise, the role of the environment directorate in the institutionalization of the norm of sustainable development goes back to the involvement of Jim McNeill, who was the executive director of the environment directorate from 1979 to 1984, in the World Commission on Environment and Development. McNeill even became secretary-general of this commission and, by drawing on the former work of the environment directorate, incorporated the polluter-pays principle and the general idea of a possible reconciliation and mutual reinforcement of the environment and the economy in the work of the commission and its definition of sustainable development (Bernstein 2000, 496).

Conclusion

The environment directorate is an actor in its own right that autonomously influences international and domestic environmental policies. Its cognitive and normative influence has been stronger than its executive influence. Governments of member and non-member countries as well as other political actors have often drawn on the analytical input the environment directorate provided, be it in public debates or scientific discourses, be it in the negotiation or implementation of international agreements. A number of concepts and principles that the environment directorate promoted have shaped approaches to environmental policy in OECD member and non-member countries. This use of the environment directorate's analytical input, the acceptance of its recommendations, and its definition of concepts best characterize its influence. By contrast, the environment directorate's record in executive influence remained poor. It succeeded neither in prompting governments to introduce new policies nor in triggering international negotiations. Overall, the environment directorate has guided actors in *how* they might pursue international or domestic environmental policies, whereas it had limited influence on fundamental political decisions of *whether* actors take action to address environmental challenges.

Different aspects of the polity, as well as the people and procedures, are crucial to understand the environment directorate's achievements and the limitations to its influence. On one hand, they define the boundaries within which the environment directorate may influence domestic and international environmental policies at all. On the other hand, they help explain its achievements. Overall, I showed that the polity defined the core potential of the environment directorate to have influence, while its internal characteristics determined and explained its actual achievements. The autonomy of the environment directorate and its influential positioning within the organization's work processes delineate the opportunity structure in which the directorate can act. They provide the environment directorate with leeway in deciding on how it carries out its research and prepares its analytical contributions. At the same time, it puts the environment directorate at the very beginning of almost every workflow within the organization. The *type* of resources that the environment directorate commands constrained its principal ability to exploit these opportunities. Lacking any financial or legal competencies, the environment directorate has to rely on its output of knowledge, ideas, concepts, and arguments. It has to convince actors but cannot compel them by adopting legally binding instruments or lure them by offering financial incentives. The *quality* of its resources— namely, the perceived authority and persuasiveness of its output—are crucial in understanding how the environment directorate has influenced actors. In turn, the expertise the environment directorate holds and controls, its organizational structure, and its organizational culture of respect and anticipating the needs and priorities of its principals help determine the quality of its output.

Acknowledgments

I owe my gratitude to all interviewees at the OECD environment directorate. I am also grateful for valuable comments and suggestions on earlier versions of this chapter to Steven Bernstein and Philipp Pattberg, as well as the MANUS project team.

Notes

1. Australia, Austria, Belgium, Canada, Czech Republic, Denmark, Finland, France, Germany, Greece, Hungary, Iceland, Ireland, Italy, Japan, Luxemburg, Mexico, Netherlands, New Zealand, Norway, Poland, Portugal, Republic of Korea, Slovak Republic, Spain, Sweden, Switzerland, Turkey, United Kingdom, United States of America (as of 2005).

2. Author's interviews at the environment directorate, Paris, April 2004.

3. Author's interview at the environment directorate, Paris, April 2004.

4. Author's interviews at the environment directorate, Paris, April 2004.

5. Author's interview at the environment directorate, Paris, April 2004.

6. Author's interview with country expert, Berlin, February 2004.

7. Some of the following evidence for the normative influence of the environment directorate has elements that might be attributed also to cognitive influence, because of the role of changes in knowledge through the output of the environment directorate. The evidence nevertheless indicates normative influence, because the changes in knowledge ultimately contributed to the creation, support, or shaping of norm building for issue-specific international cooperation.

8. Author's interviews at the environment directorate, Paris, April 2004.

9. Author's interviews at the environment directorate, Paris, April 2004.

10. Author's interviews at the environment directorate, Paris, April 2004.

11. Author's interviews at the environment directorate, Paris, April 2004.

12. Author's interviews at the environment directorate, Paris, April 2004.

13. Author's interview at the environment directorate, Paris, April 2004.

14. Author's interviews at the environment directorate, Paris, April 2004.

15. Author's interviews at the environment directorate, Paris, April 2004.

16. Author's interviews at the environment directorate, Paris, April 2004.

17. Author's interview at the environment directorate, Paris, April 2004.

18. Author's interview at the environment directorate, Paris, April 2004.

19. Author's interview at the environment directorate, Paris, April 2004 (italics added).

20. Author's interview at the environment directorate, Paris, April 2004.

21. Author's interviews at the environment directorate, Paris, April 2004.

22. Author's interviews at the environment directorate, Paris, April 2004.

23. Author's interview at the environment directorate, Paris, April 2004.

24. Author's interviews at the environment directorate, Paris, April 2004.

25. Author's interview at the environment directorate, Paris, April 2004.

26. Author's interviews at the environment directorate, Paris, April 2004.

27. Author's interviews at the environment directorate, Paris, April 2004.

28. Author's interview at the environment directorate, Paris, April 2004.

29. Author's interviews at the environment directorate, Paris, April 2004.

30. Author's interview at the environment directorate, Paris, April 2004.

31. The OECD does not publish detailed statistics on staff and their professional backgrounds (Dostal 2004). Estimates in the literature range between 700 (Dostal 2004; OECD 2004e) to 800 (Trondal, Marcussen, and Veggeland 2004) full-time employed research personnel to which approximately 500 research personnel employed on an ad hoc basis with limited time contracts added (Trondal, Marcussen, and Veggeland 2004). Altogether, including general services staff, the OECD employed some 2000 staff (OECD 2004e).

32. Author's interview at the environment directorate, Paris, April 2004.

33. Author's interview at the environment directorate, Paris, April 2004.

34. Author's interviews at the environment directorate, Paris, April 2004. See also Trondal, Marcussen, and Veggeland 2004 and Henry et al. 2001.

References

Armingeon, Klaus. 2004. "OECD and National Welfare State Development." In *The OECD and European Welfare States*, edited by Klaus Armingeon and Michelle Beyeler, 226–241. Cheltenham, UK: Edward Elgar.

Bernstein, Steven. 2000. "Ideas, Social Structure and the Compromise of Liberal Environmentalism." *European Journal of International Relations* 6 (4): 464–512.

Beyeler, Michelle. 2004. "Introduction: A Comparative Study of the OECD and European Welfare States." In *The OECD and European Welfare States*, edited by Klaus Armingeon and Michelle Beyeler, 1–12. Cheltenham, UK: Edward Elgar.

Bundesministerium für Umwelt. 2001. *OECD Confirms German Government's Course towards Ecological Modernisation in Germany.* Press release. Berlin: Bundesministerium für Umwelt, Naturschutz und Reaktorsicherheit. Available at http://www.bmu.de/en/1024/js/news/pressrelease010124/ (accessed 11 September 2004).

Bonuci, Nicola. 2004. *The Legal Status of an OECD Act and the Procedure for Its Adoption.* Paris: OECD. Available at http://www.oecd.org/dataoecd/26/29/31691605.pdf (accessed 7 September 2004).

CBD, Convention on Biological Diversity. 2001. *Incentive Measures: Proposals for the Design and Implementation of Incentive Measures.* UN Doc. UNEP/CBD/SBSTTA/7/11 of 20 September 2001. Montreal: Convention on Biological Diversity.

CBD, Convention on Biological Diversity. 2002. *Capacity-Building for Access to Genetic Resources and Benefit-Sharing: Synthesis of Submission Received on Need, Priorities and Existing Initiatives, and Additional Elements for Consideration in the Development of an Action Plan.* UN Doc. UNEP/CBD/ABS/EW-CB/1/2 of 4 November 2002. Montreal: Convention on Biological Diversity.

CBD, Convention on Biological Diversity. 2004. *Report of the First Meeting of the Conference of the Parties Serving as the Meeting of the Parties to the Protocol on Biosafety.* UN Doc. UNEP/CBD/BS/COP-MOP/1/15 of 14 April 2004. Kuala Lumpur: Convention on Biological Diversity.

Comolet, Arnaud. 1990. "How OECD Countries Respond to State-of-the-Environment Reports." *International Environmental Affairs* 4 (1): 3–17.

Dostal, Jörg M. 2004. "Campaigning on Expertise: How the OECD Framed EU Welfare and Labour Market Policies—and Why Success Could Trigger Failure." *Journal of European Public Policy* 11 (3): 440–460.

Environment Canada. 1995. *OECD's Report on Canada's Environmental Performance Released.* Press release. Environment Canada. Available at http://www.ec.gc.ca/press/oecd_p_e.htm (accessed 11 September 2004).

Haas, Peter M., and David McCabe. 2001. "Amplifiers or Dampeners: International Institutions and Social Learning in the Management of Global Environmental Risks." In *Learning to Manage Global Environmental Risks*, edited by The Social Learning Group, 323–348. Cambridge, MA: MIT Press.

Hanf, Kenneth. 2000. "The Problem of Long-Range Transport of Air Pollution and the Acidification Regime." In *International Environmental Agreements and Domestic Politics: The Case of Acid Rain*, edited by Arild Underdal and Kenneth Hanf, 21–48. Burlington, VT: Ashgate.

Henry, Miriam, Bob Lingard, Fazal Rizvi, and Sandra Taylor. 2001. *The OECD, Globalisation, and Education Policy.* Amsterdam, New York: Elsevier.

Jäger, Jill, with Nancy M. Dickson, Adams Fenech, Peter M. Haas, Edward A. Parson, Vladimir Sokolov, Ferenc L. Toth, Jeroen van der Sluijs, and Claire Waterton. 2001. "Monitoring in the Management of Global Environmental Risks." In *Learning to Manage Global Environmental Risks*, edited by The Social Learning Group, 31–48. Cambridge, MA: MIT Press.

Lehtonen, Markku. 2005. "OECD Environmental Performance Review Programme: Accountability (F)or Learning?" *Evaluation* 11 (2): 169–188.

Long, Bill L. 2000. *International Environmental Issues and the OECD 1950–2000.* Paris: OECD.

Lönngren, Rune. 1992. *International Approaches to Chemicals Control.* Stockholm: The National Chemicals Inspectorate.

Lorentsen, Lorents. 2004. "The OECD Environmental Strategy: Are We On Track?" *OECD Observer*, April 7.

Marcussen, Martin. 2004a. "Multilateral Surveillance and the OECD: Playing the Idea Game." In *The OECD and European Welfare States*, edited by Klaus Armingeon and Michelle Beyeler, 13–31. Cheltenham, UK: Edward Elgar.

Marcussen, Martin. 2004b. "The OECD as Ideational Artist and Arbitrator: Reality or Dream?" In *Decision-Making within International Organisations*, edited by Bob Reinalda and Bertjan Verbeek, 90–106. London: Routledge.

Marcussen, Martin. 2004c. "OECD Soft Governance." In *Soft Law in Governance and Regulation: An Interdisciplinary Analysis*, edited by Ulrika Mörth, 103–128. Cheltenham, UK: Edward Elgar.

OECD. 1985. *OECD*. Paris: OECD.

OECD. 1997. *Guiding the Transition to Sustainable Development*. Paris: OECD.

OECD. 2001a. *Domestic Transferable Permits for Environmental Management: Design and Implementation*. Paris: OECD.

OECD. 2001b. *Environmentally Related Taxes in OECD Countries. Issues and Strategies*. Paris: OECD.

OECD. 2002a. *Handbook of Biodiversity Valuation: A Guide for Policy Makers*. Paris: OECD.

OECD. 2002b. *OECD Environment Programme 2003–2004*. Paris: OECD. Available at http://www.oecd.org/dataoecd/48/63/19827587.pdf (accessed 12 August 2004).

OECD. 2003a. *Environmentally Harmful Subsidies: Policy Issues and Challenges*. Paris: OECD.

OECD. 2003b. *Voluntary Approaches for Environmental Policy: Effectiveness, Efficiency and Usage in Policy Mixes*. Paris: OECD.

OECD. 2004a. *Legal Instruments of the OECD* [Web site]. Available at http://www.oecd.org/document/46/0,2340,en_2649_34483_1925230_1_1_1_1,00.html (accessed 10 August 2004).

OECD. 2004b. *OECD's Environment, Health and Safety Programme*. Paris: OECD. Available at http://www.oecd.org/dataoecd/18/0/1900785.pdf (accessed 12 August 2004).

OECD. 2004c. *OECD Environment Programme 2005–2006*. Paris: OECD. Available at http://www.oecd.org/dataoecd/48/63/19827587.pdf (accessed 12 August 2004).

OECD. 2004d. *OECD Environmental Strategy: Review of Progress*. Paris: OECD.

OECD. 2004e. *OECD Online Guide to Intergovernmental Activity*. Paris: OECD. Available at http://webnet3.oecd.org/OECDgroups/ (accessed 12 August 2004).

OECD. 2005a. *Environmental Harmful Subsidies. Challenges for Reform*. Paris: OECD.

OECD. 2005b. *OECD Decisions, Recommendations and Other Instruments in Force*. Paris: OECD. Available at http://www.olis.oecd.org/horizontal/oecdacts.nsf (accessed 23 November 2005).

Pagani, Fabrizio. 2002. *Peer Review: A Tool for Co-Operation and Change—An Analysis of an OECD Working Method*. Paris: OECD.

Papadopoulos, George S. 1994. *Education 1960–1990. The OECD Perspective*. Paris: OECD.

Porter, Tony, and Michael Webb. 2004. "The Role of the OECD in the Orchestration of Global Knowledge Networks." Paper presented at the 45th Annual Convention of the International Studies Association, 17–20 March, Montreal (Quebec), Canada.

Sullivan, Scott. 1997. *From War to Wealth. Fifty Years of Innovation*. Paris: OECD.

Tolba, Mostafa, Osama A. El-Kholy, Essam El-Hinnawi, Martin W. Holdgate, D. F. McMichael, and R. E. Munn. 1995. *The World Environment 1972–1992. Two Decades of Challenges*. London: Chapman and Hall.

Trondal, Jarle, Martin Marcussen, and Frode Veggeland. 2004. "International Executives: Transformative Bureaucracies or Westphalian Orders?" *European Integration Online Papers* 8 (4): 1–18.

UNFCCC, United Nations Framework Convention on Climate Change. 2002. Review of the Implementation of Commitments and of Other Provisions of the Convention. National Communications: Green House Gas Inventories from Parties Included in Annex I to the Convention. UNFCCC Guidelines on Reporting and Review. UN Doc. FCCC/CP/2002/8 of 28 March 2002. New Delhi: United Nations Framework Convention on Climate Change.

5

The World Bank: Making the Business Case for the Environment

Robert Marschinski and Steffen Behrle

Introduction

In August 2004, the World Bank approved the largest environmental project in its history, offering Brazil USD 550 million in form of a Programmatic Reform Loan for Environmental Sustainability. Emblematic for its "making the business case" approach toward the environment, the World Bank country director justified the intervention first of all on economic grounds: "The costs to society from environmental destruction are high, rough estimates placing them at as much as 4 percent of the country's GDP."[1]

The World Bank[2] is not an environmental organization as such. But it still represents a prominent case among the world's intergovernmental bureaucracies active in the environmental arena. Established at the Bretton Woods conference in 1944, it has evolved into one of the largest international organizations of today, with an annual administrative budget of USD 1 billion (World Bank 2004a, 33) and roughly 8,800 staff working at the headquarters in Washington, DC, or in one of the over one hundred country offices. It is a public multilateral institution that is mostly known as a financier of large loans to developing countries, but also as a "source and proselytizer of ideas" on economic, social, and environmental development (Gavin and Rodrik 1995, 332).

According to article I of the the International Bank for Reconstruction and Development (IBRD) Articles of Agreement—the World Bank's constitutional document—its mandate is to assist with reconstruction and development in regions that have been disrupted by war or that are less developed. Hence, the articles make no mention of sustainable development or environmental protection. The latter became a policy goal in its own right only in 1987, after a period of strong internal resistance (Wade

1997; Nielson and Tierney 2003), when the World Bank's operational manual was amended by a series of safeguard policies, "to prevent and mitigate undue harm to people and their environment in the development process." The establishment of an environment department shortly thereafter, along with the launch of "core" environment projects, marked the World Bank's adjustment to the nascent paradigm of sustainable development.

However, many external observers remain skeptical about the World Bank's ability to adequately handle environmental issues. Environmentalists in particular point to a series of ecologically disastrous projects that the World Bank carried out in the 1970s and 1980s, promoting deforestation, destroying coastal ecosystems, and furthering soil degradation (Rich 1994). The adoption of the safeguard policies in 1987 did not prevent the World Bank's continued involvement in environmentally controversial projects, and hence sparked further critique, from nongovernmental organizations (Seymour and Dubash 1999; Alexander et al. 2002; Rich 2002), independent reviewers (Morse and Berger 1992), and even from inside the World Bank (Liebenthal 2002; World Bank 2002a).

Although the academic literature shares the criticism produced by nongovernmental organizations to some extent, scholars also point to laudable aspects in the World Bank's environmental efforts (Haas and Haas 1995; Le Prestre 1995; Nielson and Tierney 2003). For instance, Haas and Haas (1995) conclude that among thirteen international organizations, only the World Bank and UNEP exhibited traits of "learning" in the ways they integrated environmental issues into their work. Nakayama (2000) attests a generally much improved ability of the World Bank to handle environmental issues. Gutner (2002) compares the World Bank's environmental performance in Central and Eastern Europe with that of two other multilateral development banks and finds the World Bank to be the most responsive, transparent, and environmentally stringent among the three. A different and rather extensive strain of literature focuses on the World Bank's struggle for environmental reform, for example, against external pressure (Nielson and Tierney 2003; Wade 2004), or on the grounds of economic rationality (Krueger 1998; Gilbert et al. 1999). In other cases, particular aspects are emphasized, such as the World Bank's production of hegemonic knowledge (Goldman 2004; Goldman 2005), corporate culture (Nelson 2003), the role of its president (Fidler 2001; Mallaby 2004; Moog Rodrigues 2004), or its emphasis on structural adjustment lending (Kessler and Van Dorp 1998).

Addressing the controversy about the World Bank's overall impact on the environment is beyond the scope of this study. Rather, our objective is to identify causal links that explain how different types of influence that the World Bank has had on national and international environmental policy were achieved. To this end, the first part of this chapter assesses the influence of environmental activities by the World Bank along three categories; namely, cognitive, normative, and executive. In the second part, we discuss the explanatory power of several independent variables vis-à-vis the observed influence. In doing so, we refer to design characteristics of the World Bank as an *international organization*. At the same time, we demonstrate that a consistent argument can be built only if the internal characteristics of the World Bank *bureaucracy*—as represented by its staff and internal procedures—are taken into account.

Although the central environment department plays an important role in coordinating the World Bank's environmental activities, several other units may manage projects with environmental contents. For this reason, the subject of our study is defined by the entirety of the World Bank's environmental activities—including the whole environmental portfolio, not just the activities of the environment department. Doing so seems appropriate also in view of the multisectoral nature of many World Bank projects, and its multilayered internal structure, under which employees may have multiple affiliations and lines of reporting.[3]

By excluding the World Bank's large nonenvironmental portfolio, many potentially adverse impacts on the environment are a priori neglected. Our results therefore necessarily convey an overly green vision of the World Bank, and for that reason cannot be directly linked to the above-mentioned controversial debate. Having said this, such a green bias should not impair the correct identification of factors that explain how the autonomous influence of the World Bank was brought about.

Related literature mostly analyzes the World Bank's struggle to implement environmental policies in terms of several external and internal explanatory variables, especially governance, incentives, "goal congestion" (Naim 1994, c276) or "antinomic delegation" (Gutner 2005, 11), but it does not disentangle the different effects and causal pathways. So far, it has not been investigated systematically how the environmental activities of the World Bank *as an actor* influence other actors, and in how far this influence is determined by the World Bank *bureaucracy*. It is our ambition to address this gap.

The case study draws upon three types of sources: academic publications on the World Bank, original World Bank documents, and sixteen personal interviews with World Bank employees working on environmental issues. All interviews were conducted by Robert Marschinski in the headquarters in Washington, DC, in the course of a three months' stay at the World Bank.

Structure and Activities

A substantial part of the World Bank's environmental output consists of environmental projects.[4] Five to ten percent of the World Bank's yearly investments address environmental issues (World Bank 2005, 27). The World Bank finances projects that range from pollution and waste management to environmental capacity building and global issues such as biodiversity, climate change, and international waters. Hence, the World Bank has de facto become a widely present actor in this field, with cumulative lending for environmental projects reaching USD 9.2 billion over the years 1998–2003 (Acharya et al. 2004).

An overview of projects related to the environment (according to the World Bank's seven environmental themes and the type of project[5]) indicates that most core environment projects are based on small grants with USD 7 million per project on average (see table 5.1). But it also shows that core environment loan projects (about USD 50 million each) and integrated loan projects that include only some environmental components (about USD 100 million each) dwarf the grant projects in monetary terms. Strictly speaking, grants represent external funding and are mainly linked to the World Bank's role as an implementing agency of the GEF and of the Montreal Protocol Multilateral Fund, as well as to its various carbon funds. Not unexpectedly for a development agency, "Pollution Management and Environmental Health" and "Environmental Policies and Institutions" make up the largest share in the World Bank's green portfolio. "Biodiversity" receives the least resources but ranks high in number of projects, giving rise to the World Bank's claim to be "the world's largest single international funding source for biodiversity projects" (World Bank 2005, 53).

The World Bank integrates its lending by selected support measures. First, so-called Analytical and Advisory Activities encompass formal

Table 5.1
Summary of all World Bank projects from 1984 to mid 2005 that address one of the seven environmental themes[1]

	Total number of projects	Total invested amount [million USD]	Projects financed through IBRD/IDA loans				Grants (GEF, Ozone fund, and so on)	
			Number of core ENV projects	Invested amount [million USD]	Number of projects with ENV component	Invested amount[2] [million USD]	Number of projects	Invested amount [million USD]
Biodiversity	288	5,391	54	1,994	51	2,388	183	1,009
Climate change	207	14,980	8	857	111	13,517	88	606
Environmental policies and institutions	536	30,052	97	4,615	248	23,882	191	1,555
Land administration and management	296	15,694	57	2,251	180	13,143	59	300
Pollution management and environmental health	548	42,108	58	3,498	367	37,381	123	1,229
Water resource management	352	23,960	49	2,966	245	20,656	58	338
Other environmental and natural resources management	147	5,527	10	359	89	4,538	48	230
Total	1,402	90,766	155	7,696	892	80,522	355	2,548

Source: World Bank project online database (accessed 14 April 2005).
1. Excluding MIGA guarantees (five projects). Projects with environment as "old major sector" and all grant-financed projects are considered "core" environment projects. Grant projects are financed through the GEF, the ozone fund, carbon offsets, rainforest fund, or special financing. Columns do not sum up because many projects address more than one environmental theme, and thus figure in more than one row.
2. Shows total lending commitment, meaning that the amount representing the sole environmental component of the projects will be a fraction thereof.

environmental reports and studies, as well as workshops and non-lending technical assistance programs. In 2004, roughly one hundred environment-related products of this kind were finalized (World Bank 2003b, 38). Second, the World Bank has bundled most of its capacity-building and learning programs within a specialized center: the World Bank Institute. In 2003, this "capacity development arm of the World Bank" spent more than USD 50 million for the training of individuals, about 20 percent of which was allocated to "Environment and Sustainable Development" (World Bank Institute 2003, 75f).

Summing up, the World Bank has a broad environmental output, which by far exceeds the immediate products of the three hundred or so professionals of the environment department. With an annual turnout of around one hundred environmentally relevant projects (corresponding to investments between USD 1 and 2 billion), about one hundred analytical and technical assistance products, and USD 10 million worth of training days on environment and sustainable development, the World Bank constitutes by far the largest player within this book's sample of international bureaucracies. Obviously, one would expect to find a relatively stronger influence from a large implementing and financing agency such as the World Bank than from small convention secretariats. Hence, the results of this case study shall be discussed and weighed against the findings for other larger multi-issue organizations, in particular UNEP (Bauer, this volume, chapter 7) and the OECD (Busch, this volume, chapter 4), even though the OECD is not comparable to the World Bank in terms of geographical scope, since World Bank projects are almost always directed to developing countries).

A special relationship links the World Bank with the GEF (see also Andler, this volume, chapter 8). Although formally independent of each other, the World Bank hosts the GEF on its premises, acts as its trustee, and is the implementing agency that has captured more than 50 percent of GEF resources.[6] As a consequence, one could indeed raise the question of whether it is even possible to separate their influence and—as we do in this volume—analyze them separately. For the purpose of this study, we decided on the following "rules of accounting": influence of GEF-financed World Bank projects will be credited to the World Bank, while the GEF case study focuses on the GEF secretariat and its influence on external actors (see Andler, this volume, chapter 8).

The Influence of the World Bank

We analyze the influence of the World Bank with regard to the three categories of cognitive, normative, and executive influence. Cognitive influence changes the technical and scientific understanding of environmental problems, as well as the awareness or concern for them. Normative influence shapes international cooperation and the collective capacity to respond to environmental problems. Finally, executive influence is defined as that affecting the physical and institutional capacity of states to safeguard the environment.

Cognitive Influence

In terms of scholarly knowledge, World Bank staff members published more than 2000 scientific articles in peer-reviewed journals between 1995 and 2004.[7] About 10 percent of these—hence an average of 20 articles per year—relate to environmental issues, mostly from an environmental economics perspective. The World Bank's publication record stands out. For example, no other research institution has published more peer-reviewed articles on "environmental services" (referring to 1990–2005). Each article was cited on average nearly five times, and some many times more; for example, an article by Chomitz and Gray (1996) on deforestation received more than a hundred citations.

Green accounting has been a particular thrust area of World Bank research. The early theoretical discussion on the subject was influenced by the workings of current and former environmental staff members, including—among others—Hamilton, Goodland, Ledec, and Daly. Later, the theoretical concept was confronted with empirical data, leading to the innovative and well-received[8] book *Where Is the Wealth of Nations?* (World Bank 2006). Also, the World Bank's independent Operations Evaluation Department (renamed the Independent Evaluation Group in 2005) confirmed that "seminal work was done on natural capital, environmental indicators, and 'green accounting'" (Liebenthal 2002, 8). Some observers have been more reserved, questioning the originality of World Bank research and seeing its strength more in "testing theories, often developed elsewhere" (Gilbert et al. 1999, F608). Even a former World Bank chief economist, Nick Stern, found its research performance in the field of environment to be "less impressive" (Stern and Ferreira 1997, 557).

The World Bank's traditional stronghold of economic and development data has been expanded to include a wide range of environmental data and indicators, most notably in its annually published *World Development Indicators*, but also in the form of a separate publication, the *Little Green Data Book*. Moreover, both the 1992 and 2003 editions of the World Bank's flagship publication *World Development Report* have focused on the environment (World Bank 1992; World Bank 2002c). The former, entitled *Development and the Environment*, has stimulated the debate on the poverty-environment nexus, in particular by prompting "the first discussion" (Xepapadeas 2005, 1253) on the so-called environmental Kuznets curve, an inverted U-shaped relationship between pollution and income, for which it provided an "early example" (Boyce 2004, 116).

The stark influence of these publications is reflected in the high number of other publications in the field of environment that explicitly draw on these sources: more than four hundred documents cite the *World Development Indicators* and just over fifteen hundred the *World Development Report* (according to the Scopus database). The World Bank's strength within this area was also echoed in two positive external evaluations of its environment research in 2006 (Banerjee et al. 2006, 116) and 1997, the latter pointing in particular to the World Bank's success in defining pollution indices and uncovering patterns of international pollution.[9] The World Bank has also pioneered innovative data collection methods, such as remote sensing (Gastellu-Etchegorry 1990).

At the same time, several academic scholars (Mehta 2001; Wilke 2004; St. Clair 2004) question the apolitical nature of the knowledge emerging from the World Bank, and argue that underneath a disguise of objective science and a "technocratic veil" (St. Clair 2004), it actually promotes its own economistic agenda. Goldman (2004), though denouncing the highly biased environmental assessment reports produced in the context of the Nam Theun II dam project in Laos, nevertheless attests that they come to represent "cutting-edge knowledge of global significance", as the World Bank's official seal on new knowledge and data gives it "tremendous global stability, legitimacy, and circulation" (Goldman 2004, 59, 75).

To summarize, our evidence suggests that the World Bank's environmental data and knowledge production, though mainly focused on specialized areas such as environmental economics, has reached large audiences and is widely referenced. The World Bank has made scientific contributions by publishing a substantial number of articles in peer-reviewed journals. It has produced and analyzed environmental data and pioneered innovative approaches.

Normative Influence

At first sight, the World Bank's role in international environmental cooperation should be limited to help client countries to "meet the objectives of the global conventions" (World Bank 2002a, 35). However, as we argue in this section, the World Bank has influenced the normative aspects of environmental policy in at least three different ways: first, by shaping the way international agreements are operationalized and implemented; second, by facilitating transnational cooperation on the regional level; and, third, by leading partnerships.

Two specific cases illustrate how the World Bank has influenced the implementation modalities of two international environmental agreements. For the Global Mechanism of the desertification convention, it became a reform engineer. The Global Mechanism was established in 1997 with its aim being to facilitate the allocation of financial resources for the implementation of the convention. After five years of an "almost unnoticed existence" and an "identity crisis" of the Global Mechanism, the World Bank started a reform initiative.[10] Namely, it financed an independent evaluation, wrote a three-year business plan, and put forth an agenda for action, all of which were subsequently endorsed by the conference of the parties.

The Prototype Carbon Fund, established by the World Bank in 2000 in order to spur the development of a global carbon market, represents an instance in which the World Bank leaped ahead of the official negotiations. It worked toward the operationalization of the climate convention's Kyoto Protocol at a time when the protocol's ratification was highly uncertain. Thus, the World Bank took a considerable risk and acted ahead of all other players by launching a series of emissions reduction projects, which eventually needed to be certified under the protocol's rules and traded on a then nonexistent market in order to realize their value. It thereby turned a rather theoretical framework into something very concrete (Kiss et al. 2002, 1647). As a consequence, "the procedures, documentation, and methodologies developed by the Prototype Carbon Fund are helping to structure projects under the CDM [Clean Development Mechanism] and JI [Joint Implementation] projects and carbon transactions beyond the PCF [Prototype Carbon Fund]"

(Prototype Carbon Fund 2002, 49). Indeed, at one point the World Bank was even criticized for surging too far ahead of the climate negotiations,[11] though its carbon funds were eventually copied by other institutions, such as the Dutch government or the German development bank KfW (Kreditanstalt für Wiederaufbau).

In general, the field of climate policy has emerged as a World Bank thrust area: in addition to the Prototype Carbon Fund, it sponsored the elaboration of national CDM and JI strategies through its National Strategy Studies program, and provided analytical results from its aligned research activities. It perhaps even inspired a new policy proposal on the "rules of accounting" for emissions reductions stemming from biological sinks: "I have the modest claim of having invented the Colombian proposal, but the Colombians also invented it internally, so I can't directly claim the influence there."[12] Hence, within the area of climate change, the World Bank strengthened the Kyoto process through the injection of information into the negotiations, by demonstrating its practical feasibility, and by pointing out potential benefits for developing countries.

Second, the World Bank has facilitated cooperation on the regional level. It is party to three regional international environmental agreements, which were set up to resolve the dispute between India and Pakistan over the usage of freshwater from the Indus basin.[13] Through these treaties, and through the subsequent financing of the Tarbela dam, the World Bank stipulated an agreement on the sharing of a common water resource between these two antagonist countries (World Bank 2005, 23). The World Bank continues to play a mediating role in this "success story" (Nakayama 2000, 404) even today, by appointing neutral experts or members of a court of arbitration during conflicts.

In absolute terms, however, regional activities still play a marginal role. By the end of 2004, the World Bank's project database listed only twenty-nine past and ongoing cross-boundary regional environmental projects. Of these, twenty-six were GEF projects, and roughly 50 percent addressed riparian cooperation in transboundary water and marine issues. In terms of project outcomes, the assessment remains inconclusive, not least because of the World Bank's often somewhat supporting role as one of several sponsors or implementers. In one instance, a World Bank project led to the establishment of a regional organization, the Lake Victoria Fisheries Organization (World Bank 2002b, 2). On the other side, the World Bank's role in the rehabilitation of the Aral Sea was deemed a failure both by external (Nakayama 2000, 405) and internal referees

(World Bank 2004c), despite an earlier self-praise as the "best in development diplomacy" (Kirmani and Le Moigne 1997). So, though it is difficult to draw final conclusions on the overall outcome, it remains safe to say that the country level still constitutes the World Bank's main focus.

Third, the World Bank has increased international cooperation by initiating and promoting partnerships. At the time of writing, it participated in 44 (out of 308) global type-II partnerships for sustainable development,[14] of which it was leading two (the Critical Ecosystem Partnership Fund and the Global Gas Flaring Reduction Partnership).

Examples of other prominent partnerships that draw on World Bank financing and—to some extent—leadership include the World Commission on Dams, which was initiated in 1998 by the World Bank jointly with the International Union for Conservation of Nature (Dingwerth 2007), the Global Water Partnership, the World Wide Fund for Nature (WWF)/World Bank forest alliance, and the Africa Stockpiles Program (Albert 2003, 28).

To sum up, the World Bank bureaucracy demonstrates discreetness when it comes to its influence on international negotiations. It takes on supportive rather than leading roles, and its influence seems to be limited to the "injection of information on what different regimes might look like,"[15] as well as to advice and identification of "good practice" with regard to implementation, financial, and regulatory issues. Nonetheless, one should not assume that the World Bank's influence on international negotiations is wholly nonexistent, as it might occur through informal channels that are difficult to trace, not least because of the political incentive to negate such influence: "Sometimes there was an influence, you know of it, but you can't take the credit for it, for political reasons."[16]

In areas that do not fall into the domain of ongoing negotiations, the World Bank's influence becomes more evident. It actively fosters regional cooperation between states through a limited number of transboundary projects, plays a leading role in the formation of international fora, and builds public-private partnerships. But even here the World Bank often avoids prominent leadership roles, and rather works as a coordinator (in particular donor coordination), a provider of administrative and financial support, or an expert advisor.

Executive Influence

A precursor of the influence that may or may not result from World Bank projects is the financial influence of the World Bank's approval decision. This influence goes beyond the nominal amount of the World Bank loan itself, which typically covers only 40 percent of the total costs of an environmental project (calculation based on World Bank online project database). The remaining part is provided by cofinanciers such as regional or bilateral development banks, individual donor countries, and the borrowing country itself. Crucially, the approval of a project by the World Bank often guides the investment decisions of other financiers, especially for controversial projects. For instance, in case of the Nam Theun II dam project in Laos, *The Economist* reports that in view of the expected protests associated with large dam projects, commercial banks "will not stump up any money without the World Bank's approval."[17] In other words, the mere involvement of the World Bank has a strong influence on the flow of investments for development projects.

A substantial influence on national institutions results from the World Bank's advisory activities. Hunter (2001) reports that the World Bank has assisted in the development of environmental legal and institutional capacity in more than fifty developing countries since 1992. In a similar vein, Gutner points to the strong role of the World Bank in Eastern Europe, where its "intellectual and policy support" helped governments to bring about a series of policy reforms (2002, 164).

A major tool for the World Bank to influence the shaping of national policies was the National Environmental Action Plan, which all countries that receive soft loans from the International Development Association were required to develop. (It was also recommended to IBRD client countries.)

Described as a "dominant framework" of the World Bank's environmental efforts (Piddington 1992, 216), it assisted countries both by means of financial contributions and through direct participation of specialized World Bank staff in the process itself. Up to the year 2000, an overall of ninety-two National Environmental Action Plans had been completed. According to Gutner (2002, 146), they proved to be a successful "capacity building exercise," and enabled the World Bank to support countries in the formulation of an environmental policy reform agenda. At the same time, however, an review by the Operations Evaluation Department judged the overall outcome to be only of "mixed quality" (Liebenthal 2002, 8), and criticized the lack of follow-up to keep the plans up to date.

Another instance of executive influence is represented by the World Bank's environmental (and social) safeguard policies, to which every borrower must agree to adhere in order to obtain World Bank funding. The safeguard policies call for, among other things, mandatory environmental assessments and management plans whenever a project can be expected to have adverse effects on the environment. As a consequence, borrowers had to carry out environmental assessments for 64 percent of all World Bank projects (World Bank 2005, 27). In our staff interviews, safeguard policies were widely praised as a milestone in the World Bank's "environmental turnaround,"[18] and as a general justification for continued World Bank involvement, since countries would often be expected to worry less about environmental issues if they financed and implemented projects entirely on their own.

Interestingly, safeguard policies were in several cases permanently adopted by client countries. For instance, more than half of all sub-Saharan African countries have introduced laws on environmental assessments during the 1990s (Bekhechi and Mercier 2002). The World Bank has encouraged and supported this process with several projects—for example, with the "highly successful" (Lintner et al. 1996, 8) Mediterranean Environmental Technical Assistance Program and the Capacity Development and Linkages for Environmental Impact Assessment in Africa program.

At the same time, environmental staff acknowledges that "the quality of the environmental assessments and management plans is variable,"[19] and that more needs to be done to reinforce borrower compliance. The Operations Evaluation Department, too, found that safeguard procedures were not always implemented wholeheartedly by World Bank project staff (Liebenthal 2002, 11), or were carried out too late to still have a significant impact on the project design (19). Another problem could be inaccessibility: for instance, the environmental assessment report for the Nam Theun II dam project had a length of twenty-two volumes. Overall, "the Bank's performance on environmental safeguard policies remains contentious" (19).

However, the influence of the World Bank safeguard policies goes beyond the direct World Bank–client interaction. According to a staff member, World Bank environmental standards have become "world best practice," and as such are widely referenced by public and private financiers.[20] The so-called Equator Principles, which have been adopted by twenty-seven major private lending institutions, are based on the World Bank's environmental and social guidelines (World Bank 2005, 27). Likewise, with the 1998 *Pollution Prevention and Abatement*

Handbook, the World Bank has provided a best practice compilation that, according to a nongovernmental organization, is "widely referenced by export credit agencies, donor agencies, and private lenders."[21] Generally, World Bank safeguard principles are recognized—along with the OECD Common Approaches—as the international standard in project financing (Knigge et al. 2003, 26). The World Bank's pivotal role was also reflected in the way the recommendations of the World Commission on Dams were weakened when they were not fully endorsed by the World Bank (Knigge et al. 2003, 51).

Another manifestation of the World Bank's executive influence is its contribution toward the swift domestic implementation of international environmental treaties, such as the Montreal Protocol, the Kyoto Protocol, and the biodiversity convention. In case of the Montreal Protocol, it assisted developing countries in the phaseout of ozone-depleting substances, expecting to eventually eliminate "74 percent of CFCs [chlorofluorocarbons] produced in developing countries and about 58 percent of global CFC production" (World Bank 2003b, 13, Box 2.9). At the same time, projects associated with the Prototype Carbon Fund are likely to cut greenhouse gas emissions by 40–45 million tons of carbon dioxide equivalent over ten years (Prototype Carbon Fund 2004, 5). At the same time, however, greenhouse gases produced by World Bank–financed traditional energy and extractive industries projects amount to around three hundred million tons of carbon dioxide equivalent per year, according to World Bank estimates (World Bank 1999, 4), and much more according to a nongovernmental organization (Wysham 2005, 4).

In the area of biodiversity the World Bank helped establish more than thirty-three million new hectares—roughly eight times the size of Switzerland—of protected areas around the world (World Bank 2004b, 11). Moreover, with the increased usage of conservation trust funds, it has also devised an innovative instrument for the sustainable financing of such areas (World Bank 2003a, 18).[22]

To sum up, capacity building represents the World Bank's natural domain. Our data indicates that it has significantly influenced the legal and administrative capacity of its client countries, and has also financed substantial physical interventions. Nevertheless, efforts to build environmental institutions have not always been successful, and in many cases "improvements in the functioning of the institutions concerned have been elusive" (World Bank 2002a, 30). One reason for this, according to the World Bank, was that its technical assistance approach viewed capacity building merely as organizational engineering and overemphasized improvements in formal organization and physical equipment (World Bank 2002a, 31), thereby causing the World Bank to be perceived as the "elephant in the corridor."[23] So even though there is a very significant influence, it is not necessarily as strong as originally intended by the World Bank.

In conclusion of the analysis of the World Bank's overall cognitive, normative, and executive influence on environmental policy, we can summarize the first part of this case study as follows: we found the strongest influence to be on the executive side, with a particularly strong influence on international environmental standard setting for project financing. In addition, some cognitive influence—related to scholarly studies and data analysis, as well as normative influence—linked to the Bank's role as implementation engineer—can be attributed to the World Bank, albeit to a lesser extent.

We also noticed that the World Bank generally favors interventions based on market mechanisms, such as vouchers and auctions (e.g., for phaseout of chlorofluorocarbons), certification (e.g., for ornamental fishing), ecotourism (biodiversity), or emissions trading (Prototype Carbon Fund). It thrives whenever issues can be linked across sectors to create win-win situations, such as energy efficiency and emission control, erosion control and agricultural productivity, pollution control, or health. At the same time, it became evident that some areas have developed higher profiles than others. For instance, climate change mitigation has received much more attention than adaptation. Likewise, ozone depletion has been a major issue, but not so transboundary freshwater bodies or desertification, which even a staff member found "puzzling since it is an area that is so much related to much of the Bank's lending."[24]

Overall, the environmental performance of the World Bank remains characterized by the contrast between successful environmental projects and rather controversial ones, such as greenhouse gas reduction versus continued support for extractive industries, and biodiversity investments versus ongoing "totally devastating" agricultural projects.[25] Moreover, the rare but recurrent emergence of individual cases in which World Bank environmental safeguards were breached (e.g., Inspection Panel cases) negatively overshadows the World Bank's environmental track record.

On the whole, our characterization of the World Bank compares well with the findings of Tarradell (2007), who conducted a survey to assess and compare how the nine bureaucracies studied in this book are perceived by national experts in their respective field. Her findings confirm that "the World Bank excels as an executive bureaucracy," particularly by "facilitating new practices, for example energy audits or pollution abatement technologies." In line with our results, a relatively lower but still "remarkable" influence in the normative area is attributed to the World Bank.

Explaining the Influence

Problem Structure

For the World Bank, which deals with several pollution-related "brown" and conservation-related "green" environmental issues, the variable problem structure cannot be limited to the characteristics of a specific environmental problem. On a general level, however, and in comparison to other areas in development, environmental problems are perceived to be characterized by a considerable time lag between investments and returns, and as generating benefits that are often hard to express in purely pecuniary terms. This is especially the case for global environmental issues, such as climate change or biodiversity.

A repercussion of this problem structure can be seen in the "fundamental differences of view" (Liebenthal 2002, viii) among World Bank member states with regard to the cost-benefit ratio of environmental projects. Developed countries often act as environmental promoters; developing countries tend to prioritize other issues over environmental projects, such as infrastructure projects, that are seen as less "costly and rigid" (Liebenthal 2002, viii). The World Bank's client countries are indeed rather reluctant to take out large refundable loans for environmental projects when other investment opportunities in fields such as energy or infrastructure are expected to yield relatively higher, quicker, and more tangible returns. Therefore, the problem structure explains why the World Bank's influence in the environmental area remains comparably lower than in other fields of development. As was shown earlier, for its core environmental projects, the World Bank relies in fact heavily on third party–financed grants (from, e.g., the GEF) to overcome this drawback.

Polity

Polity stands for the basic legal framework that determines the organization's setup and basic functions. In the following sections, we discuss the implications of the World Bank's relatively high formal autonomy (competences), its extensive and reliable material resources (resources), and its broad scope as a multi-issue organization with practically universal membership (embeddedness).

Competences   The World Bank is characterized by a mixed bottom-up/top-down governance structure in which the governing body lays out the general roadmap, but leaves the identification and preparation of individual projects to World Bank staff. For final approval, a staff task team composes and submits a full-length blueprint of the project to the board of executive directors, the World Bank's twenty-four-member in-house governing body. At the time of writing, only eight executive directors represent solely their own country, while all others speak and vote for groups of countries. The voting power of the directors is given by the total shares their respective country holds. The United States, Japan, Germany, France, and the United Kingdom represent the five largest shareholders, with a combined voting power of roughly 40 percent.

Technically, a positive decision requires a majority of the capital-weighted votes cast (IBRD Articles of Agreement, article V, section 3), but the board mostly operates on a consensus basis (Scholar 2005). In fact, no formal voting occurred during the entire 2004 fiscal year (Department for International Development 2005, 20). Still, "the board meeting is typically the end of a long process" (Scholar 2005), consisting of behind-door negotiations, during which relative voting powers are very likely taken into account (Bretton Woods Project 2005).

These two features of World Bank governance, the active role of staff and the simple majority rule, confer a "significant degree of relative autonomy" (Naim 1994, c279) to the World Bank bureaucracy.[26] This autonomy, in turn, provides a first explanation on how this bureaucracy managed to obtain authorization for projects that did not grow out of the direct interest of any of its principals, or even conflicted with its members' interest. In the following discussion, we argue that the existence of some of the World Bank's more controversial projects—as well as some of its pioneering green projects—becomes comprehensible in view of its formal governance structure.

First, historical examples suggest that some World Bank projects became accepted largely because of deliberately overoptimistic project appraisals. With about three hundred projects per year covering fifty different sectors, it is evident that the members of the board depend heavily on information prepared for them by project staff (Gutner 2005, 29).

Relevant documents, however, might be framed in a "highly technical language, often obscuring the actions taken or the anticipated outcomes" (Nielson and Tierney 2003, 252). As a consequence, there have been cases of unpleasant surprises for the board. For instance, the full extent of resettlements in the Sardar Sarovar Dam construction project in India was revealed only after the fact by an investigative commission (Morse and Berger 1992). Allegedly, the World Bank's bureaucracy has in the past tended to treat the executive directors "like cultivated mushrooms—'kept in the dark and fed manure.'"[27] In one instance, it even withheld a critical internal report from the board, despite explicit requests for it by the U.S. executive director (Rich 2002). Hence, the World Bank's high formal autonomy implies a reduced supervisory power of the board, which helps to explain the rare but persistent occurrence of projects with *unexpected* (for a majority of principals) negative environmental repercussions.

Second, the approval of World Bank projects that are at odds with the interests of some member states can be understood as a consequence of a governing body that is divided and "full of big tensions,"[28] but decides over policies and projects by simple majority rule. Such was the case in the highly controversial 1992 Narmada River Dam project in India, which was initially approved against the votes of most industrialized countries (George and Sabelli 1994),[29] but also in the adoption of the Prototype Carbon Fund, where the U.S. and Saudi Arabian executive directors jointly abstained from the vote.[30] In other words, World Bank projects not representing the collective interests of its principals may be approved through the formation of ad hoc coalitions of member states with similar interests. Thus, whereas a high voting threshold—as, for example, in the GEF—can be expected to favor balanced projects of the least-common-denominator type, the majority rule facilitates a more direct "reflection" (Hunter 2001, 66) of the member countries' divergent views on the merits of environmental projects.

At the same time, some of the World Bank's innovative green projects would not exist if World Bank staff did not have the ability to develop and advance own project ideas, as exemplified by the case of the World Bank's official environment strategy, where "the board gives it the legitimacy, but it does not dictate it. Frankly, the board did not even know what was going on, except that we told them that this is an important process."[31]

For instance, the World Bank's move to invigorate the Global Mechanism of the desertification convention went back to an initiative of three of its staff members.[32] And, finally, also the idea of a Prototype Carbon

Fund was originally conceived by a World Bank official in a paper drawn up several years before its actual creation.[33]

Resources The main branch of the World Bank, the IBRD, has been equipped with a self-contained financing mechanism: each year it can raise billions of dollars at low costs on the private capital market, and make a profit by issuing loans at a slightly higher interest rate to its client countries. As a consequence, the World Bank's disposable resources even only those for environment—are very high compared to most other international bureaucracies. Moreover, due to the self-contained nature of this funding mechanism, it enjoys, unlike many other bureaucracies, "significant financial autonomy" (Nielson and Tierney 2003) vis-à-vis its state principals.

At first sight, the ability to issue loans of around USD 20 billion per year might seem to provide the World Bank with a strong direct influence over its clients. In reality, however, total environmental lending typically lies between one and two billion USD per year (Acharya et al. 2004), and especially the greener environmental projects are mostly funded by relatively small grants: "While for big infrastructure projects there is considerable leverage, environmental projects often are funded by grants that are generally smaller, and so there is a smaller incentive for clients to change policies."[34]

According to World Bank staff, "clients are still reluctant to take out loans for the environment," because investment returns are perceived as too low, and because of the option to receive a grant.[35] As a consequence, the availability of grant funding has almost become a necessary condition for a client country to accept a green environmental project (Liebenthal 2002, 11). The largest contribution by far to the roughly USD 200 million in grants that the World Bank mobilizes each year for environmental projects stems from the GEF (average 1989–2004, according to World Bank online project database). For instance, it finances almost all of the World Bank's cross-boundary environmental projects. With a view to biodiversity, a specialist underscored the crucial role of GEF funding: "If we didn't have the GEF funding, I don't even know where we would be."[36] Besides the GEF, a considerable amount of grant financing is provided through the Montreal Protocol Fund and the Prototype Carbon Fund. The latter draws entirely on third-party funding, proving that one of the World Bank's more successful "do-good" activities are in fact not explicable in terms of its own substantial material resources.

The World Bank's resources can indirectly create leverage by linking environmental issues to loans from other sectors by means of conditionality. One important example of this instrument are the World Bank's safeguard policies, which among other things oblige the borrower to carry out environmental impact assessments for all projects with certain characteristics. As mentioned before, this is now done for every other project, which would hardly be the case if it were not laid down as a condition for receiving a World Bank loan.

Within a second form of conditionality, the World Bank requests the insertion of green components into larger, integrated projects, often as a means of compensation for expected negative environmental impacts of the project's main component. According to World Bank staff, this has had the effect of "bringing money from development to conservation" by "getting the developers to pay for creating a park," and thus created green side effects in some large projects.[37] For instance, the energy company Exxon helped establish two nature reserves in the context of the Chad-Cameroon Pipeline project (Mallaby 2004, 350). And as part of the Nam Theun II dam project in Laos, developers were obliged to replenish fish stocks and install a "new wildlife reserve no less than nine times bigger than the area to be flooded by the dam."[38]

According to a World Bank official, "that the Bank is a bank gives it a lot of power in situations when a country really wants a loan."[39] Indeed, the World Bank's leverage fades whenever a country has access to alternative funding sources through other donor institutions or private capital markets. Having a choice between a loan with attached conditionality and safeguard requirements from the World Bank, or a modestly more expensive unconditional one available on the capital markets, many emerging market and transition countries may opt for the latter, as happened with the Central and Eastern European countries (Gutner 2002, 158). And India and China, among the World Bank's most important clients, have drawn lines with respect to the environmental and social conditions that they are willing to accept: after initially requesting World Bank funding for, respectively, the 1992 Narmada Dam and the 1999 Western China Poverty project, they withdrew their proposal once the approval became endangered or subject to modifications because of safeguard concerns.[40] They subsequently obtained financing elsewhere, and implemented the project in their own way. Similarly, Laos plans to build its next three dams without World Bank assistance, because "cynics say the Laotian authorities have learned that it is easier to do without

World Bank funding, and all the environmental and social protections that come with it."[41]

In sum, the instrument that is most directly linked to the World Bank's financial resources—environmental conditionality—constitutes an important explanatory factor vis-à-vis its "do-no-harm" agenda, but plays only a limited role with regard to the effects of its "do-good" activities. And even with green conditionality "you can push, but you can only push so far,"[42] depending on the economic strength of the country in question. For the future, the World Bank's widely publicized approval of two sizable environmental adjustment loans to Brazil (see earlier discussion) and Mexico might indicate that it wants to strengthen the leverage of its financial resources by offering large policy loans and strongly "making the business case" for the environment, eventually convincing more clients of the financial viability of green projects.

Embeddedness The World Bank was established within the Bretton Woods regime as a global development bank: its "clients" are national governments, and it addresses them on a one-to-one basis. Thus, it comes as no surprise that the World Bank's main autonomous influence was found on the executive side. But as will be seen in the following discussion, its position as a lender to governments and its multi-issue embedding give also rise to the World Bank's convening power, its "environmental ambivalence" (Hunter 2001, 66), and its role as informal standard setter.

First, article III.2 of the World Bank's Articles of Agreement explicitly requires that "each member shall deal with the Bank only through its Treasury, central bank" or some "similar fiscal agency." As a consequence, the World Bank's management traditionally enjoys a "direct and frequent access to ministers and heads of state" (Naim 1994, c281). An officer confirms: "Having access to governments at the highest level is extremely important. . . . It is frustrating here at the World Bank that it is a lending and less a grant institution, but on the other hand the access is fantastic. It has a great convening power."[43] This often-asserted convening power (Piddington 1992, 216; Kanbur 2002, 7; Liebenthal 2002, 31) enables the World Bank to launch its multiparty projects, such as transboundary water projects or the Prototype Carbon Fund, also with regard to the mobilization of cofinancing. On the other side, the constraint of always having to work with national governments might hamper the success of projects for which a more direct involvement of local stakeholders would be desirable. In one instance, reforms of the forestry sector prescribed by the finance ministry were not equally embraced by the ministry of forestry (Seymour and Dubash 2000, 2). In a similar vein, the Operations Evaluation Department has criticized that project information is often accessible only to top-level government officials, but not to people at the implementation level (World Bank Operations Evaluation Department 2003, 60).

Second, because its tasks are less defined by what to do than by what to achieve ("reduce poverty"), the World Bank pursues a wide range of activities in terms of sectors, countries, and stages of the policy cycle. Its projects range from cleanup measures to basic research and the building of public-private partnerships. This broad embedding of the World Bank is intimately linked to the controversial role it has come to play in the field of environment. With the immense range of activities pursuable under the banner of development, blatant contradictions are easily created, such as when the World Bank on one hand promotes the reduction of greenhouse gas emissions through its various carbon funds and climate-related GEF activities, and on the other hand funds the extraction of fossil fuels.

Moreover, changing "vogues" within the development field reverberate with the World Bank and have led to considerable fluctuations in the environmental budget, which declined in recent years to about 50 percent of its peak reached in the mid 1990s after the Rio summit (Acharya et al. 2004, 32). As a consequence, environmental staff must perpetually battle for resources, since "the Bank does so much—we have a large mandate—a priority this week may not be a priority next week."[44] Hence, the fact that the World Bank is not embedded as an environmental but multi-issue development organization means that critique and requests for more, less, or different environmental activities are likely to persist. Its record will continue to be characterized by the contradictions arising from the coexistence of both highly innovative "green" and environmentally controversial projects.

Third, the World Bank's embeddedness as a broad any-sector organization nevertheless constitutes an ideal breeding ground for "good environmental practice" identification and the definition of standards. This holds in particular for the brown environmental issues—that is, those related to pollution management—where an organization like the World Bank can draw on its in-house experience from many nonenvironmental projects. Arguably, this constitutes a comparative advantage over a purely environmental organization like UNEP (Bauer, this volume, chapter 7; but compare also to Campe, this volume, chapter 6). And other than its comprehensiveness in terms of sectors, the World Bank's emergence as a natural catalyst and trigger of informal standards would hardly be possible without its weight of an institution that operates in about 100 countries, and in which 184 countries are represented.

People and Procedures

In addition to the polity characteristics of the World Bank as an *intergovernmental organization*, the procedures embodied in its *bureaucracy* and the very people constituting it explain some of its influence. On the behavioral side, we discuss the expertise held by World Bank employees, the role of the World Bank's president, and the bureaucratic culture of its staff. On the structural side, we explore the formal rules and procedures that determine the workflow within the World Bank bureaucracy. Although these internal variables relate to some observed influence, they explain more the direction and quality of World Bank influence in the field of the environment than their quantity or overall existence.

Organizational Expertise   The World Bank is particularly known for its expertise in development economics. Flanked by massive investments, its research division became the world's largest development research institute (Gilbert et al. 1999) and prides itself on recruiting only the "the best and the brightest" (Kapur 2002, 60). However, perhaps because it experienced difficulties in the recruitment of highly qualified professionals from the noneconomic disciplines (Weaver 2003, 123), the World Bank is not nearly as well positioned in the environmental field. In fact, the World Bank's 236 environmental specialists account for only 2.5 percent of the total workforce (World Bank 2005, 14).[45] Nevertheless, among its environmental staff are some internationally recognized experts, notably the World Bank's chief scientific officer Robert Watson, who served as chair of the Intergovernmental Panel on Climate Change and cochair of the Millennium Ecosystem Assessment.[46]

In other words, the World Bank avails of environmental expertise, but in a highly concentrated form in or around the central environment department. Its small but prolific group of environmental researchers has produced a respectable publication record, and through its involvement in the international environmental assessments, has helped green the World Bank's appearance. However, because it has so few natural scientists, the World Bank lacks the normative power it has been said to emanate "as a generator of ideas about development" (Wade 1997, 5); for example, it would not give authoritative definitions of terms such as "critical habitats," except perhaps in particular instances at the national level (Goldman 2004).

With regard to the World Bank's bread-and-butter ground operations, an officer admits that "the World Bank first and foremost needs a well-informed staff" in order to succeed, but "does not quite achieve that," because senior managers "know a lot about project management, but not necessarily a lot about where the world around them is going scientifically."[47] As a consequence, the World Bank increasingly relies on consultants.[48] Such was the case in Laos, where the World Bank's lack of in-house capacity to assess environmental impacts led it to hire "an army of Northern consultants to do these studies" (Goldman 2004, 60). The heavy use of external expertise has also been blamed for both the production of biased environmental assessment reports (Goldman 2004, 60) and the aforementioned "mixed quality" (Liebenthal 2002, 8) of National Environmental Action Plans.

On the other side, for less technical issues of economic-environmental policy that are more accessible to the World Bank's highly trained and versatile economists, the bureaucracy's expertise does constitute a source of influence. In fact, building on its "world-class experts" (Rogoff 2004, 57), the World Bank often advises governments and even stays in continuous "policy dialogues" with them. The foremost example for this type of influence is found in the World Bank's numerous strategy and action plan exercises, which are elaborated in collaboration with (if not under the guidance of) World Bank experts. For instance, an employee described the World Bank's influence with regard to the CDM as follows: "We have been in long discussions with the Chinese and Indian governments, and eventually we got them. India is now a big supporter of CDM projects. And China is on the brink."[49]

Last but not least, many World Bank employees "have an intimate knowledge of the politics, economics, and social situation" (Piddington 1992, 216) of developing countries, which gives the World Bank a comparative advantage toward the management of projects and programs in these countries. This type of expertise explains why donors have entrusted the World Bank with the implementation of environmental programs such as the Montreal Protocol or the GEF, or, in case of the carbon funds, mandated the World Bank to spearhead CDM and JI projects. Similarly, because World Bank officials are well connected within the international donor community, the World Bank is often approached by developing countries to facilitate fundraising and coordinate donors for regional projects, as was the case in the Nile Basin initiative or the Mesoamerican Barrier Reef System project.

In sum, expertise delivers some explanatory relationships, but one has to distinguish different types of expertise. The World Bank's highly concentrated environmental expertise mainly helped improve the World Bank's credentials as an "environmental player" and explains how it brought about its cognitive influence. At the same time, some evidence suggests that lacking in-house environmental expertise at the operational level and the resulting dependency on consultants negatively affects the quality of environmental assessments and plans. Its more general policy expertise made the World Bank become an authoritative and, accordingly, an influential advisor in the executive field, that is, in questions of national environmental policy. Finally, the World Bank's project implementation expertise and developing country knowledge are important reasons for its ability to attract substantial external funding for environmental projects and its role as facilitator and coordinator of regional cooperation.

Organizational Structure   Under the Wolfensohn presidency, the World Bank adopted a matrix structure consisting of so-called networks, anchors, and sectors, which involve officers in multiple affiliations and lines of reporting. In what follows, we argue that this particular organizational structure has paved the way for the often observed discrepancy between the World Bank's green rhetoric and its mixed environmental performance on the ground.

The matrix structure prompted criticism for various reasons: to begin with, an extensive internal survey revealed the patchy understanding of its different dimensions among staff, which, in turn, has caused a "sectoral fragmentation and unclear accountabilities" (World Bank Operations Evaluation Department 2005, 31). Such reservations were echoed in our interviews with environmental staff members, who viewed the Bank's organizational structure as one reason why proenvironmental "commitments made at the very highest levels are not necessarily translated consistently throughout the World Bank."[50] Officers also complained about competition between departments and sectors for their working time, in which "staff ends up being torn in many directions."[51] Resource allocation and decision making were not always perceived as transparent: "Quotas and other internal mandates often drive decisions, and these are not necessarily transparent. The decision is made and it does not seem to be completely rational or consistent with what the regulations may be, and so there are inconsistencies which can frustrate. . . . It would help to have more transparency on how decisions and particularly resource allocation decisions are made."[52]

Second, the increased regionalization has indirectly weakened the systematic implementation of environmental objectives. In fact, under World Bank President Wolfensohn, the World Bank experienced a substantial relocation of staff into "the field," along with a transfer of decision-making power to country directors, which assumed "considerable latitude and powers" (World Bank Operations Evaluation Department 2004, 31). As a consequence, the relative importance of environment at the country level has become susceptible to personal priorities: "The Millennium Development Goals should be our guideline, and environment is one of these eight goals, but a country director might just choose to concentrate on four out of the eight, and environment might not be between them."[53]

Likewise, the fact that "every region has its way of doing things"[54] explains why environmental safeguards have been applied with varying rigor across World Bank operations. According to one officer, the environmental impacts of infrastructure projects are satisfactorily monitored in Latin America, because of a "stronger team," while she tends to "hear more complaints from Africa, that despite the safeguard policies, they don't really monitor well."[55] Similarly, an investigation of the Independent Inspection Panel found a "disturbingly wide range of divergent and, often, opposing views" (Inspection Panel 2000, xiv) regarding the safeguard policies: while some staff members insisted on strict compliance, others merely saw them as "idealized policy statements" (Inspection Panel 2000, xiv). Under such circumstances, the panel concluded, a consistent implementation of the policies is simply impossible.

The third point of contention concerns the World Bank's internal incentive system, which has been accused of fostering an "approval culture" (Wapenhans 1992) by overly rewarding output—that is, project preparation and approval, instead of supervision and evaluation (Rich 2002; World Bank Operations Evaluation Department 2004, x). With regard to the environmental safeguards, the matrix's multiple lines of reporting create an additional perverse incentive and "conflict of interest" (Liebenthal 2002, 20), when environmental specialists who depend on their regional task managers for regular work assignments are at the same time meant to ensure that these task managers comply with World Bank safeguard provisions.

Despite the criticism, one feature of the organizational structure was seen by many staff members as vital for the World Bank's environmental turnaround: its institutional feedback mechanisms. In total, the World Bank affords four monitoring bodies, including its in-house Operations Evaluation Department (renamed in 2006 to the Independent Evaluation Group) and the Independent Inspection Panel, which both report directly to the board of executive directors (see World Bank 2005, 37, for more details). The Operations Evaluation Department has provided a number of valuable—and critical—reviews on the World Bank's environmental performance (e.g., Liebenthal 2002), although long-time lags have provoked some criticism.[56] The Independent Inspection Panel, set up in 1993, starts an independent investigation whenever at least two local citizens credibly claim to be negatively affected by a World Bank project due to a safeguard violation. Interestingly, as of the year 2005 this delicate trigger had been activated in only thirty-two cases, and has for some projects—for example, the Chad-Cameroon Pipeline project and the Arun III dam project—led to remedying modifications or even the complete withdrawal of the World Bank.

In sum, the complex and highly decentralized organizational structure of the World Bank delivers a plausible explanation for the observed nonuniform environmental efforts and practices across its operations. The World Bank's inner organizational slack has nurtured the mixed rigor seen in the enforcement of environmental safeguards, and put the World Bank's environmental commitment to the discretion of local managers. At the same time, however, it has allowed individual strong leaders to form "pockets of environmental excellence," for example in carbon finance or the area of ozone-depleting substances and persistent organic pollutants. The World Bank's institutional feedback mechanisms may have helped "knock out some of the wacky ideas from earlier on,"[57] but fall short of acting as effective learning agents, as long as their valuable insights are not more systematically internalized.

Organizational Culture   The diversity of geographical and cultural backgrounds within the World Bank is remarkable. Professionals from developing countries are well represented even in higher positions; almost 50 percent in 2002 (World Bank 2001a, 21). However, many of those are graduates from Western universities, especially U.S. and British institutions. Still, people with 165 different nationalities and native speakers of more than 100 languages work for the World Bank. In addition, 52 percent of the employed are women, including 40 percent of staff in middle positions and 23 percent in higher positions (20).

Given this diversity, one cannot expect the World Bank to be characterized by a single and coherent ideology that all employees share. But neither can one deny the existence of a particular organizational culture that shapes the way the World Bank envisions and depicts its mission and the "environmental and social sustainability" of its activities. In particular, our findings suggest that the World Bank's embracement of economic and technocratic reasoning directs its influence toward areas that are susceptible to quantitative analysis and suitable for interventions based on market instruments.

The dominance of this economic reasoning lies at the core of the World Bank's theories and practices. In the literature (Kapur et al. 1997), this is explained as a historical consequence of the convergence of external interests (private commercial lenders, northern manufacturers) and political preferences of major shareholders (economic liberalization to combat communism). Moreover, as a response to the rise of policy-oriented adjustment lending and an increased focus on macroeconomic stabilization and liberalization during the 1980s, the World Bank experienced a rapid staff turnover that brought in a large number of neoclassical-oriented economists (Mosley et al. 1991, 47).[58] Today, the picture of the World Bank as a large haven for all kinds of economists is still valid (World Bank 2001c, 21; World Bank 2003c), even within the environmental sector,[59] and is also recognizable in the environment strategy's call for "making the business case."

Moreover, because its mandate imposes strict political neutrality,[60] the World Bank has embraced an apolitical and technocratic behavior, with a strong preference for the language of numbers: "We are evidence based, trying to guide our work by what is effective and what is not. . . . This can be considered a strength of the World Bank."[61] George and Sabelli (1994, 193) describe this as a rejection of all approaches that are not in conformity with quantitative, abstract models based on econometric analysis. Naim (1994, c283) confirms that "sociological-type analysis is belittled," similar to Goldman (2004), who delineates a culture that is unfamiliar and resistant to sociocultural knowledge.

The environmental officers easily recognize the dominant organizational culture as such. One staff member—noting that it is not the "natural inclination of a macro-economist to think about the environment"[62]—even spoke of a sometimes frustrating clash of different cultures. Another employee revealed that he would like to "lock up twelve of our best economists and tell them to find the solution for our huge future environmental problems. And as long as they come with answers like 'the market will solve it' or 'new technologies will emerge on time,' I would keep them locked up."[63]

Even though such statements suggest a certain deviation from the mainstream culture, the World Bank's dominating organizational culture prevails to large extent even among its environmental staff and explains direction and quality of World Bank influence. Its striving for market-based interventions can be viewed as a manifestation of its "economistic" organizational culture. In particular, this refers to the World Bank's decision to invest in emissions trading, auctions, environmental funds, and ecotourism, and its trainings on cost internalization. In a similar vein, its organizational culture also shapes the World Bank's preference for environmental issues that are tractable by quantitative approaches and rigorous cost-benefit analyses: for instance, the World Bank has played an influential role in climate change mitigation, but has been less proactive—and thus less influential—in adaptation; the same can be said for ozone protection versus desertification. Finally, the "technocratic" aspect of the World Bank's organizational culture explains the intense effort it puts into data and indicator compilation (as opposed to, e.g., more efforts into ethnological and social research), needed to strengthen its evidence-based approach and to give it an "objectivistic" character.

Organizational Leadership The World Bank's public face is first and foremost seen in its president. In the past, presidents were associated with characteristic changes and particular business styles of the World Bank. For instance, the leadership of McNamara during the 1970s led to a strong expansion of World Bank operations and the rise of adjustment lending. Our analysis of the Wolfensohn presidency suggests that although he implemented a number of reforms to green the World Bank, it remains difficult to gather sufficient data on his actions to explain the World Bank's influence, save perhaps in the field of climate change.

President Wolfensohn's leadership from 1995 to 2005 has mainly been described as "a dynamic proactive leadership" (Kapur 2002, 60). Among other things, like addressing corruption, he is generally credited for the attempt to mainstream the environment into the World Bank's projects and organizational structure (Pincus and Winters 2002). Under his tenure, the World Bank practically stopped the controversial financing of big dams (with the exception of the Nam Theun II dam), and made an effort to appease nongovernmental organizations by increasing stakeholder inclusiveness and the transparency of World Bank operations.

As with many assertions about the World Bank, not all agree: Rich (2002, 51) criticizes the "disconnect" between Wolfensohn's proclaimed ambitions and the lack of much-needed reforms in the World Bank's environmental assessment practice, and a former managing director (Einhorn 2001, 22) views the World Bank as due for a "managerial cycle" in order to clear the "goal congestion" created by the "visionary cycle" associated with Wolfensohn.

Our interviews hardly reflected this type of criticism; on the contrary, environmental officers almost uniformly described Wolfensohn as a trigger for positive changes: "It's hard to say anything without saying something about Wolfensohn. He has turned the institution around. Compared to when I joined the World Bank it is a brand new Bank now."[64] Allegedly, it was on his initiative that the World Bank adopted the proactive strategy seen in its approach to the Prototype Carbon Fund. At the time of its inception, the ratification of the Kyoto Protocol and the eventual marketability of any achieved emissions reductions could not be counted on, but Wolfensohn pushed for the project because he felt that it was precisely the role of a public institution such as the World Bank to take risk and thereby eventually allow developing countries to profit from participation in the international carbon market.[65] He defended the project—"the principals may push, but Wolfensohn pushes back"[66]—even against the reservations of the George W. Bush administration.

In sum, it is difficult to provide hard evidence that would allow World Bank influence to be traced directly to its former president. Arguably, his explicit insistence on the World Bank's active and supportive role within the Kyoto process represents one such instance. Certainly, he brought about a change in the World Bank's rhetoric and an increased involvement of civil society, but in how far these measures influenced other actors or merely improved the World Bank's public image is unclear.

Conclusion

A first result of our study regards the qualitatively different roles of the variables *polity* and *people and procedures*: whereas the former rather explains autonomous influence, the latter mainly determine its character. In what follows, we go back to our three dependent categories of influence—cognitive, executive, and normative—and discuss how they can be explained in terms of the independent variables.

The World Bank has strong influence on the national level through a mix of material incentives—pushing through conditionality for do-no-harm, pulling through grants for do-good activities—and its policy and country expertise (policy dialogues, "guided" strategy studies). Perhaps counterintuitively, the World Bank's own generous material resources (loans and soft loans) fall short of providing a salient explanation for a large part of its autonomous influence in the green environmental area, where projects are often relatively modest in financial terms and based on grants provided by third parties—in particular, the GEF.

The World Bank's overall still-mixed environmental record originates in its loosely defined mandate, which opens the door to severe goal conflicts. In practice, though, it is driven by the combination of a divisive problem structure and a weak external (low-threshold decision making, dependence on staff for information) and internal supervision (unclear accountabilities, country directors as local strongmen), which also nurtures the approval of controversial projects and the varying rigor in the enforcement of safeguard policies. At the same time, however, the relative freedom of the bureaucracy to pursue own initiatives allowed for the formation of "pockets of environmental excellence" (carbon finance, ozone unit), often driven by strong individuals from middle management. Last but not least, its embeddedness positions the World Bank at the epicenter of the global development (financing) community, vesting it with a strong influence on environmental standards in international project financing.

On the other side, the World Bank's particularly strong role within some issue areas (climate change mitigation, ozone), and its limited presence in others (adaptation to climate change, desertification) can be understood in terms of its economistic organizational culture, which lets the World Bank excel whenever a given problem structure is compatible with rigorous cost-benefit analysis and interventions based on market instruments. In the long run, however, the World Bank's "business case" approach to the environment may impair its effectiveness, standing at odds both with the public goods problematique and the well-known difficulties involved in the monetary valuation of environmental services. Even the World Bank's widely predicted "many win-win opportunities" (World Bank 2002a, 5) within the poverty-environment nexus have so far produced only "few up-scale working examples" (Varley 2005, 9).

Less pronounced but nonetheless significant was the World Bank's cognitive influence, mainly associated with its scholarly contributions in the field of environmental economics and policy, but also apparent in its provision of comprehensive environmental data. Clearly, the World Bank's ability to fund a proper research group and its successful recruitment of several high-caliber experts is the most straightforward explanation. However, the World Bank has developed a particular strength in assembling and analyzing environmental data not least because of its global embedding, which confers upon the World Bank "a comparative advantage in accessing data" (Gilbert et al. 1999) and "unusual access to what were formerly impenetrable research sites" (Goldman 2004, 62). On the whole, the World Bank's cognitive influence remains closely linked to a relatively small group of environmental researchers and analysts, and though they may have succeeded in greening the World Bank's profile, our evidence suggests that they remain somewhat detached from its bread-and-butter ground operations.

Finally, in the normative field, the World Bank has shaped the regulation and implementation of some aspects of global international cooperation and acted as a coordinator and facilitator at the regional level. Toward global issues and their negotiations, the World Bank takes up a discreet stance, and realizes its influence mainly by injecting relevant information derived from its implementation and policy expertise. But without the World Bank's ability to pursue—with some autonomy—its own initiatives against the stalemate in the official negotiations, its influential role in the Kyoto process would of course be inconceivable. On the regional level, most influence is attributed to the World Bank's convening power, that is, a mixture of its high-level government access and its ability to provide its own—or arrange external—financing. Still, even though the World Bank has more influence on the regional level, a substantial scaling up in this area is hampered by the mismatch between the physical extension of regional environmental problems and its single-country-focused institutional structure.

Acknowledgments

Many thanks go to the interviewees from the World Bank, and to the Infrastructure and Environment unit of the Development Economics

Research Group—in particular, former member Franck Lecocq. The authors are grateful for two extensive reviews of earlier versions of this chapter by Steffen Bauer and Per-Olof Busch, and for additional helpful suggestions from the MANUS project team and from Ralf Leiteritz.

Notes

1. World Bank News Release No. 2005/58/LAC (on file with authors).

2. The term "World Bank" refers only to the International Bank for Reconstruction and Development and the International Development Association, as opposed to "World Bank Group," which includes three other organizations; among them, the International Finance Corporation.

3. One year after Paul Wolfowitz became World Bank President in 2005, the environment department was reorganized and became part of a newly created division called the Sustainable Development Network. The research for this chapter, however, was carried out from 2003 to 2005, and therefore does not extend beyond the Wolfensohn presidency.

4. The perception of World Bank–financed projects as output of the World Bank is justified by the fact that—unlike a commercial bank—the World Bank plays a very active role in project selection and implementation: after a project has been identified by a joint government and World Bank team, it is the latter's responsibility to prepare the official project proposal and to supervise the project implementation.

5. Under the codification valid at the time of writing, any World Bank project is associated with up to five sectors, five themes, and five goals. Whenever at least one of the possible five project themes belongs to the environmental area, the project is classified as an environmental project. As a consequence, the environmentalism in some of these projects may be rather marginal. For instance, the environmental São Paulo Metro Line 4 Project (World Bank 2001b) essentially financed the construction of a new subway line.

6. Including projects in the pipeline. Source: GEF online project database, accessed 18 April 2005.

7. To derive this result, we consulted both the Web of Science publication database of the Institute of Scientific Information, and Scopus, an abstract and indexing database. In order to be counted, at least one author of an article had to be affiliated with the World Bank. Note that of the 2073 Web of Science records, 178 belong to either one of the World Bank's own two refereed journals, "The World Bank Research Observer" and "The World Bank Economic Review."

8. See, for example, the review in *The Economist* on 15 September 2005, 96.

9. World Bank 1997, Evaluation of Environment Research, cited from World Bank Web site, http://www.worldbank.org/html/rad/evaluation97/environ.htm (accessed October 2005). See also the 2006 thematic evaluation on environmental research by G. Heal. On file with authors.

10. Interview by Robert Marschinski with World Bank staff member, World Bank headquarters, Washington, DC, April 2004.

11. Interview by Robert Marschinski with World Bank staff member, World Bank headquarters, Washington, DC, April 2004.

12. Interview by Robert Marschinski with World Bank staff member, World Bank headquarters, Washington, DC, April 2004.

13. Two Indus Basin Development Fund agreements and the Tarbela Development Fund Agreement. Source: Environmental Treaties and Resource Indicators Web site, http://sedac.ciesin.columbia.edu/entri (accessed April 2005).

14. According to the UN database of Partnerships for Sustainable Development: http://webapps01.un.org/dsd/partnerships/public/welcome.do (accessed November 2005).

15. Interview by Robert Marschinski with World Bank staff member, World Bank headquarters, Washington DC, May 2004.

16. Interview by Robert Marschinski with World Bank staff member, World Bank headquarters, Washington DC, May 2004.

17. *The Economist*, 29 November 2003, 28.

18. Interview by Robert Marschinski with World Bank staff member, World Bank headquarters, Washington DC, May 2004.

19. Interview by Robert Marschinski with World Bank staff member, World Bank headquarters, Washington DC, April 2004.

20. Interview by Robert Marschinski with World Bank staff member, World Bank headquarters, Washington DC, April 2004.

21. See http://www.bicusa.org/bicusa/issues/environmental_and_social_policies/1399.php (accessed May 2008).

22. Even though no aggregate data was available for the area of desertification, the World Bank has financed and implemented "physical" interventions on soil and terrain, such as the China Loess Plateau Watershed Rehabilitation Project, which has been hailed as "one of the most successful erosion control programs in the world" (Varley 2005, 9).

23. Interview by Robert Marschinski with World Bank staff member, World Bank headquarters, Washington, DC, April 2004.

24. Interview by Robert Marschinski with World Bank staff member, World Bank headquarters, Washington, DC, April 2004.

25. Interview by Robert Marschinski with World Bank staff member, World Bank headquarters, Washington, DC, May 2004.

26. The World Bank's high level of autonomy also rests on the particular stability of its constitutional document. In fact, the Articles of Agreement can only be modified by a double super majority of "three-fifths of the members, having eighty-five percent of the total voting power" (article XIII), which grants a factual veto right to the United States, which holds 17 percent of the World Bank shares.

27. Cited from Herman Daly's "Farewell Speech," given after his resignation from the World Bank. Available online at http://www.whirledbank.org/ourwords/daly.html. Published in parts as Daly 1994.

28. Interview by Robert Marschinski with World Bank staff member, World Bank headquarters, Washington, DC, May 2004.

29. The borrowing country, India, later withdrew its request for World Bank financing. Other examples of environmentally controversial projects that were approved against the votes of several western executive directors include the 1999 China Western Poverty Reduction Project and the 1992 Pak Mun dam in Thailand.

30. Interview by Robert Marschinski with World Bank staff member, World Bank headquarters, Washington, DC, April 2004.

31. Interview by Robert Marschinski with World Bank staff member, World Bank headquarters, Washington, DC, April 2004.

32. Interview by Robert Marschinski with World Bank staff member, World Bank headquarters, Washington, DC, May 2004.

33. Interview by Robert Marschinski with World Bank staff member from the carbon finance group, World Bank headquarters, Washington, DC, April 2004. The 1993 paper is entitled "Mobilizing private capital against global warming: a business concept and policy issues." See http://www.carbonfinance.org/docs/LessonsLearnedCarbonFinance.doc (accessed October 2005).

34. Interview by Robert Marschinski with World Bank staff member, World Bank headquarters, Washington, DC, April 2004.

35. Interview by Robert Marschinski with World Bank staff member, World Bank headquarters, Washington, DC, April 2004.

36. Interview by Robert Marschinski with World Bank staff member, World Bank headquarters, Washington, DC, April 2004.

37. Interview by Robert Marschinski with World Bank staff member, World Bank headquarters, Washington, DC, May 2004.

38. *The Economist*, 9 April 2005, 47.

39. Interview by Robert Marschinski with World Bank staff member, World Bank headquarters, Washington, DC, May 2004.

40. World Bank press release (2000) for China Western Poverty project (on file with authors).

41. *The Economist*, 29 November 2003, 28.

42. Interview by Robert Marschinski with World Bank staff member, World Bank headquarters, Washington, DC, May 2004.

43. Interview by Robert Marschinski with World Bank staff member from the environment department, World Bank headquarters, Washington, DC, May 2004. The point that the "lending process gives [a multilateral development bank] convening power" has also been made by Birdsall and Deese (2001).

44. Interview by Robert Marschinski with World Bank staff member, World Bank headquarters, Washington, DC, April 2004.

45. As remarked by a former director of the environment department: "The level of staff effort in World Bank units is notoriously difficult to calculate, given the extensive use of consultant services" (Piddington 1992, 219).

46. He also participated in the International Scientific Assessment of Ozone, and the Global Biodiversity Assessment. Several other staff members have contributed to the Intergovernmental Panel on Climate Change and the Millennium Ecosystems Assessment; one officer received the Rose-Hulman Award from the International Association for Impact Assessment.

47. Interview by Robert Marschinski with World Bank staff member, World Bank headquarters, Washington, DC, April 2004.

48. Interview by Robert Marschinski with World Bank staff member, World Bank headquarters, Washington, DC, April 2004.

49. Interview by Robert Marschinski with World Bank staff member, World Bank headquarters, Washington, DC, May 2004.

50. Interview by Robert Marschinski with World Bank staff member, World Bank headquarters, Washington, DC, May 2004.

51. Interview by Robert Marschinski with World Bank staff member, World Bank headquarters, Washington, DC, May 2004.

52. Interview by Robert Marschinski with World Bank staff member, World Bank headquarters, Washington, DC, May 2004.

53. Interview by Robert Marschinski with World Bank staff member from the environment department, World Bank headquarters, Washington, DC, May 2004.

54. Interview by Robert Marschinski with World Bank staff member from the environment department, World Bank headquarters, Washington, DC, April 2004.

55. Interview by Robert Marschinski with World Bank staff member from the environment department, World Bank headquarters, Washington, DC, April 2004.

56. As one World Bank official stated in an interview: "The problem with OED [Operations Evaluation Department] in the past has been that they were so slow, you got feedback ten years later. That doesn't help." In fact, a survey showed that only 27 percent of the World Bank's staff made use of OED products (World Bank Operations Evaluation Department 2004, 38).

57. Interview by Robert Marschinski with World Bank staff member, World Bank headquarters, Washington, DC, May 2004.

58. On the dominance of neoclassically trained economists in the World Bank in the 1980s and 1990s, see Stern and Ferreira 1997; Wade 1997; and Kapur 2002.

59. Examples include the head of the Environmentally and Socially Sustainable Development Network, Ian Johnson, and the former director of the environment department, Kristalina Georgieva.

60. Article IV, Section 10 of the IBRD Articles of Agreement: "The Bank and its officers shall not interfere in the political affairs of any member, nor shall they be influenced in their decisions by the political character of the member or members concerned."

61. Interview by Robert Marschinski with World Bank staff member, World Bank headquarters, Washington, DC, May 2004.

62. Interview by Robert Marschinski with World Bank staff member, World Bank headquarters, Washington, DC, April 2004.

63. Interview by Robert Marschinski with World Bank staff member, World Bank headquarters, Washington, DC, April 2004.

64. Interview by Robert Marschinski with World Bank staff member, World Bank headquarters, Washington, DC, April 2004.

65. Interview by Robert Marschinski with World Bank staff member, World Bank headquarters, Washington, DC, April 2004.

66. Interview by Robert Marschinski with World Bank staff member, World Bank headquarters, Washington, DC, April 2004.

References

Acharya, Anhali, Ede Jorge Ijjasz-Vasquez, Kirk Hamilton, Piet Buys, Susmita Dasgupta, Craig Meisner, Kiran Pandey, and David Wheeler. 2004. *How Has Environment Mattered? An Analysis of World Bank Resource Allocation.* World Bank Policy Research Working Paper 3269. Washington, DC: The World Bank.

Albert, Jocelyne. 2003. "Partnerships: The Next Step in People, Planet, and Prosperity." *Environment Matters: A Magazine of the World Bank* (annual magazine), 28–29.

Alexander, Nancy, Pam Foster, Marcia Ishii-Eitermann, Ricardo Carrere, Aparna Sundar, Carol Welch, and Daphne Wysham. 2002. *Marketing the Earth: The World Bank and Sustainable Development.* Washington, DC: Friends of the Earth and Halifax Initiative.

Banerjee, Abhijit V., Angus Deaton, Nora Lustig, and Kenneth Rogoff. 2006. *An Evaluation of World Bank Research, 1998–2005.* Washington, DC: The World Bank.

Bekhechi, Mohammad A., and Jean-Roger Mercier. 2002. *The Legal and Regulatory Framework for Environmental Impact Assessments: A Study of Selected Countries in Sub-Saharan Africa.* Washington, DC: The World Bank.

Birdsall, Nancy, and Brian Deese. 2001. "Multilateral Development Banks in a Changing Global Economy." *Economic Perspectives: An Electronic Journal of the U.S. Department of State* 6 (1).

Boyce, James K. 2004. "Green and Brown? Globalization and the Environment." *Oxford Review of Economic Policy* 20 (1): 105–128.

Bretton Woods Project. 2005. "The World Bank Board of Executive Directors." *Bretton Woods Update* No. 45 (March–April). London: Bretton Woods Project. Available at http://www.brettonwoodsproject.org/art.shtml?x = 174885 (accessed May 2008).

Chomitz, Kenneth M., and David A. Gray. 1996. "Roads, Land Use, and Deforestation: A Spatial Model Applied to Belize." *World Bank Economic Review* 10 (3): 487–512.

Daly, Herman. 1994. "Fostering Environmentally Sustainable Development: Four Parting Suggestions for the World Bank." *Ecological Economics* 10 (3): 183–187.

Department for International Development. 2005. *The UK and the World Bank 2004: Report on the UK's Involvement with the World Bank, July 2003–June 2004.* London: Department for International Development.

Dingwerth, Klaus. 2007. *The New Transnationalism: Transnational Governance and Democratic Legitimacy.* Basingstoke, UK: Palgrave Macmillan.

Einhorn, Jessica. 2001. "The World Bank's Mission Creep." *Foreign Affairs* (Sept.–Oct.): 22–35.

Fidler, Stephen. 2001. "Who's Minding the Bank?" *Foreign Policy* 126 (September–October): 40–50.

Gastellu-Etchegorry, Jean P., editor. 1990. *Satellite Remote Sensing for Agricultural Projects.* World Bank Technical Paper 128. Washington, DC: The World Bank.

Gavin, Martin, and Dani Rodrik. 1995. "The World Bank in Historical Perspective." *The American Economic Review* 85(2): 329–334.

George, Susan, and Fabrizio Sabelli. 1994. *Faith and Credit: The World Bank's Secular Empire.* Boulder, CO: Westview Press.

Gilbert, Christopher, Andrew Powell, and David Vines. 1999. "Positioning the World Bank." *The Economic Journal* 109 (459): 598–633.

Goldman, Michael. 2004. "Imperial Science, Imperial Nature: Environmental Knowledge for the World (Bank)." In *Earthly Politics: Local and Global in Environmental Governance*, edited by Sheila Jasanoff and Marybeth Long Martello, 55–80. Cambridge, MA: MIT Press.

Goldman, Michael. 2005. *Imperial Nature: The World Bank and Struggles for Social Justice in the Age of Globalization.* New Haven: Yale University Press.

Gutner, Tamar L. 2002. *Banking on the Environment.* Cambridge, MA: MIT Press.

Gutner, Tamar L. 2005. "Explaining the Gaps between Mandate and Performance: Agency Theory and World Bank Environmental Reform." *Global Environmental Politics* 5 (2): 10–37.

Haas, Peter M., and Ernst B. Haas. 1995. "Learning to Learn: Improving International Governance." *Global Governance* 1 (3): 255–284.

Hunter, David. 2001. "The World Bank: A Lighter Shade of Green?" In *Yearbook of International Co-operation on Environment and Development 2001/2002*, edited by Olav Schram Stokke and Øystein B. Thommessen, 59–67. London: Earthscan.

Inspection Panel. 2000. *China Western Poverty Reduction Project Investigation Report*. Washington, DC: The World Bank Inspection Panel.

Kanbur, Ravi. 2002. *International Financial Institutions and International Public Goods: Operational Implications for the World Bank*. G-24 Discussion Paper Series 19. Geneva: United Nations Conference on Trade and Development.

Kapur, Devesh. 2002. "The Changing Autonomy of Governance of the World Bank." In *Reinventing the World Bank*, edited by Jonathan R. Pincus and Jeffrey A. Winters, 54–75. Ithaca, NY: Cornell University Press.

Kapur, Devesh, John P. Lewis, and Richard Webb, editors. 1997. *The World Bank: Its First Half Century*. Washington, DC: Brookings Institution.

Kessler, Jan J., and Mark van Dorp. 1998. "Structural Adjustment and the Environment: The Need for an Analytical Methodology." *Ecological Economics* 27 (3): 267–281.

Kirmani, Syed, and Guy Le Moigne. 1997. *Fostering Riperian Cooperation in International River Basins: The World Bank at Its Best in Development Diplomacy*. World Bank Technical Paper No. 335. Washington, DC: The World Bank.

Kiss, Agi, Gonzalo Castro, and Kenneth Newcombe. 2002. "The Role of Multilateral Institutions." *Philosophical Transactions of the Royal Society. Series A, Mathematical, Physical, and Engineering Sciences* 360:1641–1652.

Knigge, Markus, Benjamin Görlach, Ana-M. Hamada, Caroline Nufford, and Andreas Kraemer. 2003. *The Use of Environmental and Social Criteria in Export Credit Agencies' Practices*. Eschborn, Germany: Deutsche Gesellschaft für Technische Zusammenarbeit (GTZ) and Ecologic.

Krueger, Anne O. 1998. "Wither the World Bank and IMF?" *Journal of Economic Literature* 36 (4): 1983–2020.

Le Prestre, Philippe G. 1995. "Environmental Learning at the World Bank." In *International Organizations and Environmental Policy*, edited by Robert V. Bartlett, Priya A. Kurian and Madhu Malik, 83–101. Westport, CT: Greenwood Press.

Liebenthal, Andrés. 2002. *Promoting Environmental Sustainability in Development: An Evaluation of the World Bank's Performance*. Washington, DC: World Bank Operations Evaluation Department.

Lintner, Stephen F., Sherif Arif, and Marea Hatziolos. 1996. *The Experience of the World Bank in the Legal, Institutional, and Financial Aspects of Regional Environmental Programs: Potential Applications of Lessons Learned for the ROPME and PERSGA Programs*. Washington, DC: The World Bank.

Mallaby, Sebastian. 2004. *The World's Banker: The Story of Failed States, Financial Crises, and the Wealth and Poverty of Nations*. New York: Penguin Press.

Mehta, Lyla. 2001. "The World Bank and its Emerging Knowledge Empire." *Human Organisation* 60 (2): 189–196.

Moog Rodrigues, Maria G. 2004. "Advocating for the Environment: Local Dimensions of Transnational Networks." *Environment* 46 (2): 14–25.

Morse, Bradford, and Thomas Berger. 1992. *Sardar Sarovar: Report of the Independent Review.* Ottawa, Canada: Resource Futures International.

Mosley, Paul, Jane Harrigan, and John Toye. 1991. *Aid and Power: The World Bank and Policy-Based Lending. Volume I.* London: Routledge.

Naim, Moises. 1994. "The World Bank: Its Role, Governance and Organizational Culture." In *Bretton Woods: Looking to the Future*, edited by Bretton Woods Commission, c273–c287. Washington, DC: Bretton Woods Commission.

Nakayama, Mikiyasu. 2000. "The World Bank's Environmental Agenda." In *The Global Environment in the Twenty-first Century: Prospects for International Cooperation*, edited by Pamela Chasek, 399–410. Tokyo: UNU Press.

Nelson, Paul J. 2003. "Multilateral Development Banks, Transparency and Corporate Clients: 'Public-Private Partnerships' and Public Access to Information." *Public Administration and Development* 23:249–257.

Nielson, Daniel L., and Michael J. J. Tierney. 2003. "Delegation to International Organizations: Agency Theory and World Bank Environmental Reform." *International Organization* 57 (2): 241–276.

Piddington, Kenneth. 1992. "The Role of the World Bank." In *The International Politics of the Environment*, edited by Andrew Hurrell and Benedict Kingsbury, 212–227. Oxford: Clarendon Press.

Pincus, Jonathan R., and Jeffrey A. Winters, editors. 2002. *Reinventing the World Bank.* Ithaca, NY: Cornell University Press.

Prototype Carbon Fund. 2002. *Annual Report.* Washington, DC: The World Bank.

Prototype Carbon Fund. 2004. *Annual Report.* Washington, DC: The World Bank.

Rich, Bruce. 1994. *Mortgaging the Earth: The World Bank, Environmental Impoverishment, and the Crisis of Development.* Boston: Beacon Press.

Rich, Bruce. 2002. "The World Bank under James Wolfensohn." In *Reinventing the World Bank*, edited by Jonathan R. Pincus and Jeffrey A. Winters, 26–53. Ithaca, NY: Cornell University Press.

Rogoff, Kenneth. 2004. "The Sisters at 60." *The Economist* July 24: 65–67.

Scholar, Tom. 2005. "The Executive Boards of the World Bank and International Monetary Fund." *Bretton Woods Update No. 46.* London: Bretton Woods Project. Available at http://www.brettonwoodsproject.org/art-236027 (accessed May 2008).

Seymour, Frances, and Navroz K. Dubash. 1999. "World Bank's Environmental Reform Agenda." *Foreign Policy in Focus* 4 (10): 1–4.

Seymour, Frances, and Navroz K. Dubash. 2000. *The Right Conditions: The World Bank, Structural Adjustment, and Forest Policy Reform.* Washington, DC: World Resources Institute.

St. Clair, Asuncion L. 2004. "Global Knowledge, Global Politics: The World Bank as a Transnational Expertised Institution." Paper presented at the Fifth Pan-European International Relations Conference on Constructing World Orders, 9–11 September 2004, The Hague.

Stern, Nicholas, and Francisco Ferreira. 1997. "The World Bank as 'Intellectual Leader.'" In *The World Bank: Its First Half Century*, edited by Devesh Kapur, John P. Lewis, and Richard C. Webb, 523–609. Washington, DC: Brookings Institution Press.

Tarradell, Mireia. 2007. *The Influence of International Bureaucracies in Global Environmental Politics: Results from an Expert Survey*. Global Governance Working Paper 26. Amsterdam and others: The Global Governance Project.

Varley, Robert C. G. 2005. *The World Bank and China's Environment 1993–2003*. Operations Evaluation Department Working Paper. Washington, DC: The World Bank.

Wade, Robert. 1997. "Greening the Bank: The Struggle over the Environment 1970–1995." In *The World Bank: Its First Half Century*, edited by Devesh Kapur, John P. Lewis, and Richard C. Webb, 611–734. Washington, DC: Brookings Institution.

Wade, Robert. 2004. "The World Bank and the Environment." In *Global Institutions and Development: Framing the World?*, edited by Morten Bøås and Desmond McNeill, 72–94. London and New York: Routledge.

Wapenhans, Willi. 1992. *Report of the Portfolio Management Task Force*. Washington, DC: World Bank.

Weaver, Catherine. 2003. *The Hypocrisy of International Organizations: The Rhetoric, Reality, and Reform of the World Bank*. PhD thesis. Madison: University of Wisconsin-Madison.

Wilke, Alex. 2004. *The World Bank's Knowledge Roles: Dominating Development Debates*. London: Bretton Woods Project. Available at http://www.brettonwoodsproject.org (accessed May 2007).

World Bank. 1992. *World Development Report 1992: Development and the Environment*. Washington, DC: The World Bank and Oxford University Press.

World Bank. 1999. *The Effect of a Shadow Price on Carbon Emissions in the Energy Portfolio of the World Bank: A Carbon Backcasting Exercise*. Washington, DC: The World Bank.

World Bank. 2001a. *The Medium-Term Human Resources Agenda: Aligning with the Bank's Strategic Directions*. Washington, DC: The World Bank.

World Bank. 2001b. *Project Information Document: Sao Paulo Metro Line 4 Project*. Washington, DC: The World Bank.

World Bank. 2001c. *Strategic Staffing: Issues and Challenges for FY03–05*. Washington, DC: The World Bank.

World Bank. 2002a. *Making Sustainable Commitments: An Environment Strategy for the World Bank*. Washington, DC: The World Bank.

World Bank. 2002b. *Project Information Document: Lake Victoria Environmental Management Project—Supplemental Credit, Uganda.* Washington, DC: The World Bank.

World Bank. 2002c. *World Development Report 2003: Sustainable Development in a Dynamic World.* Washington, DC: The World Bank and Oxford University Press.

World Bank. 2003a. *Cornerstones for Conservation: World Bank Assistance for Protected Areas 1988–2003.* Washington, DC: The World Bank.

World Bank. 2003b. *Putting Our Commitments to Work: An Environment Strategy Progress Report.* Washington, DC: The World Bank.

World Bank. 2003c. *Strategic Staffing Update Paper.* Washington, DC: The World Bank.

World Bank. 2004a. *Annual Report 2004, Volume 2.* Washington, DC: The World Bank.

World Bank. 2004b. *Ensuring the Future: The World Bank and Biodiversity, 1988–2004.* Washington, DC: The World Bank.

World Bank. 2004c. *Implementation Completion Report for Aral Sea Water and Environmental Management Project.* Washington, DC: The World Bank.

World Bank. 2005. *Focus on Sustainability 2004.* Washington, DC: The World Bank.

World Bank. 2006. *Where Is the Wealth of Nations? Measuring Capital for the XXI Century.* Washington, DC: The World Bank.

World Bank Institute. 2003. *Annual Report 2003.* Washington, DC: The World Bank.

World Bank Operations Evaluation Department. 2003. *Sharing Knowledge: Innovations and Remaining Challenges. An OED Evaluation.* Washington, DC: World Bank Operations Evaluation Department.

World Bank Operations Evaluation Department. 2004. *Annual Report on Operations Evaluation.* Washington, DC: World Bank Operations Evaluation Department.

World Bank Operations Evaluation Department. 2005. *Annual Report on Operations Evaluation.* Washington, DC: World Bank Operations Evaluation Department.

Wysham, Daphne. 2005. "A Carbon Rush at the World Bank." *Foreign Policy in Focus* (February) [online source]. Available at http://www.fpif.org/papers/0502wbank.htm (accessed April 2006).

Xepapadeas, Anastasios. 2005. "Economic Growth and the Environment." In *Handbook of Environmental Economics Vol. 3*, edited by Karl-G. Mäler and Jeffrey Vincent, 1219–1266. Amsterdam: Elsevier.

6

The Secretariat of the International Maritime Organization: A Tanker for Tankers

Sabine Campe

Introduction

To promote "safe, secure, and efficient shipping on clean oceans" is the slogan of the International Maritime Organization (IMO), the UN specialized agency responsible for shipping safety and prevention of marine pollution from ships. This organization was founded in March 1948—first under the title of Inter-Governmental Maritime Consultative Organization—with the adoption of a convention that entered into force in 1958.[1] Marine environment protection was added to the IMO's mandate in 1967, partly as a response to the sinking of the *Torrey Canyon*. Reflecting its growing importance for maritime safety and marine pollution, the organization's name was changed in 1982 to the International Maritime Organization (Lampe 1983).[2]

The secretariat of the IMO in London has a demanding task. Shipping is a global business, and ships from different countries of origin with international crews travel through different jurisdictions and territories. The performance of the IMO has been analyzed by international lawyers,[3] by scholars of ocean management,[4] and by political scientists who focused on the formation and effectiveness of international environmental regimes.[5] Yet none of the studies has concentrated on the work of the IMO secretariat as an international bureaucracy. None has tried to measure its influence and to explain it with reference to the particular features of the secretariat. Moreover, no study has focused on the environmental division of the IMO secretariat, which stands at the center of this chapter.

In the following analysis, I argue that the secretariat of the IMO has been an influential actor regarding the provision of technical expertise on ship design and construction. This relates to the fact that its staff has predominantly seafaring or naval engineering backgrounds and good contacts to the shipping industry. However, the influence of the secretariat's marine environment division on environmental policy is less pronounced. It has seldom influenced environmental discourses, and there is not much evidence for direct influence on the international negotiations on ship-based marine pollution. This makes the marine environment division—and the overall IMO secretariat—a prototype of a technocratic and rather industry-oriented international bureaucracy in the field of global environmental governance.

My research is based on primary and secondary sources, as well as nine interviews with senior officers of the maritime safety division, the technical cooperation division, and the marine environment division at the headquarters of the IMO. In the next section, I introduce the structure and activities of the IMO secretariat and its marine environment division. I then analyze the influence of the work of the secretariat and its marine environment division, and explain the achievements and failures of the secretariat.

Structure and Activities

The IMO has 167 state members that represent 97.02 percent of the world merchant shipping tonnage (Lloyd's Register 2006). There are three associated members (IMO 2008a), and sixty-five nongovernmental organizations have been granted consultative status (IMO 2008b). In addition, the IMO has formal cooperation agreements with forty-two intergovernmental organizations (IMO 2008c). The work of the organization is conducted in four committees that are open to all members: the Maritime Safety Committee, the Marine Environment Committee, the Legal Committee, the Technical Co-operation Committee, and the Facilitation Committee.

The framework for the work of the IMO and its secretariat is the IMO Convention. According to article 1, the organization shall facilitate cooperation among governments in the field of public regulation and practices relating to technical matters affecting shipping engaged in international trade. It shall promote the general adoption of the highest practicable standards in maritime safety, efficiency of navigation, and the prevention and control of marine pollution from ships, and deal with all related administrative and legal matters. In addition, the IMO shall advance the removal of discriminatory restrictions in shipping to promote merchant shipping without discrimination. Finally, the organization shall manage the exchange of information among governments.

Initially, the sole task of the IMO secretariat was to foster maritime safety and efficiency of navigation. In practice, however, in 1959 it had already become the secretariat of the first global instrument on ship-based pollution, the International Convention for the Prevention of Pollution of the Sea by Oil (OILPOL).[6] The IMO secretariat was responsible for the continuous development of OILPOL. Consequently, a Subcommittee for Oil Pollution was installed within the IMO (M'Gonigle and Zacher 1979, 99). During the runup to the 1973 International Conference on Marine Pollution that eventually led to the adoption of the International Convention for the Prevention of Pollution of the Sea (MARPOL 73/78),[7] the subcommittee's name was changed to the Marine Environment Protection Committee. This was to reflect that the committee did not deal exclusively with oil pollution, but also with pollution by chemicals; goods in packaged form; and sewage, garbage, and air pollution (MARPOL 73/78, Annexes I to IV). Overall, the IMO secretariat is responsible for the administration of the various conventions negotiated within IMO (Campe 2008a).

The Influence of the IMO Secretariat and its Marine Environment Division

This section analyzes effects on the behavior of actors that can be attributed to activities of the IMO secretariat and its marine environment division. I do not focus on eventual environmental effectiveness. As a recent report on oil pollution from sea-based activities argues, oil inputs resulting from operational discharges and ship accidents have been reduced from 1.49 million tons in 1981 to 0.47 million tons in 1997 (GESAMP 2007, 111).[8] According to this study, this decrease can be attributed to wide ratification and implementation of MARPOL and to increasing public pressure on shipping firms, especially after tanker accidents (GESAMP 2007, 111). Critics, however, have questioned the validity of similar assessments, as data on environmental effectiveness are based on estimates (Peet 1994, 44). In any case, it remains unclear—and methodologically almost impossible to resolve—whether increasing compliance can be ascribed to any activity of the IMO secretariat. However, a number of other, indirect types of influence of the secretariat on the behavior of actors can be ascertained. These will be at the center of the following analysis.

Cognitive Influence

One of the secretariat's major tasks is to pool information about technical details concerning ship construction and nautical engineering. The IMO secretariat, however, has a rather weak record in using information provided by member states effectively. Although it receives national reports, no proper reporting system had been established by the secretariat for long—to the effect that industry then created databases independently, and that the International Chamber of Shipping and the ship-owners' association INTERTANKO published reports on reception facilities (Mitchell 1994, 129–130 and 231; 1993, 129–130; Mitchell, McConnell and Barrett 1999). Only recently has the IMO secretariat intensified its efforts in database management. One staff member even reports that his job predominantly is to "put the facts on the table," and that a growing demand for reliable data by organizations such as the European Union can be recognized.[9] Within its Global Ballast Water Management Programme, for example, the secretariat implemented a clearinghouse on new technologies: the Ballast Water Treatment Research and Development Directory.

In addition, the IMO secretariat informs on legal issues. For instance, the secretariat commissioned a review on existing international obligations and national regulatory approaches on ballast water management, and the Global Ballast Water Management Programme Legislative Review Project prepared such a report (McConnell 2002). Although the IMO secretariat typically serves as a purely technical organization, in this case it has taken a proactive stance on the development of alternative technologies (McConnell 2003, 90). Most important for the IMO secretariat's outreach is a large publications department that produces an impressive number of manuals on IMO regulations and codes. All publications are translated into several UN languages. Profit from book sales finances technical cooperation activities through the IMO Printing Fund (IMO 2001, 2004). The demand for IMO manuals and guidelines grows steadily, as sales increases show.[10]

Apart from collecting technical information about ships, the IMO marine environment division undertakes no scientific research. However, the secretariat hosts the Joint Group of Experts on the Scientific Aspects of Marine Environmental Protection (GESAMP), which was founded in 1967 by a number of UN organizations and is physically based at the

IMO secretariat. The GESAMP meets annually to advise on scientific aspects of environmental marine protection. The group is rather small: every sponsoring organization sends one technical officer (currently from the IMO, FAO, UNESCO/IOC [Intergovernmental Oceanographic Commission], WMO [World Meteorological Organization], WHO, IAEA, UN, and UNEP). It prepares periodic assessments of the state of the marine environment and publishes both reports and scholarly journal articles (Cordes 2004). Many of the reports that are published as *GESAMP Reports and Studies* reappear in shorter versions in peer-reviewed journals. In total, there are 1436 citations of GESAMP papers, and two reports are even classified as "most cited papers" in their field by ISI Web of Science (Cordes 2004, 66). Hence, publications have spread widely beyond IMO. Through GESAMP, the IMO secretariat has influenced the knowledge base on marine pollution.

The public discourse on marine pollution has always been spurred by tanker accidents, most prominently the disasters of the *Torrey Canyon*, the *Amoco Cadiz*, the *Exxon Valdez*, and the *Erika* (Birnie 1999).[11] As a result, shipping has increasingly become a subject to public debate and the IMO has been perceived as an "international lobbyist for maritime shipping" (Höfer and Metz 2003, 113). IMO Secretary-General Efthimios E. Mitropoulos reports that in "the last quarter of a century, shipping's environmental credentials have come under sharper scrutiny than ever before and this is something that is set to continue and increase."[12] Rather than being a proactive player in the environmental discourse, the IMO and its secretariat have merely responded to the international debate. For instance, with regard to air pollution from ships, the IMO refrained from any action for several years and commissioned a first study on greenhouse gas emissions only in 1999.[13] The IMO intensified its discussions only upon request from the climate secretariat; it did not initiate any action of its own (Oberthür 2003, 195).

The IMO secretariat has only reacted to the environmental discourse, and shipping as a means of transport has not been called into question (McConnell 2003, 71). Rather, the IMO secretariat may have helped framing shipping as an environmentally safe means of transport. Former IMO Secretary-General William O'Neill emphasized that "the existence of a strong transport and communication infrastructure is essential to sustainable development,"[14] and the current IMO secretary-general, Efthimios Mitropoulos, confirms that "there can be no doubt that transport and communication are crucial for sustainable development in the global environment."[15]

In sum, the IMO secretariat provides a pool of information on technical issues related to shipping and legal aspects of possible regulations. Yet it is less effective in making use of compliance data and national reports. Through membership in GESAMP, the IMO has contributed to a better scientific understanding of marine pollution. Yet the secretariat has always been rather reactive in environmental discourses; overall, it has helped frame shipping as an appropriate form of transportation at a global level.

Normative Influence

To foster international cooperation on the regulation of shipping is a central task of the IMO. Therefore, the secretariat's most important activity is to facilitate negotiations among IMO member states. By providing an arena for negotiations, the IMO secretariat facilitates discussions and has often been called a "broker."[16] In addition, the IMO member organization issues codes that eventually may obtain the status of customary law, and develops guidelines on the implementation of conventions negotiated within the intergovernmental meetings of IMO.

The secretariat staff reports that most work is dedicated to preparing meetings, collecting documents and drafting agendas, but rarely to introducing new topics to negotiations.[17] The secretariat seems rather reluctant to push the public discourse into one direction, presumably out of fear that IMO member states could lose confidence in its work.

Generally, different regulations in different jurisdictions make the adherence to standards complicated and costly, and thus inhibit an effective environmental policy (Kim 2003). The shipping industry in particular has a strong interest in clear regulation and standards, because international standards usually represent the lowest common denominator.[18] Strict unilateral regulation endangers the effectiveness of international regimes and imposes high costs on the shipping industry (Ilg 2001, 31). Also, a mosaic of different regimes and regulations might constrain the freedom of merchant shipping (Ilg 2001, 99). For instance, in the case of the MARPOL negotiations, a compromise was possible because the shipping industry finally supported international regulation in order to avoid unilateral action by environmental leaders (Carlin 2001, 335). With its 1972 Ports and Waterways Safety Act, the U.S. Coast Guard *could* have required segregated ballast water tanks, although no international convention was signed yet. Unilateral action could thus be prevented through negotiations within the Marine Environment Protection

Committee, when the parties finally agreed on the ambitious U.S. target that required segregated ballast water tanks for new tankers weighing more than 70,000 deadweight tons (Hartje 1995, 387).

However, these are effects of the IMO as a member organization. The direct influence of its secretariat on negotiations is harder to trace. All civil servants interviewed for this study have stressed that they only serve the member states and do not push toward one political direction. The secretariat predominantly fulfils a "service function" (Breitmeier 1997, 108) and provides a forum for negotiations, including preparing the meetings, distributing the submissions among the participants, taking minutes, and briefing the chairpersons.

One of the rare exceptions are the negotiations on the Convention to Control Harmful Antifouling Systems on Ships (AFS Convention), where the IMO secretariat proactively promoted research on alternative technologies and influenced outcomes.[19] The AFS Convention regulates the use of tributyltin in coatings to prevent aquatic organisms from attaching to a ship's hull, which is known as "fouling" and causes a higher flow resistance and thus higher fuel consumption.[20] It has harmful effects on the environment (Goldberg 1986; Stewart 1996). The use of tributyltin in antifouling coatings was first discussed in an international arena at the meeting of the parties to the Convention of Marine Pollution from Land-based Sources (PARCOM) in 1987,[21] but a total ban of tributyltin did not seem feasible for economic reasons. PARCOM deals with land-based pollution in the North-East Atlantic, and the global regulation of ship-based marine pollution falls under the responsibility of the IMO, which is why the issue was referred to the IMO (Campe 2003). The IMO secretariat took a proactive stance and offered to draft a review on the state of the art of alternative technologies. In addition, the secretariat suggested collecting information on the removal of tributyltin coatings to support developing countries. In the final round of negotiations, the IMO secretariat actively influenced the negotiation's outcomes. It submitted a resolution on technical cooperation that was then—albeit slightly modified—adopted by the diplomatic conference.

In sum, promoting negotiations is a core task of the IMO secretariat, and it can fulfil this function well because of its perceived neutrality. By providing an arena for discussions, it helps to avoid a mosaic of unilateral regulations that would be the most costly option for most members. Yet the IMO secretariat primarily fulfils supportive functions. Only in few cases (e.g., the negotiations of the AFS Convention) has the secretariat deliberately influenced negotiations. Overall, the secretariat appears rather service-oriented than driven by a policy agenda.

Executive Influence

Though the facilitation of negotiations has been the focus of the work of the IMO secretariat for long, technical cooperation is now perceived as essential for compliance with and enforcement of IMO regulations. The IMO secretariat develops and implements projects that aim to improve the compliance by flag states and the enforcement of IMO conventions by port states.

The IMO secretariat has increased its technical cooperation efforts in recent years, and capacity building has become an increasingly important topic for the IMO, reflected by the fact that the World Maritime Day, which is celebrated annually to draw attention to shipping, had in 2006 the theme "Technical Cooperation: IMO's Response to the 2005 World Summit."[22] Within the IMO secretariat, the technical cooperation division is responsible for implementing the Integrated Technical Cooperation Programme (ITCP). It has focused on policy formulation support and institutional capacity building through the deployment of advisory missions, the provision of model legislation and the coaching of trainees to foster compliance (IMO 2004). Recently, the Integrated Technical Cooperation Programme was reorganized; it now uses integrated financial data to make the operative management more efficient. The IMO also tried to boost flag state implementation through an initiative in developing countries. An impact study shows that problem awareness has increased (Fakhry 2003, 95). In addition, a Voluntary Audit Scheme is also intended to foster compliance among developing countries. It will be used as an instrument for capacity building, as it will "help to identify where capacity-building activities would have the greatest effect and it will also enable appropriate action to be much more precisely focused."[23]

The technical cooperation division works closely with the specialist departments (maritime safety and marine environment) to further the development and the implementation of projects.[24] Broken down to the different departments, roughly 29 percent of all activities relate to the Marine Environment Division and 61 percent are implemented through the Maritime Safety Division (IMO 2004). Maritime safety is also focus of capacity building within the IMO: "The activities delivered covered a wide range of subjects with maritime safety issues remaining central to the Programme."[25] The funds for technical cooperation stem from voluntary contributions and are less than 2 percent of the annual budget of the

IMO. Almost half of the funds stem from the Technical Cooperation Fund, which is financed through the IMO's Printing Fund, which administers the production and sale of publications (IMO 2001, 2004). The GEF accounts for another third of the funds, followed by UNEP (8 percent), Norway (7 percent), and the European Union (4 percent). The budget of the ITCP and especially donor funding has increased considerably in recent years, which also reflects the growing importance capacity building efforts have within IMO.[26] The regional focus of IMO's capacity building has been West and Central Africa. The governments of Côte d'Ivoire, Ghana, and Kenya have signed three memoranda of understanding with the IMO to extend the IMO's presence in their countries.[27] In addition, the IMO tries to align its projects in Africa with the New Partnership for Africa's Development. For instance, through the new Forum on the Establishment of an Integrated Sub-regional Coastguard Function Network for West and Central African Countries, the IMO tries to promote the sustainable use of the Exclusive Economic Zone in these countries.[28]

To train professionals, three institutions have been founded under the auspices of the IMO. The World Maritime University, established in 1983 and based in Malmö, Sweden, provides postgraduate education for about two hundred students. In addition, in 1990 the International Maritime Law Institute was founded in Malta, with about two hundred lawyers participating in graduate classes. Finally, the International Maritime Academy—founded in 1989 and based in Trieste, Italy—trains professionals and government officials in short-term courses. The IMO secretariat also sporadically evaluates the performance of officers trained by the IMO.[29]

In sum, the IMO secretariat has intensified capacity building, but data on its effects are still scarce. IMO staff members agree that helping developing countries to implement the conventions should be a focus of the IMO's work. As one IMO officer estimates, only 40–60 percent of all IMO member states are able to follow developments, and at most a third of them are able to implement them.[30]

Explaining the Influence

Problem Structure

The IMO deals with transport issues that—at least in the case of the large shipping nations—touch vital interests that governments want to keep under control. Because the IMO is a multi-issue organization, it can be expected that conflicts, especially with regard to multiple-principal problems, will arise. The IMO secretariat generally deals with problems in two very different and often conflicting issue areas, that is, economics and marine environmental protection, as maritime transport relates to both of them. Ship owners, traders, and oil companies strive for most efficient and low cost shipping, while representatives of environmental, tourism and fishing interests call for strict environmental policies (Tan 2006, 35 and 67–69). The problem of oil pollution has thus been evaluated in some studies as "malign," as preferences of different actors diverge strongly and costs of regulation are high (Carlin 2001, 335–336). In addition, intentional oil pollution belongs to the group of "pollution externality imposed on a global commons by a relatively concentrated industry in which actors are susceptible to regulation by both domestic and foreign authorities" (Mitchell 1994, 23).

Transport is a big business, and ship owners try to maximize their profits. They often try to reduce personnel costs and costs resulting from safety and pollution prevention measures (Alderton and Winchester 2002). The restrictions of many shipping nations—for example, the United States, Norway, and Greece—are very tight. Many ship owners thus decide to register their ships in other countries with open registers, which are often called "flags of convenience" (see DeSombre 2006 for more details). In addition, traditional shipping nations created systems of so-called second registers that exempt ship owners from strict labor and safety standards. Roughly 54 percent of the world fleet tonnage is registered in open registers (Llácer 2003). According to the Flag State Conformance Index, second registers such as those established by for instance Norway, the United Kingdom, Denmark, the Netherlands, and Germany, rank much higher than newly consolidated open registers such as, for example, Cambodia, Equatorial Guinea, or Belize. Recently, some large flags of convenience such as Liberia, Panama, and the Bahamas have improved their efforts to collaborate with other IMO members (Höfer and Metz 2003, 115; Ilg 2001, 120). The discrepancy between the traditional shipping nations and the flags of convenience is not as clear-cut as it has been two decades ago, but they still favor different types of regulations (Alderton and Winchester 2002, 42). To sum up, different actors have conflicting interests, which complicates rather than eases policy regulation.

Tanker accidents like the sinking of the *Torrey Canyon* in 1967 worked as exogenous shocks and influenced the development of the liability and oil-spill response. They did not directly trigger an international regime, but led the United States into its frontrunner position pushing for international regulation (Carlin 2001, 342). Even the (then) IMO Secretary-General Sir Colin Goad called the *Torrey Canyon* incident a "stroke of luck" for the organization, because it fueled the importance of environmental matters within the organization (Ilg 2001, 12). In addition, several external factors influenced the adoption and implementation of MARPOL. The ship-building industry boomed in the early 1970s due to the opening of the U.S. oil market in 1973. Because of the Organization of Arab Petroleum Exporting Countries' boycott of the United States and the Netherlands, trade in oil decreased by 8 percent until 1975. At the same time, the tanker fleet had grown by 25 percent, resulting in free capacities (Höfer and Metz 2003, 109). Both the rising oil prices and the shipping industry's over-capacities boosted the adoption of segregated ballast tanks. On one hand, oil became too expensive to be wasted through discharges, and on the other hand, segregated ballast tanks could reduce the global tanker capacity. Finally, new shipping routes and the overall decrease in transport volume of oil reduced the number of accidents (Höfer and Metz 2003, 109).

The level of compliance of the tanker industry has varied greatly and has mainly depended on the type of regulation. As Mitchell and colleagues (1999) show, discharge standards have not altered the performance of the tanker industry, but equipment standards have indeed changed the behavior of the shipping operators. Still, governments have largely failed to provide their ports with necessary reception facilities, and if they have done so, this can be traced back to local lobbying rather than to the international instrument or organization (Mitchell 1994). Public pressure induced a compliance pull, thereby decreasing the amounts of oil entering the sea (GESAMP 2007, 111).

In sum, the problem structure of ship-based marine pollution is rather malign, because the costs of regulation are high and the preferences vary greatly. Flag states opt for weak regulation; coastal states call for strict laws. However, two factors have worked in the opposite direction: rising oil prices minimized oil discharges because wasting oil simply became too expensive, and tanker accidents accelerated political action inasmuch as they boosted public attention for marine environmental pollution.

Polity

Competences   Paradoxically at first sight, the secretariat's lack of autonomy allows for some influence on negotiations, within certain limits.

Perceived as neutral broker loyal to its member states without the ability to act against the will of its principals, the secretariat is trusted by the member states and its submissions are generally regarded as a good basis for negotiations. This characteristic adds to an explanation why the IMO secretariat does not work as a strong advocate and has comparatively little influence on environmental discourses.

The IMO has the status of a specialized agency of the UN and is largely independent within the UN family. The UN General Assembly and the UN Economic and Social Council can merely submit recommendations to the IMO. Every year, an external financial auditing following UN standards takes place, which however only relates the adequacy of accounting systems and does not include a review of the work. Although largely independent from the UN system, the IMO secretariat has low autonomy regarding its member states (Carlin 2001, 352). Activities that go beyond the IMO mandate are rare.[31]

The dominance of shipping interests over environmental concerns is reflected in the voting procedures within the IMO as a member organization. The IMO has seven organs. The assembly is the highest organ and all members are part of it. Usually the assembly meets biennially; it decides on the work program and budget, elects the council, and approves the secretary-general. A two-thirds majority is required for changes in the IMO constitution. All decisions require a simple majority of votes, yet most decisions are taken by consensus (Ilg 2001, 24). The council is the executive organ of the IMO. Its forty members represent the ten largest shipping nations, the ten largest seaborne trading nations, and twenty countries with a maritime interest that at the same time represent all major world regions (article 17, IMO Convention). Due to this allocation mechanism, coastal states that are most vulnerable to marine pollution are underrepresented (Biermann 1994, 192), and the large flag states possess a de facto veto. Flag states, which are responsible for enforcing IMO conventions on ships flying their flag, play a major role within the IMO. They provide large parts of its budget, and have great influence on decision making within IMO. This influence can be seen in the entry-into-force provisions of the conventions negotiated within IMO: international agreements often enter into force when a number of countries that represent a certain percentage of the world fleet have ratified the convention.

The IMO as an organization has proven to be an adequate forum for negotiations, which has been promoted by tacit acceptance, a procedure that allows for speedy amendment of technical annexes. International legally binding agreements usually include terms on how to change both the convention and its annexes, and parties to an agreement typically reserve the right to amend a convention, requiring an explicit consent of all parties. This procedure has proven to be very slow and inadequate; because technology changes rapidly, technical specifications included in annexes to the conventions continuously need to be adapted (Lang 1992). In light of the *Torrey Canyon* disaster of 1967, several approaches to speed up amendments to technical annexes of conventions were discussed within IMO meetings. The legal department compiled a review of amendment procedures of other intergovernmental organizations.[32] Through tacit acceptance, technical amendments automatically enter into force unless a third of the member states object within twelve months. Because tacit acceptance allows technical changes to be made very efficiently, it has been judged a major advancement in combating marine pollution (Ilg 2001). It grants IMO staff considerable influence, and IMO secretariat staff has reported that this opportunity has been used quite frequently to update the regulations. The tacit acceptance procedure has thus increased the secretariat's ability to influence conventions.

To sum up, the IMO secretariat has rather restricted competencies vis-à-vis its member states, at least in constitutive issues. It has little control over its budget, and decisions are usually taken by consensus. Tacit acceptance allows for timely amendments, but it grants the IMO secretariat further autonomy only with regard to technical matters. The IMO secretariat's low political profile and pronounced technical knowledge explains its major strength, which is to provide a forum for negotiations and technical expertise.

Resources   The financial resources of the IMO secretariat are scarce, although it has a relatively stable budget derived from membership fees that depend on the size of a member state's fleet (in gross tonnage) and its UN contributions. The budget of the IMO amounted to £46,194,900 (USD 92,294,927) for the biennium 2004–2005. The three largest contributors are Panama (19.2 percent of total budget), Liberia (7.89 percent), and the Bahamas (5.19 percent), and the fact that they are poorer developing countries has led to temporary cash shortages in the past. Therefore, the IMO set up a "Working Capital Fund" to bridge liquidity squeezes. So far, member states have not suspended their payments for disapproval of IMO secretariat's work and no major conflicts with member states were experienced.[33] Unlike many other UN agencies, the IMO secretariat has not undergone any nominal budget cuts—a fact that has been interpreted as general approval of the IMO secretariat's work by member states.[34] However, staff complains that "states are not willing to pay for the service they get."[35] Due to the tight budget, vacancies can often not be filled. The council allocates practically every cent of the budget, and due to rather strict terms of reference, the IMO secretariat cannot reallocate money on its own.

The IMO secretariat has no hard sanction mechanisms at its hand. Furthermore, it has not used softer means to sanction compliance failure to full capacity. The IMO secretariat has a weak record in collecting national reports and monitoring compliance (Mitchell 1994, 140). Although the OECD publishes data to shame governments by blaming them for not meeting their goals (Busch, this volume, chapter 4), the IMO secretariat did not even synthesize available data (Mitchell 1993, 231). Although it received reports on OILPOL and MARPOL enforcement by governments, the secretariat did not issue any overview or synthesis reports until 1984, when it published a two-page document claiming that there are no general trends available. It also failed to issue a standardized reporting form until 1985 (Mitchell 1994, 140).

In sum, neither the IMO secretariat nor the IMO as a member organization have any formal sanctioning mechanisms. Despite available data on enforcement, no monitoring took place within IMO and softer sanction mechanisms such as the publishing of enforcement data have not been used to full capacity, either.

Embeddedness Fighting marine pollution is one of the two tasks of IMO; the other one—arguably the more important one—is promoting safety at sea. The combination of those two issues represents a typical multiple-principal problem. Although maritime safety is under the responsibility of the transport, shipping, or economic ministries, the agency concerned with marine pollution is usually the environment ministry. This issue has led to incoherent policies and conflicts in the respective ministries (de La Fayette 2001, 144).[36]

The lack of cooperation between the IMO and other international environmental organizations further illustrates this point. The IMO is one of three main UN organizations responsible for ocean governance (the others are UNESCO/IOC and UNEP). Although some cooperation exists, there seems to be insufficient policy coordination at the global level (Hinds 2003, 351). The World Commission on the Oceans judges this coordination as sometimes more symbolic than operational (1998, 147–152). The IMO is chiefly responsible for the prevention of vessel-source marine pollution at a global scale, and UNEP is the organization dealing with land-based marine pollution and regional cooperation. UNEP's task is to link "assessments of the marine environment and the causes of its deterioration, with response actions for management and development of the marine and coastal environment" through its Regional Seas Programme (Akiwumi and Melvasalo 1998, 230). Through the Global Programme for Action for the Protection of the Marine Environment from Land-based Sources, UNEP attempts to support regional authorities in developing countries in preventing ship-based marine pollution. Although the IMO is listed among the nine key players of the pollution monitoring and assessment program of the Mediterranean Action Plan, it was apparently not part of any of the eleven projects implemented under the Global Programme for Action for the Protection of the Marine Environment from Land-based Sources.[37] The UN Commission on Sustainable Development also called for better cooperation between the IMO and UNEP (Birnie 1999, 369–370), and the UNEP Governing Council asked for a closer cooperation between the regional programs and the IMO (Adler 2003, 14).

This shows that the cooperation of the IMO secretariat with UNEP has been rather limited. It seems, however, that at least for regional projects, the cooperation between the IMO and UNEP is getting more substantial. For instance, the IMO and UNEP jointly implement the "International Assistance Action Plan" to assist Lebanon in addressing coastal oil pollution.[38] Related to the adoption of the International Convention for the Control and Management of Ships Ballast Water and Sediments, the IMO founded the Global Ballast Water Management Programme, which is funded by the GEF through UNDP. To administer this initiative, a coordination unit has been created within the IMO secretariat. The project started its first phase in 2000, and funding for the next phase has now been provided by the GEF.[39] The program aims to foster exchange between representatives from industry, nongovernmental organizations, governments and international organizations. In sum, while we find cooperative arrangements between the IMO secretariat and other organizations, the driving forces behind this cooperation are rather outside the IMO bureaucracy.

People and Procedures

Organizational Expertise   The IMO secretariat provides data on technical issues yet is rather reactive to the environmental discourse. This difference can be explained by its strong technical expertise and its close contacts to business and industry. "Ninety percent of my work is talking to external people," illustrates a technical officer.[40] The professional backgrounds of IMO staff reflect the fact that marine environmental protection is less important within IMO. Overall, members of both the marine environment and the maritime safety division have mostly seafaring backgrounds. Those working in the technical cooperation division have been trained in international relations or related fields. The lack of environmental experts was perceived as a disadvantage.[41]

The most important source for expertise are the classification societies. Classification societies assess the state of repair of ships and issue classifications, which then determine what kind of policy ship owners are offered by insurance carriers (Campe 2008b). The International Association of Classification Societies is especially influential: with the highly technical issues being addressed within the IMO, staff reports that the expertise of classification societies is crucial for judging the technical feasibility of new solutions.[42] A representative of the American Bureau of Shipping describes the classifications societies as "technical advisor[s]" to IMO (Somerville 2004, 5). In addition, the ship-owner associations are very active at meetings of the Marine Environment Protection Committee and often submit documents. Although the secretariat has cooperated with environmental nongovernmental organizations, there is a bias in favor of the shipping industry that is reflected in the network in which IMO officers act.

Overall, the IMO avails itself of strong technical expertise and is well connected to the outside world with a bias for the shipping industry. The secretariat maintains especially close contacts to the classification societies, which explains why the secretariat predominantly has effects on technical matters of shipbuilding and construction, while the influence on environmental issues is significantly smaller.

Organizational Structure   The secretariat of the IMO is located in London and comprises a staff of three hundred. Only a small fraction of this staff works on environmental issues. The secretariat is organized in a number of divisions: the Maritime Safety Division with thirty-six staff members, the Marine Environment Division with twenty, the Legal Affairs and External Relations Division with twenty-three, and the Technical Cooperation Division with twenty. In these divisions, 60 percent of staff are technical officers or higher (UN salary categories P, D), and 40 percent are support staff. The remaining two hundred staff of the

IMO secretariat work in the Administrative Division and the Conference Division.

Staff reports clearly defined responsibilities combined with highly formalized decision-making procedures. Several staff members claim that communication structures predate modern communication technologies and are no longer adequate. Also, day-to-day decisions are made in a very hierarchical way that was perceived as inadequate. Staff members report on "small kings" within IMO who protect their small sphere of influence, which has not necessarily led to greater efficiency and transparency. The IMO has a precise mandate that includes furthering maritime safety and marine pollution prevention. Some interviewees stressed that technical cooperation has become more important than the drafting of new conventions, and that the IMO is moderately equipped for that. Because the IMO is not very open for change and its decision-making procedures are highly formalized, there is little proactive engagement of IMO staff. Hierarchies are perceived to be too strong and communication structures are not up to date. This explains why the IMO secretariat is rather reluctant to become proactive and rather hesitant to influence discourses.

Organizational Culture   Staff members usually join the IMO secretariat at an advanced level of their career, and many members have worked for national administrations before. IMO staff members come from very diverse cultural backgrounds. Technical officers are often appointed for political reasons, and not exclusively for their expertise.[43] Finally, UN salaries are more attractive than many government salaries, but not competitive with salaries paid in industry. No internal staff workshops take place, and there are no formal learning mechanisms. The IMO undergoes external audits that are common in the UN system, and that relate only to accounting and finance.[44] The overall learning aptitude of the IMO secretariat is thus rather low.

IMO staff perceives itself as a broker for negotiations among its member states, and staff shows remarkable successes in this capacity. Staff underscores that neutrality is the most important feature of the IMO secretariat.[45] Moreover, the IMO secretariat presents its policies as purely pragmatic and technical solutions (Birnie 1999, 366). In the past, the IMO has somewhat resisted responding to any demands for restructuring. In light of the UNCED process, the IMO was asked to incorporate the precautionary principle into the work of all IMO bodies. Yet instead of mainstreaming environmental concerns, the IMO basically argued for the status quo and against major organizational reform. In the 1990s, IMO officers referred to two rather outdated resolutions that regulated the work program for the 1980s to avoid structural change (372–373).[46] The organizational culture of the bureaucracy tends to favor efficient shipping over sustainable development goals, and the dominating professional culture of seafarers promotes this culture.

In sum, IMO officers try to be as "neutral" as possible and advocate for technical solutions with a pragmatic reasoning. Strong hierarchies and outdated communication channels hamper innovation. The specific institutional design impeded the mainstreaming of the precautionary principle, and economic efficiency concerns and the inherent interest of free maritime transport dominate.

Organizational Leadership   Since the 1970s, the terms for the IMO secretary-generals have been quite long: Chandrika Prasad Srivastava from India served from 1974–1989, William A. O'Neil from Canada served from 1990–2003, and Efthimios E. Mitropoulos from Greece has served from 2004, and was reappointed for his second term until 2011. William O'Neil supported the opening of the IMO for organizations from "all sectors of the industry" and thus arguably promoted the IMO's standing as the key hub for technical regulations and standards.[47] Efthimios E. Mitropoulos has dedicated his second term to "deliver high-quality services," while at the same time "sharpening the focus of the Organization."[48] Though staff reported that the secretary-generals have always been active in promoting specific policies and regulations, no data about the style of leadership could be generated, and therefore, the explanatory power of this variable is very limited in this case.

Conclusion

The IMO secretariat has some cognitive influence, mainly related to technical matters of ship construction. A growing demand for reliable data voiced by other organizations such as the EU confirms this strength. Cognitive influence can be explained by the ability of IMO staff to pool technical knowledge, which has been reinforced by its excellent contacts to the shipping industry. Our hypothesis—the higher the expertise, the higher the influence of a bureaucracy will be—can therefore be confirmed. Through cosponsoring of the scientific advisory body GESAMP, IMO staff contributed to furthering scientific findings about marine environmental protection. Nevertheless, this task is of lower priority than the provision of technical knowledge. The embedding of the organization explains this: contacts to the shipping industry are closer than are those to environmental nongovernmental organizations. Cooperation with other environmental intergovernmental organizations such as UNEP has been rather limited until very recently. In addition, the IMO secretariat as an international bureaucracy has not been a very active player in the environmental discourse. The IMO is well designed to craft technical standards of ship construction. Yet it is less able to lobby for environmental protection.

Capacity building is of increasing importance, and although no conclusive evidence could be found, there appears to be a positive trend. The flag state implementation initiative improved environmental awareness in developing countries. The three research and training institutes associated with the IMO receive good evaluations, and sporadic assessments of the impact of workshops organized by the technical cooperation division show positive results. In addition, internal features account for increasing efforts to promote capacity building. The internal restructuring of development assistance that led to a mainstreaming through the Integrated Technical Cooperation Programme accounts for this rather positive outlook.

The IMO as a member organization provides an excellent forum for negotiations. In most cases, the IMO secretariat managed to keep all parties at the table, thereby avoiding a costly mosaic of different regulations. Eventually, the IMO secretariat staff influences the course of the negotiations in a few instances; this could be observed, for example, in the case of negotiations of the AFS convention. The secretariat introduced a resolution on technical cooperation that was then adopted. Somewhat counterintuitively, its influence on international cooperation can be explained with reference to the little autonomy of the IMO secretariat. Exactly this feature shapes its character of an honest, neutral broker that enjoys its member states' trust. Formal autonomy is thus not a necessary condition for influence. The problem structure explains its small autonomy: the IMO's main objective is to promote safe and efficient shipping, while environmental standards often increase shipping costs. The hypothesis of this project—the higher the costs of regulation, the smaller the influence of the international bureaucracy—can thus be confirmed. Interestingly, its autonomy with regard to technical amendments of IMO convention annexes has been increased through the tacit acceptance procedure. This confirms that the IMO secretariat is perceived as a technical expert capable of pooling technical knowledge on the global business of shipping. In sum, however, the IMO secretariat can be described, in the context of this study, as a reactive, more technocratic bureaucracy. In a sense, it is after all like a tanker for the tankers.

Acknowledgments

I owe my gratitude for fruitful comments and suggestions on earlier versions of this text to Steinar Andresen, Manfred Elsig, Thomas Höfer, Heike Hoppe, Philipp Pattberg, Marco Schäferhoff, and to the MANUS project team.

Notes

1. Convention on the Intergovernmental Consultative Maritime Organization, adopted 6 March 1948, entered into force: 17 March 1958, United Nations Maritime Conference. Held at Geneva, Switzerland, from 19 February to 6 March 1948. Final Act and Related Documents. Lake Success, New York. United Nations Publication 1948 VIII.2.

2. The Japanese delegation first objected to this name, because "Imo" means "hot potato" in Japanese. The delegates then agreed to pronounce it as single letters: "I-M-O" (see Lampe 1983, 86).

3. Brubaker 1993; Dempsey 1984; Ilg 2001; Lauwaars 1984; M'Gonigle and Zacher 1979.

4. Cicin-Sain and Knecht 1993; Foders 1989; Hinds 2003; Huber et al. 2003; Kimball 2003; World Commission on the Oceans 1998.

5. Biermann 1994; Breitmeier 1997; Carlin 2001; Haas 1989; Jones 1999; Kim 2003; Mason 2003; Mitchell et al. 1999; Mitchell 1994; Peet 1994; Peterson 1997. For an excellent overview of the political dynamics behind rule-making processes within the IMO, see Tan 2006 (especially 29–106).

6. International Convention for the Prevention of Pollution of the Sea by Oil, entered into force 26 July 1958, 9 International Legal Materials 1.

7. International Convention for the Prevention of Pollution from Ships, 1973, as modified by the Protocol of 1978 relating thereto (MARPOL 73/78), entered into force 2 October 1983, 17 International Legal Materials 546.

8. The last value refers to an average oil input per year in the period from 1989 to 1997 (GESAMP 2007, 111).

9. Author's interview with senior staff member, Marine Environment Division, IMO headquarters, June 2003.

10. Author's interview with senior staff member, Maritime Safety Division, IMO headquarters, June 2003.

11. Author's interview with senior staff member, Marine Environment Division, IMO headquarters, June 2003.

12. IMO News 1/2007, 4.

13. IMO Doc. MEPC 43/10/2. For a review on air pollution from ships, see also Michaelowa and Krauser 2000.

14. IMO News 3/2007, 6.

15. "Message from the Secretary-General." IMO News 3/2005, 4.

16. Author's interview with senior staff member, Marine Environment Division, IMO headquarters, June 2003.

17. Author's interview with senior staff member, Marine Environment Division, IMO headquarters, June 2003; see also Tan 2006, 369. One exception is the 1995 Code that specifies the requirements of the 1978 International Convention on Standards of Training, Certification and Watch-keeping for Seafarers; the negotiations for this code have been advocated by the IMO secretary-general (Dirks 2001).

18. Author's interview with senior staff member, Maritime Safety Division, IMO headquarters, June 2003.

19. This section draws on Campe 2003.

20. The AFS Convention enters into force on 17 September 2008, following accession to the treaty by Panama on 17 September 2007. See "Harmful ships paint systems to be outlawed as international Convention meets entry into force criteria" (IMO News 4/2007, 6).

21. Convention of Marine Pollution from Land-based Sources (13 International Legal Materials 1974), entry into force 6 May 1978. PARCOM was replaced by the Convention for the Protection of the Marine Environment of the North-East Atlantic (OSPAR) (32 International Legal Materials 1069), which entered into force 25 March 1998.

22. IMO News 3/2006, 4–5. See also IMO resolution A.986(24) "The Importance and Funding of Technical Co-operation as a Means to Support the United Nations Millennium Declaration and the Millennium Development Goals," adopted in 2005.

23. "Voluntary audit scheme adopted at IMO's 24th Assembly." IMO News 1/2006, 18–19.

24. Author's interview with senior staff member, Technical Cooperation Division, IMO headquarters, June 2003.

25. IMO News 3/2006, 14.

26. "Integrated programme delivers widespread benefits." IMO News 3/2003, 18.

27. "Technical co-operation in 2004–2005 'best ever' results." IMO News 3/2006, 14.

28. "The naval contribution to sustainable development in West and Central Africa." IMO News 4/2007, 10.

29. Author's interview with senior staff member, Technical Cooperation Division, IMO headquarters, June 2003.

30. Author's interview with senior staff member, Marine Environment Division, IMO headquarters, June 2003.

31. Author's interview with senior staff member, Marine Environment Division, IMO headquarters, June 2003.

32. These were the International Civil Aviation Organization, the International Telecommunication Union, and the World Meteorological Organization. See IMO Doc. A VII/12 "Amendment Procedures in Conventions for which IMCO is Depositary," cited in Ilg 2001, 31.

33. Author's interview with senior staff member, Marine Environment Division, IMO headquarters, June 2003.

34. Author's interview with senior staff member, Marine Environment Division, IMO headquarters, June 2003.

35. Author's interview with senior staff member, Marine Environment Division, IMO headquarters, June 2003.

36. Author's interview with senior staff member, Marine Environment Division, IMO headquarters, June 2003.

37. See the Web site of the UNEP Regional Seas Programme, http://www.unep.ch/seas/main/partners/hpart.html, 31 July 2004.

38. IMO News 3/2006, 6.

39. "Funding approved for next phase of GloBallast Partnerships." IMO News 3/1997, 10.

40. Author's interview with senior staff member, Marine Environment Division, IMO headquarters, June 2003.

41. Author's interview with senior staff member, Marine Environment Division, IMO headquarters, June 2003.

42. Author's interview with senior staff member, Maritime Safety Division, IMO headquarters, June 2003. See also Tan 2006, 43.

43. Author's interview with senior staff member, Marine Environment Division, IMO headquarters, June 2003.

44. Author's interview with senior staff member, Marine Environment Division, IMO headquarters, June 2003.

45. Author's interview with senior staff member, Marine Environment Division, IMO headquarters, June 2003.

46. "Objectives of the Organization in the 1980s," IMO Doc. A 500; "Work methods and organization of work in committees and their subsidiary bodies," IMO Doc. A 777.

47. "International Maritime Prize awarded to IMO Secretary-General emeritus, Mr. William A. O'Neil." IMO Press Briefing, 16 November 2004. Available at http://www.imo.org/Newsroom/mainframe.asp?topic_id=848&doc_id=4443 (accessed 12 February 2008).

48. "Mr. Efthimios Mitropoulos of Greece is the seventh Secretary-General of the International Maritime Organization, the United Nations agency concerned

with maritime safety and security and the prevention of marine pollution from ships." IMO Web site (2008). Available at http://www.imo.org/Newsroom/mainframe.asp?topic_id=85 (accessed 12 February 2008].

References

Adler, Ellik. 2003. "A World of Neighbours: UNEP's Regional Seas Programme." *Tropical Coasts* (July): 12–18.

Akiwumi, Paul, and Terttu Melvasalo. 1998. "UNEP's Regional Seas Programme: Approach, Experience, and Future." *Marine Policy* 22 (3): 229–234.

Alderton, Tony, and Nik Winchester. 2002. "Globalisation and De-regulation in the Maritime Industry." *Marine Policy* 26:35–42.

Biermann, Frank. 1994. *Internationale Meeresumweltpolitik: Auf dem Weg zu einem Umweltregime für die Meere?* Frankfurt am Main: Peter Lang.

Birnie, Patricia. 1999. "Implementation of IMO Regulations and Oceans Policy Post-UNCLOS and Post-UNCED." In *Current Maritime Issues and the International Maritime Organization*, edited by Myron H. Nordquist and John Norton Moore, 361–390. The Hague: Kluwer Law International.

Breitmeier, Helmut. 1997. "International Organizations and the Creation of Environmental Regimes." In *Global Governance: Drawing Insights from the Environmental Experience*, edited by Oran R. Young, 87–114. Cambridge, MA: MIT Press.

Brubaker, Douglas. 1993. *Marine Pollution and International Law. Principles and Practice.* London: Belhaven Press.

Campe, Sabine. 2003. *Die Wirksamkeit und Funktionsweise von internationalen Organisationen—Die Rolle der Internationalen Seeschifffahrts-Organisation (IMO) in den Verhandlungen zur AFS-Konvention.* Master Thesis. Berlin: Freie Universität Berlin.

Campe, Sabine. 2008a. "International Maritime Organization (IMO)." In *Encyclopedia of Tourism and Recreation in Marine Environments*, edited by Michael Lück, 249–250. Oxford: CABI.

Campe, Sabine. 2008b. "Class Society, or Classification Society." In *Encyclopedia of Tourism and Recreation in Marine Environments*, edited by Michael Lück, 91. Oxford: CABI.

Carlin, Elaine M. 2001. "Oil Pollution from Ships at Sea: The Ability of Nations to Protect a Blue Planet." In *Environmental Regime Effectiveness: Confronting Theory with Evidence*, edited by Edward L. Miles, Arild Underdal, Steinar Andresen, Jørgen Wettestad, Jon Birger Skjærseth, and Elaine M. Carlin, 331–356. Cambridge, MA: MIT Press.

Cicin-Sain, Biliana, and Robert W. Knecht. 1993. "Implications of the Earth Summit for Ocean and Coastal Governance." *Ocean Development and International Law* 24 (4): 323–353.

Cordes, Ruth. 2004. "Is Grey Literature Ever Used? Using Citation Analysis to Measure the Impact of GESAMP, an International Marine Scientific Advisory Body." *The Canadian Journal of Information and Library Science/La Revue Canadienne des Sciences de l'Information et de Bibliothéconomie* 28 (1): 49–69.

de La Fayette, Louise. 2001. "Protection of the Marine Environment in 2000." *Environmental Policy and Law* 31 (3): 140–149.

Dempsey, Paul Stephen. 1984. "Compliance and Enforcement in International Law: Oil Pollution of the Marine Environment by Ocean Vessels." *Northwestern Journal of International Law and Business* 6:459–561.

DeSombre, Elizabeth R. 2006. *Flagging Standards: Globalization and Environmental, Safety, and Labor Regulations.* Cambridge, MA: MIT Press.

Dirks, Jan. 2001. *Decision Making in International Organizations: The IMO.* Grenoble: European Consortium for Political Research.

Fakhry, Aref. 2003. "Capacity-Building in International Marine Environmental Law: Perspectives of Developing Countries." In *International Maritime Environmental Law. Institutions, Implementation, and Innovations*, edited by Andree Kirchner, 93–99. The Hague, New York, London: Kluwer Law International.

Foders, Federico. 1989. "International Organizations and Ocean Use: The Case of Deep-Sea Mining." *Ocean Development and International Law* 20 (5): 519–530.

GESAMP. 2007. "Estimates on Oil Entering the Marine Environment from Sea-Based Activities." *GESAMP Reports and Studies* 75. London: International Maritime Organization.

Goldberg, E.D. 1986. "TBT: An Environmental Dilemma." *Environment* 28:17–44.

Haas, Peter M. 1989. "Do Regimes Matter? Epistemic Communities and Mediterranean Pollution Control." *International Organization* 43 (3): 377–403.

Hartje, Volkmer. 1995. "Ocean Pollution by Tankers: Regulating Operational Discharges as a Partial Policy Success." In *Successful Environmental Policy. A Critical Evaluation of 24 Cases*, edited by Martin Jänicke and Helmut Weidner, 379–393. Berlin: Edition Sigma.

Hinds, Lennox. 2003. "Oceans Governance and the Implementation Gap." *Marine Policy* 27 (4): 349–356.

Höfer, Thomas, and Lutz Metz. 2003. "Effectiveness of International Environmental Protection Treaties on the Sea Transport of Mineral Oil and Proposals for Policy Revision." In *International Marine Environmental Law: Institutions, Implementation, and Innovations*, edited by Andree Kirchner, 101–121. The Hague: Kluwer Law International.

Huber, Michael E., Robert A. Duce, J. Michael Bewers, David Insull, Ljubomir Jeftic, and Stjepan Keckes. 2003. "Recent Development: Priority Problems Facing the Global Marine and Coastal Environment and Recommended Approaches to their Solution." *Ocean and Coastal Management* 46:479–485.

Ilg, Christoph. 2001. *Die Rechtsetzungstätigkeit der International Maritime Organization: Zur Bedeutung der IMO bei der Weiterentwicklung des Meeresumweltrechts.* Doctoral Dissertation, University of Tübingen.

IMO, International Maritime Organization. 2001. *Work Programme and Budget for the Twenty-Second Period, Financial Period 2002–2003,* IMO Doc. A22/Res. 906. London: IMO.

IMO, International Maritime Organization. 2004. *Technical Co-operation Fund: Final Report on the 2002–2003 Programme.* IMO Doc. TC 54/3/1. London: IMO.

IMO, International Maritime Organization. 2008a. *IMO Member States with Year of Joining.* http://www.imo.org/home.asp (accessed 25 February 2008).

IMO, International Maritime Organization. 2008b. *Non-Governmental Organizations which Have Been Granted Consultative Status with IMO.* http://www.imo.org/home.asp (accessed 25 February 2008).

IMO, International Maritime Organization. 2008c. *Inter-Governmental Organizations which Have Concluded Agreements of Cooperation with IMO.* http://www.imo.org/home.asp (accessed 25 February 2008).

Jones, Carol A. 1999. "Compensation for Natural Resource Damages from Oil Spills: A Comparison of U.S. Law and International Conventions." *International Journal of Environment and Pollution* 11 (1): 86–107.

Kim, Inho. 2003. "A Comparison between the International and U.S. Regimes Regulating Oil Pollution Liability and Compensation." *Marine Policy* 27 (3): 265–279.

Kimball, Lee A. 2003. *International Ocean Governance. Using International Law and Organizations to Manage Resources Sustainably.* Gland, Switzerland, and Cambridge, UK: International Union for Conservation of Nature.

Lampe, Wilhelm H. 1983. "The 'New' International Maritime Organization and Its Place in Development of New Law." *Journal of Maritime Law and Commerce* 14:305–314.

Lang, Winfried. 1992. "Diplomacy and International Environmental Law-Making. Some Observations." *Yearbook of International Environmental Law* 3: 117–122.

Lauwaars, Richard H. 1984. "The Interrelationship between United Nations Law and the Law of Other International Organizations." *Michigan Law Review* 82 (5–6): 1604–1619.

Llácer, Francisco J. Montero. 2003. "Open Registers: Past, Present, and Future." *Marine Policy* 27 (6): 513–523.

Lloyd's Register. 2006. *World Fleet Statistics.* London: Fairplay Publishers.

Mason, Michael. 2003. "Civil Liability for Oil Pollution Damage: Examining the Evolving Scope for Environmental Compensation in the International Regime." *Marine Policy* 27 (1): 1–12.

McConnell, Moira L. 2002. "GloBallast Legislative Review. Final Report." *GloBallast* [Global Ballast Water Management Programme] *Monograph Series*, 1. London: International Maritime Organization.

McConnell, Moira L. 2003. "Inter-Agency Collaboration or Inter-Agency Competition: A Challenge for the UN System." In *International Marine Environmental Law. Institutions, Implementation, and Innovations*, edited by Andree Kirchner, 69–99. The Hague: Kluwer Law International.

M'Gonigle, R. Michael, and Mark W. Zacher. 1979. *Pollution, Politics, and International Law*. Berkeley: University of California Press.

Michaelowa, Axel, and Karsten Krauser. 2000. "International Maritime Transport and Climate Policy." *Intereconomics* 35 (3): 127–136.

Mitchell, Ronald B. 1993. "Intentional Oil Pollution of the Oceans." In *Institutions for the Earth. Sources of Effective International Environmental Protection*, edited by Peter M. Haas, Robert O. Keohane, and Marc A. Levy, 183–248. Cambridge, MA: MIT Press.

Mitchell, Ronald B. 1994. *Intentional Oil Pollution at Sea. Environmental Policy and Treaty Compliance*. Cambridge, MA: MIT Press.

Mitchell, Ronald B., Alexei Roginko McConnell, and Ann Barrett. 1999. "International Vessel-Source Oil Pollution." In *The Effectiveness of International Regimes: Causal Connections and Behavorial Mechanisms*, edited by Oran R. Young, 33–90. Cambridge, MA: MIT Press.

Oberthür, Sebastian. 2003. "Institutional Interaction to Address Greenhouse Gas Emissions from International Transport: ICAO, IMO, and the Kyoto Protocol." *Climate Policy* 3:191–205.

Peet, Gerard. 1994. "International Co-operation to Prevent Oil Spills at Sea: Not Quite the Success It Should Be." In *Green Globe Yearbook of International Co-operation on Environment and Development 1994*, edited by Helge Ole Bergesen and Georg Parmann, 41–54. Oxford: Oxford University Press.

Peterson, M.J. 1997. "International Organizations and the Implementation of Environmental Regimes." In *Global Governance: Drawing Insights from the Environmental Experience*, edited by Oran R. Young, 115–152. Cambridge, MA: MIT Press.

Somerville, Robert D. 2004. "Protecting the Marine Environment. The Role and Responsibilities of Class." Paper presented at the 10th International Oil Spill Conference, Brisbane, 23–27 August 2004.

Stewart, Carol. 1996. "The Efficacy of Legislation in Controlling Tributyltin in the Marine Environment." In *Tributyltin: Case Study of an Environmental Containment*, edited by Stephen J. De Mora, 264–295. Cambridge, UK: Cambridge University Press.

Tan, Alan Khee-Jin. 2006. *Vessel-Source Marine Pollution. The Law and Politics of International Regulation*. New York: Cambridge University Press.

World Commission on the Oceans. 1998. *The Oceans of Our Future*. Cambridge, UK: Cambridge University Press.

7

The Secretariat of the United Nations Environment Programme: Tangled Up in Blue

Steffen Bauer

Introduction

The United Nations Environment Programme (UNEP) was the major institutional outcome of the 1972 United Nations Conference on the Human Environment in Stockholm. Since then it has operated as the United Nations' principal body for environmental affairs. Even though the need to reform the organizational architecture of international environmental governance has long been debated (Bauer and Biermann 2005, with further references), the international bureaucracy at the core of this architecture has met with relatively little scholarly attention. However, as "the leading global environmental authority that sets the global environmental agenda, that promotes the coherent implementation of the environmental dimension of sustainable development within the United Nations system and that serves as an authoritative advocate for the global environment" (Nairobi Declaration, see UNEP Governing Council 1997, para. 2), UNEP and its secretariat warrant scrutiny.

The constitution of UNEP is very different from the host of specialized agencies that were established by the United Nations in the immediate aftermath of World War II. Yet since the UNEP secretariat was established in Nairobi, Kenya, in 1973, it has evolved as an eminent player in international environmental governance. In particular, it has played a lead role in the facilitation of a number of groundbreaking multilateral environmental agreements, in the development and promotion of international environmental law, and in raising general awareness for and knowledge about the environmental challenges facing the international community. This chapter traces and explains the influence of the UNEP secretariat in international environmental governance and relates its findings to UNEP's mandate to catalyze and coordinate international environmental politics.

In spite of an abundant literature on international environmental institutions, few studies have systematically focused on the performance of UNEP as an actor in international environmental politics (for a recent exception, see Ivanova 2005). As an organization, UNEP has not been of particular interest to most scholars of international relations: institutionalists were occupied with international regimes instead of organizations such as UNEP, and realists typically did not care much about environmental policy in the first place (D'Anieri 1995; Mitchell 2002). Scholars of international environmental governance, on the other hand, have shown a tendency to take the inadequacy of UNEP as a starting point for discussion rather than as an analytical result (also Tarasofsky 2002; Najam 2005).

Many studies on the organization of international environmental politics, however, address the role that was played by UNEP at least to some extent (e.g., McCormick 1989; Thacher 1992; Imber 1993, 1996; Timoshenko and Berman 1996; Desai 2000; Andresen 2001; Biermann 2002; Kimball 2002; Bauer and Biermann 2004; Elliott 2004, 2005). In particular, the prospects of UNEP are hotly debated among proponents and skeptics of a specialized agency for the environment, such as a United Nations Environment Organization or a World Environment Organization (see the edited volumes by Biermann and Bauer 2005; Chambers and Green 2005; and Rechkemmer 2005). In addition, a number of in-depth studies of specific multilateral environmental agreements have contributed to a better understanding of UNEP's contribution to international environmental governance (e.g., Andresen and Rosendal [in press]; Downie 1995; Mee 2005; Nicholson 1998; Rosendal and Andresen 2004). Yet overall knowledge on the influence of UNEP remains severely limited; hence, its influence is the starting point of this chapter.

This study builds on the analysis of primary and secondary sources as well as a five-week research visit to the secretariat's Nairobi headquarters in the fall of 2003, a brief visit to its New York liaison office in spring 2004, and continuous personal communication with secretariat officers, governmental stakeholders, and academic observers. Complementary information on the secretariat's Paris-based Division on Technology, Industry, and Economics was obtained through a study of project colleague Steffen Behrle (2004); further data on outside perceptions of the performance of UNEP was generated from a specifically designed expert survey on international environmental bureaucracies.[1]

Structure and Activities

The United Nations Environment Programme is legally not an international organization, but a subordinate entity of the United Nations Organization. Its existence is based on resolution 2997 (XVII) of the United Nations General Assembly of 15 December 1972, in which the United Nations decided on distinct institutional and financial arrangements for international environmental cooperation (United Nations General Assembly 1999). The General Assembly also decided to endow the new entity with "a small secretariat" in Nairobi, Kenya, to be governed by a Governing Council with fifty-eight members that represent the five United Nations regions.[2] The UNEP secretariat operates under the auspices of the UN secretary-general, who also appoints its executive director. The latter is required to report back to the General Assembly through the United Nations Economic and Social Council. UNEP was the first major UN body to be headquartered in a developing country.

UNEP's formal background is indicative of two things in the context of this study. First, as a distinct United Nations entity with its own governing body, secretariat, and budget, UNEP qualifies as an international bureaucracy. Second, the political and bureaucratic constraints resulting from its subordinate position within a considerably larger organization—namely, the United Nations—imply a low degree of organizational autonomy from the outset.

Moreover, the UNEP secretariat has to deal with a broad range of international environmental policies, rather than just one specific issue. Though this indicates its central role as the United Nations principal environmental authority, it also entails the prioritization of environmental issues over others. Consequently, it is to be expected that it will perform better on some issues than on others, which should be kept in mind when judging UNEP's overall performance.

UNEP's original organizational structure was based on environmental issues. In 1998–1999, the secretariat was fundamentally reorganized by former executive director Klaus Töpfer. Issue-specific departments were replaced by functional divisions, which concentrate the secretariat's expertise on environmental law, policy development, policy implementation, environmental conventions, regional cooperation, and early warning and assessment. This reform had also been helped by the report of a Task Force on Environment and Human Settlements, which Töpfer had been asked to chair by UN Secretary-General Annan in pursuit of his overall reform agenda "Renewing the United Nations" (Annan 1997).[3]

Adjustments to the 1999 restructuring enacted after 2006 by the new executive director have not affected the basic setup of the secretariat (see UNEP 2007b for details).

The UNEP secretariat employs some four hundred professional officers, mostly at its Nairobi headquarters, but also at regional and other outposted offices and in its Paris-based Division on Technology, Industry, and Economics.[4] Its main budget, the UNEP Environment Fund, has varied between some thirty and just over sixty million USD per year, averaging USD 48.3 million over 1996–2005. This accounts for roughly three hundred of the secretariat's professional staff.[5] The fund's volatility depends on member states' voluntary contributions, which has long been seen as a major problem in international environmental governance.

A comprehensive assessment of UNEP's resource base also needs to take into account a host of trust funds, earmarked contributions, and, notably, projects financed through the Global Environment Facility (GEF) that are also administered by the UNEP secretariat (see Ivanova 2005, 34–36, for greater detail). For instance, the funds the secretariat acquires as an implementing agency of the GEF account for an increasing share of UNEP's total workforce. In 2003 alone they provided for 59 professional and 32 general service posts, that is, 91 out of a total staff of 861 (UNEP 2004, 64).

The Influence of the UNEP Secretariat

Ultimately, the policies enacted through UNEP are supposed to generate positive ecological impacts. Indeed, as former executive director Töpfer acknowledged, "The state of the environment tells us whether our policies and programmes are effective" (2002). It is beyond this study to establish a direct connection between these policies and changes in environmental parameters. Yet this chapter will attribute some developments in international environmental governance to specific activities of the UNEP secretariat.

Cognitive Influence

In particular, the work of the UNEP secretariat has contributed to shaping the cognitive sphere of international environmental governance. Although a distinction between the international organization and its bureaucracy is rarely made in the literature, many studies that hail UNEP's role as a major force in the setting of an agenda on international environmental politics implicitly refer to the secretariat. Indeed, many such references are spread throughout the literature on the evolution of an international environmental agenda since the early 1970s and the emergence of a number of issue-specific treaty regimes.[6]

To name but a few examples, the UNEP secretariat provided the international arena with early consultations and deliberations on ozone layer depletion and on the loss of biological diversity; framed international discourses on chemical pollutants and hazardous wastes; has catalyzed international action on desertification; incited governments to address marine pollution; and, in conjunction with the World Meteorological Organization, successfully initiated the Intergovernmental Panel on Climate Change.

Mostly, these initiatives emanated from the UNEP secretariat's environmental assessments, which draw on a broad network of collaborative research centers, such as the UNEP Global Resources Information Database and the UNEP World Conservation Monitoring Centre. These assessments have become a primary tool for environmental information and are "highly recognized in the field" (Ivanova 2005, 16). They often convey a persuasive sense of urgency that eventually leads governments to action. Accordingly, the effective functioning of the UNEP secretariat as an agenda-setting authority is often highlighted even in studies that view the agency's general performance as inefficient, ineffective, and inadequate (see, for instance, von Moltke 1996; Downie and Levy 2000; and Tarasofsky 2002).

The image of a successful agenda setter was reflected by interviewees within the secretariat. Many emphasized UNEP's achievements in staging groundbreaking international conferences and negotiations, but were reluctant to discuss the effectiveness of policy outcomes.[7] Moreover, 40 percent of respondents to the expert survey for this book considered UNEP as "highly influential" in shaping domestic debates on environmental issues. Though the underlying data do not allow for robust conclusions, they indicate UNEP's capacity to influence global discourses on environmental policy.

Considering the widespread recognition of this influence on the agendas and discourses of international environmental politics, I will not go into further detail here, but turn to its normative and executive influence.

Normative Influence

Normative influence of the UNEP secretariat relates to a variety of processes in international environmental governance that cannot all be comprehensively covered in this chapter. I will focus on two areas:

influence on issue-specific intergovernmental cooperation (notably multilateral environmental agreements) and influence on the general institutional architecture of international environmental governance.

Facilitating Intergovernmental Environmental Negotiations   Substantive normative influence of the UNEP secretariat can be observed in intergovernmental negotiations in particular. The secretariat is the host bureaucracy to numerous environmental treaties for which it provides key secretariat services on both negotiation and implementation. As such, it has facilitated a number of groundbreaking multilateral environmental agreements since the mid-1970s—for example, the 1979 Convention on the Conservation of Migratory Species of Wild Animals, the 1987 Montreal Protocol, the 1992 Convention on Biological Diversity, and the 2001 Stockholm Convention on Persistent Organic Pollutants. UNEP also serves as the "institutional memory" for a range of intergovernmental negotiations—for instance, in the case of its ozone secretariat (Bauer, this volume, chapter 9).

The influential role of international civil servants in such processes has been particularly well documented in the case of the Regional Seas Programme, which is considered one of UNEP's first major successes (Haas 1990; Nicholson 1998; Tolba and Rummel-Bulska 1998).[8] In the negotiation of the initial Mediterranean Action Plan and subsequent 1976 Barcelona Convention, governments were brought to the negotiation table that did not even maintain official diplomatic relations at the time, namely Israel and Egypt. Hence, the collaborative success of the initiative is considerable, even as its behavioral impact may be questioned (Skjærseth 2001, 311). The Regional Seas Programme illustrates the catalytic role and convening power of international civil servants even under highly politicized actor constellations (McCormick 1989, 115; see also Tolba and Rummel-Bulska 1998, 38–45).[9]

These activities of the secretariat to stimulate and sustain intergovernmental negotiations and interagency cooperation through strategically combining legal, scientific, and management approaches have become exemplary for the international institutionalization of environmental policy (see also Boxer 1983). For instance, within a few years, the program to protect the Mediterranean Sea was emulated in a series of international agreements for other regional seas. These now provide for a comprehensive contractual framework that comprises 17 regional treaties and numerous protocols that cover 130 coastal states and approximately 50 international agencies (see UNEP 2002d; Desai 2004, 172n102).[10]

The success of the UNEP Regional Seas Programme gave the secretariat a key position also in international pollution control, supported by UNEP's focus on international legal action on chemical pollutants and hazardous wastes. For instance, UNEP contributed significantly to the negotiation of the 1989 Basel Convention on the Control of Transboundary Movements of Hazardous Wastes and Their Disposal, the 1998 Rotterdam Convention on Prior Informed Consent (see following), the 2001 Stockholm Convention on Persistent Organic Pollutants, and many regional chemical conventions such as the 1991 Bamako Convention on the transboundary movement of hazardous wastes within Africa (also Desai 2004, 176–177 and nn. 119–121; Andresen and Rosendal [in press], with further references). Consequently, most multilateral environmental agreements that relate to hazardous substances are now overseen by the UNEP secretariat. Compared to other environmental issues, this led to relatively high coherence in international law and policy, which is manifested through two "essential building blocks"—namely, the Rotterdam and Stockholm conventions (von Moltke 2005).

The Rotterdam Convention is a good illustration of the normative influence of the UNEP secretariat in intergovernmental environmental negotiations. Guiding a coalition of developing countries and nongovernmental organizations, the UNEP secretariat emerged as a key driver to alter the contractual environment of international trade in pesticides when it forged the consensus for the establishment of a prior informed consent procedure in spite of strong opposition from pesticide-producing countries such as Germany, Great Britain, and the United States (Paarlberg 1993; Victor 1998). Notably, it had developed the Cairo and London guidelines for the exchange of information on chemicals in international trade, which proved groundbreaking for the institutionalization of regulation regarding the production, trade, and consumption of pesticides.[11] In parallel, it garnered the eventual support of the UN Food and Agricultural Organization (FAO), with which it now jointly administers the convention. Moreover, the UNEP secretariat's success in facilitating the Rotterdam Convention has been set forth when negotiators of the Stockholm Convention deliberately drew from the proceedings of the Rotterdam Convention (IISD 2005b, 12). Since then, the position of the UNEP secretariat at the hub of the hazardous substances cluster has been strengthened by the invitation of parties to propose administrative changes to enhance synergies between the Basel, Stockholm, and Rotterdam conventions (IISD 2005c, 7).

Shaping International Environmental Governance   A second main area of normative influence is the protracted reform debate in international environmental governance. Here, the UNEP secretariat is a stakeholder in its own right, and it understands how to bring its views into the discussion. In the wake of the Malmö Declaration of the Global Ministerial Environment Forum (2000), the reform debate has intensified and been structured by what is now known as the "Cartagena Process." This term refers to the open-ended deliberations of governments on international environmental governance that are basically organized by the UNEP secretariat. A report by the executive director has been endorsed by a decision of the UNEP Governing Council in Cartagena, Colombia, at its seventh special session (see IISD 2002 for details; UNEP 2001a). The process warrants that the reform debate continues within the confines of UNEP and is thus organized first and foremost through the UNEP secretariat.

Major issues under the Cartagena process include strengthening of UNEP's role, authority, and financial basis; coordination and coherence between multilateral environmental agreements; capacity building, technology transfer, and country-level coordination; strengthening UNEP's scientific basis; and cooperation and coherence within the United Nations system.

Within the debate on strengthening UNEP's role, the question of universal membership (as opposed to the exclusive fifty-eight-member Governing Council) again illustrates how the UNEP secretariat influences the institutions and procedures of international environmental governance. The issue has been on the agenda of many intergovernmental sessions and was tabled for the UNEP Governing Council after governments failed to address it at the World Summit on Sustainable Development (UNEP 2002b). Universal membership was debated both at the council's twenty-second session and at its eighth Special Session at Jeju, and adjourned for further consideration by the UN secretary-general and member states. It remains controversial (UNEP 2007a). Opponents of universal membership fear a precedent for turning UNEP into a specialized agency, and proponents of universal membership strive to at least keep the issue on the agenda (see, for instance, IISD 2004a, 2005a).

Against this background, the UNEP secretariat has arranged for de facto universal membership already through establishing the Global Ministerial Environment Forum. Upon the initiative of then–executive director Töpfer in 1999, it is by now common practice to convene the Global Ministerial Environment Forum and recurrent "special sessions" of the Governing Council in the intervals between the biennial regular sessions of the Governing Council. Moreover, the Global Ministerial Environment Forum is now always invited to convene back to back with regular council sessions, which considerably enhances their political clout. Though the Governing Council with its restricted membership continues to be de jure the decision-making body of UNEP, the secretariat has successfully institutionalized a complementary forum that cannot be ignored by the Governing Council.[12]

Similarly, the secretariat has addressed the strengthening of its financial basis by informally introducing a "voluntary indicative scale of contributions" to appreciate the relative commitment of individual governments. Although this is hardly a panacea for UNEP's financial problems, it has helped frame budgetary discussions and broadened the donor base and thus the legitimacy of the Environment Fund (also Ivanova 2005, 36).[13]

Executive Influence

UNEP has no operative mandate and was never meant to be an implementing agency "on the ground." Its mandate to build national capacities in environmental law has long been the sole exception. This situation has been changed to some extent by the secretariat's expanding GEF portfolio and by the priority that the Governing Council gives to the Bali Strategic Plan on Technology Support and Capacity Building, which expanded UNEP's mandate (IISD 2004b, 2005a). Even in earlier years, the UNEP secretariat was involved in activities at national and local levels, many of which entail explicit capacity-building components (see UNEP 2002a for an overview). Indeed, the secretariat has deliberately increased its respective efforts over the years.[14] Institutionally, this is reflected in a strengthened Division for Environmental Policy Implementation that claims responsibility "for the implementation of environmental policy ... at global, regional, *and national* levels."[15] Likewise, increasing governmental requests force the UNEP secretariat to pursue more capacity-building projects that may stretch its own capacities (Ivanova 2005, 27–28). However, the secretariat does not seem to oppose this overload. Fuelled by an intrinsic desire to matter "in the field," it even encourages the incremental shift toward an operational mandate. One senior officer insisted that it would be "completely stupid" to strictly adhere to UNEP's regional and global mandate.[16]

In the following, I illustrate, first, how the UNEP secretariat engages at national and local levels. Secondly, I highlight its capacity-building role in environmental law.

Interagency Cooperation and Partnership Initiatives   In the absence of its own capacities to engage in policy implementation at domestic levels, the UNEP secretariat is generally bound to cooperate with UN agencies that have both the mandate and the facilities to do so. Hence, in spite of typical frustrations with partner agencies that are eager to distinguish their brand and anxious to protect their turf, the UNEP secretariat has often sought to maximize its output through interagency cooperation within the United Nations (Bauer and Biermann 2004). Joint programs became a viable option to circumvent the formal restrictions of UNEP's nonoperational mandate.[17]

The joint Sustainable Cities Programme with UN-HABITAT, the United Nations program for human settlements, is one example.[18] First established in 1990, the Sustainable Cities Programme is now running in its second decade, albeit with discontinuous support from secretariat and donor agencies. The program builds local capacities for environmental governance, mainly through the provision and periodic refinement of a set of Environmental Planning and Management tools that are replicated through a network of developing cities in some thirty countries around the world. Though the effective application of the program's Environmental Planning and Management approach varies considerably across participating countries (see, e.g., United Nations Centre for Human Settlements and Danish International Development Agency 2000), it provides the UNEP secretariat with valuable results to show to national delegates and local stakeholders, and it proves its general ability to engage in local activities.

In a similar vein, the UNEP secretariat supports capacity building as a lead partner and organizational platform for a number of public-private partnerships that have been launched in the wake of the 2002 World Summit on Sustainable Development. The outcome of these partnerships is not yet clear, and will be diverse in any case (Andonova and Levy 2003; Ivanova 2003; Biermann et al. 2007). Early assessments of energy-related partnerships indicate, however, that an active role of the UNEP secretariat is commonly welcomed by private partners who have a high demand for the services that UNEP provides (Behrle 2004). Again, the secretariat's aspiration to engage in public-private partnerships such as the Partnership for Clean Fuel and Vehicles indicates the push toward on-the-ground policy implementation.

Moreover, the UNEP secretariat contributes to national capacity building in environmental monitoring and assessment, at least indirectly. The

Division of Early Warning and Assessment's collaborative approaches to aggregate environmental data from around the world have led to the diffusion of environmental reporting methods that feed into UNEP's periodical Global Environmental Outlook.[19] Since the publication of the first report in 1997, many regional environmental forums and national governments have applied its methodology to produce or improve their own environmental assessments. Even in countries where no reporting was carried out, it still catalyzed national reports on the state of the environment (Ivanova 2005, 16).

Building Legal Capacities UNEP's effectiveness in promoting and advancing international environmental law goes hand in hand with efforts to build legal capacities in developing countries. This is largely achieved through consecutive Programmes for the Development and Periodic Review of Environmental Law (commonly referred to as the Montevideo Programme) and the UNEP-led Partnership for the Development of Environmental Law and Institutions in Africa. Both programs have been developed and are implemented through the secretariat's Law Branch, which thus administers numerous capacity-building projects to train university lecturers and civil servants or to advise parliaments and policy makers. The latter was prominently the case with the comprehensive Environmental Management and Coordination Act that was passed by the legislature in the UNEP's host country Kenya in 1999. Likewise, the secretariat's legal experts have contributed to the development of substantive environmental laws in Mozambique (fifteen laws and regulations), Uganda (thirteen), Burkina Faso (twelve), Malawi (nine), Kenya (eight), Tanzania (seven), and São Tomé and Príncipe (five) under the Partnership for the Development of Environmental Law and Institutions in Africa between 1994 and 2000 (UNEP 2003, 12–26).

The Montevideo Programme, which is now in its third ten-year cycle since 1982, generates the major thrust for UNEP's domestic activities and has evolved into the secretariat's main tool to catalyze the creation of international environmental law (Loibl 2001, 63).[20] Moreover, it was crucial in the evolution of the secretariat's own legal capacity from initial ad hoc activities to systematic worldwide promotion of "co-ordinated and coherent development of environmental law" (Loibl 2001, 61).

In recent years, the UNEP secretariat has expanded its promotion of international environmental law by activities that specifically address national judiciaries. The reasoning of the secretariat's senior legal experts is that judges represent the single most powerful stakeholders for the actual application of environmental laws and regulations. Often, progressive legislation is formally in place, but is not applied with the rigor required to make it effective. Though parliaments have limited reach in bringing legislation to bear on the ground, the UNEP secretariat's legal experts observed that people commonly adhere to the authority of judges even where governmental agencies are reluctant to enforce environmental law.[21]

Yet the initiative to actively involve national judiciaries was not greeted with enthusiasm by governments when the UNEP secretariat convened a Global Judges Symposium in the immediate runup to the World Summit on Sustainable Development in 2002, which eventually adopted the Johannesburg Principles (UNEP 2002c). Although governments criticized the secretariat for overstretching its competencies, they could hardly ignore the outcomes of the symposium. The secretariat, to its defense, referred to its Montevideo mandate, even though one senior legal officer admitted "no government, not even judges themselves would dare think of involving judges in international environmental governance."[22] While governments may argue that they, and not judges, are UNEP's stakeholders, Executive Director Töpfer reiterated that the secretariat would continue to support judges in their capacity to transform the "paper tigers" of international environmental law into effective legal tools.[23]

Explaining the Influence

Problem Structure

Two major aspects define the problem structure in which UNEP operates: first, the need to square environmental concerns and development priorities in a North–South context, and second, the multiplicity of issues under UNEP's purview. The environment-development context placed the UNEP secretariat from the outset in a challenging international environment. The North–South divide has burdened the work of many United Nations agencies created in a post-colonial international system,[24] and UNEP is no exception. From the 1972 United Nations Conference on the Human Environment onwards, Indira Gandhi's widely quoted statement at this conference that poverty is the biggest polluter has been hovering over UNEP ever since. Moreover, the environment has been considered traditionally an issue of low politics in the North, too. Considering these adverse conditions, the UNEP secretariat is doing remarkably well.

The divergent priorities of North and South are well known and are reiterated at every meeting of the UNEP Governing Council. On the one hand, developing countries emphasize their right to development and the North's responsibility for global pollution. Many developing countries are still rather wary of environmental protection, which some view as a potential threat to economic development. Developed countries, on the other hand, argue that the right to development does not entail a right to pollute and that developing countries must not repeat rich countries' mistakes in a view of a deteriorating world environment and the many ecological interdependencies that were not understood until long after the industrial revolution. Moreover, they emphasize that environmental protection is not at odds with economic development and that it will in fact benefit developing countries by improving the livelihoods of the poor.

This notion is captured in the slogan of "environment for development," which the secretariat adopted to reflect the balance that it seeks to maintain. While the protection of the world environment is its very raison d'être, the cooperation of developing countries is pivotal both for international environmental governance to be effective and for the survival of UNEP as a meaningful international bureaucracy. Developed countries, too, seek the cooperation of developing countries to address environmental problems that cannot be tackled within their jurisdiction, but they would hardly go out of their way to preserve UNEP if it were merely pursuing a Southern agenda. In other words, the problem structure requires the UNEP secretariat to make international environmental governance palatable to developing countries in a manner that also caters to the expectations of the industrialized world.

This daunting balancing act is facilitated by a second main characteristic of UNEP's problem structure, that is, its variety. Pollution and protection of the world environment at global and regional levels has many facets that vary considerably regarding both costs and saliency.[25] Yet all are covered by the general mandate of UNEP. The secretariat can thus pick and choose from a broad array of environmental issues—at least to the extent that resulting policies can be convincingly linked to its mandate vis-à-vis the Governing Council. Hence, issues tabled by the secretariat can simply be dropped as premature, as in the case of "Asian Brown Cloud."[26] Conversely, they can be prioritized and exploited to full public relations potential, if they trigger the right buttons with both developed and developing countries, such as the Partnership for Clean Fuels and Vehicles or the Great Apes Survival Project.

On balance, the problem structure of international environmental governance thus restrains the secretariat's room for maneuver and forces it to act cautiously. At the same time, it creates opportunities to set agendas and priorities in accordance with its own preferences and, ideally, comparative advantages, which may then be exploited to generate success stories.

Polity

Although not the only program under the auspices of the United Nations secretariat, UNEP's position within the UN system is rather unique. On the one hand, it is designed as the United Nations' preeminent agency for all of its environmental policy, whereas for comparison the United Nations Development Programme is surrounded by a host of other agencies with closely related development mandates. On the other hand, UNEP is but a small entity with limited formal competences and scant resources.

Competences   Although the UNEP Governing Council has embraced Agenda 21, the secretariat is still grappling with its formal institutional repercussions. In hindsight, it was ill-prepared for the challenges imposed on its lead role in international environmental governance, notably through the creation of the Commission on Sustainable Development and the Global Environment Facility, and the expansion of activities into UNEP's traditional turf by developing agencies like the United Nations Development Programme and the World Bank, which pursue their own reading of sustainable development (for illustrations, see the contributions in Werksman 1996; also Brack and Hyvarinen 2002, in the context of the World Summit on Sustainable Development). Moreover, two major policy areas were cut off from UNEP's traditional domain through the adoption of the UN climate convention and later the UN convention to combat desertification, both of which are administered by independent United Nations secretariats (Busch, this volume, chapter 10; Bauer, this volume, chapter 12). Hence the emergence of new players on an already overcrowded field amounted to a de facto depreciation of the UNEP secretariat, even as governments regularly affirm UNEP's pivotal position in international environmental governance.

Conversely, the work of UNEP also relates to the implementation of the Millennium Development Goals and the Johannesburg Plan of Implementation, bringing with it opportunities for the UNEP secretariat. As a consequence, also UNEP is increasingly seen as interfering with the work of UN agencies that deal with socioeconomic development, education, and health. UNEP policies pertaining to the Millennium Development Goals and the Johannesburg Plan are thus wind in the sails of those who wish to see the UNEP secretariat moving into on-the-ground implementation, and who have been particularly encouraged by the Bali Strategic Plan.

In sum, sailing under the flag of sustainable development may have proven to be more useful for developing agencies like UNDP to acquire environmental projects, than the other way around. It is telling, for example, that Craig Murphy's comprehensive history of the UNDP discusses the program's environmental activities under the heading "new sources of funding" (Murphy 2006, 268; see also Bauer and Biermann 2004).

Resources   In any case, on-the-ground activities are severely constrained by the secretariat's budgetary realities. This is unsurprising inasmuch as UNEP is not a funding agency. Still, the secretariat could achieve much more with a budget that was commensurate to the expanding scope of its two-year program of work (see, among others, Imber 1996; Andresen 2001; Wapner 2003; Andresen and Rosendal [in press]). Indeed, the resources of UNEP do not match the budgets of many environmental ministries or even some of the major environmental nongovernmental organizations (Biermann 2005). Though UNEP's financial clout has benefited from tapping complementary resources beyond the Environment Fund, this hardly translates into greater operational leeway. Quite the opposite: the transaction costs imposed by the administration of a multitude of small funds, many of which need to be accounted for bilaterally vis-à-vis donor countries, are stretching thin administrative capacities and curtailing the secretariat's ability to plan strategically ahead.

Subsequently, the increasing proportion of extra-budgetary activities has given rise to criticism both inside and outside the secretariat. For one thing, the deployment of bilaterally acquired earmarked contributions is, by definition, restricted to specific policies and thus leaves the secretariat with little latitude in terms of implementation.[27] Moreover, there is concern that the handling of extra-budgetary resources promotes mission creep and takes secretariat attention from its regular work program as determined by the Governing Council.

Embeddedness   Caught in the institutional tangle that emanates from the United Nations' pursuit of sustainable development, the UNEP secretariat is notoriously unlikely to fulfill its coordinative mandate in international environmental politics (see Elliott 2005 for a comprehensive assessment of attempts to coordinate environmental policies within the UN). In a highly fragmented policy arena in which a range of competitive agencies claim their stakes in international environmental governance, UNEP is not in a position appropriate to this task. The institutional constraints thus facing the UNEP secretariat have been further exacerbated by a profound discursive change in the polity in which it is embedded. In particular, the international paradigm shift toward the concept of sustainable development—as manifested by the 1987 World Commission on Environment and Development ("Brundtland Commission"), the 1992 United Nations Conference on Environment and Development (UNCED), and the 2002 World Summit on Sustainable Development—has blurred the delineation of competences between agencies dealing with environmental and development affairs (Bruyninckx 2005; also Elliott 2005; Henry 1996; Imber 1993). Although a mainstreaming of environmental and development objectives is not contested in principle, it hardly facilitates the coordination of international environmental governance—in particular since development concerns have gradually taken precedence in the sustainable development discourse.

People and Procedures

Organizational Expertise   Authoritative in-house expertise on the state of the world environment and international environmental law is probably the strongest source of the political influence of the UNEP secretariat. Based on comprehensive environmental assessments, it has in many cases identified environmental risks and projected ecological trends with a persuasive sense of urgency upon which governments reacted.

This is typically achieved either through its own capacity for assessment and early warning or by convening and facilitating expert networks. In some cases, the secretariat can also be credited for generating strategic knowledge and expertise in a manner that created the impetus to institutionalize epistemic communities, as has most prominently worked in the case of the Intergovernmental Panel on Climate Change, but also relates to less spectacular examples. The systematic backup of policy making by independent expertise, which has been championed by the UNEP secretariat since its inception, has now become a standard in international environmental politics as elaborate procedural components for environmental assessment and monitoring are routinely included in virtually all multilateral environmental agreements. Indeed, the capacity of the UNEP secretariat to aggregate, process, and distribute data on the state of the world environment may well reflect the biggest area of congruence between its original 1972 mandate and its actual performance.

UNEP is by no means the only global player in terms of environmental expertise. Yet it has established itself as the authoritative environmental voice at the intergovernmental level. As such, it is well interlinked with nongovernmental organizations and research institutions and maintains a network with public experts at domestic levels. Although specific expertise on complex ecological processes will naturally be stronger in university departments and major research institutions, the UNEP secretariat is the hub of global environmental information.[28]

The Global Environment Outlook series has become not only UNEP's public information flagship, but also a standard reference for domestic policy makers and journalists working on the environment. It quickly evolved into the environmentalists' match to the World Bank's World Development Report and the Human Development Report of the United Nations Development Programme.[29] Accordingly, the UNEP secretariat is also a major contributor to the reports of the World Resources Institute and was assigned as the lead agency for the coordination and compilation of the United Nations' Millennium Ecosystem Assessment.

The respective expertise is concentrated in the secretariat's Division of Early Warning and Assessment. The scientific capacity of the division does not extend to genuine research, but it occasionally commissions external experts to provide data on its behalf (Behrle 2004).[30] Moreover, the UNEP secretariat invites input from eminent experts to engage in substantive consultations. For instance, Executive Director Töpfer highlighted the contributions of Nobel laureates Wole Soyinka and Rigoberta Menchú to identify interlinkages between biological diversity and cultural diversity—an issue that has subsequently spawned controversial debates between the secretariat and parties.[31] Inside the secretariat, however, such initiatives were appreciated, because "sometimes you need new ideas, you need new thinking, you need someone to come in and thinking out of the box."[32]

In addition to environmental expertise, the UNEP secretariat has also become the leading intergovernmental authority on international environmental law. This is another key source for influence, because the demand for legal expertise and capacity building in environmental law continues to be high and has traditionally been one of the major priorities in the secretariat's program of work (Sand 1985; Birnie and Boyle 2002; Desai 2004). Though the international system lacks robust means to enforce international law, formal legal arrangements as well as informal norms and regulations are suitable means to affect state behavior, not least in the environmental field (see, for instance, Chayes, Handler Chayes, and Mitchell 1998; Abbott and Snidal 2000). Consequently, multilateral treaties and soft law agreements have been a key area of the work of the UNEP secretariat and continue to be seen as "one of the central mechanisms by which international cooperation can be fostered" (Töpfer 1998, 11; see also Tolba and Rummel-Bulska 1998, 11–24).

The secretariat's legal expertise is concentrated in a Law Branch that is responsible for, among other things, the implementation of the Montevideo Programme for the Development and Periodic Review of Environmental Law. In a unique manner, the mandate on which the Montevideo Programme is based has been given to the secretariat not from the UNEP Governing Council but by the United Nations General Assembly during its thirtieth session.[33] With regard to the success of the Montevideo Programme, two factors have been crucial. First, the legal experts in the UNEP secretariat have been credited for steering a thorough preparation process that led to the establishment of the program in the first place. Secondly, the untypical ten-year cycles of the program allow for long-term strategies that are impossible for policies and projects designed to match the two-year program of work.[34]

In sum, the combination of substantive expertise in environmental assessment and international law with the technocratic expertise of the UNEP secretariat as the institutional memory of international environmental cooperation is a major source for the bureaucracy's capacity to influence international negotiations, despite its limited financial means and formal autonomy. This capacity is supported by a professional staff that is committed to the environmental cause and well trained.

Organizational Leadership   Political leadership of the UNEP secretariat is another important factor in explaining its considerable influence on international environmental cooperation. It has made a difference in a number of intricate negotiations and often in a fashion that has made the "personality culture" surrounding its leadership a notorious feature of the organization as such (Mee 2005, 235). Oran Young (1991) employed the example of former executive director Mostafa Tolba's crucial role in international ozone negotiations to develop a concept of entrepreneurial leadership for his tripartite typology of political leadership in institutional bargaining. Although this example has been particularly prominent (Bauer, this volume, chapter 9), similar importance has been attributed to the leadership of senior UNEP officers in a number of international environmental negotiations, including the Mediterranean Action Plan; the Convention on Biological Diversity; the development of the prior informed consent procedure in the trade with pesticides, which paved the way for the Rotterdam Convention; and the Stockholm Convention on persistent organic pollutants. Hence, UNEP's impressive record in advancing the contractual environment of international environmental politics is closely linked to the skillful and authoritative political leadership of the UNEP secretariat.

To this end, it was pivotal that executive directors like Tolba and Töpfer knew how to play their cards in a problem structure of principled North–South confrontation. As an Egyptian, Tolba may have had a natural credit with developing countries, but he also appealed to the developed world by emphasizing his background in science while at the same time avoiding co-optation by industrial interests. Instead, he managed "to frame issues in ways that foster integrative bargaining and to put together deals that would otherwise elude participants" (Young 1991, 293); he showed long-term "strategic thinking" as well as a "bullying style in negotiation" (Mee 2005, 235).

Töpfer, on the other hand, drew personal authority from his political career in the North. As former German minister of the environment, he had emerged as a protagonist of the 1992 Rio Summit and as a chair of the Commission on Sustainable Development thereafter. Once at the helm of the UNEP secretariat, he knew to credibly emphasize the link between environment for development "better than anyone during his two terms in office" (Steiner 2007, 3). During his tenure, he thus acquired staunch support among developing countries, particularly in Africa, while maintaining his links with developed countries. By way of his energetic and distinctly political leadership style, he was pivotal in regaining government's confidence in UNEP and in strengthening the position of the UNEP secretariat in international environmental governance. Notably in comparison to the mid-1990s, Töpfer has been successfully "marking out his territory among the competitive hounds in the UN system" (Sandbrook 1999, 174; see also Mee 2005).

Different from the tenures of Tolba and Töpfer, a major crisis of UNEP coincided with the comparatively weak leadership of Elizabeth Dowdeswell from Canada, who served as executive director from 1993–1997. In spite of the generally positive momentum for international environmental policy in the aftermath of the Rio Summit, developed countries voiced an increasing discontent with the performance of the UNEP secretariat during the tenure of Dowdeswell. The crisis culminated when major donors—the United States and Japan—froze their contributions to the Environment Fund. Richard Sandbrook's assessment appears harsh—that Dowdeswell "was not ready for the rough and tough UN game. . . . From all accounts her political and management skills could not match the entrenched UN ways of doing business and associated numerous vested interests" (Sandbrook 1999, 172). However, it reverberates with more diplomatic comments of long-serving UNEP officers.[35]

The history of the UNEP secretariat thus shows that strong organizational leadership enables a maximization of the influence that can be generated from even modest resources endowed to an international bureaucracy.

Organizational Structure   Contrasting the background of strong leadership vis-à-vis its organizational environment, a look inside the UNEP secretariat yields mixed results. Though professional staff unanimously praised Töpfer's achievement to have revitalized UNEP as a global agency, they also point to the expenses in terms of internal organization and management. In spite of the secretariat's reasonably flat hierarchy, concerns have been voiced regarding a lack of accessibility at executive levels, the prevalence of a top-down management approach, and internal politicking.

A functional organizational chart of the UNEP secretariat in 1998–2006 shows eight parallel substantive divisions, subordinate only to the offices of the executive director and deputy executive director. A senior management group—comprised of the executive director, the deputy executive director, and the division directors—meets regularly to coordinate and harmonize the work within the secretariat. In the words of a division director, this exclusive group serves as "a management tool for the [executive director] to manage the corporate interest of the organization [and] to improve the corporate understanding of activities we are having."[36] A rather exclusive body, the group represents top-down decision making within the secretariat, which is also found to be prevalent "in all divisions and at most levels" in a recent study by Andresen and Rosendal (in press).[37] Moreover, in spite of the formally flat hierarchy, the divisions do not necessarily operate at the same level, which fosters internal power games and "empire building."

Notably, the Division of Technology, Industry, and Economics—physically detached from headquarters at the UNEP's Paris premises—enjoys a special de facto status and has thus developed an organizational culture that is markedly different from the one at headquarters (Behrle 2004). At headquarters, the Division of Policy Development and Law has acquired *primus inter pares* status, as interviewees both inside and outside this division have highlighted its proximity to the Office of the Executive Director.[38] Environmental law has traditionally been a flagship of UNEP and policy development is characterized as "the backyard of the [Executive Director]."[39] Different again, the division that coordinates UNEP's activities vis-à-vis the Global Environment Facility operates independently from other divisions and gets internal clout from the considerable resources under its portfolio.

These internal hierarchies are prone to nourish jealousy and conflicts of interest between divisions as well as between senior management and the rank and file (also Sandbrook 1999; Downie and Levy 2000; Andresen and Rosendal [in press]). Still, most interviewees have emphasized that their working environment is generally cooperative and rarely affected by turf battles.

The heart of the problem thus rather seems to be that internal tensions are not coherently addressed by the executive level. At least partially, this can be explained by the notorious traveling schedule of Executive Director Töpfer, who had been often absent, or when in Nairobi, also burdened with oversight of the United Nations Offices at Nairobi which he served as director general. (After Töpfer's departure, the administration of the United Nations Offices at Nairobi was transferred to the executive director of UN-HABITAT.) One program officer thus argued that many of the internal problems could be easily "alleviated if [Executive-Director Töpfer] would be here more often and if he would act firmer on turf-battles between divisions, but he's hardly ever in Nairobi and if he's around he's too busy to care for such issues. I am convinced . . . he knows how to keep a large administration in order, but this potential is not used when you're hardly around."[40]

The adverse impacts of poor internal management were felt by some to be exacerbated by "staggering red tape" in internal communication.[41] This negative perception was not shared by all program officers, however, and some even consider the UNEP bureaucracy "a well-oiled machinery" that would not be less efficient than most governmental bureaucracies at domestic levels.[42] In any case, core bureaucratic functions such as staff and budget matters have even been delegated to the United Nations Offices at Nairobi to lighten the administrative burden of the UNEP secretariat.[43] Although this is not always perceived as an improvement to the status quo ante (see for instance Andresen and Rosendal [in press]), it does release professional staff from nonsubstantive duties.[44]

On balance, the organizational structure of the UNEP secretariat certainly provides its new executive director, Achim Steiner, with room for improvement. He has duly proclaimed "not least, more effective and efficient management" to be one of four priority themes for his first term in office (Steiner 2007, 3). Yet, even as he takes office, the secretariat does not appear to be inefficient to the extent that bureaucratic procedures would severely inhibit its capacity to have the influence that stems from the factors discussed previously.

Conclusion

In many ways, the secretariat of UNEP is the hub of international environmental governance. At the very least, it has the clear mandate to represent the "environmental pillar" of the UN system. Nonetheless, it is merely a small, underfunded, and formally low-ranking player within this system, and it has always struggled to coordinate the increasingly fragmented policy arena in which a plethora of agencies and institutions with less comprehensive, but nonetheless environmental mandates have mushroomed over the past decades, in particular since the environmental agenda has been transformed into the agenda of sustainable development. Still, the influence of the UNEP secretariat as a key actor of international environmental governance can be seen and felt in many ways: most notably in the cognitive and normative spheres of intergovernmental politics, but also in the executive realm of on-the-ground policy implementation.

In terms of cognitive influence, the UNEP secretariat draws from its organizational expertise and the ability to zoom in on specific issues comprised in its broad general mandate. Brokering of environmental knowledge for policy makers has been and continues to be one of its staunchest assets. It bears the potential to become even more useful, if the corresponding capacities of the secretariat and its network of partners are systematically enhanced. Although governments have repeatedly expressed the imperative need to do so, they have yet to walk the talk.

In terms of normative influence, UNEP's achievements may be less spectacular than the groundbreaking results that could be obtained at the outset of international environmental politics in the 1970s and 1980s. Yet as multilateral environmental negotiations continue to become ever more specific and complex, the UNEP secretariat continues not only to provide the vital services and organizational expertise to keep these processes going, but also to further them through dynamic organizational leadership.

In terms of executive influence, the UNEP secretariat faces considerable restrictions through both its problem structure and its polity. Nonetheless, organizational leadership and incremental changes in its formal competences allowed for notable influence as the secretariat occasionally circumvented its nonoperative mandate and capitalized on its mandate to build domestic capacities in international law. Though it has still little to show in comparison to bigger implementing agencies with operational mandates and much larger funds, capacity building and subsequent executive influence may prove a dynamic area for organizational change in the future. This has long been a more or less secret ambition inside the secretariat, and governments are now seen to incrementally expand UNEP's agenda accordingly.

In sum, it is largely the people and procedures of the UNEP secretariat that allow for its remarkable influence in spite of the severe constraints entailed by its problem structure and polity. Strong organizational leadership and reformed organizational structures have enabled UNEP to recuperate from the challenges it faced in the mid 1990s. Even so, it remains tangled up amid a motley crew of competitive UN agencies that will not be coordinated by the UNEP secretariat. The lack of coordination, coherence, and consistency in international environmental governance thus continues to inhibit a more effective performance. There is hence a larger picture that reflects a consistent unwillingness of governments to back the United Nations' key environmental bureaucracy with adequate means and substantive political decisions rather than with symbolic actions that, at the end of the day, signify only for UNEP to be off limits.

It remains to be seen whether the recent changes at the helm of both the United Nations and the UNEP secretariat, a revived Environmental Management Group, or renewed calls for a United Nations Environment Organization will yield greater penetration in the context of the United Nations' overall effort to enhance system-wide coherence in the areas of development, humanitarian assistance, and the environment (UN 2006, see also UN Doc. A/61/583). The history of international environmental governance does not bode well, even as the ostensible momentum for "a climate of change" (UNEP 2007b) supports cautious optimism.

Acknowledgments

I am indebted to my interviewees at the UNEP offices in Nairobi and New York and at the United Nations Offices in Nairobi. I am particularly grateful to Halifa Drammeh, who facilitated my research stay at the UNEP headquarters. I am also indebted to the respondents of the MANUS expert survey and thank the MANUS project team for valuable comments. Earlier versions of this study have been presented at the European conferences on the human dimensions of global environmental change in Potsdam (2005) and in Amsterdam (2007), and at the 2007 annual meeting of the Academic Council on the United Nations System in New York.

Notes

1. Of 35 respondents that referred to UNEP, 63 percent were from developed countries; 43 percent represented nongovernmental organizations; 17 percent science or research institutions; and 14 percent public agencies (roughly one-fifth of respondents did not specify a country or a stakeholder category).

2. Accordingly, 16 council members are from Africa, 13 from Asia, 10 from Latin America and the Caribbean, 6 from Eastern Europe and 13 from the group of "Western Europe and Others."

3. The 1998 report of the Task Force was eventually adopted by the UN General Assembly as Report of the Secretary General on Environment and Human Settlements on 28 July 1999 (UN Doc. A/RES/53/242 of 10 August 1999).

4. Specifically, 27 professional and 16 general service posts for UNEP's Nairobi headquarters are financed through the United Nations core budget. If these are included, UNEP's total payroll accounted for 456 professional and 405 general posts in 2003 (UNEP 2004) compared to 337 professional and 339 general posts in 1999 (UNEP 2000). The increase in staff is largely explained by UNEP's increasing role as an implementing agency of the GEF (see following).

5. The Environment Fund reached an average of USD 55 million during the second term of Executive Director Töpfer (2002–2005), after USD 43.2 million in his first term (1998–2001); figures aggregated from the secretariat's annual reports.

6. See, among others, McCormick 1989; Thacher 1992; Downie 1995; Imber 1996; Tolba and Rummel-Bulska 1998; Chasek 2001; Najam 2005; Elliott 2004, 2005; Ivanova 2005; and Mee 2005.

7. Author's interviews at UNEP headquarters, Nairobi, September and October 2003.

8. See Mee 2005, 241–243, for a survey of problems typically encountered under the Regional Seas Programme.

9. Also author's interview, UNEP headquarters, Nairobi, 24 September 2003.

10. Also author's interviews at UNEP headquarters, Nairobi, 17 and 24 September 2003.

11. For instance, the Cairo and London guidelines for exchange of information on chemicals in international trade were originally developed within the UNEP secretariat. Author's interview, UNEP headquarters, Nairobi, 29 September 2003.

12. This interpretation has been confirmed in senior level interviews at UNEP headquarters, Nairobi, September and October 2003.

13. Author's interviews at the United Nations Offices at Nairobi and UNEP headquarters, Nairobi, 25 September and 7 October 2003, and interview with the executive director, Nairobi, 6 October 2003.

14. Author's interview, UNEP headquarters, Nairobi, 9 October 2003.

15. Author's emphasis; see http://www.unep.org/DEPI/; last visited 8 March 2007.

16. Author's interview at UNEP headquarters, Nairobi, 9 October 2003.

17. Author's interview at UNEP headquarters, Nairobi, 9 October 2003.

18. At the beginning of the program, UN-HABITAT was still known as United Nations Centre for Human Settlements (United Nations Centre for Human Settlements/Habitat).

19. Author's interview at UNEP headquarters, Nairobi, 29 September 2003.

20. Following decision GC.21/L.6 at the twenty-first session of the UNEP Governing Council (IISD 2001, 7; for further details, see UNEP 2001b).

21. Author's interview, UNEP headquarters, Nairobi, 29 September 2003.

22. Author's interview, UNEP headquarters, Nairobi, 29 September 2003.

23. Author's interview with the executive director, UNEP headquarters, 6 October 2003.

24. For instance, the UNCTAD has evolved into a talking shop where developing countries air their frustrations; the United Nations Industrial Development Organization is all but starved by donor countries since developing countries insisted to upgrade it into a specialized agency; and the implementation of the desertification convention is severely mired by outright North–South antagonism (chapter 12).

25. For an attempt to cluster the host of environmental issues under UNEP, see von Moltke 2005.

26. UNEP and Center for Clouds, Chemistry, and Climate 2002, and author's interviews at UNEP headquarters, Nairobi, 29 September and 6 October 2003. Meanwhile, the issue reemerged under the less controversial header of "Atmospheric Brown Cloud."

27. This is not necessarily the case, though. One program officer has singled out the Netherlands and the Scandinavian countries that would want "the UN and UNEP to be in a better position to act on their own." These countries would

sometimes provide extra-budgetary contributions that are "linked to an overall policy area . . . but not strictly earmarked." UNEP would thus be flexible in how to use these extra funds "as long as proposals [are] sensible." Author's interview, UNEP headquarters, Nairobi, 22 September 2003.

28. For an overview of international organizations' capacity to assess the global environment, see Doyle and Massey 2000.

29. For instance, thirty-four out of thirty-five respondents to the MANUS Expert survey stated that they regularly draw on UNEP publications in their own work; one-third of them at least once a month.

30. For a recent example, see the role of the Denmark-based Risoe National Laboratory in the UNEP-led Global Network on Energy for Sustainable Development (Behrle 2004, 64); also author's interview at UNEP headquarters, Nairobi, 29 September 2003.

31. Author's interview with the executive director, Nairobi, 6 October 2003.

32. Author's interview at the UNEP headquarters, Nairobi, 1 October 2003.

33. For an account of the evolution of the Montevideo Programme, see Desai 2004, 88–93.

34. Author's interview at UNEP headquarters, 29 September 2003.

35. Personal communications at UNEP headquarters, Nairobi, September and October 2003.

36. Author's interview, UNEP headquarters, Nairobi, 9 October 2003.

37. Also author's interviews at medium management levels, UNEP headquarters, Nairobi, September 2003.

38. This has been further enhanced by new Executive Director Steiner, who rearranged the division by attaching its policy development capacity directly to his office (personal communication at UNEP headquarters, Nairobi, February 2007).

39. Author's interview at UNEP headquarters, Nairobi, 9 October 2003.

40. Author's interview at the UNEP headquarters, Nairobi, 22 September 2003.

41. Author's interviews and personal communications at UNEP headquarters, Nairobi, throughout September and October 2003; see also Andresen and Rosendal (in press).

42. Author's interview at UNEP headquarters, Nairobi, 24 September 2003.

43. The agencies present at the United Nations Offices at Nairobi include the UN-HABITAT headquarters as well as regional and country chapters of United Nations Children's Fund, UNDP, World Food Programme, Joint United Nations Programme on HIV/AIDS, United Nations High Commissioner for Refugees, FAO and others.

44. Author's interviews and personal communications at UNEP headquarters throughout September and October 2003.

References

Abbott, Kenneth, and Duncan Snidal. 2000. "Hard and Soft Law in International Governance." *International Organization* 54 (3): 421–456.

Andonova, Liliana B., and Marc A. Levy. 2003. "Franchising Global Governance: Making Sense of the Johannesburg Type II Partnerships." In *Yearbook of International Co-operation on Environment and Development 2003/2004*, edited by Olav Schram Stokke and Øystein B. Thommessen, 19–31. London: Earthscan.

Andresen, Steinar. 2001. "Global Environmental Governance: UN Fragmentation and Co-ordination." In *Yearbook of International Co-operation on Environment and Development 2001/2002*, edited by Olav Schram Stokke and Øystein B. Thommessen, 19–26. London: Earthscan.

Andresen, Steinar, and Kristin Rosendal. In press. "The Role of the United Nations Environment Programme in the Coordination of Multilateral Environmental Agreements." In *International Organizations in Global Environmental Governance*, edited by Frank Biermann, Bernd Siebenhüner, and Anna Schreyögg. London: Routledge.

Annan, Kofi. 1997. *Renewing the United Nations. A Programme for Reform*. New York: United Nations.

Bauer, Steffen, and Frank Biermann. 2004. *Partners or Competitors? Policy Integration for Sustainable Development between United Nations Agencies*. Paper presented at the 2004 Berlin Conference on the Human Dimensions of Global Environmental Change, 3–4 December.

Bauer, Steffen, and Frank Biermann. 2005. "The Debate on a World Environment Organization: An Introduction." In *A World Environment Organization: Solution or Threat for Effective International Environmental Governance?*, edited by Frank Biermann and Steffen Bauer, 1–23. Aldershot, UK: Ashgate.

Behrle, Steffen. 2004. *Neue Mechanismen der Global Governance: Partnerschaften in der internationalen Umweltpolitik. Funktionen internationaler Organisationen in globalen Partnerschaften für nachhaltige Entwicklung—das Beispiel UNEP*. Otto Suhr Institute for Political Science, Freie Universität Berlin, Germany. Unpublished manuscript (on file with author).

Biermann, Frank. 2002. "Strengthening Green Global Governance in a Disparate World Society: Would a World Environment Organization Benefit the South?" *International Environmental Agreements: Politics, Law, and Economics* 2:297–315.

Biermann, Frank. 2005. "Re-launching the UN Environment Programme: The Rationale for a World Environment Organization." In *A World Environment Organization: Solution or Threat for Effective International Environmental Governance?* edited by Frank Biermann and Steffen Bauer, 117–144. Aldershot, UK: Ashgate.

Biermann, Frank, and Steffen Bauer, editors. 2005. *A World Environment Organisation. Solution or Threat to Effective International Environmental Governance?* Aldershot, UK: Ashgate.

Biermann, Frank, Man-san Chan, Ayşem Mert, and Philipp Pattberg. 2007. "Multi-stakeholder Partnerships for Sustainable Development: Does the Promise Hold?" In *Partnerships, Governance, and Sustainable Development. Reflections on Theory and Practice*, edited by Pieter Glasbergen, Frank Biermann, and Arthur P. J. Mol, 239–260. Cheltenham: Edward Elgar.

Birnie, Patricia W., and Alan E. Boyle. 2002. *International Law and the Environment.* 2nd edition. Oxford: Oxford University Press.

Boxer, Baruch. 1983. "The Mediterranean Sea: Preparing and Implementing a Regional Action Plan." In *Environmental Protection. The International Dimension*, edited by David A. Kay and Harold K. Jacobson, 267–309. Totowa, NJ: Allanheld, Osmun, and Co.

Brack, Duncan, and Joy Hyvarinen, editors. 2002. *Global Environmental Institutions. Perspectives on Reform.* London: Royal Institute of International Affairs.

Bruyninckx, Hans. 2005. "Sustainable Development: The Institutionalization of a Contested Policy Concept." In *International Environmental Politics*, edited by Michele M. Betsill, Kathryn Hochstetler, and Dimitris Stevis, 265–298. Basingstoke, UK: Palgrave Macmillan.

Chambers, Bradnee W., and Jessica F. Green, editors. 2005. *Reforming International Environmental Governance.* Tokyo: United Nations University Press.

Chasek, Pamela S. 2001. *Earth Negotiations: Analyzing Thirty Years of Environmental Diplomacy.* Tokyo: United Nations University Press.

Chayes, Abram, Antonia Handler Chayes, and Ronald B. Mitchell. 1998. "Managing Compliance: A Comparative Perspective." In *Engaging Countries. Strengthening Compliance with International Environmental Accords*, edited by Edith Brown Weiss and Harold K. Jacobson, 39–62. Cambridge, MA: MIT Press.

D'Anieri, Paul. 1995. "International Organizations, Environmental Cooperation, and Regime Theory." In *International Organizations and Environmental Policy*, edited by Robert V. Bartlett, Priya A. Kurian, and Madhu Malik, 153–169. Westport, CT: Greenwood.

Desai, Bharat H. 2000. "Revitalizing International Environmental Institutions: The UN Task Force Report and Beyond." *Indian Journal of International Law* 40 (3): 455–504.

Desai, Bharat H. 2004. *Institutionalizing International Environmental Law.* Ardsley, NY: Transnational.

Downie, David Leonard. 1995. "UNEP and the Montreal Protocol." In *International Organizations and Environmental Policy*, edited by Robert V. Bartlett, Priya A. Kurian, and Madhu Malik, 171–185. Westport, CT: Greenwood Press.

Downie, David Leonard. and Marc A. Levy. 2000. "The UN Environment Programme at a Turning Point: Options for Change." In *The Global Environment in the Twenty-First Century: Prospects for International Cooperation*, edited by Pamela S. Chasek, 355–377. Tokyo: United Nations University Press.

Doyle, Michael W., and Rachel I. Massey. 2000. "International Organizations and the Environment: Looking Towards the Future." In *The Global Environment in the Twenty-First Century: Prospects for International Cooperation*, edited by Pamela S. Chasek, 345–354. Tokyo: United Nations University Press.

Elliott, Lorraine. 2004. *The Global Politics of the Environment.* 2nd edition. London: Palgrave Macmillan.

Elliott, Lorraine. 2005. "The United Nations' Record on Environmental Governance: An Assessment." In *A World Environment Organization: Solution or Threat for Effective International Environmental Governance?*, edited by Frank Biermann and Steffen Bauer, 27–56. Aldershot, UK: Ashgate.

Global Ministerial Environment Forum. 2000. *Malmö Ministerial Declaration. Declaration of the Global Ministerial Environment Forum and the United Nations Environment Programme Governing Council.* UN Doc. UNEP/GCSS VI/L.3, 31 May. Nairobi: UNEP.

Haas, Peter M. 1990. *Saving the Mediterranean. The Politics of International Environmental Cooperation.* New York: Columbia University Press.

Henry, Reg. 1996. "Adapting United Nations Agencies for Agenda 21: Programme Coordination and Organizational Reform." *Environmental Politics* 5 (1): 1–24.

IISD, International Institute for Sustainable Development. 2001. Summary of the 21st Session of the UNEP Governing Council and Second Global Ministerial Environment Forum: 5–9 February 2001. *Earth Negotiations Bulletin*, 12 February.

IISD, International Institute for Sustainable Development. 2002. Summary of the Seventh Special Session of the UNEP Governing Council, Third Global Ministerial Environment Forum and Final Open-Ended Group of Ministers or Their Representatives on International Environmental Governance: 12–15 February 2002. *Earth Negotiations Bulletin*, 18 February.

IISD, International Institute for Sustainable Development. 2004a. Summary of the Eighth Special Session of the United Nations Environment Programme's Governing Council/Global Ministerial Environment Forum: 21–29 March 2004. *Earth Negotiations Bulletin*, 2 April.

IISD, International Institute for Sustainable Development. 2004b. Summary of the Third Meeting of the Open-Ended High-Level Intergovernmental Working Group on an Intergovernmental Strategic Plan on Technology Support and Capacity Building: 2–4 December 2004. *Earth Negotiations Bulletin*, 6 December.

IISD, International Institute for Sustainable Development. 2005a. Summary of the 23rd Session of the UNEP Governing Council/Global Ministerial Environment Forum: 21–25 February 2005. *Earth Negotiations Bulletin*, 28 February.

IISD, International Institute for Sustainable Development. 2005b. Summary of the First Conference of the Parties to the Stockholm Convention: 2–6 May 2005. *Earth Negotiations Bulletin*, 9 May.

IISD, International Institute for Sustainable Development. 2005c. Summary of the Second Conference of Parties to the Rotterdam Convention on the Prior Informed Consent Procedure for Certain Hazardous Chemicals and Pesticides in International Trade: 27–30 September 2005. *Earth Negotiations Bulletin*, 3 October.

Imber, Mark F. 1993. "Too Many Cooks? UN Reform after the Rio United Nations Conference on Environment and Development." *International Affairs* 69:55–70.

Imber, Mark F. 1996. "The Environment and the United Nations." In *The Environment and International Relations*, edited by John Vogler and Mark F. Imber, 138–154. London: Routledge.

Ivanova, Maria H. 2003. "Partnerships, International Organizations, and Global Environmental Governance." In *Progress or Peril? Partnerships in Global Environmental Governance*, edited by Jan M. Witte, Charlotte Streck, and Thorsten Benner, 9–36. Washington, DC, and Berlin: Global Public Policy Institute.

Ivanova, Maria H. 2005. "Can the Anchor Hold? Rethinking the United Nations Environment Programme for the 21st Century." Report Number 7. New Haven: Yale School of Forestry and Environmental Studies.

Kimball, Lee A. 2002. "The Debate over a World/Global Environment Organization: A First Step Toward Improved International Arrangements for Environment and Development." In *Global Environmental Institutions: Perspectives on Reform*, edited by Duncan Brack and Joy Hyvarinen, 19–31. London: Royal Institute of International Affairs.

Loibl, Gerhard. 2001. "The Role of International Organisations in International Law-making: International Environmental Negotiations—An Empirical Study." *Non-State Actors and International Law* 1:41–66.

McCormick, John. 1989. *The Global Environmental Movement. Reclaiming Paradise*. Bloomington: Indiana University Press.

Mee, Laurence D. 2005. "The Role of UNEP and UNDP in Multilateral Environmental Agreements." *International Environmental Agreements: Politics, Law and Economics* 5:227–263.

Mitchell, Ronald B. 2002. "International Environment." In *Handbook of International Relations*, edited by Walter Carlsnaes, Thomas Risse, and Beth A. Simmons, 500–516. London: Sage.

Murphy, Craig N. 2006. *The United Nations Development Programme. A Better Way?* Cambridge, UK: Cambridge University Press.

Najam, Adil. 2005. "Neither Necessary, Nor Sufficient: Why Organizational Tinkering Will Not Improve Environmental Governance." In *A World Environment Organization: Solution or Threat for Effective International Environmental Governance?*, edited by Frank Biermann and Steffen Bauer, 235–256. Aldershot, UK: Ashgate.

Nicholson, Michael. 1998. "A Rational Choice Analysis of International Organizations: How UNEP Helped to Bring About the Mediterranean Action Plan." In *Autonomous Policy Making by International Organizations*, edited by Bob Reinalda and Bertjan Verbeek, 79–90. London: Routledge.

Paarlberg, Robert L. 1993. "Managing Pesticide Use in Developing Countries." In *Institutions for the Earth: Sources of Effective International Environmental Protection*, edited by Peter M. Haas, Robert O. Keohane, and Marc A. Levy, 309–350. Cambridge, MA: MIT Press.

Rechkemmer, Andreas, editor. 2005. *UNEO—Towards and International Environment Organization. Approaches to a Sustainable Reform of Global Environmental Governance.* Baden-Baden, Germany: Nomos.

Rosendal, G. Kristin, and Steinar Andresen. 2004. *UNEP's Role in Enhancing Problem-Solving Capacity in Multilateral Environmental Agreements: Coordination and Assistance in the Biodiversity Conservation Cluster.* FNI Report 10/2003. Lysaker: Fridtjof Nansen Institute.

Sand, Peter H. 1985. "Environmental Law in the United Nations Environment Programme." In *The Future of International Law of the Environment*, edited by Renè J. Dupuy, 51–88. Dordrecht: Martinus Nijhoff.

Sandbrook, Richard. 1999. "New Hopes for the United Nations Environment Programme (UNEP)?" *Global Environmental Change* 9 (2): 171–174.

Skjærseth, Jon Birger. 2001. "The Effectiveness of the Mediterranean Action Plan." In *Environmental Regime Effectiveness. Confronting Theory with Evidence*, edited by Edward L. Miles, Arild Underdal, Steinar Andresen, Jørgen Wettestad, Jon Birger Skjærseth, and Elaine M. Carlin, 311–330. Cambridge, MA: MIT Press.

Steiner, Achim. 2007. "A Year of Change, a Year of Reform." In *UNEP in 2006. Annual Report*, edited by the United Nations Environment Programme, 3–5. Nairobi: UNEP.

Tarasofsky, Richard G. 2002. *International Environmental Governance: Strengthening UNEP.* UNU Working Paper. Tokyo: UNU Press.

Thacher, Peter S. 1992. "The Role of the United Nations." In *The International Politics of the Environment. Actors, Interests, and Institutions*, edited by Andrew Hurrell and Benedict Kingsbury, 183–211. Oxford: Oxford University Press.

Timoshenko, Alexander, and Mark Berman. 1996. "The United Nations Environment Programme and the United Nations Development Programme." In *Greening International Institutions*, edited by Jacob Werksman, 38–54. London: Earthscan.

Tolba, Mostafa K., and Iwona Rummel-Bulska. 1998. *Global Environmental Diplomacy. Negotiating Environmental Agreements for the World, 1973–1992.* Cambridge, MA: MIT Press.

Töpfer, Klaus. 1998. *United Nations Task Force on Environment and Human Settlements.* Nairobi: United Nations Offices at Nairobi.

Töpfer, Klaus. 2002. *Statement by the Executive Director of the United Nations Environment Programme at the 57th Session of the United Nations General Assembly, Second Committee, Agenda Item 87: Environment and Sustainable Development.* New York, 14 November 2002.

UN, United Nations. 2006. *Delivering as One. Report of the Secretary-General's High-Level Panel on System-Wide Coherence.* New York: United Nations.

United Nations Centre for Human Settlements and Danish International Development Agency. 2000. *Evaluation of Urban Environment (SCP) City Projects in Six African Countries. Final Evaluation Report.* October 1999. Nairobi: United Nations Centre for Human Settlements.

UNEP, United Nations Environment Programme. 2000. UNEP Annual Report 1999. Nairobi: UNEP.

UNEP, United Nations Environment Programme. 2001a. International Environmental Governance: Report of the Executive Director. UN Doc. UNEP/IGM/1/2, 3 April 2001. Nairobi: UNEP.

UNEP, United Nations Environment Programme. 2001b. *The Programme for the Development and Periodic Review of Environmental Law for the First Decade of the Twenty-First Century.* Nairobi: UNEP.

UNEP, United Nations Environment Programme. 2002a. *Capacity Building for Sustainable Development: An Overview of UNEP Environmental Capacity Development Initiatives.* Nairobi: UNEP Division of Environmental Policy Implementation.

UNEP, United Nations Environment Programme. 2002b. *Issue Paper Concerning the Question of Universal Membership of the Governing Council/Global Ministerial Environment Forum of the United Nations Environment Programme. Note by the Executive Director.* UN Doc. UNEP/GC.22/INF/36 of 19 December. Nairobi: UNEP.

UNEP, United Nations Environment Programme. 2002c. *Johannesburg Principles on the Role of Law and Sustainable Development. Adopted at the Global Judges Symposium held in Johannesburg, South Africa on 18–20 August 2002.* Nairobi: UNEP.

UNEP, United Nations Environment Programme. 2002d. *Regional Seas. Strategies for Sustainable Development.* Nairobi: UNEP.

UNEP, United Nations Environment Programme. 2003. *Partnership for the Development of Environmental Law and Institutions in Africa, last updated September 2003.* Nairobi: UNEP. Powerpoint Presentation.

UNEP, United Nations Environment Programme. 2004. *UNEP in 2003. Annual Report.* Nairobi: UNEP.

UNEP, United Nations Environment Programme. 2007a. *President's Summary of the Discussions by Ministers and Heads of Delegation at the Twenty-fourth session of the Governing Council/Global Ministerial Environment Forum of the United Nations Environment Programme, Nairobi, 5–9 February 2007.* Nairobi: UNEP.

UNEP, United Nations Environment Programme. 2007b. *UNEP in 2006. Annual Report*. Nairobi: UNEP.

UNEP, United Nations Environment Programme, and Center for Clouds, Chemistry and Climate. 2002. *The Asian Brown Cloud: Climate and Other Environmental Impacts*. Pathumthani, Thailand: UNEP Regional Resource Centre for Asia and the Pacific.

UNEP Governing Council. 1997. *Nairobi Declaration of the Heads of Delegation*. Nairobi: UNEP.

United Nations General Assembly. 1999. *Report of the UN Task Force on Environment and Human Settlements Annex to the Report of the Secretary-General on Environment and Human Settlements*. UN Doc. A/53/463. New York: United Nations.

Victor, David G. 1998. " 'Learning by Doing' in the Non-binding International Regime to Manage Trade in Hazardous Chemicals and Pesticides." In *The Implementation and Effectiveness of International Environmental Commitments. Theory and Practice*, edited by David G. Victor, Kal Raustiala, and Eugene B. Skolnikoff, 221–281. Cambridge, MA: MIT Press.

von Moltke, Konrad. 1996. "Why UNEP Matters." In *Green Globe Yearbook on International Co-operation on Environment and Development 1996*, edited by Helge O. Bergesen and Georg Parmann, 55–64. Oxford: Oxford University Press.

von Moltke, Konrad. 2005. "Clustering International Environmental Agreements as an Alternative to a World Environment Organization." In *A World Environment Organization: Solution or Threat for Effective International Environmental Governance?*, edited by Frank Biermann and Steffen Bauer, 175–204. Aldershot, UK: Ashgate.

Wapner, Paul. 2003. "World Summit on Sustainable Development: Toward a Post-Jo'burg Environmentalism." *Global Environmental Politics* 3 (1): 1–10.

Werksman, Jacob, editor. 1996. *Greening International Institutions*. London: Earthscan.

Young, Oran R. 1991. "Political Leadership and Regime Formation: on the Development of Institutions in International Society." *International Organization* 45 (3): 281–308.

8

The Secretariat of the Global Environment Facility: From Network to Bureaucracy

Lydia Andler

Introduction

When the international community decided to take action against global environmental problems such as climate change, biodiversity loss, and desertification in the early 1990s, the need for a multilateral funding mechanism was obvious to many in the field. Already one year before the 1992 Rio summit, the Global Environment Facility (GEF) was established to fund projects that address global environmental problems. However, through its centralized structure that bundled financial mechanisms for several environmental problem areas as well as through its closeness to the World Bank, the GEF raised concerns with numerous groups. Strong criticism from nongovernmental organizations and developing countries led to the restructuring of the GEF in 1994. The GEF now has a unique institutional structure that draws on three implementing agencies: the UN Development Programme, the UN Environment Programme, and the World Bank. Today, it serves as the financial mechanism for four environmental conventions: the UN Framework Convention on Climate Change, the Convention on Biological Diversity, the Convention on Persistent Organic Pollutants, and the UN Convention to Combat Desertification. The GEF receives its funds from countries that have committed themselves to assisting developing countries under these conventions. It then channels funds to eligible projects, which are designed and executed by the three implementing agencies. The administration of all GEF-related processes rests with a small secretariat in Washington, DC. In the following sections, the term "secretariat" refers to this bureaucracy and the expression "GEF" relates to the entire GEF network.

The case of the GEF secretariat differs from the group of secretariats of intergovernmental environmental treaties through its legal status and its position between powerful implementing agencies. Even though the secretariat serves similar political and technical functions, it addresses several environmental problems and serves different roles in terms of the interaction with the other bodies of the GEF network. Given this variation in central explanatory factors—namely, problem structure and polity—the GEF secretariat was of particular interest for the comparative analyses in this book.

Scholars from political science, international law, and organization theory became interested in both its institutional arrangements and its development over time. Nearly all reflect on the extraordinary institutional structure of the GEF (Keohane and Levy 1996; Silard 1995; Ehrmann 1997; Payne 1998; Jordan 1995; Reinicke and Deng 2000; Matz 2005). Werksman (2004) focuses on the secretariat's inability to enter into formal legal relationships with other international bureaucracies; Streck (2000) analyzes the particularities of the network structure and GEF's strong partnerships with international bureaucracies, nongovernmental organizations, and to some extent the private sector. Other authors focus on GEF projects (Gerlak 2004) and their effects in specific regions such as China (Heggelund, Andresen, and Ying 2005). The dominant focus of this literature, however, is on the "GEF network" composed of the assembly, the GEF council, the GEF secretariat, the three implementing agencies, the science and technical advisory panel, as well as the connected conventions and their secretariats. Yet the particular role and influence of the GEF secretariat remained largely outside the focus of these studies.[1] However, as an integral part of the network, the secretariat closely interacts with GEF units in the implementing agencies and has thus remained the "centerpiece of the GEF galaxy" (de Chazournes 2003, 13).

This case study analyzes the autonomous influence of this bureaucracy and attempts to explain this influence. The analysis does not focus on the effectiveness of GEF projects on the ground (see, e.g., Heggelund, Andresen, and Ying 2005). Data for this study were collected during a field visit to GEF headquarters in Washington, DC. Personal interviews have been conducted with eight staff members. A research colleague held a second round of interviews. This was complemented by telephone interviews. Additional data on expert perceptions of the influence of the GEF secretariat were provided by the expert survey (Tarradell 2007).

Structure and Activities

After lengthy debates on how to implement a financial mechanism for global environmental problems, a joint initiative by the French and German governments led to the foundation of the GEF in 1991. Three institutional features characterized its "pilot phase." First, the GEF was limited to a three-year operating phase as an experiment in the funding for global environmental protection and sustainable development (GEF 1992). Second, the GEF had informal, loosely structured and nonbureaucratic governance rules: participation by interested governments was voluntary, the members met twice a year to review and approve GEF projects, decisions were taken by consensus, and the final project approval was left to the three implementing agencies. Third, the three implementing agencies administered and jointly executed GEF's operations according to their comparative advantages. No distinct GEF bureaucracy had been established at this stage.

During the pilot phase, relationships between the three implementing agencies deteriorated, as the World Bank and the UN Development Programme competed over power, control, and financial resources (Fairman 1996). In addition, nongovernmental organizations and developing countries strongly criticized the GEF for its close association with the World Bank and its lack of transparency and accountability (Streck 2001). By 1992, it was clear that the GEF would need to change its structure and operational modalities if its mandate was to be extended beyond the pilot phase and if it were to become the formal financial mechanism of the biodiversity and climate conventions (Sjöberg 1996). After a long negotiation process, seventy-three member countries and the three implementing agencies signed the "Instrument for the Establishment of the Restructured Global Environment Facility" in 1994 (in the following the "instrument"), which laid down the rules and the institutional arrangements for the future operations of the GEF.

The mandate remained unchanged as compared to the pilot phase. It assigned the GEF to "operate, on the basis of collaboration and partnership among the implementing agencies, as a mechanism for international cooperation for the purpose of providing new and additional grant and concessional funding to meet the agreed incremental costs of measures to achieve agreed global environmental benefits in the following focal areas" (GEF 2004b, paragraph 2): biological diversity; climate change;

international waters; ozone layer depletion; land degradation, primarily desertification and deforestation (added in 2002); and persistent organic pollutants (added in 2002).

The GEF operates under the guidance of and is accountable to the conferences of the parties of all related conventions, which decide the policies, program priorities, and eligibility criteria of their respective convention processes. At the annual conferences of the parties to the conventions, the GEF receives new guidance and reports on former activities and achievements. In partnership with the Montreal Protocol, GEF grants are eligible for countries in central and eastern Europe (those that do not qualify for funding from the Montreal Protocol) to phase out the use of ozone-depleting chemicals. Regional water agreements influence GEF's initiatives to protect international waters.

One of the major changes compared to the pilot phase was the strengthened institutional structure of the GEF. This includes the assembly consisting of representatives of all participating countries (176 countries, as of 2004). The assembly meets every three years to review GEF's general policy. The council, which meets biannually, is the main governing board responsible for developing, adopting, evaluating operational policies, and approving all full-scale GEF projects. Since 1994, the assembly and the council have been able to make decisions by a double-weighted majority; that is, approval of decisions requires 60 percent of the votes of all countries, as well as votes representing 60 percent of the contributions.

The three implementing agencies carry out GEF projects and are accountable to the council for their GEF-related activities. Since 1999, seven executing agencies (mostly regional development banks) have also gained access to GEF funding and can execute GEF projects.[2] The implementing agencies work with the recipient countries together to assist in project identification, manage project preparation, and supervise project implementation.

Another crucial innovation compared to the pilot phase—and the focus of this chapter—was the establishment of the functionally independent secretariat. The problems that the GEF was designed to address have been "so closely tied to intergovernmental negotiations that policy decisions could hardly be delegated to a set of implementing agencies" (Fairman 1996, 78). Therefore, the founding states had emphasized the need for a "neutral" intermediary body between the governments and the implementing agencies in the form of a secretariat. The major tasks of this GEF secretariat are to implement effectively the decisions of the assembly and the council, to coordinate the formulation and oversee the implementation of program activities, to ensure in consultation with the implementing agencies the implementation of the operational policies adopted by the council, to review and report to the council on the adequacy of arrangements made by the implementing agencies, and to coordinate with the secretariats of other relevant international bodies (GEF 2004b, paragraph 21).

One of the main assignments of the secretariat is to serve the council and to interpret the conventions' guidance, and, based on this, to develop operational policies that lay down the foundation for the GEF's efforts in the six focal areas. The latter is carried out through interagency task forces with the GEF units of the implementing agencies. Although GEF projects are initiated, prepared, implemented, and evaluated by the respective implementing agency, the secretariat has a significant review role throughout the project cycle. The main function is to review the project proposals according to their conformity with GEF policies and to decide whether they are eligible for council approval. Furthermore, the secretariat prepares most of the documents for the biannual council meetings such as project reviews, operational policies, and other information reports. It is also responsible for reporting to the related conferences of the parties. The relatively small secretariat consists of a chief executive officer, a deputy, and eight teams—in total about fifty staff (as of 2004). Since 1996, the secretariat has also hosted the monitoring and evaluation unit for GEF project reviews.

Although the GEF governance structure is complex, the secretariat is crucial to the overall performance of the GEF. The following section analyzes whether, where, and how the secretariat has generated a meaningful influence on GEF activities.

The Influence of the GEF Secretariat

The secretariat is intended to serve as the permanent bureaucracy of the GEF network. Therefore, it can be expected to have an influence, mainly on the diverse entities of the GEF network, and less so at the actual project level or on broader international environmental politics.

This analysis thus largely reflects the influence of the GEF secretariat in relation to other bureaucracies involved in GEF activities. This does not imply that the GEF in terms of its grants has not helped ameliorate some of the problems it addresses. As stated in its annual reports, GEF projects achieved a wide range of important environmental improvements such as the reduction of greenhouse gas emissions or the expansion of protected areas in selected countries (GEF 2004a). According to Heggelund, Andresen, and Ying (2005), the GEF contributed to effectively combating environmental problems in China and also yielded global environmental benefits. The analytical approach taken in this chapter, however, restricts the analysis to the actual role of the secretariat, which can influence environmental conditions only indirectly through its funding mechanism.

Cognitive Influence

The official task of the secretariat is to serve as a "facilitator" among the several institutions involved in GEF activities, rather than to influence the international discourse. Thus, in a narrow sense, the secretariat has no function for cognitive influence in terms of changing the understanding and rising the awareness of environmental problems.

Nevertheless, the secretariat represents the GEF network to the external world, as it is responsible for the Web page and GEF publications. To achieve this, the secretariat collects and administers the environmental knowledge gained at all stages of the GEF's projects. Together with the monitoring and evaluation unit, the secretariat prepares and publishes reports on GEF activities.

Although the secretariat has produced several publications and maintains a comprehensive Web page, public awareness of the GEF is limited according to interview sources and the expert survey. Its visibility is still low among governments (particularly in developing countries) or other potentially relevant groups such as the private sector. Staff members assert that the GEF secretariat is not yet perceived as an actor in its own right.[3] According to the expert survey, the influence of GEF publications on environmental discussions is moderate and neither media coverage nor public awareness has been increased through the communication strategies of the secretariat (Tarradell 2007). CEO Leonard Good reflects on this issue: "I've had this comment made to me as well—that the GEF is not that well known or understood. I've met people from the private sector and people within the IMF who have not actually heard of the GEF. I don't think we're that well known in donor countries, not very well at all" (Good 2003).

In sum, the secretariat has hardly managed to present the GEF to the international community. Until now, the GEF is too little known to have cognitive influence on the international community in terms of changing their knowledge and belief systems.

Normative Influence

The GEF as such can be considered a "joint international effort," for which the instrument lays down the common rules and institutional arrangements. According to the instrument, the secretariat serves the council by preparing the documents for the council decisions. In this function, the secretariat translates and operationalizes decisions by the conferences of the parties and, based on this guidance by the conventions and in cooperation with the implementing agencies, develops strategies and operational programs for all GEF-related activities. In doing so, the secretariat fulfills similar functions as other treaty secretariats, with the sole difference that the products of negotiation are not binding international treaties, but general policies for the GEF activities. However, as the following two examples demonstrate, the secretariat has been able to influence the modalities on how to prioritize and implement GEF grants.

The first is the "operational strategy" developed by the secretariat and approved in 1995, which lays the foundation for GEF efforts in the focal areas. The strategy incorporates guidance from the conventions for which the GEF serves as the financial mechanism. Consistent with this strategy, the secretariat established "operational programs" to provide strategic frameworks for the development of projects. According to a senior program officer, the operational programs have been an important step in the history of the GEF to clarify and focus with regard to its mandate and the focal areas.[4] The secretariat was central in these processes as coordinator of the process among the different agencies involved.

A second major achievement has been the "strategic priorities" developed by the secretariat and approved in 2003. Until 2000, the GEF relied on so-called eligibility criteria. At this time, the demand for GEF projects by far exceeded the supply, and the addition of new focal areas rendered the situation even more complex. As a consequence, the secretariat was assigned by the council to improve the management of demand and supply. Consequentially, it effectively introduced twenty-two strategic priorities for project selection and funding. They reflect the major themes and approaches under which resources are programmed within each of the focal areas. The strategic priorities regarding climate change, for example, aim to accelerate the shift from technology-based approaches toward those that are market-based and application-oriented, emphasizing policies and institutions that enhance sustainable development benefits. According to interview sources, the strategic priorities significantly changed the ways how GEF projects are administered and managed in all implementing agencies.⁵ The secretariat itself developed the strategy and promoted its implementation within the network.

The secretariat as the core bureaucracy within the GEF network acts as the institutional advocate for GEF policies. Its prime target group is the implementing and executing agencies. With them, the secretariat generates normative influence in their decision-making process on project designs and funding. The secretariat effectively urges them to adhere to the respective GEF criteria that have been developed under the responsibility of the secretariat.

In sum, the secretariat's normative influence is mainly related to the facilitation of the modalities of the GEF itself. The positive influence is executed through setting up strategies and operational policies on how to manage and implement the scarce GEF resources. These policies manifested themselves in subsequent reallocation of resources and competences among the different organizations involved in the implementation of GEF projects. By actively promoting these GEF policies, the secretariat has an ongoing normative influence with the relevant GEF entities.

Executive Influence

With regard to executive influence, the GEF secretariat is mostly focused on strategic capacity-building issues such as the definition of operational guidelines for national capacity needs. These strategic issues have gained increased attention in the early 2000s. The actual "capacity building" on the ground is left to the implementing agencies.⁶

Given its diverse institutional arrangements, the GEF at large has not succeeded in developing an integrated and systematic approach for its capacity-building activities. In 2001, the conventions stipulated that the capacity needs of recipient countries should be addressed more systematically to enable countries to effectively implement the conventions (GEF 2001). Following a request by the GEF council, the secretariat took the lead in the collaboration with the implementing agencies and developed a "strategic approach to enhance capacity building" in GEF activities. The secretariat thereby used the opportunity to shape and influence the activities of the other partners in the GEF network regarding capacity building. As of 2003, a proposal was submitted that mainly focused on "national capacity self-assessment" projects (GEF 2003b). It contained an operational program for national self-assessment projects and a guideline for the GEF decision-making process on where capacity-building projects are needed most urgently and have to be funded. For the countries, the approach provided the opportunity to gauge their capacity needs and priorities based on systematic self-assessments. This element became operational in 2004.

In sum, the influence of the secretariat regarding capacity building has merely conceptual components. As such, the influence in this field is rather indirect. By means of its unified strategy, the secretariat developed direct leverage to shape and focus the capacity-building activities of the implementing agencies and the target countries. This also shows how the secretariat develops a new strategic approach and promotes the GEF capacity-building approach among the implementing agencies.

Explaining the Influence

This analysis has identified two major fields of autonomous influence in relation to the other agencies of the GEF network, namely normative and indirect executive influence. It shows that the secretariat has no role as an executive bureaucracy and is not expected to have a direct influence as such. Its influence in this field is merely indirect through the provision of strategic guidelines for the other implementing agencies. The subsequent sections will develop an explanatory pattern for the observed normative and indirect executive influence of this bureaucracy.

Problem Structure

The secretariat deals with six different environmental topics. These environmental areas are very diverse in terms of their problem structure; most of the topics are dealt with by the case studies of the secretariats in this volume (see on climate policy, Busch, this volume, chapter 10; on biodiversity policy, Siebenhüner, this volume, chapter 11; on desertification policy, Bauer, this volume, chapter 12). As it is hardly feasible to separate the influence of the secretariat regarding the six issue areas, the problem structure of each focal area does not serve as an explanatory factor for the secretariat's influence in particular in normative and executive fields. Nevertheless, the plurality of problems the secretariat addresses at once renders it difficult for the small bureaucracy to formulate and implement targeted awareness raising campaigns. Interview sources confirmed that the secretariat deals with too many problems at the same time and thus has not enough resources to focus in depth on one of the environmental concerns. Hence, the wide scope in terms of issue areas can explain the little cognitive influence of the secretariat.[7]

Polity

Competences   The legal status of the GEF is a source of much debate among international law scholars (Ehrmann 1997; Werksman 2004), and features of it can explain the influence of the secretariat, particularly in terms of its normative influence. Zoe Young (2002) emphasizes that the GEF secretariat has many principals, namely all the members of the GEF network. Yet legally, the council is the most relevant. The relationship between the council and the secretariat is crucial for understanding what the formal competences of the secretariat are and why they confine the secretariat's autonomous influence.

The secretariat has strict terms of reference, although it enjoys the liberty of interpreting guidance by the conferences of the parties and of preparing most documents for council decisions. Though more fundamental matters require council decisions, the day-to-day operations are left to the secretariat. Therefore, the secretariat has considerable leeway through the drafting of most council decisions—for instance, the twenty-two strategic priorities. These competences apply particularly to technical matters. When controversies arise that do not allow for a final decision, the secretariat is regularly asked to prepare new drafts for the following council meeting. In doing so, it is the secretariat's "central task [to] balance the political needs of major interests in the GEF" (Young 2002, 105). The council members approve other proposals that need less discussion during the biannual meetings.

Formally, decision making in the council requires a double-weighted majority. The majority of both the donor countries and the recipient countries need to agree to a final decision and to resolve disputes. In practice, the council has never resolved a conflict by majority vote but instead does so by consensus building among all parties. The latter process offers the secretariat as a mediating bureaucracy the opportunity to build trust and provide common grounds for the conflicting parties, similar to other convention secretariats.

Resources   The budget for the GEF secretariat amounts to USD 8.3 million (2004). This amount is almost doubled from its 1995 level (USD 4.3 million). Each year, the council approves the budget for the secretariat as part of the overall GEF budget. Additionally, the overall budget provides the annual funding for all core corporate management activities in the GEF units within the implementing agencies. They are paid for their support in developing and reviewing GEF operational policies. Costs incurred through project preparation and implementation are covered by a separate budget. In 1999, a new fee-based system was installed to ensure better control over these costs.

Mostly, OECD countries finance the GEF through replenishments into the Global Environmental Trust Fund every four years. However, the role of the GEF as a catalyst for the mobilization of additional resources has been a key objective since its foundation. Cofinancing arrangements with one of the three implementing agencies is the predominant pattern of GEF funding. GEF projects must include a sustainable source of non-GEF funding. Therefore it funds only the "incremental costs," that is, the part of a project that will bring global environmental benefits. As of 2004, the GEF had provided USD 4.5 billion in grants for over 1,300 projects in 140 countries and generated about USD 14.5 billion in cofinancing from other partners.[8]

The financial resources of the secretariat are restricted and decided annually by the council. Staff members face these constraints through, for example, limited travel expenses and restrictions on other necessary research and monitoring tasks (Young 2002, 158). Several secretariat members emphasized the high workload. Yet additional staff is not anticipated in future budgets in order to keep the secretariat lightweight and to avoid overlap with the implementing agencies. The secretariat receives secondments from donor countries, which keeps wage costs down and allows the secretariat to fill key staff positions with well-qualified individuals.

The council in its position as the governing board decides upon GEF projects and thus upon the resource allocation in terms of implementing agencies and focal areas. Nevertheless, as indicated previously, the secretariat reviews the project proposals at four stages of the project cycle for conformity with GEF operational programs and general project review criteria (GEF 2003a, 7). Besides this, the chief executive officer of the secretariat is entitled to approve medium-sized projects (those below USD 1 million) and part of the enabling activities (those below USD 350,000), which amounts to approximately 5 percent of GEF grants, but about 47 percent of GEF projects, as of 2005.[9]

At first sight, the financial resources of the secretariat appear to be small. However, the influence of the secretariat on the project cycle and therefore on the allocation of GEF grants and the right to decide upon small-sized projects explains the normative influence in terms of promoting GEF policies within the GEF network.

Embeddedness   Besides the broadness of the environmental problems addressed, the secretariat operates in a narrowly defined working environment. The GEF itself has been set up as a network rather than a new organization in its own right. It is defined explicitly as the financial mechanism of the four conventions. Hence, the GEF secretariat solely channels grants for GEF projects to implementing agencies. Likewise, the secretariat has no regional outreach as it disposes of its office only in Washington.

As a consequence, the close cooperation between the secretariat as the permanent body of the GEF and the other organizations involved is paramount. Some scholars emphasize the strengths of the network character of the GEF (Streck 2000). The secretariat is, according to Zoe Young, "at the centre of the wheel with many spokes" (2002, 105), with close and good relationships and information exchanges, particularly with other international bureaucracies.

Yet this network character of the GEF does not always deliver the desired outcomes. Although the secretariat maintains contacts with all member states, the cooperation with the operational focal points in recipient countries has been ineffective in several cases. According to an overall performance study, the operational focal points lack information, capacity, and financial resources. Furthermore, the secretariat does not provide simple information and easily accessible documents (GEF 2002). The fact that the secretariat itself is not present in the recipient countries renders the communication more difficult to manage. This undermines the awareness for the GEF itself and renders the task for the secretariat to increase the awareness of global environmental problems in member states and the wider international community more challenging.

In addition, external stakeholders associate most projects with the implementing agencies rather than with the secretariat or GEF at large. This common external perception also tends to undermine the efforts by the secretariat to increase the awareness of its existence and role as well as of the problems addressed by GEF.[10]

Closely related to this, the GEF at large and the secretariat in particular are often seen as instruments of the World Bank. Even after it was restructured in 1994, several countries and nongovernmental organizations still perceived it as such, because the World Bank supports the secretariat in an administrative sense. Its human resources department manages the secretariat's staff contracts. The secretariat also shared e-mail addresses with the World Bank until 2003. In 2001, the secretariat prepared a document on the institutional authority proposing increased autonomy for the secretariat. This document has not been supported by any implementing agency, since it appeared as if they have a "common concern that GEF's consolidating role should not expand to the extent that it becomes an institutional rival" (Werksman 2004, 49). According to a senior program officer, the strategic priorities introduced in 2002 strengthened the role of the secretariat, as it now decides which projects are to be introduced in the GEF portfolio. The introduction of the fee-based system in 1999 for the implementing agencies and the integration of seven executing agencies to directly access GEF funds increased its self-confidence (Streck 2001). Consequently, the secretariat gained some new means to influence the implementing agencies. In the end, however, the implementing agencies remain powerful in the actual implementation of GEF policies. They have to internalize them into their work programs and implement the projects according to general GEF policies, giving the secretariat only an indirect leverage on actual project implementation.

This sheds light on the influence of the secretariat according to the promotion of GEF policies within the GEF network, in particular the implementing agencies. Regarding financial resources, the intervention into the project cycle and the approval of small-sized projects provides the secretariat with means to influence other actors. These financial means are supported by the increased independence of the secretariat through the strategic priorities. Notwithstanding, the implementing agencies are accountable to the council and revert to their expertise for issues related to the implementation of projects.

The embeddedness of the secretariat between highly autonomous bureaucracies of the GEF network also explains the absence of direct executive influence. Through the institutional setup and the limited competences of the secretariat, its normative influence is largely restricted to a strategic level, leaving the operational decisions to the implementing agencies.

People and Procedures

Organizational Expertise   The small size of the secretariat does not guarantee that it has experts for all relevant topics. For short-term tasks, it relies on the support of consultants. Although the network character of the GEF can lead to complex institutional relations, the secretariat has the ability to build partnerships for each respective task in terms of gaining expertise. Through the science and technical advisory panel that provides independent strategic advice to the GEF, the secretariat has access to a roster of technical and scientific experts. The close coordination with the three implementing agencies provides the secretariat with very specific expertise necessary for relevant activities. Therefore, the close coordination of the GEF with other international bureaucracies allows the secretariat to draw on external expertise when necessary.

This lack of its own technical and scientific expertise is part of the explanation for the agency's lack of cognitive influence. The secretariat has not come to represent a competence center for any of the focal areas. Thus the international community will hardly refer to this bureaucracy when expertise on any of the covered environmental problems is needed. This function is mostly occupied by the convention secretariats (Bauer, this volume, chapter 9; Busch, this volume, chapter 10, and Siebenhüner, this volume, chapter 11).

Although most technical and scientific expertise rests outside the secretariat, its field of expertise is largely procedural. As mediator and administrator of the GEF project approval and the GEF funding procedures, the secretariat has developed significant expertise with regard to the management of processes. In addition, the acceptance of its strategic priorities and the operational strategy can be credited to the external perception of a rather neutral agent with expertise in matters of process design and negotiations.

Organizational Structure   The GEF secretariat is small in size and characterized by its flat hierarchy and the dominance of informal working arrangements and short bureaucratic procedures. Staff members of the secretariat have well-defined responsibilities, but this does not fully apply to decision making. The style of leadership and decision making has changed since 2003 under the new chief executive officer Lennart Good. It developed from a top-down approach into a more consultative one. Yet the responsibility of who takes the final decision is not well defined. In many cases, the final decision is left to the chief executive level. Nevertheless, the secretariat seems quite able to organize itself in order to respond to given tasks. This might partially explain the influence in terms of its normative effects, namely the elaboration of GEF policies and their operational framework.

It is often argued that the GEF has "a strong ability of adaptation to a changing environment" (Streck 2001, 71), or is a "work in progress" (de Chazournes 2003, 24). Looking at the evolution of the entire

GEF since 1991, several changes to the institutional structure and processes have taken place, which were mostly triggered by external demands. The most fundamental change has been the restructuring, which was completed in 1994. Since then, the GEF has institutionalized several instruments to review and critically analyze its activities—for example, external reviews and studies conducted by the monitoring and evaluation unit.

Despite the several instruments to review GEF activities, the entire GEF network struggles with an unworking feedback mechanism and an ineffective knowledge management. Lessons from GEF projects are learned by the implementing agencies. They are fed back to the secretariat by means of annual portfolio reviews or the interagency task forces. Nevertheless, the secretariat is criticized for its inefficient internal knowledge management and lack of "feedback loops."[11] A former GEF senior program officer concluded that the secretariat is "good in listening and absorbing things. . . . It can less act upon and translate what it is told to do."[12] Although the secretariat has failed to overcome the communication problems of the network structure, it plays a major role in developing and implementing the strategy for the knowledge management of the entire GEF.

These difficulties have implications also for the external influence of the secretariat as such. The limited expertise and the insufficient knowledge management within the GEF network contribute to the explanation of the secretariat's limited cognitive influence within the GEF family as well as beyond the network.

Organizational Culture The organizational culture of the secretariat cannot explain much of its normative and indirect executive influence. The staff composition might give an indication about an organizational culture that is shaped by professionals from academic backgrounds. Technical specialists and natural scientists form the majority among all staff members. This culture at times produces problems with implementing agencies with differing organizational cultures, such as UNDP. Restraints on the secretariat's influence on them can also be attributed to these differences. Differences to the World Bank and its organizational culture, however, are rare due to the vicinity of both agencies, the support by the World Bank in administrative matters, and the fact that staff often switches back and forth between the Bank and the GEF secretariat.

Organizational Leadership   The former chief executive officer, Mohamed El-Ashry, managed to put the secretariat in the position to play a key role in the political navigation between the different actors within the GEF network. He was a central figure in the secretariat's interaction with the council members, the conventions, and the implementing agencies. Accordingly, the behavior of the executive officer has been crucial for the strategic and operational work the secretariat undertook. He was most active in managing the modalities of the entire GEF.

Consensus building among council members had been one of the major challenges faced by El-Ashry. Before council meetings, he regularly consulted the different member states in order to develop consensual positions. Persistent patterns in the behavior of the charismatic chief executive officer were to treat southern states like "kings" (Young 2002, 10), but remain aware that donor states pay their shares. Once characterized as the "stage manager" (Young 2002, 156), El-Ashry had much influence on the discussion at the council meetings, and on the entire course of the GEF construction. He had been in office since the foundation of the GEF secretariat in 1994 and is still known as the person with the best institutional knowledge on the GEF. Among staff members, he was a well-respected and "very much present" leader.[13]

In 1994, most GEF member states opposed the idea of creating a new distinctive bureaucracy. Nevertheless, soon after its creation, the secretariat had thirty employees. The development of the secretariat regarding personnel and functions is observed critically not only by implementing agencies, but also by council members. Both are concerned that this development leads to duplication of activities and that the original idea of relying on existing organizations becomes obsolete. By contrast, El-Ashry pushed for the well-staffed, separate, and independent agency trying to establish his "own kingdom."[14]

The personal skills and abilities of El-Ashry had a significant influence on the way the secretariat operated and on decisions made prior and during the biannual council meetings. Therefore, to understand the mainly normative influence the secretariat had on its target group—notably the council and the implementing agencies—leadership of El-Ashry has to be seen as crucial.

Conclusion

The GEF secretariat has some normative influence; however, not in a sense directly comparable to other bureaucracies in international environmental politics. It influences the facilitation of the modalities of the GEF itself instead of the actual negotiations of environmental treaties. Successful formulation and implementation of strategic policies and programs for the GEF operations manifest this influence. The secretariat also influences the behavior of the implementing agencies in terms of promoting the policy guidelines for GEF projects. This generates an indirect executive influence on capacity-building processes. Yet so far the secretariat has not been able to directly influence project implementation on the ground.

Regarding cognitive influence, the secretariat acts as a public mouthpiece for the entire GEF. It takes responsibility to reach the wider community dealing with environmental problems mainly through the Web page. Although not its core function, the analysis shows that the awareness among the public for the GEF itself and its objectives is not satisfactory. The secretariat thus had hardly any observable cognitive influence.

Features of its polity, but also its procedures and the people involved in it can explain these normative and indirect executive influences. The limited but well-detectable normative influence regarding the modalities of the GEF can be understood as a consequence of the secretariat's relatively extended competences with regard to technical matters. The secretariat translates the broad policy guidelines of its principals into strategies and operational programs, and benefits from a great leeway in shaping these programs. In addition, it operates under low supervision, as the council meets only twice a year. Regarding its people, the former chief executive officer El-Ashry played a major role as well. Through his leadership skills and very good institutional knowledge, El-Ashry had an important function in maneuvering the secretariat between conflicting actors. He urged for an independent bureaucracy in the form of the secretariat in order to have a body representing the GEF. His abilities to convene the parties at one table and to establish a well-functioning secretariat strongly contributed to the secretariat's influence in terms of managing the modalities of the GEF. These features assist the secretariat in developing effective GEF policies.

Promoting GEF policies and project criteria is another major task of the secretariat. According to its mandate, the secretariat shall influence the implementing agencies as they implement GEF projects. Thus, the secretariat ensures that these projects comply with GEF policies. With regard to financial resources, the secretariat occupies a powerful position through the four review points in the project cycle and the right of approval of the chief executive officer for smaller GEF projects. This constitutes an incentive for the implementing agencies to accept and adopt GEF requirements. Yet the secretariat is not fully perceived as an actor in its own right, which undermines its influence in terms of promoting GEF policies among powerful implementing agencies. Its organizational embeddedness with some overlap of responsibilities and resulting institutional rivalries significantly limits the overall autonomous influence of the secretariat, and the leverage on project implementation and capacity building in particular.

To understand the very small cognitive influence, one will also have to turn to the polity of the secretariat. The competences of the GEF do not allow for larger research or awareness raising activities. Nevertheless, the secretariat is responsible for representing the GEF in the international environmental community. Operating as a largely technocratic agent in the background, the secretariat has not yet lived up to this ambition. Nevertheless, the secretariat is the permanent actor and hence the public mouthpiece for the GEF as such. Due to limited competences, restricted financial resources, and the close observation through the implementing agencies, the secretariat faces difficulties in promoting public awareness. Moreover, the diversity of the problems addressed render the formulation of targeted awareness raising campaigns a most difficult task hardly to be accomplished by a small bureaucracy. The lack of high-profile in-house scientific and technical expertise and the problems in terms of the internal knowledge management add to this.

In conclusion, it is remarkable that an institution that was not intended to become an independent bureaucracy has nevertheless taken significant steps toward generating influences on "adjacent" bureaucracies. The secretariat's polity that positioned it between powerful implementing agencies while maintaining drafting rights under low supervision and decision power over the allocation of GEF grants, explains the normative and the limited executive effects. In addition, among the internal factors, leadership by the chief executive officer El-Ashry partially explains the analyzed normative influence. Nevertheless, other features of its polity—mainly the narrowly defined role in the project cycle and its role as an agent in the background and the lacking knowledge management within the GEF network—hinder the secretariat to fully develop its influence.

Acknowledgments

I am grateful for all interviewees in the secretariat of the GEF, the World Bank, and the UN Development Programme. Many thanks for valuable comments on earlier versions of this chapter also to Philipp Pattberg, the editors, and the MANUS project team.

Notes

1. A prominent exception is a book by Zoe Young (2002), who provides a detailed description of the GEF secretariat's functions and roles.

2. The status as the executing agencies enables them to prepare and implement GEF projects on behalf of the GEF, to submit project proposals directly to the GEF and not through an implementing agency, and to receive grants from the GEF Trustee (Heggelund, Andresen, and Ying 2005).

3. Author's interview with GEF officer, Washington, DC, May 2003.

4. Author's interview with senior GEF officer, Washington, DC, May 2003.

5. Author's interview with senior GEF officer, Washington, DC, May 2003.

6. For the example of the World Bank see Marschinski and Behrle, this volume, chapter 5.

7. Author's interview with senior GEF officer, Washington, DC, May 2003.

8. According to the GEF project database: http://www.gefonline.org and the GEF Web page: http://www.gefweb.org (accessed July 2005).

9. According to the GEF project database: http://www.gefonline.org (accessed May 2005).

10. Author's interview with senior GEF officer, Washington, DC, May 2003.

11. Author's interview with senior GEF officer, Washington, DC, May 2003.

12. Author's interview with senior GEF officer, Washington, DC, May 2003.

13. Author's interview with senior GEF officer, Washington, DC, May 2003.

14. Author's interview with senior GEF officer, Washington, DC, May 2003.

References

de Chazournes, Laurence B. 2003. *The Global Environment Facility as a Pioneering Institution: Lessons Learned and Looking Ahead.* Working Paper. Washington, DC: Global Environment Facility.

Ehrmann, Markus. 1997. "Die Globale Umweltfazilität." *Zeitschrift für ausländisches und öffentliches Recht und Völkerrecht* 57 (2/3): 565–614.

Fairman, David. 1996. "The Global Environment Facility: Haunted by the Shadow of the Future." In *Institutions for Environmental Aid. Pitfalls and Promise*, edited by Robert O. Keohane and Marc A. Levy, 55–88. Cambridge, MA: MIT Press.

GEF, Global Environment Facility. 1992. *The Pilot Phase and Beyond.* Working Paper Nr. 1. Washington, DC: Global Environment Facility.

GEF, Global Environment Facility. 2001. *Elements of Strategic Collaboration and a Framework for GEF Action for Capacity Building for the Global Environment*. Washington, DC: Global Environment Facility.

GEF, Global Environment Facility. 2002. *The First Decade of the GEF*. Second Overall Performance Study. Washington, DC: Global Environment Facility.

GEF, Global Environment Facility. 2003a. *GEF Project Cycle: An Update*. Washington, DC: Global Environment Facility.

GEF, Global Environment Facility. 2003b. *Strategic Approach to Enhance Capacity Building*. Washington, DC: Global Environment Facility.

GEF, Global Environment Facility. 2004a. *Annual Report 2004. Producing Results for the Global Environment*. Washington, DC: Global Environment Facility.

GEF, Global Environment Facility. 2004b. *Instrument for the Establishment of the Restructured GEF*. Washington, DC: Global Environment Facility.

Gerlak, Andrea K. 2004. "One Basin at a Time: The Global Environment Facility and Governance of Transboundary Waters." *Global Environmental Politics* 4 (4): 108–141.

Good, Leonard. 2003. Speech given by Len Good at the GEF Council Meeting, November 19, 2003. On file with authors.

Heggelund, Gørild, Steinar Andresen, and Sun Ying. 2005. "Performance of the Global Environment Facility (GEF) in China: Achievements and Challenges as Seen by the Chinese." *International Environmental Agreements* 5:323–348.

Jordan, Andrew. 1995. "Designing New International Organizations: A Note on the Structure and Operation of the Global Environment Facility." *Public Administration* 73:303–312.

Keohane, Robert O., and Marc A. Levy, editors. 1996. *Institutions for Environmental Aid. Pitfalls and Promise*. Cambridge, MA: MIT Press.

Matz, Nele. 2005. "Financial Institutions between Effectiveness and Legitimacy: A Legal Analysis of the World Bank, Global Environment Facility, and the Prototype Carbon Fund." *International Environmental Agreements* 5:265–302.

Payne, Rodger A. 1998. "The Limits and Promise of Environmental Conflict Prevention: The Case of the GEF." *Journal of Peace Research* 35 (3): 363–380.

Reinicke, Wolfgang H., and Francis Deng. 2000. *Critical Choices. The United Nations, Networks, and the Future of Global Governance*. Ottawa: International Development Research Centre.

Silard, Stephen. 1995. "The Global Environment Facility: A New Development in International Law and Organization." *The George Washington Journal of International Law and Economics* 28 (3): 607–654.

Sjöberg, Helen. 1996. "The Global Environment Facility." In *Greening International Institutions*, edited by Jacob Werksman, 148–162. London: Earthscan.

Streck, Charlotte. 2000. *The Network Structure of the Global Environment Facility*. UN Vision Project on Global Public Policy Networks. Available at www .globalpublicpolicy.net (accessed September 2004).

Streck, Charlotte. 2001. "The Global Environment Facility: A Role Model for International Governance?" *Global Environmental Politics* 1 (2): 71–94.

Tarradell, Mireia. 2007. *The Influence of International Bureaucracies in Global Environmental Politics: Results from an Expert Survey*. Global Governance Working Paper No. 26. Amsterdam and others: The Global Governance Project.

Werksman, Jacob. 2004. "Consolidating Global Environmental Governance: New Lessons from the GEF?" In *Emerging Forces in Environmental Governance*, edited by Norichika Kanie and Peter M. Haas, 35–50. Tokyo: UNU Press.

Young, Zoe. 2002. *A New Green Order? The World Bank and the Politics of the Global Environment Facility*. London: Pluto Press.

9

The Ozone Secretariat: The Good Shepherd of Ozone Politics

Steffen Bauer

Introduction

The international regime for the protection of the stratospheric ozone layer is considered one of the major successes in international environmental politics. The literature on its emergence, evolution, and effectiveness is abundant and has been a major catalyst for the study of international environmental regimes.[1] Yet few scholars have systematically looked at the role of the international secretariat that administers the Vienna Convention for the Protection of the Ozone Layer and the Montreal Protocol on Substances that Deplete the Ozone Layer: the ozone secretariat within the United Nations Environment Programme in Nairobi. Although other explanatory factors may be more significant in explaining the regime's overall success, it is intriguing that hardly anyone has looked at the role of the bureaucracy that has served the parties to the Montreal Protocol for over two decades now. Even Edward Parson's *Protecting the Ozone Layer* (2003), which is arguably the most thorough analysis of the ozone regime available, draws hardly on insights from the ozone secretariat.[2]

The general relevance of the ozone secretariat has been addressed in a section of Jørgen Wettestad's study on the effectiveness of the Montreal Protocol (2001). Penelope Canan and Nancy Reichman (2002) approached the ozone regime from a sociological perspective and identified the treaty secretariat as one component in a complex network of "ozone connections." The ozone secretariat has also been included as one of five cases in Rosemary Sandford's comparative study of environmental treaty secretariats (1994; see also Sandford 1992, 1996). I used examples from the ozone secretariat and the secretariat of the UN Convention to Combat Desertification to analyze the "bureaucratic authority" of intergovernmental secretariats (Bauer 2006). Finally, officers of the ozone secretariat have provided an inside account that stresses the conducive role of their bureaucracy (Andersen and Sarma 2002).

Based on this literature, one can plausibly assume that the secretariat, despite its small size, has contributed to the overall performance of the regime, "perhaps more so than envisioned in the regime-creation phase" (Wettestad 2001, 162). In the following study, I further substantiate this argument and trace where, how, and to what extent the work of the ozone secretariat has influenced the outcomes of the overall regime.

A number of factors make the ozone secretariat a unique case study in this volume. First, the ozone secretariat is by far the smallest bureaucracy in the sample. Hence one would hardly expect the secretariat to have a sizable impact on international ozone politics. Given the technical specificity of the ozone problem and the advanced institutional arrangements that result from it, one could expect the ozone secretariat to make a difference, especially in dealing with expert knowledge in a manner that may affect the international ozone discourse and international cooperation. Conversely, the small bureaucracy can hardly be expected to directly alter the behavior of governments or to provide them with additional capacities.

The small size of the secretariat also presents a methodological challenge. Given that the secretariat employs merely six to eight program officers, including the executive secretary and its deputy, the explanatory power of some analytical categories in this book's case study design are here reduced to anecdotal information. There is little use, for instance, in analyzing the organizational structure of such a small secretariat. This point needs to be considered when the secretariat is credited for flat hierarchies and swift internal decision making. Likewise, a relevant share of the empirical material available for this case study represents microperspectives from within the secretariat. The information is relevant, yet cannot be expected to match the empirical clout of other case studies presented in this book that could extract and synthesize data from dozens of interviews.

A second feature unique to this case study is the formal status of the secretariat; namely, its close organizational link to UNEP. That the ozone secretariat could be seen as an extension of UNEP rather than as a bureaucracy in its own right might lower its standing vis-à-vis governments. However, it could also be assumed that the authority of its international civil servants is enhanced precisely because they are part of a larger UN agency with some clout in international environmental governance. For instance, vis-à-vis the United Nations secretary-general and the United Nations General Assembly, the ozone secretariat is formally represented by the UNEP executive director.

The ozone secretariat is responsible for the administration of both the Vienna Convention on the Protection of the Ozone Layer and the more specific Montreal Protocol on Substances that Deplete the Ozone Layer. To keep the analysis focused, the statements made in this chapter refer to the administration of the Montreal Protocol unless the Vienna Convention is mentioned, too.

Structure and Activities

The international regime for the protection of the stratospheric ozone layer builds on a multilateral environmental agreement typical for international environmental politics of the 1980s (see Sandford 1994). Both the Vienna Convention and the Montreal Protocol provide for a secretariat to administer the regime's implementation, namely "to organize future meetings, prepare and transmit reports, and perform functions assigned to it by any future protocols" (Downie 1995, 179). The bureaucracy that results from these provisions is one component of the overall ozone regime that has developed since the mid 1970s. The regime comprises, among other components, the legal framework of the Vienna Convention and the Montreal Protocol, plus its London, Copenhagen, Beijing, and Vienna amendments; an Open-Ended Working Group of the Parties; a variety of expert panels, such as the Technology and Economic Assessment Panel; and the Multilateral Fund.

The Vienna Convention stipulated that the secretariat shall be hosted by UNEP as a distinct entity answerable to the convention's conference of the parties. However, the ozone secretariat is often perceived as a subordinate unit of UNEP, and the formal legal relationship between the two is hard to grasp. In practice, the ozone secretariat formally reports to the UN General Assembly through the UNEP executive director, and official communication with parties or publications of the ozone secretariat formally come under the UNEP label. Secretariats of other multilateral environmental agreements, such as the one serving the Convention on Biological Diversity or the Convention on International Trade in Endangered Species (CITES), operate under similar formal arrangements, but are more easily recognized as entities of their own, if only for the marked difference that they are hosted outside the UNEP headquarters. Moreover, the biodiversity secretariat has its own logo, whereas the ozone secretariat uses the overall UNEP emblem. The ozone secretariat also relies on the UNEP secretariat and the UN Offices at Nairobi for conference services and administrative assistance. UNEP officials are eager to emphasize that UNEP is indeed catering for the ozone secretariat and that its own Coordinating Committee on the Ozone Layer, established in 1977 in accordance with the World Plan of Action on the Ozone Layer, constituted the secretariat's institutional predecessor.[3]

The setup of the ozone secretariat is simple. Each program officer represents what would be one functional unit or division in bigger international bureaucracies; the executive secretary and its deputy constitute the secretariat management. They supervise one senior legal officer, one senior scientific affairs officer, one administrative officer, and one information and communications officer. In 2004, two more program officers were seconded to strengthen the secretariat: one covering monitoring and compliance, the other serving as a database manager. The parties' decision to approve these additional posts has been welcomed by the secretariat management. It is perceived as an overdue step that acknowledges the ever increasing workload resulting from the different reporting schemes for the consecutive amendments to the Montreal Protocol.[4] In sum, with its general support staff, the ozone secretariat now employs eighteen people, who are all formally employees of the United Nations Environment Programme. At the helm of the secretariat, Marco Gonzalez succeeded Madhava Sarma in 2002 as its third executive secretary.[5]

The annual budget of the secretariat amounts to roughly USD 1 million with respect to administering the Vienna Convention and an additional annual average of about USD 3–5 million to cover its activities related to the Montreal Protocol. With these resources, the ozone secretariat administers formal conferences and meetings of the parties and its subsidiary bodies, the Open-Ended Working Group, as well as informal consultative meetings and public outreach measures. The major share of the secretariat's budget is spent on conference services, which include the organization and financing of the travels of developing country delegates. Hence, only 10–15 percent of the budget remains for nonconference activities.[6]

The funds of the ozone secretariat are independent from the multimillion dollar Multilateral Fund for the Implementation of the Montreal Protocol in Montreal. As of 2002, the ozone fund had disbursed roughly

USD 1.5 billion to over 100 developing countries. In 2002, governments agreed to replenish the fund with USD 573 million for 2003–2005 (IISD 2003, 4; see Biermann 1997 for details on the setup of the fund).

Other than conference management, the secretariat provides technical advice for the parties and drafts decisions, as well as treaties and amendments on their behalf. Moreover, it convenes review panels and coordinates the reporting and compliance issues to which the parties have committed themselves.

The Influence of the Ozone Secretariat

Cognitive Influence
The framing of "ozone discourses" (Litfin 1994) that was pivotal in bringing about the contractual environment of the ozone regime was dominated by situational factors—notably, the discovery of a substantial thinning of the stratospheric ozone layer ("ozone hole")—and the epistemic community involved in this discourse (Haas 1992; also Parson 2003, 84). Scientists and civil servants of UNEP, the World Meteorological Organization, the British Antarctic Survey, and the U.S. National Aeronautics and Space Administration were part of this discourse many years before the establishment of the ozone secretariat. Yet the ozone secretariat continues to play an important role in keeping ozone depletion on the agenda. This is politically important, because to some extent, the Montreal Protocol's success is its current weakness. Media attention to the problem has dropped dramatically since the late 1980s and early 1990s, and environmental organizations—most of which typically depend on media attention—have turned to more visible issues such as climate change. As the regulation of ozone depleting substances advances to ever more complex levels, it is an important role of the ozone secretariat to maintain attention of political decision makers and awareness for the vulnerability of the stratospheric protective shield among a wider public.[7] Thus, the secretariat's role in shaping the discourse by brokering complex knowledge to all kinds of stakeholders is hardly less important today than it was in the regime creation phase, when the Vienna Convention would have been stillborn were it not for the intervention of UNEP's Ozone Unit (Benedick 1998).

Indeed, the secretariat remains active in state-of-the-art knowledge dissemination and information brokering. Its output ranges from the provision of ready-to-go information kits to children's comics and teaching kits. International Ozone Day, which is annually organized by the secretariat since 1988, has become one of the more noteworthy ones among the many "world days" under the banner of the United Nations.[8] Moreover, the ozone secretariat seeks the limelight by presenting the Outstanding National Ozone Units Award, for which parties compete by presenting their efforts in implementing the Montreal Protocol and protecting the ozone layer. Beyond keeping governments' general attention, many informal meetings that convene to facilitate decision making are based on the specific knowledge that is provided for by the secretariat's officers.[9]

Normative Influence
In addition, the ozone secretariat has furthered international cooperation under the Montreal Protocol on Substances that Deplete the Ozone Layer. For one, the secretariat advises and supports national ozone officers to raise awareness within their countries and to advance the implementation of international commitments on the ground.[10] As the status of implementation reflects positively upon the advancement of the overall regime, this facilitates international cooperation quite significantly. As a notable example, it promotes ratification of progressive amendments to the Montreal Protocol inasmuch as it helps parties to live up to their commitments.[11]

It is an institutional peculiarity of the ozone regime that there are different numbers of parties to the protocol and each of its amendments. Although there is almost universal membership to the Vienna Convention and the Montreal Protocol, membership is lessening with each succeeding amendment. Out of 191 parties to the Montreal Protocol, 186 have ratified the 1990 London Amendment, 179 the 1993 Copenhagen Amendment, 159 the 1998 Montreal Amendment, and 135 the 2000 Beijing Amendment.[12] This renders the administration of reporting requirements and the provisions for meetings of the parties more complex and labor-intensive compared with other environmental treaties. Technically, each amendment of the Montreal Protocol has largely to be dealt with like a convention in its own right.[13] The secretariat has thus a stake in convincing parties to ratify all amendments, and it can even refer to its formal mandate to invite non-parties to meetings and to provide them with appropriate information (UNEP 2003, 344).

Another issue is the negotiation of Critical Use Nominations and Critical Use Exemptions, which regulate the domestic production and consumption of ozone-depleting substances that are subject to being phased out. Decisions on critical uses are typically based on recommendations by the Technology and Economic Assessment Panel, a subsidiary body of the conference of the parties, and its subsidiary committees, such as the Methyl Bromide Technical Options Committee. Offering its own technical and procedural expertise, the ozone secretariat could facilitate progress in deliberations within the Technology and Economic Assessment Panel on a number of occasions.[14]

Notably, the secretariat's scientific and legal staff assists parties in identifying industrial branches or ozone-depleting substances that may be critical but have not been regulated yet. These may then be tabled for consideration by the Technology and Economic Assessment Panel. However, this is even more vigorously pursued by nongovernmental organizations such as Greenpeace International or the Environmental Intelligence Agency.[15] Once the parties have decided on critical use exemptions, the ozone secretariat is again involved through the administration of the respective reporting requirements. Yet it is the parties that report to the secretariat, which ultimately leaves control of information at the hands of national governments. For instance, the U.S. administration has repeatedly caused outrage among party delegations by withholding data of its methyl bromide–producing companies (IISD 2004).[16]

Executive Influence

The successful development of technical and financial capacities in developing countries, based on an unprecedented willingness of major developed country parties to mobilize resources at a scale of billions of dollars, is a major reason for the achievements of the Vienna Convention and the Montreal Protocol. However, the administration of these substantive resources is the domain of the Multilateral Fund and, to some extent, of the Global Environment Facility, both of which are institutionally detached from the ozone secretariat.

The implementation of capacity-building activities under the Montreal Protocol are basically the domain of four implementing agencies: the World Bank, the United Nations Industrial Development Organization, the UN Development Programme and, to a lesser extent, UNEP's Ozone Action Programme, which is located at its Paris-based Division of Technology, Industry, and Economics. It is these international bureaucracies that brought about the installation of so-called Ozone Units in the capitals in the developing world. These are small administrative units, usually linked to the national environment ministry, with staff trained and financed by the implementing agencies to draft and implement national programs on the phaseout of ozone-depleting substances (see Biermann 1997 for details). The Ozone Units have thus acquired a quasi-diplomatic status regarding the communication flows between the ozone secretariat and the parties. Officers in Nairobi emphasized that the overall achievements of the Montreal Protocol would not be conceivable without the provision of these effective interlinkages between national levels and the international regime through the Ozone Units and the ozone secretariat.[17]

As for the contribution by the ozone secretariat itself, it has no mandate to build technical or financial capacities. Its capacity to build institutional capacities is also limited, due in no small part to lack of staff.

However, the executive secretary notes that the secretariat does occasionally provide workshops as well as support to networks that are crucial in disseminating knowledge and building capacity.[18] In this respect, one senior officer provided concrete examples of contributing in person to regional network workshops in developing countries. Such meetings convene regularly in developing country regions to prepare the technical experts from national Ozone Units for upcoming conferences such as the annual meeting of the parties or the Open-Ended Working Group. These officers provide background information for national delegates and thus function as intermediaries between the international processes and policy makers at the domestic level. Participation in such regional network conferences offers an opportunity for the secretariat to clarify to the domestic ozone officers the wider political implications of their technical briefs.[19] Ultimately, such workshops enable the secretariat to narrow the gaps at the domestic levels between the rather apolitical experts that care for the subject matter of ozone policy implementation, and political negotiators who represent national interests in the intergovernmental forums of ozone politics. Other than many national representatives, the secretariat's officers are in the position to flag crucial issues and to extract the pertinent pieces out of the massive information that is brought to it by the parties. This however, needs to be done in a cautious, strictly noninstructive manner. Again, the secretariat always remains neutral and does not take sides, but "plays the role that governments want us to play."[20] The approach seems to be to clarify important issues without being perceived as giving advice, because governments do not like to be advised by the secretariat, at least not in public forums.

In sum, participation in regional workshops and practical assistance from the ozone secretariat for governments plays a role, but hardly qualifies this small secretariat as a significant capacity builder compared to other bureaucracies analyzed in this volume.

Explaining the Influence

Problem Structure

The potential of the ozone secretariat to influence regime outcomes is constrained or enabled by external factors, notably the complexity of the problem at stake and political or other contextual contingencies in which all of the regime's stakeholders are embedded. In the literature scrutinizing the success of the ozone regime, the characteristics of stratospheric ozone layer depletion have been given particular explanatory power. In opposition to many other environmental problems, and despite evident variation in terms of vulnerability around the world, ozone depletion is a genuine global commons problem that directly affects the functioning of the atmosphere and thereby indirectly all flora and fauna on the planet. In short, a depleted ozone layer leaves everyone worse off. As no country or region could gain from an increase in harmful ultraviolet radiation, concepts of "winners" and "losers" are irrelevant (Wettestad 2001, 156).

This insight, however, does not equal consensus and swift cooperation in international politics. Leaving initial uncertainty with regard to the scope and complexity of the environmental threat aside, two major factors were responsible for the contentiousness of the issue in international politics: the economic importance of chlorofluorocarbons and other ozone-depleting substances for powerful chemical industries and national economies in Europe and North America, and imbalances along the North–South divide.[21] Though the former has been largely ameliorated during the process of regime formation as it boiled down to manageable questions of economic competitiveness, the latter remains to be contested and infringes upon the overall success of the regime to protect the ozone layer. Indeed, the North–South conflict appears as the main obstacle to ensuring "smooth sailing with regard to complete problem solving" (Wettestad 2001, 167) of an otherwise exceptionally effective regime. This problem is further intensified by the fact that the countries in transition of Middle and Eastern Europe bear a closer resemblance to developing countries than to industrialized countries, as far as their capacities to comply with the Montreal Protocol are concerned.[22]

Effective international regulation was further helped by high concern among many governments in the industrialized world. Adverse health effects, such as increased risk of skin cancer and eye cataracts due to higher levels of ultraviolet radiation, received much public attention in the developed world and required politicians to respond to the fears of their electorate. Many analysts have emphasized the importance of the discovery of the ozone hole, which served as a "smoking gun" for advocates of a ban on chlorofluorocarbons vis-à-vis skeptical decision makers, notably among the conservative governments of Germany and the United Kingdom (Litfin 1994; Benedick 1998).

Although this overall problem structure remains largely stable, political stakes and perceptions of saliency have varied over time. These shifts within the larger problem structure are typically the result of new information and subsequent additions to the list of ozone depleting substances (see also Parson 2003). And though the salience of ozone layer protection seemed to be waning at the turn of the century, new controversies about specific ozone depleting substances and established substitutes that have now emerged as potent greenhouse gases point in the opposite direction. Adding yet more layers of complexity to ozone politics, they will strengthen rather than weaken the position of the secretariat.

Polity

Competences   The overall autonomy of the ozone secretariat is rather small. This bureaucracy is at the service of two governing bodies—the conferences to the Vienna Convention and the meetings of the parties to the Montreal Protocol—and is subordinate to UNEP, which in itself has limited formal autonomy as a mere program. Likewise, the senior management of the secretariat has hardly any leverage in terms of financial resources or legal mandate.

Resources   The resources of the secretariat are modest. Its staff is stretched thin, and a few program officers struggle to handle all requirements coming out of party meetings and related to the different amendments of the protocol. Few resources are available for strategic expenditures, as preparation and servicing of the party and committee meetings account alone for about 90 percent of the annual budget (see previous).

Embeddedness   Despite limited resources, there is some room for influence that stems from the secretariat's thick embeddedness within the regime. Despite the unwillingness of governments to expand the competencies of the secretariat, its executives took great care to establish the ozone secretariat as an efficient hub of the overall ozone regime. As such, the secretariat is credited for smooth cooperation with parties around the globe. To this end, it aptly employs its interlinkages with the altogether 110 national Ozone Units that have been created following ratification of the Montreal Protocol. The resulting network provides for efficient communication flows between national authorities that are responsible for the on-the-ground implementation of the Montreal Protocol and the regime's switchboard that is the ozone secretariat, which ultimately feeds back into the intergovernmental processes. This is appreciated in particular by civil servants in developing country parties, who depend on the institutional and technical assistance provided by the ozone secretariat for lack of own administrative capacities, notably when it comes to the processing of national reports.

People and Procedures
To actually exploit the limited room for influence that opens itself to the ozone secretariat, people and procedures are the key explanations. This relates to the expertise vested in the bureaucracy, and its leadership, which has been exemplary on many accounts. Both organizational expertise and organizational leadership could flourish, partially because of the organizational culture of the ozone secretariat.

Organizational Culture   The organizational culture of the secretariat is best described as a technocratic organizational culture that builds on strong in-house expertise of both scientific and political aspects of the protection of the stratospheric ozone layer. It is further characterized by the small size of the ozone secretariat, which grants close working relationships between officers and a flat hierarchy. Although there is a formal bureaucratic structure, several officers stated that top-down hierarchy would hardly be felt in their everyday work and thereby positively distinguish their workplace from other UN agencies. Hence, a good "team spirit" generally prevails in the secretariat. Occasional internal difficulties are mostly handled informally and constructively, and information flows easily. This was also felt to ensure efficiency in the performance of the secretariat.

There is also a remarkable level of identification with the objectives of the Montreal Protocol among professional staff and, in particular, a strong sense of pride regarding the secretariat's good reputation among governments.

Organizational Expertise   If it comes to technical, legal, and even political knowledge relating to any of the ozone treaties, the expertise available within the ozone secretariat is probably second to none. National bureaucrats responsible for the implementation of the Montreal Protocol often find themselves overwhelmed with the ever more complex requirements of the protocol and its amendments.[23] Many thus rely on advice from the secretariat and appreciate the practical help provided by the "ozone officers" in Nairobi. This service function of the secretariat is particularly important for administrators in developing countries, whose domestic capacities to meet reporting requirements and other treaty obligations are severely limited. As the ultimate institutional memory of the regime and the main provider of general information and technical advice, the ozone secretariat can thus directly influence how compliance issues are handled at the domestic level. Secretariat officers themselves emphasize that they are mere service providers whose advice would exclusively serve the letters of the treaty as agreed by the parties. Yet their advice is essential to the actions of those who depend on it. Indeed, it epitomizes rational-legal authority in Max Weber's understanding of bureaucratic rule.

In addition, the secretariat has some influence through drafting reports and decisions on behalf of the meeting of the parties. The executive secretary emphasizes that the drafts provided by the secretariat have no relevance for governments unless they adopt them, and he downplays the role of the secretariat.[24]

However, several program officers indicate that by acting as the institutional memory of the ozone regime and by acquiring levels of technical knowledge superior to those of most party delegates, the significance of documents drafted by the secretariat are high.[25] Quite explicitly, it has been argued that in acknowledgment of the profound expertise embodied by the ozone secretariat, the drafts provided through it are widely perceived as authoritative. Accordingly, the wording of draft decisions or other documents that are put before the parties are a significant source of influence. Secretariat officers can anticipate which elements of a draft decision or report will be controversial, and can thus phrase them so that they are acceptable for governments or even slip the attention of delegates. Conversely, the secretariat can ensure that certain issues will receive the attention of delegates, and thus initiate discussion even if some governments would have the issue rather ignored. For instance, a provision may be included in a draft decision that requires the secretariat to monitor progress on the implementation of an obligation. If the report goes without amendments, the secretariat will eventually be mandated to make inquiries at pursuant party meetings. If, however, some governments wish to exclude the monitoring provision, they must make an explicit effort to this end, which also raises attention to the issue.[26]

Moreover, it should prove particularly insightful to investigate the specific contributions of the ozone secretariat in the expert panels and committees that serve as the consultative basis of most substantive negotiations in the ozone regime. As Karen Litfin (1994) has shown in her analysis of "ozone discourses," the interface of scientific expertise and intergovernmental cooperation has been crucial in shaping the ozone regime. The role of the ozone secretariat in providing for the Technology and Economic Assessment Panel would promise to be of particular interest in that respect.[27]

Organizational Leadership   Finally, a central means for the ozone secretariat to influence ozone politics are its senior bureaucrats and their diplomatic activities. Throughout the history of the ozone regime, its executives have actively interfered with intergovernmental negotiations either to facilitate consensus among parties or to seek ways for them to comply with the commitments made under the Montreal Protocol. Naturally, the executive secretary of the ozone secretariat is at the forefront of such activities, but they may also involve the UNEP executive director or, on occasion, professional officers of the secretariat (for instance, if several breakout groups consult in parallel at a meeting of the parties).

Although the ozone secretariat may not pressure parties, its staff can emphasize the adverse effects that noncomplying parties can have on other parties, which are always wary to see free-riders benefit from their own commitment. The executive secretary has described the precautionary principle as an important tool in this respect: "We are here to serve the parties' will, but we are also reminding them of their responsibilities."[28]

Arguably, the diplomatic skills of the ozone secretariat's top executives have brought about the most visible manifestations of its practical influence within the ozone regime. Both Mostafa Tolba and Madhava Sarma are commonly described as very proactive executive secretaries who have been influential in furthering the institutionalization and implementation of international ozone politics. Numerous insiders to the Montreal Protocol have expressed the general importance for the secretariat to have a strong and proactive leadership to be effective; almost always they refer to one or both of them in order to illustrate their point. According to one senior officer, both of them typically sought informal ways to incite the parties to eventually concede what they intended them to concede. In particular, they often succeeded in brokering consensus on controversial issues *before* formal negotiations between parties began. Conversely, an anxious executive secretary would have little grip on the directions in which intergovernmental negotiations evolve and would thus risk diminishing the regime's progress.[29]

Joanna Depledge (2007) addressed the climate change negotiations to scrutinize the pivotal role of executive secretaries at conferences of the parties by means of their direct interactions with the ever-changing chairpersons. Although the specific relationship between secretariat executives and conference chairpersons was not systematically studied in this case study, it is reasonable to assume that similar mechanisms are at work every time the parties convene. In fact, when I presented Depledge's findings during a follow-up interview and asked about parallels to the ozone negotiations, this was emphatically affirmed.[30]

The crucial role of organizational leadership in ozone politics can be traced back to before the emergence of the permanent ozone secretariat, when intergovernmental ozone negotiations were provided for by the Ozone Unit of UNEP. Although scholars generally hesitate to attribute prominence to individual leadership in relation to other explanatory variables, the appraisal of Mostafa Tolba's contribution in furthering the formation of a substantive ozone regime is unanimous. Talking to participants of early ozone negotiations or screening the literature on the origins of the Vienna Convention, it is hard to avoid what leadership researcher Alan Bryman mocks as "hagiographic pen pictures of successful leaders" (1996, 288). In the world of ozone negotiators, Tolba appears to enjoy a larger-than-life status in terms of charismatic leadership, diplomatic skill, and personal authority. Peter M. Haas (1992, 194), for instance, praised him as "instrumental in hammering out the final compromises" of the Montreal Protocol, and to Oran Young (1991), Tolba exemplifies an ideal typical "entrepreneurial leader" who capitalized on individual skills and formal stature to substantially advance the cause of the ozone regime.[31] Own communications with officers of the ozone secretariat and officials who have been involved with ozone negotiations acknowledge Young's caption, albeit with varying degrees of enthusiasm.[32] Edward Parson (2003, 205) deemed it worth noting that a proposal of Tolba at the 1990 meeting of the parties was "unusually timid," thereby underscoring that usually he was quite the opposite.

Madhava Sarma, Tolba's successor and the first executive secretary of the new ozone secretariat in 1987, is also credited with strong leadership. Like his predecessor, he has been described as a charismatic and skillful diplomat who was respected by industrialized and developing countries alike. In particular, he has been credited for breaking negotiation deadlocks through personal interventions that were crucial in bringing about ambitious amendments to the Montreal Protocol at meetings of the parties. It does not diminish the genuine contributions of Sarma to note that his first years as executive secretary were facilitated by the fact that Tolba was still present in ozone politics as UNEP's executive director.

As far as the new executive secretary, Marco Gonzalez, is concerned, officers have been reluctant to compare him to his predecessors. For one, it was too early to pass a fair judgment at the time most interviews were undertaken (2003); secondly, the Montreal Protocol has entered a phase that is unlikely to see similarly groundbreaking developments as the 1980s and early 1990s. It was noted, however, that he appears to prefer a comparatively cautious approach vis-à-vis the parties.[33]

Conclusion

This chapter investigated the ozone secretariat's contribution to the overall success of the international ozone regime. Major explanations for this success story thus far emphasize the influence of a strong epistemic community; the availability of and business interests in economically attractive technical solutions; genuine concern among decision makers in powerful industrial countries; and the provision of authoritative leadership by committed individuals. Given this set of explanatory factors, did the work of the ozone secretariat make any difference?

Following from this analysis, it did. In an unspectacular way, the ozone secretariat contributed to ozone politics by facilitating highly constructive intergovernmental negotiations—on stage and behind the scenes. This activity was helped by the good reputation that the ozone secretariat enjoys among parties, which in turn reflects the successful realization of its core functions and in particular a record of smooth servicing of the parties. In the complex institutional web of international ozone politics, the ozone secretariat really is the hub.

From this vantage point, the institutional maze of the ozone regime and the increasing complexity of the policy issues it is dealing with create opportunities for the ozone secretariat to influence ozone politics in spite of its miniscule size and modest resources. The potential stemming from the secretariat's thick embeddedness is aptly exploited, namely through the strong expertise vested in the bureaucracy and an organizational leadership that maintains a clever balance between keeping a low profile while instigating parties to move ahead.

This organizational behavior was enabled, in particular, by the authoritative expertise represented by the organization as a whole, as well as by its officers. Arguably, there are few policy makers at domestic levels that could possibly match the comprehensive grasp of the secretariat of the myriad legal and technical provisions around the Montreal Protocol.

Moreover, the secretariat is widely credited for its neutrality and professionalism, as well as transparency in its activities. This is perceived as its most precious asset inside the secretariat in view of its standing vis-à-vis the parties. Accordingly, officers at all levels emphasized the need to sustain this level of satisfaction among their "clients." Indeed, there was a sense of pride within the ozone secretariat over its smooth relations with parties in both industrialized countries and developing countries. Thus, inside the secretariat it is seen as a reward for good performance that governments approved additional program officers, even at a time when there is a tendency to cut back on international civil servants.

Though the challenge to halt ozone layer depletion is no longer in the limelight of international environmental politics, the ozone secretariat is still required to oversee that governments keep dealing with it. Indeed, as intricate conflicts between ozone policy and climate policy need to be mastered, parties may soon turn to a proved and tested agent for further guidance.

Acknowledgments

I am grateful to my interviewees at the ozone secretariat in Nairobi and in particular to Deputy Executive-Secretary Michael Graber for facilitating my participation at the First Extraordinary Meeting of the Parties to the Montreal Protocol in Montreal, Canada, 24–26 March 2004. For valuable comments on this case study, I am indebted to the MANUS project team.

Notes

1. For comprehensive assessments and further references, see the United Nations' own account (Andersen and Sarma 2002) and the seminal volume of Edward A. Parson (2003); for early case studies of ozone politics with a lasting impact on the study of international regimes see, in particular, Young 1989 and Haas 1992.

2. His impressive list of interviewees covers 124 interviews over twelve years (1990–2001), but merely two UNEP officers (see Parson 2003, 281–284).

3. Wettestad suggests that the establishment of the ozone secretariat was a compromise between governments that wanted to bestow the administration of the Vienna Convention on the World Meteorological Organization, which is predominantly staffed with scientists, and governments that wanted UNEP to perform this function, as an organization that is shaped by more "political" UN career officers (2001, 161).

4. Author's interview with the deputy executive secretary, Nairobi, 30 September 2003.

5. Sarma served the Vienna Convention and the Montreal Protocol from 1987 to 2000. He had followed Mostafa Tolba, who, as the then-incumbent UNEP executive director, was acting as the first executive officer of the Vienna Convention. Deputy Executive-Secretary Michael Graber served as acting executive secretary prior to Marco Gonzalez's arrival in 2002.

6. Author's interview at the ozone secretariat, Nairobi, 30 September 2003.

7. Author's interview at the ozone secretariat, Nairobi, 5 October 2006.

8. Author's interview at the ozone secretariat, Nairobi, 6 October 2003.

9. Author's interview with the executive secretary, Nairobi, 26 September 2003; author's interview at the ozone secretariat, Nairobi, 5 October 2006.

10. Author's interview with the executive secretary, Nairobi, 26 September 2003.

11. Author's interview with the deputy executive secretary, ozone secretariat, Nairobi, 30 September 2003.

12. See http://ozone.unep.org/ratification_status/ (accessed 21 May 2008).

13. Author's interview at the ozone secretariat, Nairobi, 7 October 2003.

14. Author's interviews at the ozone secretariat, Nairobi, 6 October 2003 and 5 October 2006.

15. Personal communication at Extraordinary Meeting of the Parties–1, Montreal, 24–26 March 2004; see also IISD 2004.

16. In the meantime, a U.S. court required the U.S. government to disclose the respective information; author's interview at the ozone secretariat, Nairobi, 5 October 2006.

17. Author's interviews at the ozone secretariat, Nairobi, 30 September, 1 October and 6 October 2003.

18. Author's interview with the executive secretary, Nairobi, 26 September 2003.

19. Author's interviews at the ozone secretariat, Nairobi, 30 September and 6 October 2003.

20. Author's interview at the ozone secretariat, Nairobi, 6 October 2003.

21. For a comprehensive analysis of the costs and salience of international ozone politics and how they changed over time, see Parson (2003).

22. This problem has been addressed by making these countries' efforts to phase out ozone-depleting substances eligible for funding through the GEF. The Multilateral Fund thus remains a preserve of developing countries.

23. On the specific requirements of the Montreal Protocol including its amendments, see the handbook that is published and regularly updated by the ozone secretariat (UNEP 2003).

24. Author's interview at the ozone secretariat, Nairobi, 6 October 2003.

25. Author's interviews at the ozone secretariat, Nairobi, 6 and 7 October 2003; for further anecdotal evidence, see Churchill and Ulfstein (2000).

26. Author's interview at the ozone secretariat, Nairobi, 7 October 2003.

27. Author's interview at the ozone secretariat, Nairobi, 6 October 2003 and 5 October 2006.

28. Author's interview with the executive secretary, Nairobi, 26 September 2003.

29. Author's interview at the ozone secretariat, Nairobi, 7 October 2003; similar, if typically more cautious statements were made by other officers that were interviewed at the ozone secretariat, Nairobi, 30 September, 1 and 6 October 2003, and 5 October 2006.

30. Author's interview at the ozone secretariat, Nairobi, 5 October 2006.

31. For further praise see the account of Richard Benedick (1998), who was the U.S. chief negotiator throughout Tolba's term of office, or Canan and Reichman's (2002, 48–52) caption of Tolba "at the intersection of history, biography and personality."

32. A few more critical narrators suggested that there have been difficulties, too, referring to a larger-than-life ego of the UNEP's longest-serving executive director and a rather peculiar leadership style.

33. Author's interviews at the ozone secretariat, Nairobi, 6 October 2003 and 5 October 2006. In the more recent interview, it was suggested that Gonzalez's rather cautious stance might be linked to increased anxiety in a view of the

U.S. administration, an issue that had even led, at one point, to tangible differences of opinion inside the secretariat.

References

Andersen, Stephen O., and K. Madhava Sarma. 2002. *Protecting the Ozone Layer: The United Nations History.* London: Earthscan.

Bauer, Steffen. 2006. "Does Bureaucracy Really Matter? The Authority of Intergovernmental Treaty Secretariats in Global Environmental Politics." *Global Environmental Politics* 6 (1): 23–49.

Benedick, Richard E. 1998. *Ozone Diplomacy. New Directions in Safeguarding the Planet.* Enlarged edition. Cambridge, MA: Harvard University Press.

Biermann, Frank. 1997. "Financing Environmental Policies in the South: Experiences from the Multilateral Ozone Fund." *International Environmental Affairs* 9 (3): 179–219.

Bryman, Alan. 1996. "Leadership in Organizations." In *Handbook of Organization Studies*, edited by Stewart R. Clegg, Cynthia Hardy, and Walter R. Nord, 276–292. London: Sage.

Canan, Penelope, and Nancy Reichman. 2002. *Ozone Connections. Expert Networks in Global Environmental Governance.* Sheffield, UK: Greenleaf.

Churchill, Robin R., and Geir Ulfstein. 2000. "Autonomous Institutional Arrangements: A Little-noticed Phenomenon in International Law." *American Journal of International Law* 94:623–659.

Depledge, Joanna. 2007. "A Special Relationship: Chairpersons and the Secretariat in the Climate Change Negotiations." *Global Environmental Politics* 7 (1): 45–68.

Downie, David L. 1995. "UNEP and the Montreal Protocol." In *International Organizations and Environmental Policy*, edited by Robert V. Bartlett, Priya A. Kurian, and Madhu Malik, 171–185. Westport, CT: Greenwood Press.

Haas, Peter M. 1992. "Banning Chlorofluorocarbons: Epistemic Community Efforts to Protect Stratospheric Ozone." *International Organization* 46:187–224.

IISD, International Institute for Sustainable Development. 2003. Summary of the Fifteenth Meeting of the Parties to the Montreal Protocol: 10–14 November 2003. *Earth Negotiations Bulletin*, 17 November.

IISD, International Institute for Sustainable Development. 2004. Summary of Extraordinary Meeting of the Parties to the Montreal Protocol: 24–26 March 2004. *Earth Negotiations Bulletin*, 29 March.

Litfin, Karen T. 1994. *Ozone Discourses: Science and Politics in Global Environmental Cooperation.* New York: Columbia University Press.

Parson, Edward A. 2003. *Protecting the Ozone Layer: Science and Strategy.* New York: Oxford University Press.

Sandford, Rosemary. 1992. "Secretariats and International Environmental Negotiations. Two New Models." In *International Environmental Treaty Making*, edited by Lawrence E. Susskind, Eric J. Dolin, and J. William Breslin, 27–51. Cambridge, MA: Program on Negotiation at Harvard Law School.

Sandford, Rosemary. 1994. "International Environmental Treaty Secretariats: Stage-Hands or Actors?" In *Green Globe Yearbook of International Cooperation on Environment and Development 1994*, edited by Helge O. Bergesen and Georg Parmann, 17–29. Oxford: Oxford University Press.

Sandford, Rosemary. 1996. "International Environmental Treaty Secretariats: A Case of Neglected Potential?" *Environmental Impact Assessment Review* 16:3–12.

UNEP. 2003. *Handbook for the International Treaties for the Protection of the Ozone Layer. The Vienna Convention (1985). The Montreal Protocol (1987)*. 6th edition. Nairobi: UNEP.

Wettestad, Jørgen. 2001. "The Vienna Convention and Montreal Protocol on Ozone-Layer Depletion." In *Environmental Regime Effectiveness. Confronting Theory with Evidence*, edited by Edward L. Miles, Arild Underdal, Steinar Andresen, Jørgen Wettestad, Jon Birger Skjærseth, and Elaine M. Carlin, 149–170. Cambridge, MA: MIT Press.

Young, Oran R. 1989. "The Politics of International Regime Formation: Managing Natural Resources and the Environment." *International Organization* 43 (3): 349–375.

Young, Oran R. 1991. "Political Leadership and Regime Formation: On the Development of Institutions in International Society." *International Organization* 45 (3): 281–308.

10

The Climate Secretariat: Making a Living in a Straitjacket

Per-Olof Busch

Introduction

"We support cooperative action by States to combat climate change and its impacts on humanity and ecosystems."[1] So reads the introductory clause in the staff vision of the intergovernmental bureaucracy that states created to assist them in their struggle to confront climate change: the climate secretariat. It services states in the negotiation and implementation of what has been described as "being one of the most ambitious treaties ever adopted" (Oberthür and Ott 1999, 95) and "the most profound and important global agreement of the late twentieth century" (Grubb et al. 1999, xxxiii), which in many respects "is without precedent in international affairs" (Grubb et al. 1999, xvii).

In 1992, alarmed by increasing scientific evidence on anthropogenic interference with the climate system, governments had adopted the UN Framework Convention on Climate Change ("climate convention"). Its ultimate objective is "to achieve . . . stabilization of greenhouse gas concentrations at a level that would prevent dangerous anthropogenic interference with the climate system" (climate convention, article 2). In 1997, they adopted the Kyoto Protocol, which specifies legally binding reduction targets for greenhouse gas emissions in developed countries. In 2001, they agreed upon the Marrakech Accords, which lay down implementation rules for the Kyoto Protocol.

In this chapter, I investigate how the climate secretariat has supported states in the negotiation and implementation of the climate regime, whether it had autonomous influence, and what explains its influence. Although the negotiations and the implementation of the climate regime have attracted considerable attention in the literature, the academic literature has neglected the secretariat apart from very few studies (Depledge 2005, 62–79; Depledge 2007; Yamin and Depledge 2005, 500–508).

Structure and Activities

The climate secretariat is a single-issue bureaucracy. Since its creation in 1996, the organization of departments has been oriented toward the major functional areas of the climate regime: information (including science and inventories), negotiation (including legal affairs and conference organization) and implementation (including capacity building, adaptation, and technology transfer). It services the main convention bodies, that is, the conference of the parties to the convention, and since the Kyoto Protocol entered into force, the meeting of parties to the protocol; two subsidiary bodies (the subsidiary body for implementation and the subsidiary body for scientific and technological advice); and several specialized permanent or temporary bodies—for example, the compliance committee of the Kyoto Protocol (for more details, see Yamin and Depledge 2005, chap. 13).

The climate secretariat is above all the information hub of the regime. It stores and compiles all factual information that is essential for the regime and that parties are obliged to submit. It makes available this information in publications, documents and online databases. On its Web site, it ensures the availability of all official documents since the start of the negotiations in 1991, thereby providing a more comprehensive documentation of the regime evolution than any other secretariat studied in this book. Occasionally—and less than the biodiversity secretariat (Siebenhüner, this volume, chapter 11)—the climate secretariat develops information products, publishes press releases, or gives interviews to inform the public (Depledge 2005, 68). Overall, this output serves the purpose of facilitating the intergovernmental process and keeping parties and stakeholders informed.

The climate secretariat facilitates, supports, and coordinates negotiations. It analyzes specific technical and methodological issues and, like the biodiversity secretariat (Siebenhüner, this volume, chapter 11), prepares almost every draft for decisions, proposals, conclusions, resolutions, or negotiating texts (Depledge 2005). It gives advice to the presiding officers of the negotiations, who are responsible for the smooth conduct of the negotiations, together with the climate secretariat (Depledge 2005, 35–53). It identifies options and makes strategic proposals on the conduct of negotiations—for example, on possible outcomes, on the appropriate negotiating arena, on procedural hurdles and how they might be overcome, or on qualified chairs. Moreover, it supports the presiding officers by preparing speaking notes, by giving technical advice on proposals, or by counseling on procedural issues. Between 1996—the year when it began its operations—and 2005, the climate secretariat organized more than 120 sessions and meetings of permanent and temporary bodies of the convention and the Kyoto Protocol. Moreover, it arranged more than 60 expert workshops and intersession consultations. Altogether, more than 82,000 delegates of parties, representatives of observer states, intergovernmental organizations, nongovernmental organizations, and journalists attended the conferences of the parties and sessions of subsidiary bodies.

Together with experts from parties, the climate secretariat supports the implementation of the climate regime and reviews the implementation progress by collecting, processing, and making available information on implementation, such as in the greenhouse gas emissions inventories.

The Influence of the Climate Secretariat

Cognitive Influence

The climate secretariat has not generated new knowledge or contributed to the scientific understanding of climate change. Unlike the desertification secretariat (Bauer, this volume, chapter 12), it has not shaped public or scientific discourses or pushed these in a specific political direction. Nor has it—like the ozone secretariat (see Bauer, this volume, chapter 9)—played an important role in keeping climate change on the agenda.

Nevertheless, in political and scientific assessments and related discourses, policy makers, negotiators, media, science, and civil society often draw on information from the climate secretariat. In particular, governments and their delegates use this output.[2] In an internal review, parties expressed their satisfaction with the information and documents provided by the climate secretariat. They requested even more such support and urged it to publish more in languages other than English (UNFCCC 2005). Likewise, stakeholders appreciated the output of the climate secretariat. In a survey about the climate secretariat's online database on climate friendly technologies, 85 percent of 303 respondents from 81 countries found the information relevant for their work (UNFCCC 2004). The expert survey, which was conducted for this book, supports these results: 23 of the 28 respondents (82 percent) judged the climate secretariat's output to be relevant for their work (Tarradell 2007). The use of the climate secretariat's Web site underscores this assessment. From 1999 to 2004, roughly 80,000 return visitors visited the Web site, on annual average. During the same period, downloads amounted to over 24 million.[3] In 2004, the climate secretariat estimated that 50,000 to 60,000 people around the globe follow the climate regime by utilizing its Web site.[4] Moreover, between 1996 and 2005, more than 800 academic articles quoted documents prepared by the climate secretariat (according to the SCOPUS database, www.scopus.com).

Normative Influence

A review of studies on the climate regime negotiations suggests that the climate secretariat has not shaped political outcomes or convinced parties to agree on specific measures (see, e.g., Grubb et al. 1999; Grubb and Yamin 2001; Ott 2001b; Schröder 2001; Vrolijk 2002; Depledge 2005; Oberthür and Ott 1999). Such indications also lack in the reports of the Earth Negotiations Bulletin, which reports independently and on a daily basis about negotiations of twenty-six international environmental agreements. These reports usually devote a separate section to the roles of treaty secretariats. The more than three hundred reports on the climate regime negotiations, however, do not contain a single section on the role of the climate secretariat. As in the academic analyses, the majority of references to the climate secretariat in these reports describe input of the climate secretariat or requests of parties to it. Likewise, not a single interviewee in the climate secretariat was willing to attribute autonomous political influence to it.[5]

The climate secretariat nevertheless assumes a pivotal role in the negotiations and contributed to their smooth progress by providing advice—mainly on technical issues—and by organizing the negotiations (Yamin and Depledge 2005, 432 and 507; see also Depledge 2005, 73). On a number of occasions, parties expressed their appreciation for the climate secretariat's role in the negotiations, too (e.g., ENB 2005, 18; 2000, 17; 1996a, 11). The facilitation of outcomes was however limited to the translation of political agreements among parties into hands-on technical approaches.[6] By and large, the climate secretariat supported the parties in three ways.

First, the climate secretariat facilitated negotiations by providing useful technical advice, which external experts judge to have been "extremely important" (Depledge 2005, 74). Its advice facilitated the adoption of the Marrakech Accords, by helping parties to make sense of the complex technical issues and to embark on the final stage of negotiations (Ott 2001a; Depledge 2005, 154). In the aftermath of the seventh conference of the parties, many parties appreciated the invaluable contributions of the climate secretariat to the negotiation progress (ENB 2001, 1). Moreover, the climate secretariat facilitated negotiations by removing inconsistencies in negotiation texts and by identifying options for agreement.[7] During the negotiation of the Kyoto Protocol, the climate secretariat, together with the conference chair Raul Estrada, identified options on which parties reached consensus (Oberthür and Ott 1999, 83 and 85; see also Depledge 2005, 68 and 73; Grubb et al. 1999, 64). It made indispensable contributions in the preparation of the negotiating text, which was positively received by a majority of parties (Depledge 2005, 159–161). In the post-Kyoto negotiations, the climate secretariat had "coordination teams" in place, which were indispensable in removing inconsistencies in the negotiation texts and the final decisions (Depledge 2005, 122).

Conversely, the lack of the climate secretariat's advice has occasionally complicated the negotiations. Observers of negotiations at The Hague, where parties struggled with the specification of implementation rules for the Kyoto Protocol, conclude that among others, the limited involvement of the climate secretariat caused the failure of parties to agree. The then-president of the conference of the parties, Jan Pronk, had not as extensively as other presidents resorted to the advice of the climate secretariat (Ott 2001b; see also Depledge 2005, 68 and 162). An additional reason for the failure was the delay in bringing in controversial issues into the negotiations, for which the climate secretariat has to take partial responsibility (Depledge 2005, 76).

Second, the climate secretariat facilitated negotiations by ensuring a good organization and management of negotiations. Through its advice on the appropriate negotiation arenas and its time management, the climate secretariat enabled parties to progress in negotiations (Depledge 2005, chaps. 9 and 12). It was given credit for its skillful support in managing the negotiations of the Geneva Ministerial Declaration (Oberthür and Ott 1999, 54), which increased the pressure on parties to agree upon a legally binding protocol in Kyoto and gave the negotiations additional momentum (Depledge 2005, 179). In Kyoto the climate secretariat together with chair Estrada maintained time pressure, thereby contributing to the successful conclusion of the negotiations (Depledge 2005, 179–181). Conversely, when parties failed to agree on implementation rules of the Kyoto Protocol in The Hague, the climate secretariat and the conference chair performed comparatively poorly in the negotiation management (see Depledge 2005, 183–189; Ott 2001b).

Third and finally, the climate secretariat has supported the negotiation progress by providing logistics, which must not be underestimated. "No meeting ever succeeded, because the logistics were great. But if the logistics are bad, the negotiations can fail" (interview with official at the climate secretariat, cited in Depledge 2005, 71). The organization is particularly challenging in the climate regime, since the negotiations involve a larger number of delegates and stakeholders than in any other multilateral negotiations (Barrett and Chambers 1998, 15). In an internal review, parties "generally appreciated the work of the secretariat in organizing sessions and meetings" and praised the conference scheduling and the logistics (UNFCCC 2005, 4). The provision of appropriate meeting space upon short-term notice is a particular organizational challenge, which the climate secretariat mastered when parties requested. At the resumed sixth conference of the parties, it had to provide at very short notice meeting facilities for selected groups of delegates, taking into account all necessary requirements such as security batches, country flags, and unusual seating arrangements (Depledge 2005, 71). That it accomplished all of this "in the required time frame was extremely important to maintaining the momentum of negotiations" (Depledge 2005, 71).

Executive Influence

Similar to the other treaty secretariats studied in this book, the executive influence of the climate secretariat is the weakest compared to its cognitive and normative influence. It has not triggered the adoption of new policies or the creation of institutions.[8] Nor has it assisted governments at the domestic level to implement the climate regime (unlike the desertification secretariat; see Bauer, this volume, chapter 12). At best, it has supported parties in the implementation by developing adequate implementation procedures and systems. It has developed the methodologies of these inventories, designed a computer-based registry and transaction log to make emissions trading systems work, and helped the CDM executive board create feasible assessment procedures.[9] As all other secretariats studied in this book, it has organized workshops that served to build capacities—for example, in reporting methodologies.

The climate secretariat's support satisfied parties: neither the internal review nor the literature give any indications that parties complained about its support in that area what they usually do if they are dissatisfied (see following). Parties even demanded additional support from the climate secretariat for the development of effective and smooth implementation procedures (UNFCCC 2004, 7–8).[10] In the internal review of the climate secretariat's activities, parties gave positive feedback, in particular on its coordination and support of the in-depth reviews of national communications (UNFCCC 2004, 7–8).

Explaining the Influence

Overall, the influence of the climate secretariat has been limited. The climate secretariat is a "technocratic bureaucracy" that has not had any autonomous political influence—as opposed to the desertification secretariat that Bauer describes as "activist bureaucracy" (Bauer, this volume, chapter 12). It has not promoted its own agenda or pursued specific approaches, but has responded to requests of parties. It has functioned as an important and valuable but passive information hub in the climate regime that does not autonomously interfere with any political, scientific, or public discourses. It facilitated successful negotiations through its advice, it supported parties in the development of implementation procedures, and it helped operationalize political agreements among parties by setting up functioning systems and procedures or by translating political decisions into workable solutions.

Problem Structure

Above all, the problem structure has limited the influence of the climate secretariat. Scholars describe climate change as a "malign problem" (e.g., Depledge 2005; Miles et al. 2001; Wettestad 1999). When addressing climate change, policy makers face high scientific complexity, persistent scientific uncertainties about causes and impacts, substantial differences in the contributions and the vulnerability to climate change between developed and developing countries, long time delays between high short-term costs of regulations and benefits that materialize in the long run, and low visibility. On many occasions, these characteristics have complicated the negotiations and impaired an effective regime implementation (Schröder 2001, 1–92; Ott 2001b; Grubb et al. 1999, 61–114; Depledge 2005, 18–34; and Oberthür and Ott 1999). Given that the biodiversity and desertification secretariats had more autonomous influence in policy processes (see Siebenhüner, this volume, chapter 11; Bauer, this volume, chapter 12), despite similar problem characteristics between desertification and loss of biodiversity, these alone cannot explain the differences in influence.

The problem of climate change is however unique on another dimension: domestic and international responses to global warming and inaction alike are perceived to involve higher political stakes than any other international environmental agreement. These perceptions have impaired the climate secretariat's potential to influence, and confined it to its role as technocratic bureaucracy. Above all, the perception of high stakes results from the magnitude of expected changes when addressing climate change. Effective responses to climate change are expected to have comparatively drastic consequences on prevailing economic and social structures, because they challenge the mode of economic and social development that has been pursued ever since the industrial revolution (Depledge 2005, 20; Ott 2001b, 278). Ultimately, they may culminate in a new international economic order (Ott 2001b, 278). "The climate change issue is essentially about an alternative economic development, choice of energy, and industrial economic processes. Parties have to change practically the way the whole world economy is running."[11] Climate change became a matter of "high politics" in international relations (Oberthür and Ott 1999, 1). In April 2007, the UN Security Council even discussed the implications of climate change for international peace and security (Biermann and Boas 2007; German Advisory Council on Global Change 2008). At the domestic level, responses to climate change are likewise perceived to involve high politics (e.g., Lee 1999, 279; Nitze 1994, 190; Andresen and Butenschon 2001, 351), including concerns about economic growth and competitiveness, energy and infrastructure development, or industry and transport (Depledge 2005, 32; Eckersley 2004, 82). Because energy use constitutes the basis of almost any human activity, all individuals contribute to the problem. Hence, responses to global warming potentially affect all individuals (Depledge 2005, 19). "At its heart the climate regime is about how people use resources and how we organize ourselves."[12]

At the same time, concerns related to inaction are high, given that "the stakes associated with projected changes in the climate are high" (Intergovernmental Panel on Climate Change 2001, 21). The effects of climate change are global and threaten systems that sustain human societies across the world, culminating in, for example, catastrophic and devastating weather events. Climate change may cause "substantial and irreversible damage to or loss of some systems within the next century" (Intergovernmental Panel on Climate Change 2001, 21), and may considerably affect the welfare of nations and individuals around the globe, albeit to varying extents (Intergovernmental Panel on Climate Change

2001; Stern 2007). Climate change "could result in destabilization and violence, jeopardizing national and international security to a new degree," thereby drawing "ever-deeper lines of division and conflict in international relations, triggering numerous conflicts between and within countries over the distribution of resources . . . over the management of migration, or over compensation payments between the countries mainly responsible for climate change and those countries most affected" (German Advisory Council on Global Change 2008, 1).

This combination of uniquely high political stakes with the characteristics outlined in the beginning of this section has led to fundamental—in some cases insurmountable—differences in national interests, which prompted all parties to proceed very cautiously in the negotiations. It has also motivated parties to be wary of any activities of the climate secretariat and to impose severe constraints on its potential to influence others. These constraints and the caution of parties are again not particular to the climate regime. Yet compared to other global environmental challenges and related regimes, as well as to the other treaty secretariats studied in this book, they are more pronounced, because the climate regime involves unmatched high political stakes.

Polity

Competences   The convention and the rules of procedure, which formally lay down the duties, responsibilities, and means of the climate secretariat, define competencies that are common to all treaty secretariats studied in this book (see also Yamin and Depledge 2005, chap. 10). The climate secretariat does not have any financial resources for the implementation of projects or the supply of financial incentives. Similar to the biodiversity and desertification regimes (Siebenhüner, this volume, chapter 11; Bauer, this volume, chapter 12), the GEF funds the implementation of the climate regime. Neither has the climate secretariat any regulatory competencies, as all other intergovernmental bureaucracies except for the environmental department of the World Bank (see Marschinski and Behrle, this volume, chapter 5). It cannot adopt legal decisions or enforce formal sanctions that would allow it to mandate parties or other actors to change their behavior. All legal decision-making powers lie with the conference of the parties and the meeting of parties to the Kyoto Protocol. As all other treaty secretariats studied in this book, the climate secretariat has no scientific research tasks. Within the climate regime, the responsibility for scientific input lies with the

Intergovernmental Panel on Climate Change (Yamin and Depledge 2005, chapter 15). The single competency of the climate secretariat is the provision of informatory, technical, and analytical knowledge and advice. This restriction helps to understand that the climate secretariat could not have autonomous and direct normative or executive influence or shape scientific debates. Given that all treaty secretariats studied in this book face similar restrictions, the lack of regulatory and financial competencies however cannot be the only reason that the climate secretariat had less autonomous influence.

Above all, the climate secretariat had less influence, because ever since its creation, it has faced what I describe as its "straitjacket," that is, severe constraints on its autonomy. Like any other treaty secretariat, the climate secretariat is mandated to impartiality (Yamin and Depledge 2005, 485). In the climate regime, however, many powerful parties or groups of parties have a particular strong interest in preventing the climate secretariat from pressing ahead with the regime or from carrying out activities beyond what they mandate and request. In view of the problem structure, most powerful parties or groups of parties fear the drastic economic and social consequences of an increasingly effective climate regime. Many governments in developing countries refuse to adopt effective obligations to reduce greenhouse gas emissions, because they perceive these as threats the economic development and catching-up process of their countries. Governments in developed countries, including the U.S. government, in turn fear substantial disadvantages for their economic prospects and competitiveness if they agree on mandatory emission reductions without similar obligations for major developing countries. Governments of oil exporting countries, like many countries on the Arabian Peninsula, fear substantial income losses if the consumption of oil and natural gas decreases in the wake of an effective climate regime (for an overview of positions and interests, see Oberthür and Ott 1999, 13–32; Biermann 2005; Yamin and Depledge 2005, chap. 3). Hence most parties do not want a strong and independent climate secretariat, which advances the climate regime by pursuing its own agenda and thereby possibly favors the interests of one group of parties over those of another, because it could be to their disadvantages with severe repercussions on the wealth and prosperity of their countries. "The secretariat is expected to help to steer the negotiations to a successful conclusion. Yet this expectation does not extend to one of true leadership; the parties do not expect the secretariat to lead, but rather to assist them.

In the minds of the parties the secretariat is their servant, not their leader" (Depledge 2005, 65).

In contrast to the desertification secretariat (see Bauer, this volume, chapter 12), parties do not at all tolerate if the climate secretariat advocates own ideas (Depledge 2005, 85). Parties immediately react, in some cases harshly, when the climate secretariat presents input that contradicts positions and interests of parties, puts an undue emphasis on specific approaches and aspects of a given problem, or favors one group of parties over another. "Whenever we kind of stretch our mandate beyond what they want us to do, there is immediate feed-back and the feed-back will be quite effective"[13] (see, e.g., Depledge 2005, 67 and 76–77; ENB 1996b, 10; ENB 2002, 1). Parties then force the climate secretariat to revise or even withdraw its input (Depledge 2005, 77).[14] If the input relates to politically controversial questions, the straitjacket becomes particularly evident. The parties expect the climate secretariat to consider a broad range of different positions and interests in a way acceptable to all parties. It needs to carefully balance the differing expectations of parties and to justify any action against its mandate (Depledge 2005, 64–65 and 165). If the climate secretariat fails to live up to these expectations, it risks losing the trust and confidence in its impartiality, which it has built up over time (Depledge 2005, 69). Only when it advises parties on technical questions, it has some scope for its own ideas.[15] Even then, it provides input on the request of parties, which define the terms of reference quite narrowly.

The climate secretariat faces similar constraints when it prepares information on the compliance of parties with their obligations. It must not assess the political implications and relevance of the information that parties submit (Depledge 2005, 68). In fact, it is inconceivable that the climate secretariat feeds this information into public discourses to pursue own purposes or to directly name and blame a party for noncompliance. At best, it identifies a number of options for further action. The compilation and synthesis of the information must not involve any criticizing political assessments of the results or policy recommendations. "Criticism is not wanted. An assessment is immediately seen as being an assessment of whether the party is doing its job and then it becomes political. The parties do not want us to get into those areas."[16]

Resources   The climate secretariat has the largest funds of all treaty secretariats studied in this book. Its core budget steadily increased from roughly USD 16 million for the biennium 1995/1996 to USD 53 million for the biennium 2006/2007. Likewise, staff steadily increased from 44 in 1996 to 199 in 2007. Evidence is missing, though, that the allocation of resources and staff positively or negatively affected the autonomous influence of the climate secretariat. Even the very few staff members in the climate secretariat who complained about a mismatch between resources and workload did not link this perceived lack to the limited influence of the secretariat.

Embeddedness   The organizational setup of the climate secretariat fits comparatively well to the challenges it has to cope with, and mirrors the major functional areas of the climate regime. Despite an isolated complaint about the speed with which the climate secretariat had adapted the allocation of staff to the increasing importance of its tasks in regime implementation, a systematic and noticeable effect on the influence of the climate secretariat could not be observed.

Its formal mandate and actual activities give the climate secretariat a key position in the larger organizational setting. In fact, in the climate secretariat everything related to the climate regime comes together. Almost any input that parties, convention bodies and formally affiliated organizations feed into the climate regime crosses the desks in the climate secretariat. A considerable share of input originates in the secretariat itself. Moreover, the climate secretariat is the only body of the climate regime that maintains close links to all convention bodies, affiliated organizations, the major stakeholders, and the media. In this sense, "the secretariat is the heart of the international process that is surrounding the climate change issue."[17]

The climate secretariat, however, was unable to convert its key position into noteworthy influence, because of the previously described constraints that parties impose on its autonomy. The relationship between the climate secretariat and the presiding officers during meetings of the conference of the parties or its subsidiary bodies best illustrates how this straitjacket reduces the potential for the climate secretariat to effectively exploit its key position and to have autonomous influence. Although the rules of procedure even mandate the climate secretariat to support and advise the presiding officers during negotiations or consultations (rule 28.2), it is entirely dependent on the good will of presiding officers. They decide whether to ask the climate secretariat for advice and whether to use the advice. The "presiding officers will always have the final say in whether a particular approach—substantive or procedural—is taken" (Depledge 2005, 67; see also Depledge 2007). If the presiding officer decides not to draw on the input or advice of the climate secretariat—as happened, for example, during the conference of the parties at The Hague, where parties failed to agree upon implementing rules for the Kyoto Protocol—it is condemned to inactivity. Yet apart from being unable, the secretariat was simply unwilling to exploit its key position in the climate regime and convert it into autonomous influence. I will demonstrate this unwillingness in the next section on organizational culture.

People and Procedures

Organizational Culture Overall, staff working at the climate secretariat has internalized the expectations of parties and has accepted their definition of boundaries, thereby limiting itself to a technocratic and politically neutral approach in any of its activities. In contrast to the desertification secretariat, which often behaves like an autonomous political actor and pursues its own goals (Bauer, this volume, chapter 12), and the biodiversity secretariat, which takes initiative and puts through particular issues (Siebenhüner, this volume, chapter 11), staff in the climate secretariat has not tried to tell parties what they should agree upon, but rather presents a variety of options. At best, it has assisted parties in their efforts to agree upon approaches acceptable to them whenever parties requested, and only then.[18] As reaction to criticism by parties when it went too far, "secretariat staff have been extremely reluctant to paraphrase or simplify complex negotiated text . . . for fear of inflaming sensitivities and being accused of bias" (Depledge 2005, 68). The secretariat has never attempted to shape public or scientific discourses or to push these toward a specific political direction. Neither has the climate secretariat tried to convince parties to adopt certain actions to improve their implementation record or to criticize parties for the lack of implementation. It deliberately refrained from initiating discussions on issues that are taboo in the perception of parties, for example, the question on future reductions of greenhouse gas emissions after the first compliance period of the Kyoto Protocol.[19]

Instead, the climate secretariat strives to ensure that parties perceive it as impartial body that does not favor one party's views over those of another or advocate specific approaches. It sees itself as provider of factual information that never takes sides with one or another party or comments explicitly on any activity of parties.[20] Staff cleanses all information from political or policy-sensitive implications and presents information without adding any evaluation. The deliberate decision of the climate secretariat to adopt a relatively minimalist approach to public relations mirrors the dominant organizational culture (Depledge 2005, 68).[21]

Paradoxically, this organizational culture of a technocratic bureaucracy is also an important if not indispensable prerequisite for its ability to have some influence at all and to promote successful negotiations and effective implementation of the regime (Yamin and Depledge 2005, 485; Depledge 2005, 78).[22] The climate secretariat needs to keep up its impartial appearance: "Perceptions of partiality within the secretariat would be a . . . persistent problem that could put the whole process in jeopardy" (Depledge 2005, 65). Staff members share this assessment. The climate secretariat would be able to influence the regime evolution only "if we are balanced and if we try to meet the demands of the parties. This is our big plus that we are following what we are told to do and that we are doing this in an objective and non-biased way."[23]

Organizational Leadership   In contrast to the biodiversity and desertification secretariats (see Siebenhüner, this volume, chapter 11; Bauer, this volume, chapter 12), staff members of the climate secretariat, including the executive staff, deliberately abstain from exercising leadership vis-à-vis parties and from pursuing openly a proactive role in the regime.[24] The first executive secretary, Michael Zammit Cutajar, has already urged staff to abstain from any proactive involvement in the negotiation or implementation of the climate regime (Depledge 2007). Every interviewed staff member in the secretariat was reluctant and often unwilling to attribute any kind of autonomous influence to the climate secretariat, which shows that this behavior is a constitutive part of its general organizational culture. "The job of the secretariat is not to shape or influence any international climate politics. Our house philosophy is that we see our process as being very much government driven. We are not an independent think tank that can just develop and throw ideas into the process. We are here to serve a particular process and we are paid for doing this job according to the instructions that are given by parties."[25] Every interviewed staff member stressed that any perception of leadership would severely conflict with its mandate and the expectations of parties. In fact, the climate secretariat "has very rarely attempted to exercise open substantive leadership by brokering agreements among parties" (Depledge 2005, 73).

Organizational Expertise   Similar to the other intergovernmental bureaucracies studied in this book, the influence of the climate secretariat rests
mainly on its expertise. Actors use the climate secretariat's information,
because the climate secretariat—like the other treaty secretariats studied in
this book—is the only authoritative source of information on the legal,
procedural, and technical issues of the regime—not to be confused with the
scientific expertise that the International Panel on Climate Change makes
available to parties. For example, the climate secretariat's database on
greenhouse gas inventories is the most comprehensive and reliable source
of information on greenhouse gas emissions. Likewise, the climate secretariat administers and disseminates all official documents related to the
negotiation and implementation of the climate regime. Hence, actors interested in regime evolution must draw on information of the climate secretariat. In fact, also the parties have no other choice than to use the climate
secretariat's Web site if they want up-to-date information on the regime
progress, since the Web site serves as an important negotiating tool.[26]

More importantly, the climate secretariat's outstanding expertise
enables it to provide parties with useful advice on any legal, procedural,
or technical issue in the negotiation and implementation of the regime.
Similar to the other treaty secretariats studied in this book, the political
and technical expertise that the climate secretariat has accumulated since
its creation allows it to carry out targeted analyses on specific negotiation
and implementation issues (Yamin and Depledge 2005, 485) as well as
to counsel presiding officers (Depledge 2005, 72). Its ability to provide
input "closely tailored to the parties' needs" is an indispensable prerequisite for its achievements. In an internal review, parties commended the
advice of the climate secretariat and its input with regard to technical and
legal issues (UNFCCC 2005, 7; see also Depledge 2005, 77). The skill of
the climate secretariat in developing balanced and impartial input mainly
results from its experience with the political sensitivities and the technical
issues (Depledge 2005, 73).[27] Staff members could gather important inside
knowledge about the parties because of their exclusive access to the delegates. The opportunity to follow the discussions between parties during
the negotiations further strengthens their expertise (Depledge 2005). On
that basis, the climate secretariat is capable of grasping what formulation
or which option(s) look promising and could constitute the basis for a
consensual decisions of parties (Depledge 2005).[28]

Comparable to the ozone secretariat (Bauer, this volume, chapter
9), the staff of the climate secretariat has a "competitive advantage"
vis-à-vis government officials in terms of expertise, because of the full-

time occupation at the climate secretariat with political and technical questions of the regime.[29] Government officials often lack time for a thorough preparation or must first become acquainted with the issues. For example, the lesser experience and competence the presiding officer has, the more important the climate secretariat's expertise becomes (Depledge 2005, 66 and 72; Yamin and Depledge 2005, 507). And yet the above-described straitjacket and the organizational culture of the climate secretariat prevented staff from converting expertise and competitive advantages into stronger autonomous influence.

Organizational Structure   The internal procedures and the staff composition ensured that the climate secretariat could live up to the expectations of parties to provide balanced input and advice. The preparation of advice usually involves several staff members, who contemplate and play through the range of conceivable scenarios and options from a broad range of different angles and seek to identify those options that promise to emerge as the basis for consensual decisions.[30] The staff comes from countries and regions across the world and has different professional backgrounds, which has facilitated the consideration and incorporation of distinct perspectives.[31]

Conclusion

The climate secretariat has largely operated as a technocratic bureaucracy. Unlike the biodiversity and desertification secretariats (Siebenhüner, this volume, chapter 11; Bauer, this volume, chapter 12), the climate secretariat has not advocated its own political ideas or proposed specific technical approaches. It has not influenced *whether* and *which* political decisions or technical solutions parties adopt. At best, it has facilitated negotiations and assisted parties to achieve what they wanted to achieve. Whenever requested, it has supported them in identifying options for political agreements and facilitated their decisions on *how* they might implement these. The climate secretariat has facilitated progress only within the confines parties defined and above all, has executed what governments intended and requested. It has, however, not shaped international climate politics and did not even attempt to leave a genuine footprint on it.

The problem structure—in particular, the fears of powerful groups of parties that effective responses to climate change will have drastic consequences on their economic and social development—are the nucleus of the limitations in the influence of the climate secretariat. These concerns of parties resulted not only in severe constraints on the autonomy of the climate secretariat; they also reduced considerably the potential as well as the willingness and ability of the climate secretariat to convert its key position in the climate regime into actual leverage. Essentially, the strait-jacket that parties imposed through formal and informal rules on the climate secretariat left it with no other choice than acting as technocratic bureaucracy and performing its duties and responsibilities in anticipatory obedience to the expectations of parties. The straitjacket ruled out any proactive role or autonomous initiatives by the climate secretariat. It culminated in an organizational culture that bars staff in the climate secretariat from exercising any leadership vis-à-vis parties and from assuming a more independent role. This behavior has appeased the majority of parties and made it possible for the climate secretariat to use its political and technical expertise to the benefit of the climate regime evolution and realize its comparatively minor cognitive and normative influence.

Acknowledgments

I owe my gratitude to all interviewees at the climate secretariat. I am also grateful for valuable comments and suggestions on earlier versions of this text to Joanna Depledge, Philipp Pattberg, and the MANUS project team.

Notes

1. http://unfccc.int/secretariat/items/1629.php, cited 29 December 2005.
2. Author's interview at the climate secretariat, Bonn, July 2004.
3. http://unfccc.int/essential_background/about_the_website/items/3358.php, cited 29 December 2005.
4. Author's interview at the climate secretariat, Bonn, July 2004.
5. Author's interviews at the climate secretariat, Bonn, July 2004.
6. Author's interviews at the climate secretariat, Bonn, July 2004.
7. Author's interviews at the climate secretariat, Bonn, July 2004.
8. Author's interviews at the climate secretariat, Bonn, July 2004.
9. Author's interviews at the climate secretariat, Bonn, July 2004.
10. Author's interview at the climate secretariat, Bonn, July 2004.
11. Author's interview at the climate secretariat, Bonn, July 2004.

12. Author's interview at the climate secretariat, Bonn, July 2004.

13. Author's interview at the climate secretariat, Bonn, July 2004.

14. Author's interview at the climate secretariat, Bonn, July 2004.

15. Author's interview at the climate secretariat, Bonn, July 2004.

16. Author's interview at the climate secretariat, Bonn, July 2004.

17. Author's interview at the climate secretariat, Bonn, July 2004.

18. Author's interviews at the climate secretariat, Bonn, July 2004.

19. Author's interview at the climate secretariat, Bonn, July 2004.

20. Author's interview at the climate secretariat, Bonn, July 2004.

21. Author's interview at the climate secretariat, Bonn, July 2004.

22. Author's interviews at the climate secretariat, Bonn, July 2004.

23. Author's interview at the climate secretariat, Bonn, July 2004.

24. Author's interviews at the climate secretariat, Bonn, July 2004.

25. Author's interview at the climate secretariat, Bonn, July 2004.

26. Author's interview at the climate secretariat, Bonn, July 2004.

27. Author's interview at the climate secretariat, Bonn, July 2004.

28. Author's interview at the climate secretariat, Bonn, July 2004.

29. Author's interview at the climate secretariat, Bonn, July 2004.

30. Author's interview at the climate secretariat, Bonn, July 2004.

31. Author's interview at the climate secretariat, Bonn, July 2004. As of June 2005, of the seventy-six program officers employed at the secretariat, thirty-three came from Western Europe and other industrialized countries, sixteen from countries in Asia and the Pacific, eleven from countries in Latin America and the Caribbean, eight from countries in Africa, and eight from countries in Eastern Europe. Over time, these patterns have changed only slightly.

References

Andresen, Steinar, and Siri Hals Butenschon. 2001. "Norwegian Climate Policy: From Pusher to Laggard?" *International Environmental Agreements: Politics, Law and Economics* 1 (3): 337–356.

Barrett, Brendan F. D., and W. Bradnee Chambers, editors. 1998. *Primer on Scientific Knowledge and Politics in the Evolving Global Climate Change Regime: Cop 3 and the Kyoto Protocol.* Tokyo: UNU Press.

Biermann, Frank. 2005. "Between the United States and the South. Strategic Choices for European Climate Policy." *Climate Policy* 5 (3): 273–290.

Biermann, Frank, and Ingrid Boas. 2007. *Preparing for a Warmer World. Towards a Global Governance System to Protect Climate Refugees.* Global Governance Working Paper No 33. Amsterdam and others: The Global Governance Project. Available at www.glogov.org (accessed 10 September 2008).

Depledge, Joanna. 2005. *The Organization of Global Negotiations: Constructing the Climate Change Regime*. London: Earthscan.

Depledge, Joanna. 2007. "A Special Relationship: Chairpersons and the Secretariat in the Climate Change Negotiations." *Global Environmental Politics* 7 (1): 45–68.

Eckersley, Robyn. 2004. "Soft Law, Hard Politics, and the Climate Change Treaty." In *The Politics of International Law*, edited by Christian Reus-Smit, 80–105. Cambridge, UK: Cambridge University Press.

ENB, Earth Negotiations Bulletin. 1996a. *Report of the Meetings of the Subsidiary Bodies of the UN Framework Convention on Climate Change: 9–18 December 1996* (Vol. 12, No. 39). Available at http://www.iisd.ca/linkages/download/pdf/enb1239e.pdf (accessed 27 November 2004).

ENB, Earth Negotiations Bulletin. 1996b. *Summary of the Second Conference of the Parties to the Framework Convention on Climate Change: 8–19 July 1996* (Vol. 12, No. 38). Available at http://www.iisd.ca/linkages/download/pdf/enb1238e.pdf (last accessed 27 November 2004).

ENB, Earth Negotiations Bulletin. 2000. *Summary of the Sixth Conference of the Parties to the UN Framework Convention on Climate Change: 13–25 November 2000* (Vol. 12, No. 163). Available at http://www.iisd.ca/linkages/download/pdf/enb12163e.pdf (accessed 27 November 2004).

ENB, Earth Negotiations Bulletin. 2001. *Seventh Conference of the Parties to the Un Framework Convention on Climate Change: Monday, 29 October 2001* (Vol. 12, No. 170). Available at http://www.iisd.ca/download/pdf/enb12179e.pdf (accessed 18 August 2004).

ENB, Earth Negotiations Bulletin. 2002. *Highlights from UNFCCC COP-8, Wednesday, 23 October 2002* (Vol. 12, No. 202). Available at http://www.iisd.ca/linkages/download/pdf/enb12202e.pdf (accessed 27 November 2004).

ENB, Earth Negotiations Bulletin. 2005. *Summary of the Eleventh Conference of the Parties to the UN Framework Convention on Climate Change and First Conference of the Parties Serving as the Meeting of the Parties to the Kyoto Protocol: 28 November–10 December 2005* (Vol. 12, No. 291). Available at http://www.iisd.ca/linkages/download/pdf/enb12291e.pdf (accessed 13 January 2006).

German Advisory Council on Global Change. 2008. *World in Transition: Climate Change as Security Risk*. London: Earthscan.

Grubb, Michael, Christiaan Vrolijk, and Duncan Brack. 1999. *The Kyoto Protocol: A Guide and Assessment*. London: Royal Institute of International Affairs, Energy and Environmental Programme.

Grubb, Michael, and Farhana Yamin. 2001. "Climate Collapse at The Hague: What Happened, Why, and Where Do We Go from Here?" *International Affairs* 77 (2): 261–276.

Intergovernmental Panel on Climate Change. 2001. *IPCC Third Assessment Report. Climate Change 2001: Impacts, Adaptation and Vulnerability*. Cambridge, UK: Cambridge University Press.

Lee, Geoff. 1999. "Environmental Policy: Too Little Too Late?" In *Political Issues in Britain Today*, edited by Bill Jones, 245–280. Manchester, UK: Manchester University Press.

Miles, Edward L., Arild Underdal, Steinar Andresen, Jørgen Wettestad, Jon Birger Skjærseth, and Elaine M. Carlin, editors. 2001. *Environmental Regime Effectiveness. Confronting Theory with Evidence*. Cambridge, MA: MIT Press.

Nitze, William A. 1994. "A Failure of Presidential Leadership." In *Negotiating Climate Change: The Inside Story to the Rio Convention*, edited by Irving M. Mintzer, and J. Amber Leonard, 187–200. Cambridge, UK: Cambridge University Press.

Oberthür, Sebastian, and Hermann E. Ott. 1999. *The Kyoto Protocol: International Climate Policy for the 21st Century*. Berlin, Heidelberg, and New York: Springer.

Ott, Hermann E. 2001a. "The Bonn Agreement to the Kyoto Protocol: Paving the Way for Ratification." *International Environmental Agreements: Politics, Law and Economics* 1 (4): 469–476.

Ott, Hermann E. 2001b. "Climate Change: An Important Foreign Policy Issue." *Foreign Affairs* 77 (2): 277–296.

Schröder, Heike. 2001. *Negotiating the Kyoto Protocol: An Analysis of Negotiation Dynamics in International Negotiations*. Münster: LIT Verlag.

Stern, Nicholas. 2007. *The Economics of Climate Change. The Stern Review*. Cambridge, UK: Cambridge University Press.

Tarradell, Mireia. 2007. *The Influence of International Bureaucracies in Global Environmental Politics: Results from an Expert Survey*. Global Governance Working Paper 26. Amsterdam and others: The Global Governance Project.

UNFCCC, United Nations Framework Convention on Climate Change. 2004. *Results of the Survey on the Effectiveness of the Use of the UNFCCC Technology Information Clearing House. Note by the Secretariat*. UN Doc. FCCC/SBSTA/2004/INF.8. Available at http://unfccc.int/resource/docs/2004/sbsta/inf08.pdf (accessed 29 December 2005).

UNFCCC, United Nations Framework Convention on Climate Change. 2005. *Report on the Internal Review of the Activities of the Secretariat. Note by the Executive Secretary*. UN Doc. FCCC/SBI/2005/6. Available at http://unfccc.int/resource/docs/2005/sbi/eng/06.pdf (accessed 29 December 2005).

Vrolijk, Christiaan. 2002. *A New Interpretation of the Kyoto Protocol. Outcomes from The Hague, Bonn, and Marrakesh*. London: Royal Institute of International Affairs.

Wettestad, Jørgen. 1999. *Designing Effective Environmental Regimes: The Key Conditions*. Cheltenham, UK: Edward Elgar.

Yamin, Farhana, and Joanna Depledge. 2005. *The International Climate Change Regime: A Guide to Rules, Institutions and Procedures*. Cambridge, UK: Cambridge University Press.

11

The Biodiversity Secretariat: Lean Shark in Troubled Waters

Bernd Siebenhüner

Introduction

The secretariat of the Convention on Biological Diversity ("biodiversity secretariat") has been established as a treaty secretariat comparable to those of the climate convention or the desertification convention. Yet even though the mandates of these bureaucracies are rather similar, the biodiversity secretariat appears significantly more successful in generating normative influence compared with other treaty secretariats. Several experts even argue that the implementation of the convention would not have been as advanced without the work of the secretariat, which has been described as a small but effective "lean shark."[1] On the other hand, the secretariat has been less able to generate significant cognitive or executive influence.

The Convention on Biological Diversity ("biodiversity convention") was the attempt of the international community to address the challenges of the massive human-induced loss of biodiversity that exceeded the natural rate by about fifty to one hundred times over the past decades (Pimm et al. 1995). It is generally regarded as one of the major achievements of the UN Conference on Environment and Development in Rio de Janeiro in 1992. Resulting from a five-year negotiation under the auspices of UNEP, the convention was opened for signature at the Rio Summit and entered into force in December 1993. As of 2008, 189 states have ratified the convention—with the prominent exception of the United States.

Parties to the convention commit to three obligations: to the conservation of biological diversity, to its sustainable use, and to the fair and equitable sharing of the benefits arising from the use of genetic resources (SCBD 2003, Swanson 1999). The convention paved the road for future negotiations and international action to conserve biological diversity.

First, in contrast to previous attempts to combat biodiversity loss that exclusively focused on nature conservation[2], the convention pioneered in integrating conservation and economic use of biodiversity. Thereby, environmental and development interests were integrated to meet both conservation interests of the North and the development interests of the South (Boisvert and Caron 2002, Rojas and Thomas 1992). Second, the convention was the first legally binding treaty to acknowledge the sovereign rights of nation-states over their genetic resources (Kothari 1994, Svarstad 1994). Third, negotiators included a passage about technology transfer to facilitate access and conservation of genetic resources that was targeted at development goals and was partly conflicting with the interests of the emerging biotechnology industry. Overall, the convention brought several new regulations and orientations on biological diversity, but was unable to halt the accelerating loss of biodiversity all over the world (Le Prestre 2002b; Rosendal 1995).

As integral part of the convention process, the secretariat is responsible for the provision of support for implementation at large by facilitating negotiations, providing information, and monitoring. As it is a comparatively small convention secretariat formally under the auspices of UNEP, one would expect it to have limited influence on governments and business actors. Dealing with highly controversial issues between business and environmentalist interests, between environment and development concerns and between owners of and aspirants for related technologies, the secretariat has to maneuver through troubled waters.

The literature on the secretariat and its activities is scant and hardly suffices for an in-depth analysis. Although many sources discuss the convention[3] and its functioning and influence, the role of the secretariat is rarely discussed in detail. Only Le Prestre (2002a) examined the role of the secretariat within the governance system of the convention with regard to size, the role of its executive secretary, financial resources, location, and status. His study remains skeptical about the influence of the secretariat with regard to the governance of biodiversity in general, but it does not cover a detailed empirical analysis of the influence vis-à-vis national governments and other stakeholders. In his study on coordination problems among environmental treaty agencies, Andresen (2001) merely touched upon the conflict-laden relationship between the biodiversity secretariat and UNEP.

Data for this case study have been drawn from desk studies of existing documents from the secretariat and other sources. A group interview with five staff members of the secretariat as well as four additional personal interviews and a written questionnaire delivered data on internal processes as well as the external influence of the secretariat. Additional interviews and follow-up inquiries with five staff members were conducted in October 2004 and in January and February 2006. The senior expert survey with experts in Germany, India, Mexico, and the United States was answered by twenty individuals (Tarradell 2007).[4]

Structure and Activities

During the short history of the biodiversity secretariat, the internal structures and procedures have undergone several revisions and changes. Most of them were triggered by new external demands and the personal initiative of the executive secretaries.

In the first phase, starting in 1993 upon the convention's entry into force, the secretariat came into being as an interim secretariat based in Geneva under the control of UNEP. The first meeting of the parties designated UNEP to carry out the functions of the convention secretariat while ensuring its autonomy to discharge its main functions as described by the biodiversity convention. Approved by a decision of the first conference of the parties in 1994, this interim solution persisted until 1996. The interim secretariat consisted of a small number of staff and was to a large extent occupied with establishing its own structure and the bodies of the convention.

The first significant change took place when the secretariat moved to Montreal in 1996 following an offer by the Canadian government. It became a separate bureaucracy with an independent budget, even though it continued to be formally a part of UNEP. The responsibilities of the executive secretary at that time—Calestous Juma from Kenya—and UNEP were an issue of intense debates.[5] Following a process of emancipation from UNEP, the relationship between UNEP and the biodiversity secretariat was clarified through the adoption of the administrative arrangements at the fourth conference of the parties in Bratislava in 1998. At that time, the secretariat had four divisions with a staff of about twenty.[6] In addition, a small implementation unit existed under the administration of the GEF that dealt with biodiversity-related reports from national governments.

A second significant change of internal processes and structures took place in 2000, initiated by the then–executive secretary, Hamdallah

Zedan. He decided to amend the structure of the Division for Scientific, Technical, and Technological Matters, to separate the implementation part from the scientific matters, and to form a new division responsible for social, economic and legal affairs. At the same time, he established a new division responsible for resource management and conference services. These changes were not based on an organization-wide review or evaluation but mainly on the decision of the executive secretary.

Following the adoption of the target to reduce the global loss of biodiversity significantly by 2010,[7] the secretariat decided to shift its emphasis toward implementation and monitoring. It is the explicit ambition of Executive Secretary Ahmed Djoghlaf, who assumed office in 2006, to take steps toward more applied work and to advance biodiversity-related projects.

Article 24 of the biodiversity convention lays down the mandate of the secretariat: it has to arrange for and service meetings of the conference of the parties; perform the functions assigned to it by any protocol; prepare reports on the execution of its functions under this convention; coordinate with other international bodies; and perform such other functions as may be determined by the conference of the parties.

When compared to other secretariats analyzed in this book, and most other environmental treaty secretariats (Sandford 1994, 1996), this mandate is rather similar regarding the assigned tasks. During the preparation of the convention, little controversy arose over this mandate except for debates on the financial mechanism for project funding that was not given to the secretariat but to the GEF in coordination with other agencies, including the secretariat (Rosendal 1995).

In 2004, the secretariat had a staff of seventy, which is rather small compared to other international bureaucracies and to national environmental administrations. Most staff is funded through the convention's Trust Fund as approved by the conference of the parties; some are funded by UNEP, the FAO, and individual governments. The secretariat is now organized into four divisions and two units.[8] The secretariat is directed by the executive secretary, Ahmed Djoghlaf from Algeria, who also heads the Executive Direction, Management, and Intergovernmental Affairs Division.

As part of the convention process, the secretariat has to serve other bodies, such as the conference of the parties, the Subsidiary Body for Scientific, Technical, and Technological Advice (SBSTTA) and the working groups established by the conference of the parties. Representing all states that ratified the treaty, the conference of the parties is the governing body of the convention and reviews the progress of the implementation, identifies new priorities, and decides about work plans for the secretariat, contracting parties, and other relevant actors, as well as the budget of the secretariat. The conference of the parties can also decide upon amendments and adopt protocols to the convention. SBSTTA, by contrast, is a subsidiary body composed of experts from member governments with expertise in relevant fields. It plays a key role in preparing decisions of the conference of the parties and in giving advice on scientific and technical issues (Koetz et al. 2008). All conferences of the parties, SBSTTA, and working group meetings are prepared, organized and documented by the secretariat. The secretariat also prepares the background documents for the meetings. Other bodies of the biodiversity convention comprise expert panels as well as a clearinghouse mechanism.

Funding for biodiversity-related projects in developing countries is provided by the GEF. The conference of the parties provides guidance on policies, priorities, and eligibility criteria to GEF as the financial mechanism of the convention.

The Influence of the Biodiversity Secretariat

Based on the criteria for measuring the influence of international bureaucracies as presented in chapter 3, this section examines the kinds of influence the biodiversity secretariat had. It follows the distinction between cognitive, executive and normative influence.

Cognitive Influence

Even though the biodiversity secretariat has neither the means nor the mandate for scientific research, one of its main tasks is to collect and disseminate (scientific) knowledge. Yet it maintains close links with the scientific community through international assessments, international scientific cooperative programs such as DIVERSITAS (an international programme of biodiversity science), and the participation of staff members in scientific symposia. The secretariat gathers scientific information on biodiversity conservation, as well as on administrative, social, legal, and economic aspects, for example, of access and benefit sharing. This knowledge is processed and made available mostly to representatives of national governments and administrators through preparatory documents, the secretariat's Web site, series of reports, a newsletter, and a comprehensive handbook. Moreover, the secretariat has commissioned the drafting and publication of the Global Biodiversity Outlook, a voluminous report on the status and the policy measures to achieve the goals of the convention. It compiles a broad range of scientific knowledge available to the secretariat. The first report of this kind was published in 2001 (SCBD 2001). In addition, the secretariat is involved in the well-connected Millennium Ecosystem Assessment, which was supported by governments, several convention processes, and nongovernmental stakeholders such as the business community and environmentalist groups.[9]

Nevertheless, the outcomes of these activities are limited to select target groups that make regular use of these products. Whereas the information provided by the secretariat is much welcomed and frequently used by most national delegates to the international negotiations as well as by nongovernmental organizations, neither the scientific community at large nor business actors draw on this information source. According to the expert survey conducted for this research program (Tarradell 2007), representatives of national governments and nongovernmental organizations acknowledge primarily the scientific information, and 37 percent of all respondents draw on it on a monthly basis. Yet only 47 percent of the responding experts regard the information provided by the secretariat as relevant for their work, which is the lowest percentage for a bureaucracy analyzed in this volume. The quality of the information provided is by and large seen as scientifically credible and politically neutral. This influence can be viewed as a success of the secretariat's information policy in establishing trust with parties and other stakeholders.

The influence of the biodiversity secretariat on public discourses internationally and domestically remains limited. Media attention to the press releases, press conferences, and the other material provided by the secretariat is low. Members of the secretariats and external stakeholders gave consistent responses on this issue.[10] Yet respondents acknowledged by a large majority a positive effect of the identification of new environmental issues in domestic public debates.

A comprehensive communication strategy was developed with the help of external communication experts to reach broader audiences with its information. As part of an education and public awareness program, the strategy aims at bringing the problems of biodiversity and biodiversity conservation to the minds of different target groups such as the media, schools, governments, or indigenous communities. (Because the campaign was launched in 2003, its success could not be assessed in this study.)

Normative Influence

International cooperation and the support for negotiations and meetings is the most obvious influence of the biodiversity secretariat. The convention itself has almost universal membership, excluding from the major countries only the United States. The convention's most prominent protocol, the Cartagena Protocol on Biosafety, has been ratified by more than one hundred countries and entered into force in 2003 (Gupta 2004, 2006; Gupta and Falkner 2006).

During its existence, the secretariat had no urgent need to increase the number of participants to the biodiversity convention. But keeping parties at the table of the negotiations over highly controversial issues such as biosafety or access and benefit sharing poses a significant challenge for international bureaucracies such as the secretariat. Conflicting interests, heterogeneous cultures, and personal differences constantly jeopardize these processes.

Our expert survey conveys that most stakeholders regard the secretariat as effective with regard to drawing governments into international negotiations. Its balanced and continuous efforts in facilitating dialogues and negotiations on biosafety contributed immensely to the successful adoption of the protocol—notwithstanding weak and imprecise formulations in the convention and the protocol that allowed some critical countries to join. The secretariat was also conducive to the negotiations on the access and benefit provisions of the biodiversity convention as decided by the fourth conference of the parties in February 2004 in Kuala Lumpur (Siebenhüner and Suplie 2005).

With regard to the inclusion of nongovernmental actors, the convention designed its processes highly inclusive in contrast to other UN conventions where nongovernmental organizations are restricted to passive observer functions (Heijden 2002). Most respondents of the expert survey conducted for this book acknowledge the influence of the secretariat to increase participation of nongovernmental organizations in international policies. For example, the secretariat promoted the inclusion of indigenous and local communities in the Working Group on article 8j (traditional knowledge), where they now play a similar role as government delegates (even though technically they are still observers). This working group provided a platform for indigenous and local communities to articulate their concerns and interests regarding the preservation, respect and protection of traditional biodiversity-related knowledge, innovations, and practices (Coombe 2001).

The secretariat was also successful at including items on the agenda in international negotiations. For instance, it is considered the secretariat's success to include the ecosystem approach prominent in the biodiversity convention into other conventions such as the 1971 Ramsar Convention on Wetlands of International Importance Especially as Waterfowl Habitat.

This approach has been applied to biodiversity conservation policies.[11] The secretariat was also instrumental with respect to the inclusion of the 2010 biodiversity target and elements of the convention's programs of work, including access to genetic resources and benefit-sharing, in the Plan of Implementation agreed upon at the 2002 World Summit on Sustainable Development.[12]

Since 2000, the secretariat has also been entrusted with the drafting of decisions of the conference of the parties and SBSTTA. Based on positive experiences over past years, governmental delegations consider the secretariat's position on topics under debate as neutral and accept it as a valuable input in negotiations. In highly contested issues such as the access and benefit-sharing provisions of the biodiversity convention, the suggestions of the secretariat are usually amended or completely redrafted by the conference of the parties. In more technical issues, however, such as the development of indicators for the 2010 target or the results of the Millennium Ecosystem Assessment, the secretariat prepared texts that passed with minor amendments. One member of the secretariat explained: "As a national delegate it was my highest ambition to change at least one word in the text of the decision, as part of the secretariat I can influence the whole text."[13]

Since the biodiversity convention exists in parallel to similar multilateral agreements related to biodiversity issues, such as the Ramsar convention on wetlands, CITES, and the climate convention, the secretariat has to collaborate with other international bureaucracies.[14] The secretariat has managed to develop collaborative relationships with most of these organizations. It developed joint programs of work with a number of conventions and international organizations, including the Ramsar Convention on Wetlands, the desertification convention, the Convention on the Conservation of Migratory Species, and the International Union for Conservation of Nature. As one member of the secretariat explained with regard to the recommendations of the biodiversity convention, "We work with them, we can convince them that it is important to respond positively to these recommendations."[15] Advice on the integration of biodiversity concerns into the implementation of the climate convention and its Kyoto Protocol, prepared by an expert group under the biodiversity convention, was welcomed by the climate convention's subsidiary body on scientific advice which encouraged countries to make use of it. This influence has also been apparent in the case of the World Intellectual Property Organization, which took up the issue of traditional knowledge as a problem for the provision of intellectual property rights, due to interventions from the conference of the parties of the biodiversity convention brought forward through the secretariat: "They know that if they don't do it [to deal with this problem], it will be done here and it will have serious implications for them." In 2004, the secretariat followed an initiative by UNEP and took the lead in a liaison group on biodiversity-related conventions that included the Bonn Convention on the Conservation of Migratory Species, CITES, the Ramsar Convention on Wetlands of International Importance Especially as Waterfowl Habitat, and the World Heritage Convention. The group is composed of all the executive heads of the convention bureaucracies and has to coordinate the implementation of the conventions. In this function, the executive secretary of the biodiversity secretariat has potential leverage also on conventions other than the biodiversity convention.

The widely acknowledged activities of the secretariat in facilitating the implementation of the convention and promoting international cooperation in this matter were also somewhat counterproductive. Delegates of formerly highly committed governments in the field reduced their level of activity due to effective work of the secretariat in promoting the objectives of the convention. Therefore, more work and initiative is left to the secretariat, as governmental officials saw an opportunity to reduce their inputs.

In sum, the secretariat has been comparatively successful in fostering international cooperation in implementing the biodiversity convention. It helped organize the processes inclusively and is trusted by many governments as a credible and balanced facilitator of international cooperation. Unlike other medium-sized convention secretariats that require decisions of the conference of the parties for almost all relevant activities, the biodiversity secretariat is given considerable leeway in its operations, as the "conference of the parties is very flexible," as a member of the secretariat put it.[16] Thereby, the secretariat could influence the formulation of decisions of the conference of the parties and SBSTTA.

Executive Influence

Despite the ambitious announcements by the executive secretary in early 2006 to further implementation, the biodiversity secretariat is not primarily a capacity-building bureaucracy. It lacks the necessary resources to conduct or fund projects on a larger scale. The main contribution to capacity building lies in the provision of knowledge on how to implement the biodiversity convention at a national level. Through the publication of best practice examples, guidelines, and compilations of existing political and legal responses and administrative practices, the secretariat informs national practitioners about how capacities can be developed. Moreover, the secretariat increasingly organizes capacity-building workshops on issues such as monetary evaluation of biodiversity or data collection for the clearinghouse mechanism. The expert survey conducted for this project shows that these skills-oriented capacity-building activities of the secretariat play a more prominent role than technology transfer programs. Respondents perceived the secretariat primarily as a facilitator for new technological or educational policy programs, rather than for new practices, instruments, or national laws and decrees.[17]

Explaining the Influence

Although the biodiversity secretariat could influence other actors, the question arises of how to explain the normative influence as well as the (moderate) cognitive and executive influence.

Problem Structure

Regarding problem structure, the preservation of biological diversity is highly complex. It is estimated that about 23 percent of mammals and 12 percent of bird species are globally threatened (UNEP 2007). Since 1970, severe declines in population sizes have been recorded. The related global index for tropical forests shows a decline by 14 percent, as well as declines of 35 percent for marine ecosystems and 50 percent for freshwater ecosystems (Loh 2000). Most losses occurred in developing countries, where species diversity is highest.

Counterstrategies are costly and must address several frontiers. First, conservation of species and their habitats is inevitable; this includes also the protection of entire ecosystems as a functioning web of interactions among species. Second, global action is necessary, because most ecosystems cross national borders, and because biodiversity as precondition for functioning ecosystem services is a common interest of all humans. Third, economic and aesthetical values of species need to be acknowledged and institutional arrangements for the sustainable use of species are needed.

The problem of maintaining the Earth's biodiversity is global in scope, is hardly visible, and lacks public interest. One representative from the secretariat described the dilemma of the biodiversity debate: "We don't have big disasters caused by a spider, we don't have big calamities caused by a cockroach."[18] Hence, public awareness is generally low and the extinction of a species is invisible and does not entail catastrophic repercussions. Consequentially, policy makers still have a low sensitivity to the problems and to the role of biodiversity in sustainable development and poverty eradication, even though almost all countries are affected by the loss of biodiversity on their territories and by the loss of possibly valuable species and genetic resources. Moreover, no easy and ready-made solutions are available. Large-scale conservation programs are politically highly controversial, potentially costly, and not very popular with most decision makers.

Likewise, the provisions of the biodiversity convention concerning access to genetic resources and the fair and equal sharing of benefits have caused controversies between developing and developed countries and between the advocating groups—from indigenous and local communities to business and industry. In fact, the positions on the related provisions were, and to some extent still are, highly polarized. Because representatives from countries providing genetic resources and many nongovernmental organizations view companies and researchers involved in bioprospecting[19] as "biopirates," members of the business community regard the biodiversity convention as an ill-structured and uninformed UN process, governed by politicians who overestimate the value of genetic resources (Blais 2002; ten Kate 2002; ten Kate and Laird 1999). Nevertheless, the fair and equitable sharing of benefits from genetic resources is a global transnational problem that requires an international response.[20] The problem has a strong North–South dimension. Benefits are expected to be generated in industrialized countries, and genetic diversity is highest in the developing countries of the South. The structure of this problem with highly divergent interests ranging from development aid over profit interests in the pharmaceutical industry and agro-industry to pure research interests left the biodiversity secretariat with limited room for maneuver. In this severely contested area, the secretariat has to find common ground and to forge compromises in a neutral and balanced manner in order to avoid losses of trust and credibility. This limits also the normative influence and explains why the secretariat is not able to generate more influence on negotiations and final agreements.

Moreover, the convention itself limits the secretariat's scope of activities and defines its objectives rather vaguely. Since entry into force, the convention has lacked clear quantifiable targets that could give the issue higher priority on the political agenda of national governments and the international community. A strategic plan adopted in 2002 and the formulation of the target to significantly reduce the loss of biodiversity by 2010 address this problem and give the secretariat some authority for its implementation.

The limited cognitive influence can be attributed to this nature of the problem that does not lead to media-catching catastrophic events and large-scale damages of private and public properties. The loss of a species of butterflies might not even be recognized and is less spectacular for any form of media coverage than reports on major weather disasters like hurricanes or flooding.

Polity

Competences   When compared to other international bureaucracies analyzed in this book, the biodiversity secretariat's formal competences are limited. It has several areas of competence that have evolved over time, but it is at the same time restricted with regard to direct influence on states and nongovernmental actors. Everyday operational decisions remain with the secretariat, whereas the main tasks of the secretariat and other major operational matters require decisions of the conference of the parties. As formal competences are largely similar to other convention secretariats analyzed in this book, the explanatory power of this variable for the normative influence remains low. Nonetheless, limited competences can explain the limited executive and cognitive influence.

In comparison to the climate and desertification secretariats that are directly affiliated with the UN secretariat in New York, the biodiversity secretariat is still administratively attached to UNEP. Until the late 1990s, UNEP largely denied the biodiversity secretariat's autonomy and fought against any of its moves toward independence (Le Prestre 2002a;

Skjærseth 1999). Finally, on the basis of the "Administrative Arrangement between UNEP and the Secretariat of the CBD" of 1997, the secretariat managed to moderately increase its formal competences with regard to its core budget, which exclusively has to be approved by the conference of the parties. Yet the secretariat remains dependent from UNEP, as "the financial and common support services of the CBD Secretariat will be provided by UNEP, the United Nations Offices at Nairobi or any other United Nations entity, as appropriate, and as agreed by the Executive Director of UNEP in full cooperation with the Executive Secretary of the Convention" (SCBD 2003, 519). Staffing decisions also remained under control of UNEP, and the secretariat's executive secretary is appointed by the executive director of UNEP upon consultation with the conference of the parties. All staff members of the secretariat have to be appointed by the UNEP executive director "in full consultation with the Executive Secretary of the CBD" (SCBD 2003, 517). Since 2003, the secretariat has gained more freedom to recruit its own staff under a new UN-wide recruitment system. It allows the executive secretary to decide on the selection of staff in the general service category. UNEP merely checks compliance with several process criteria. By contrast, UNEP still determines the nomination of the executive secretary.

The constant struggle for more competences continued even after the 1997 agreement and kept the secretariat's formal status bounded. It remains accountable to both of its principals: the conference of the parties and UNEP. Though UNEP tried to influence the work of the secretariat through the nomination of former UNEP members as executive secretaries of the secretariat,[21] the conference of the parties assigns tasks and responsibilities to the secretariat largely independent of UNEP directives. Through this system of a twofold accountability, the secretariat's formal room for maneuver is additionally limited.

Formal means to influence external stakeholders also are restricted in the case of the biodiversity secretariat. They can explain the limited executive influence that it has on other actors. It has little leverage on the behavior of governments or nongovernmental actors, as it cannot directly fund biodiversity projects and it does not have any direct regulatory powers with such influence. The lack of leverage is most obvious in the relationship between the secretariat and national governments. Even though all parties agreed to deliver a biennial report on the domestic implementation of the biodiversity convention to the secretariat, response rates are low. In general, reporting is seen as sensitive. According to a member of the secretariat, "governments do not want to be controlled and do not want to have national monitoring obligations."[22] When the secretariat developed a monitoring scheme for national reports to include more quantifiable measures, it was welcomed as an initiative by the parties, but they refused to adopt it.

The international capacity-building mechanisms in biodiversity issues is not in the hands of the secretariat either, but is coordinated by the GEF. The role of the biodiversity secretariat in decision making on biodiversity-related projects is restricted to commenting on the evaluation of project proposals. It does not have any formal veto powers, but so far all funding decisions taken by the GEF have complied with the recommendations of the secretariat.[23] Actual funding decisions remain with the implementing agencies of the GEF mechanism (see Andler, this volume, chapter 8). Thus, the secretariat also has no formal means of influencing project funding and capacity building, which contributes to the explanation of the limited executive influence.

Sanctioning power is almost nonexistent. The secretariat has no direct influence on national implementation. One interviewee at the secretariat explained: "We at the secretariat have no say or power on the implementation of the decision addressed to the parties or the international organizations."[24]

Taken together, the formal and informal bounds of the secretariat's competences provide a reliable explanation for the limited influence on the executive and—to a lesser extent—also on the cognitive side. Limited by its mandate and the status as an intergovernmental body highly dependent on the decisions by the conference of the parties and UNEP, the secretariat has little means to pursue capacity building and policy implementation in countries. What is more, the limited competences also restrict its information and communication policies that cannot effectively reach domestic public debates. Also, in its communication activities, the secretariat is dependent on the collaboration by national authorities or initiatives to be heard by larger audiences in member states.

Resources   The normative influence can hardly be explained by the financial and personnel resources of the secretariat. Budget lines are tight and have almost stagnated over the past years. The budget requires the secretariat to remain small and highly efficient, which contributes to the explanation of the limited cognitive and executive influence.

The budgets of the secretariat are divided into different Trust Funds with varying degrees of reliability. The General Trust Fund is based on the UN scale of assessments and additional funding from, for example, the host country (Canada). It is a highly reliable source of funding. Its spending is mostly bound to the approved tasks, but the executive secretary, in consultation with the bureau of the conference of the parties, has some discretion as regards its use. The General Trust Fund, which covers all vital expenses of the secretariat, amounted to USD 10.9 million in 2006. A special voluntary trust fund provides funds for special purposes approved by the conference of the parties, such as meetings, particular initiatives such as awareness raising programs, or consultants. It is fed by voluntary contributions by national governments. Another special voluntary trust fund finances travel costs of delegates from developing countries and countries with economies in transition. In addition, the executive secretary invites governments to donate for certain meetings or events, such as ad hoc technical expert group meetings that are not covered by the other funds. These funds are generally earmarked for these specific purposes. The special trust fund for additional purposes cannot serve as a reliable funding source for long-term engagements.

Embeddedness   The secretariat's activities and its normative influence can be better understood in light of its embedding in the UNEP context. When the secretariat was founded under the auspices of UNEP, a bias toward environmental concerns was predetermined. With its clear environmental focus, UNEP strengthened the environmental stance in the interpretation and implementation of the biodiversity convention. Through its role vis-à-vis the emerging secretariat, it had the means to set up this bureaucracy to strengthen environmental concerns over industry or trade interests that might have been stronger if the secretariat had been embedded in another organizational context.

By contrast, the intergovernmental nature of the secretariat hampers its executive influence on the ground. As an intergovernmental body, the secretariat is not entitled to conduct projects in member countries, such as habitat conservation and ecosystem management, or to establish international schemes to distribute the benefits from genetic resources fairly. In all its capacity building and implementation activities, the secretariat depends on collaboration and support by member states. It is merely entitled to offer expertise and policy advice to national governments, such as through workshops and trainings.

In addition, the secretariat is highly centralized and has no regional offices. This inhibits direct contacts with local and regional-level actors, as well as with a number of other organizations based in Geneva, Nairobi, or elsewhere. This setup keeps the secretariat from effectively addressing the root causes of the problems of biodiversity loss on the ground.

With governments, the secretariat maintains well-established collaborative relations through the national focal points. To date, all formal communication between the secretariat and national governments and its experts is channeled through national focal points. As the secretariat is dependent on additional funding for specific purposes, it maintains close contacts to a number of national governments that have signaled particular interest in specific issues, such as ecotourism, in the case of the German government. Even though this system of channeled communication helps to establish expertise in member countries, the secretariat has no influence on the focal points in the national administration. Even though most focal points are not located close to national decision making at the ministerial level, the secretariat could have normative influence vis-à-vis national governments also through this communication system.

People and Procedures

Organizational Expertise   Similar to other convention secretariats, also the biodiversity secretariat serves as the "information hub" of the treaty and thereby has cognitive as well as normative influence (Sandford 1996, 7). It developed significant expertise in the field of biodiversity governance that explains its normative influence.

Of the seventy staff members, forty are professionals with an academic background. This proportion indicates a lean administration and an emphasis on issue-specific professionals. Due to highly selective recruitment, professional staff members often have academic qualifications in the fields for which they have been hired.

Over the years, the secretariat has established an additional roster of experts that it draws upon as an information source. Following a recommendation of the fifth conference of the parties, experts have been identified in nine thematic areas[25] to make their specific expertise available to the convention process. Direct advice is sought from consultants, who give recommendations on topics such as the disclosure of origins and the protection of intellectual property rights, in the case of traditional knowledge on genetic resources in the field of the access and benefit sharing provisions.[26] In addition, the secretariat was responsible for establishing the Clearing House Mechanism of the convention. It builds on interacting national Clearing House Mechanism focal points. As of 2003, 147 of these focal points were established in participating countries, and it was left to the secretariat to review and to facilitate their work through the provision of guidance and guidelines, protocols, and standards, as well as best practice cases.

Because of this expertise, the secretariat is entrusted with the documentation and preparation of negotiations in which it has been able to generate normative influence. Government representatives as well as other delegates to the SBSTTA and meetings of the conference of the parties rely on the material provided by the secretariat. The secretariat's efforts to compile scientific expertise and to distribute it effectively grant the bureaucracy a high level of trust among the negotiators and selected audiences of its publications and information campaigns. Yet the specific form of science-oriented expertise inhibits further cognitive influence in the broader public.

Organizational Structure   With its rather small organization, the secretariat successfully manages a large and complex convention process. Effective organizational procedures, a clear hierarchical structure, and the ability to adapt to new challenges and implementation requirements provide the factors that enable the bureaucracy to have influence; in particular, in a normative sense.

Decision-making procedures at the secretariat are highly centralized with a powerful position of the organization's head: the executive secretary. He has extended sanctioning powers against his staff members due to the short duration of most contracts. Employees are hired on the basis of two-year contracts, excluding administrative staff and the D-level officers (division heads). It is left to the executive secretary to extend the contracts or not.

As a rather small organization with an immediate need to collaborate across the organizational units, the biodiversity secretariat has a high potential for internal reflection and self-improvement. The secretariat has review and evaluation mechanisms that helped spur adaptive changes. Every conference of the parties has one standing item on the review of the progress of work programs, for most of which the secretariat is fully or partially responsible. Technical and financial matters are regularly checked by auditors from UNEP. Yet there is no serious external evaluation of the secretariat's work, because the conference of the parties does not allow other evaluations than through the conference of the parties.[27] Control and possible improvement of the secretariat's effectiveness is thereby left to the national governments.

Because learning processes need to diffuse through an organization to reach the organizational level, the flow and exchange of knowledge within an organization is crucial. In the case of the biodiversity secretariat, there is an exchange of knowledge across different divisions through the formation of issue-specific teams that also have to include economic and legal aspects when recommendations for the conference of the parties are being prepared. Professional interaction and exchange of views also take place in regular staff meetings, seminars, and presentations by staff members on key issues and developments in their disciplines.

Individual learning as the prerequisite of collective learning is supported by a general Staff Development Policy adopted in July 2002. It has been developed in consultation with other UN agencies and proposed by the executive secretary to the conference of the parties which adopted it. The policy encourages employees to engage themselves in "competency-based learning" and includes a check list for the self-evaluation of every employee in "core values," "core competencies," and "managerial competencies." The self-evaluation is intended to serve as a starting point for "good individual learning plans" (SCBD 2002). Yet only limited funds are available for individual training.

Organizational Culture   The offices of the secretariat are located in the business district of Montreal. Most office doors are closed during working hours and informal communication between employees during leisure time is the exception, not the rule. Yet these indicators for a rather sealed-off organizational culture seem not to compromise the organization's abilities to effectively organize its work processes and the interaction among the employees and with the external stakeholders.

The composition of staff is highly heterogeneous. The staff seems to be comparatively young and international, with representatives from all major regions of the world. Developing countries are slightly in the majority, with twenty-two professionals coming from developing countries and eighteen from developed countries.[28] With regard to professional background, both academics and practitioners occupy functions at the secretariat. Professional backgrounds vary according to the different units: scientific groups are staffed with more biological scientists, whereas the social, economic, and legal affairs unit employs more lawyers and social scientists. Economists are rare in all units. Due to the initial focus on conservation (Le Prestre 2002b), individuals with natural science backgrounds still hold a majority. This highly diverse structure of the secretariat does not allow for any suspicion of regional, professional, or gender biases. The diversity explains, however, the ability of the secretariat to speak to audiences from different world regions and from scientific as well as policy-making communities.

Organizational Leadership   The biodiversity secretariat's influence on decisions of the conference of the parties through the preparation of draft decisions can be explained not merely through the bureaucracy's expertise, but also through the neutral and balanced appearance of staff members of the secretariat in these negotiations. Most notably, the executive secretary usually plays a key role in facilitating and promoting negotiations. For instance, in funding negotiations at each conference of the parties, the secretariat's executive secretary is most active and presents cost calculations of the decisions taken so far. Thereby, he contributes to the normative influence of the secretariat, in particular with regard to the budget committee and to increasing governments' willingness to donate funds.

The personal skills and abilities of the executive secretary have a significant influence on the relationship to the parties of the convention and to other intergovernmental organizations and their executives. Through his dominating role in the secretariat, the person of the executive secretary also affects the behavior of the entire organization. He or she has to maintain a delicate balance between developing strong, informal, trust-based ties to key individuals in the policy arena, while ensuring the neutrality and balanced action of the secretariat. Calestous Juma from Kenya, the first executive secretary of the biodiversity secretariat from 1993 to 1998, tried to establish the secretariat as an autonomous international bureaucracy. In so doing, he entered into continuous disputes with UNEP officials and the UNEP executive director, but succeeded in settling a formal agreement and in locating the secretariat far away from UNEP's Nairobi headquarters.

When the second executive secretary, Hamdallah Zedan of Egypt, was appointed in 1998, many observers expected an increasing influence of UNEP on the secretariat. Yet even the former career officer from UNEP stepped up as head of a largely autonomous international bureaucracy and continued on the path of separating the secretariat from UNEP. He established the secretariat as a well-respected bureaucracy that is given much leeway by the parties of the convention. As head of the secretariat, he kept control of almost all major processes within the organization, and took decisions on the basis of consultations with the management committee of the division heads, and other relevant staff members and external experts where appropriate. Thus, his style of leadership has been described as consultative.[29] Although this style allows for expeditious decision making, it cannot always prevent conflicts or a lack of commitment from the staff members.

Since 2006, Ahmed Djoghlaf has served as executive secretary. His first announcements point toward a stronger emphasis on capacity building and implementation issues in the convention process. His style of management seems comparable to Zedan.[30]

Conclusion

The biodiversity secretariat provides an example of a well-functioning environmentalist international bureaucracy that has developed significant influence on international negotiations and cooperation as well as (to a lesser extent) on scientific discourses. The findings of this research underline the conclusion that the secretariat is a well-managed organization that has a significant degree of leeway for its activities, due to its balanced and neutral appearance. It is trusted by governments and nongovernmental stakeholders and can be described as a considerably effective environmentalist international bureaucracy. Within the confines of its mandate, the secretariat has managed to develop external influence, especially in the normative sense. In these activities, it has tried to advance environmental protection objectives with regard to nature conservation and the preservation of species and genetic resources.

The fact that the secretariat has only limited influence with regard to cognitive dimensions can be attributed to both the complexity of the underlying problem and the limited formal competences given to the secretariat by its mandate. Biodiversity loss is hardly visible as an environmental problem, and when its consequences become visible, such as in the extinction of specific fish stocks, connection lines to biodiversity are rarely drawn. New implementation challenges such as biosafety, access, and benefit sharing, however, are more closely linked to other issues of high relevance to national and international public and policy discourses such as global trade, North–South conflicts, and modification of genetic resources. The increasing activities of the secretariat in these fields give rise to the expectation of greater cognitive influence in the broader public as well.

The most severe barrier to more executive influence is the formal setup of the secretariat. Its global scope and the formal status keep it from unfolding more influence on the ground. The aspired-to increase in capacity building and practical implementation as announced in 2006 require a thorough reconsideration of this formal structure toward endowing the secretariat with stronger financial and legal means to fulfill this task.

Due to its effective internal organization and the strict style of management of its executive secretaries, the secretariat is able to be more influential than other convention secretariats with regard to normative influence. Over time, the secretariat has developed effective practices in facilitating international negotiations and in promoting the objectives of the convention. It has also exhibited a moderate ability to adjust its internal procedures and proved the secretariat's flexibility to react to new demands.

The direct influence of the secretariat on the loss of biodiversity as an environmental indicator remains meager. So far, the loss of biodiversity has been accelerating, according to available data (UNEP 2001, 122). Nevertheless, any possible impact of the secretariat on environmental improvements on the ground and on national, regional, and global levels will be delayed due to the indirect leverage. On these grounds, most actors in the field attach high expectations to the 2010 target to significantly reduce the loss of biodiversity by that year. If the target is met through effective international policies, the secretariat will deserve a share of the credit for it.

Acknowledgments

The author is grateful for the time and effort provided by the interviewees at the biodiversity secretariat and the respondents of the senior expert survey. Detailed comments from members of the secretariat and from the MANUS project team are also gratefully acknowledged. Steffen Behrle provided excellent research support.

Notes

1. Author's interview with a member of the biodiversity secretariat, October 2003.

2. Related international agreements in the field of biodiversity conservation include the 1971 Ramsar Convention on Wetlands of International Importance Especially as Waterfowl Habitat, the 1973 Convention on International Trade in Endangered Species of Wild Fauna and Flora, and the 1979 Bonn Convention on the Conservation of Migratory Species. For an extended overview, see de Klemm and Shine 1993 and Koester 2002.

3. See for example Boisvert and Caron 2002; Kimball 1997; Le Prestre 2002a, 2002b; McGraw 2002; Rojas and Thomas 1992; Rosendal 1995; and ten Kate 2002.

4. Eight answers came from officials in national governments; in each case, three from research institutions and nongovernmental organizations (six respondents did not indicate their actor group). Although stakeholders in four countries were approached, five came from Germany, four from Mexico and India each, and only one from the United States (five respondents did not indicate their country of origin).

5. This relationship between UNEP and the biodiversity secretariat seems to have both a structural and a personal component (Le Prestre 2002a; Skjærseth 1999). As the host organization for many international environmental agreements, UNEP can claim some ownership of these institutions, but governments also withdrew authority from UNEP in several cases by creating more independent administrative structures, that is, convention secretariats. In this regard, one can maintain that UNEP's success can be seen in its decreasing authority, as UNEP's executive director Klaus Töpfer put it (personal communication, January 2005). In the case of the biodiversity secretariat, additional personal conflicts between the top level executives of both organizations have been reported (Skjærseth 1999).

6. These were (1) Executive Direction and Management, (2) Scientific, Technical and Technological Matters, (3) Biosafety Unit, and (4) Implementation and Communication (SCBD 1997, 19f).

7. Decision VI/26 indicating the strategic plan of the biodiversity convention reads as "to effectively halt the loss of biodiversity so as to secure the continuity of its beneficial uses through the conservation and sustainable use of its components and the fair and equitable sharing of benefits arising from the use of genetic resources" (SCBD 2003).

8. These are the (1) Executive Direction, Management and Intergovernmental Affairs Division; (2) Scientific, Technical and Technological Matters Division; (3) Social, Economic and Legal Matters Division; (4) Implementation and Outreach Division; (5) Biosafety Unit; (6) Resources Management and Conference Services Unit.

9. For details, see Millennium Ecosystem Assessment 2003. Members of the secretariat served as contributing authors to chapters and the synthesis report of

this assessment. The secretariat was also represented in the board of the Millennium Ecosystem Assessment.

10. Specifically, 53 percent of the respondents maintained that the secretariat's activities had no influence on related media coverage in their home countries (24 percent agreed; 24 percent gave no answer). The majority ranked the influence of the secretariat on public discourse, policy agendas and media coverage as medium (35 percent) or low (29 percent), and 24 percent observed a high influence.

11. See decision V/6 of the conference of the parties in SCBD (2003) for further details.

12. Author's interview with a member of the biodiversity secretariat, October 2003.

13. Author's interview with a member of the biodiversity secretariat, October 2003.

14. For the discussion on overlap between different biodiversity related regimes and the related international bureaucracies, see Kimball 1997; Koester 2002; Rosendal 2001; Skjærseth 1999.

15. Author's interview with a member of the biodiversity secretariat, October 2003.

16. Author's interview with a member of the biodiversity secretariat, October 2003.

17. This is most obvious the case of the access and benefit sharing provisions where best practice cases for bioprospecting contracts and existing national laws are presented on the secretariat's Web site (Dedeurwaerdere 2005; Polski 2005).

18. Author's interview with a member of the biodiversity secretariat, October 2003.

19. Bioprospecting has been defined by Artuso (2002, 1355) as the "purposeful evaluation of wild biological material in search of valuable new products." For the history and connotations of the term, see Eisner 1989 and Scholz 2004.

20. Benefits from genetic resources arise in most cases in the field of agricultural and pharmaceutical applications. These could be generated by the commercial use of new sorts of plant species, which provide specific tastes or characteristics, by the use of natural substances for medical treatment, or for pharmaceutical uses—for example the development of new drugs. Most of these benefits are expected to be generated in markets in industrialized countries with an expanding biotechnological industry.

21. Both Hamdallah Zendan and Ahmed Djoghlaf are former officers of UNEP in Nairobi. Zedan served for fifteen years as UNEP's expert on biodiversity and biosafety before he was appointed executive secretary of the biodiversity secretariat. Dioghlaf had been the director and coordinator of UNEP's GEF unit since 1996 and became assistant executive director of UNEP in 2003.

22. Author's interview with a member of the biodiversity secretariat, October 2003.

23. Author's interview with a member of the biodiversity secretariat, October 2003.

24. Author's interview with a member of the biodiversity secretariat, October 2003.

25. Thematic areas are: access and benefit-sharing, agricultural biodiversity, dry and subhumid lands, forest biological diversity, Global Taxonomy Initiative, biodiversity indicators, marine and coastal biodiversity, inland waters, and biosafety (SCBD 2003, 242).

26. Author's interview with a member of the biodiversity secretariat, October 2004.

27. Author's interview with a member of the biodiversity secretariat, October 2003.

28. Data drawn from an interview with a biodiversity secretariat member, October 2003.

29. Written questionnaire from members of the biodiversity secretariat, October 2003.

30. Telephone interview with biodiversity secretariat staff member, February 2006.

References

Andresen, Steinar. 2001. "Global Environmental Governance: UN Fragmentation and Co-ordination." In *Yearbook of International Co-operation on Environment and Development 2001/2002*, edited by Olav Schram Stokke and Øystein B. Thommessen, 19–26. London: Earthscan.

Artuso, Anthony. 2002. "Bioprospecting, Benefit Sharing and Biotechnological Capacity Building." *World Development* 30 (8): 1355–1368.

Blais, Francois. 2002. "The Fair and Equitable Sharing of Benefits from the Exploitation of Genetic Resources: A Difficult Transition from Principles to Reality." In *Governing Global Biodiversity: The Evolution and Implementation of the Convention on Biological Diversity*, edited by Philippe Le Prestre, 145–157. Aldershot, UK: Ashgate.

Boisvert, Valérie, and Armelle Caron. 2002. "The Convention on Biological Diversity: An Institutionalist Perspective of the Debates." *Journal of Economic Issues* 36 (1): 151–166.

Coombe, Rosemary J. 2001. "Recognition of Indigenous Peoples' and Community Traditional Knowledge in International Law." *St. Thomas Law Review* 14:275–285.

de Klemm, Cyrille, and Clare Shine. 1993. *Biological Diversity and the Law. Legal Mechanisms for Conserving Species and Ecosystems*. International Union for Conservation of Nature Environmental Policy and Law Paper No. 29. Gland, Switzerland, and Cambridge, UK: International Union for Conservation of Nature.

Dedeurwaerdere, Tom. 2005. "From Bioprospecting to Reflexive Governance." *Ecological Economics* 53:473–491.

Eisner, Thomas. 1989. "Prospecting for Nature's Chemical Riches." *Issues in Science and Technology* 6 (2): 31–34.

Gupta, Aarti. 2004. "When Global Is Local: Negotiating Safe Use of Biotechnology." In *Earthly Politics: Local and Global in Environmental Governance*, edited by Sheila Jasanoff and Marybeth Long Martello, 127–148. Cambridge, MA: MIT Press.

Gupta, Aarti. 2006. "Problem Framing in Assessment Processes: The Case of Biosafety." In *Global Environmental Assessments: Information and Influence*, edited by Ronald B. Mitchell, William C. Clark, David W. Cash, and Nancy Dickson, 57–86. Cambridge, MA: MIT Press.

Gupta, Aarti, and Robert Falkner. 2006. "The Influence of the Cartagena Protocol on Biosafety: Comparing Mexico, China and South Africa." *Global Environmental Politics* 6 (4): 23–44.

Heijden, Hein-Anton van der. 2002. "Political Parties and NGOs in Global Environmental Politics." *International Political Science Review* 23 (2): 187–201.

Kimball, Lee A. 1997. "Institutional Linkages Between the Convention on Biological Diversity and Other International Conventions." *Reciel* 6 (3): 239–248.

Koester, Veit. 2002. "The Five Global Biodiversity-related Conventions: A Stocktaking." *Reciel* 11 (1): 96–103.

Koetz, Thormas, Peter Bridgewater, Sybille van den Hove, and Bernd Siebenhüner. 2008. "The Role of the Subsidiary Body on Scientific, Technical, and Technological Advice to the Convention on Biological Diversity as Science-Policy Interface." *Environmental Science and Policy* 11:505–516.

Kothari, Ashish. 1994. "Beyond the Biodiversity Convention. A View from India." In *Biodiplomacy: Genetic Resources and International Relations*, edited by Vincente Sanchez and Calestous Juma, 67–85. Nairobi: ACTS Press.

Le Prestre, Philippe. 2002a. "The Operation of the CBD Convention Governance System." In *Governing Global Biodiversity: The Evolution and Implementation of the Convention on Biological Diversity*, edited by Philippe Le Prestre, 91–114. Aldershot, UK: Ashgate.

Le Prestre, Philippe. 2002b. "Studying the Effectiveness of the CBD." In *Governing Global Biodiversity: The Evolution and Implementation of the Convention on Biological Diversity*, edited by Philippe Le Prestre, 57–89. Aldershot, UK: Ashgate.

Loh, Jonathan. 2000. *The Living Planet Report 2000*. Gland, Switzerland: WWF, The Global Environment Network.

McGraw, Desiree M. 2002. "The Story of the Biodiversity Convention: From Negotiation to Implementation." In *Governing Global Biodiversity: The Evolution and Implementation of the Convention on Biological Diversity*, edited by Philippe Le Prestre, 7–38. Aldershot, UK: Ashgate.

Millennium Ecosystem Assessment. 2003. *Ecosystems and Human Well-Being. A Framework for Assessment.* Washington, DC: Island Press.

Pimm, Stuart I., Gareth J. Russell, John L. Gittelman, and Thomas M. Brooks. 1995. "The Future of Biodiversity." *Science* 269:347–350.

Polski, Margaret. 2005. "The Institutional Economics of Biodiversity, Biological Materials, and Bioprospecting." *Ecological Economics* 53:543–557.

Rojas, Martha, and Chris Thomas. 1992. "The Convention on Biological Diversity. Negotiating a Global Regime." In *International Environmental Treaty Making,* edited by Lawrence E. Susskind, Eric J. Dolin, and J. William Breslin, 143–162. Cambridge, MA: Program on Negotiation at Harvard Law School.

Rosendal, G. Kristin. 1995. "The Convention on Biological Diversity: A Viable Instrument for Conservation and Sustainable Use?" In *Green Globe Yearbook of International Co-Operation on Environment and Development 1995,* edited by Helge Ole Bergesen, Georg Parmann, and Øystein B. Thommessen, 69–81. Oxford: Oxford University Press.

Rosendal, G. Kristin. 2001. "Overlapping International Regimes. The Case of the Intergovernmental Forum on Forests (IFF) Between Climate Change and Biodiversity." *International Environmental Agreements: Politics, Law and Economics* 1:447–468.

Sandford, Rosemary. 1994. "International Environmental Treaty Secretariats: Stage-Hands or Actors?" In *Green Globe Yearbook of International Co-operation on Environment and Development 1994,* edited by Helge Ole Bergesen and Georg Parmann, 17–29. Oxford: Oxford University Press.

Sandford, Rosemary. 1996. "International Environmental Treaty Secretariats: A Case of Neglected Potential?" *Environmental Impact Assessment Review* 16:3–12.

SCBD, Secretariat of the Convention on Biological Diversity. 1997. *Quarterly Report on the Administration of the Convention on Biological Diversity.* UN Doc. UNEP/CBD/QR/1 of 26 May. Montreal: Secretariat of the Convention on Biological Diversity.

SCBD, Secretariat of the Convention on Biological Diversity. 2001. *Global Biodiversity Outlook.* Montreal: Secretariat of the Convention on Biological Diversity.

SCBD, Secretariat of the Convention on Biological Diversity. 2002. *Staff Development Policy.* Internal document. Montreal: Secretariat of the Convention on Biological Diversity. On file with author.

SCBD, Secretariat of the Convention on Biological Diversity. 2003. *Handbook of the Convention on Biological Diversity.* Montreal: Secretariat of the Convention on Biological Diversity.

Scholz, Astrid. 2004. "Merchants of Diversity: Scientists as Traffickers of Plants and Institutions." In *Earthly Politics. Local and Global in Environmental Governance,* edited by Sheila Jasanoff and Marybeth Long-Martello, 217–238. Cambridge, MA: MIT Press.

Siebenhüner, Bernd, and Jessica Suplie. 2005. "Implementing the Access and Benefit Sharing Provisions of the CBD: A Case for Institutional Learning." *Ecological Economics* 53:507–522.

Skjærseth, Jon Birger. 1999. *Can International Environmental Secretariats Promote Effective Co-operation?* Paper presented at the UNU International Conference on Synergies and Co-ordination between Multilateral Environmental Agreements. Tokyo: UNU Press.

Svarstad, Hanne. 1994. "National Sovereignty and Genetic Resources." In *Biodiplomacy: Genetic Resources and International Relations*, edited by Vincente Sanchez and Calestous Juma, 46–65. Nairobi: ACTS Press.

Swanson, Timothy. 1999. "Why Is There a Biodiversity Convention? The International Interest in Centralized Development Planning." *International Affairs* 75 (1): 307–331.

Tarradell, Mireia. 2007. *The Influence of International Bureaucracies in Global Environmental Politics: Results from an Expert Survey*. Global Governance Working Paper 26. Amsterdam and others: The Global Governance Project.

ten Kate, Kerry. 2002. "Science and the Convention on Biological Diversity." *Science* 295:2371–2372.

ten Kate, Kerry, and Sarah A. Laird. 1999. *The Commercial Use of Biodiversity. Access to Genetic Resources and Benefit-Sharing*. London: Earthscan Publications.

UNEP, United Nations Environment Programme. 2001. *Global Environment Outlook 3. Past, Present, and Future Perspectives*. London: Earthscan.

UNEP, United Nations Environment Programme. 2007. *Global Environmental Outlook 4—Global Environment Outlook. Environment for Development*. Nairobi: UNEP.

12

The Desertification Secretariat: A Castle Made of Sand

Steffen Bauer

Introduction

Many stakeholders of the United Nations Convention to Combat Desertification in Those Countries Experiencing Serious Drought and/or Desertification, Particularly in Africa ("desertification convention") do not necessarily view the fight against desertification as an environmental issue or conceive of the convention as an environmental treaty. Rather, they consider it a development convention and an instrument to fight poverty in the developing world.

This stance is reflected by the secretariat of the convention, which is eager to promote the desertification convention as "*the* sustainable development convention" and hence as an institution different from its "sister conventions," the United Nations Framework Convention on Climate Change and the Convention on Biological Diversity.

Yet the convention is a substantive component of international environmental governance, too. For instance, the interdependence of environmental degradation and socioeconomic conditions is ubiquitous in international environmental governance. Second, desertification is a concept that converges around qualitative changes in the environmental conditions of the earth's land surface. Third, as I will elaborate shortly, desertification was put on the international agenda first and foremost by environmentalists. In fact, a legal convention to deal with the problem of desertification was called for by Agenda 21, which makes the desertification convention the only treaty to originate from the 1992 United Nations Conference on Environment and Development (UNCED) at Rio de Janeiro.[1]

Fifteen years after this conference, the desertification convention is still only at the beginning of its implementation phase (IISD 2005b).

Consequently, scholars have not yet studied the performance of the desertification regime with the scrutiny that distinguishes numerous case studies on other environmental regimes. Yet scholarly attention has notably risen over the years,[2] and a substantive literature is now available on the negotiations that led to the convention.

Elisabeth Corell (1999), for example, provides a comprehensive account of the convention's evolution, which illuminates in particular the crucial role of expert knowledge throughout the negotiation process.[3] Adil Najam (2004) employs the desertification negotiations to scrutinize North–South relations and the collective behavior of the "South," despite increasing heterogeneity. Others have addressed the involvement of civil society groups in the negotiation process, the extent of which was arguably without precedent in international environmental negotiations (Corell and Betsill 2001; Knabe 2006).

The history of the desertification convention dates back to the late 1960s. The trigger event for desertification to enter the international agenda was the major drought and subsequent famine that hit the Sahel region in the late 1960s and early 1970s. The UN reacted with the creation of a Sudano-Sahelian Office to provide assistance, while nine Sahelian countries established an Inter-State Permanent Committee on Drought Control in the Sahel in 1973. UNEP embraced the emerging issue by calling for the 1977 UN Conference on Desertification, at which representatives of ninety-four governments agreed on a Plan of Action to Combat Desertification. Although the plan failed to generate meaningful support (McCormick 1989, 116–122; Corell 1999, 69–72), desertification was now effectively an issue of international environmental politics and no longer discussed as an exclusive problem of the Sahel region. Indeed, the initiative of the United Nations Environment Programme, fueled by persistent demands of African governments, was essential to forge desertification into a global issue (Corell 2003). Ultimately, it led the process that culminated in substantive negotiations for an international legal instrument on desertification (on the negotiations, see Toulmin 1995; Corell 1999; Najam 2006). The convention was adopted on 17 June 1994 in Paris and entered into force on 26 December 1996. In May 2008, it had 193 parties, the closest approximation to universal membership any multilateral environmental agreement has achieved to date.

The complex institutional setting of the desertification regime, which involves various UN agencies as well as regional institutions and a diverse array of banks and funding agencies, has been described in detail by Chasek and Corell (2002) and Falloux, Tressler, and Mayrand (2006). In the following discussion, I focus on the specific role of the desertification secretariat.

This research builds predominantly on primary sources obtained mostly through a research visit to the desertification secretariat in Bonn, Germany, and five management-level interviews, including extensive interviews with the executive secretary and the deputy executive secretary.[4] In addition, a sample of complementary questionnaires on internal decision making and communication, which could be obtained from program officers, data from the survey of experts from Germany, India, and Mexico (Tarradell 2007), and a number of informal expert consultations with national delegates to conferences of the parties and ministerial officials, as well as academic observers of the desertification convention and officers of partner agencies, notably from UNEP.

I first describe the institutional particulars of the desertification secretariat, assess its influence in global desertification politics, and then explain this influence drawing on the framework developed by Biermann et al. (this volume, chapter 3). The chapter concludes with a discussion of the secretariat's activities in view of its influence on the implementation of the convention.

Structure and Activities

The desertification secretariat was transformed into a permanent UN secretariat only in 1997, following decision 5 of the first conference of the parties in Rome in 1997 (UNCCD 1997, 31). It was relocated to Bonn, Germany, in January 1999.[5] To facilitate interagency cooperation, the secretariat posted liaison officers at major United Nations locations, notably with the FAO and the International Fund for Agricultural Development in Rome and with UN headquarters in New York, as well as at the European Commission in Brussels.

The official mandate and functions of the secretariat are laid down in article 23.2 of the convention (UNCCD 2002a, 31): the secretariat must service the conference of the parties and its subsidiary bodies—that is, the Committee on Science and Technology, an expert body open to government representatives of all parties, and the Committee for the Review of the Implementation of the Convention. Moreover, the secretariat must compile and transmit reports; facilitate assistance to developing country parties in compiling and communicating information required under the convention; coordinate its activities with the secretariats of other international bodies; make the necessary contractual arrangements pertaining to its functions; report to the conference of the parties on the execution of its functions; and "perform such other secretariat functions as may be determined by the Conference of Parties" (UNCCD 2002a, 31; also Bauer 2006).

Like the climate convention, the convention to combat desertification has the status of a UN convention, which brings a higher status in the UN system in comparison to most environmental treaty secretariats under UN auspices. Still, like any other treaty secretariat, the desertification secretariat was set up to assist treaty parties in governing the international legal agreement that they have committed to.

In 2005, the desertification secretariat had a staff of fifty-six (Ortiz and Tang 2005, Annex III). The position of executive secretary of the secretariat has been since 1999 at the level of assistant secretary-general to the United Nations, and it was held by Hama Arba Diallo of Burkina Faso until 19 June 2007. Before, Diallo had served as the head of the secretariat to the Intergovernmental Negotiating Committee on Desertification (1993–1994) and the Geneva-based interim secretariat that served the first conferences of the parties (1994–1998). Luc Gnacadja, former environmental minister of Benin, succeeded Hama Arba Diallo at the helm of the secretariat on 1 October 2007 (UN Doc. SG/A/1092 of 11 September 2007; see also IISD 2007, 3).

With regard to budgetary requirements, the first conference of the parties determined in decision 3.4 that the secretariat must "enjoy the administrative and financial autonomy necessary to ensure efficient servicing of the convention and of its implementation" (UN Doc. ICCD/COP(1)/11/Add.1). The regular budget of the secretariat was USD 17 million for 2004–2005.[6] A Special Trust Fund for Participation, a Trust Fund for Supplementary Activities, and a Trust Fund for the Supplementary Contribution to the Convention Activities by the Host Government (the so-called Bonn Fund) have been created mainly to cover the travel costs of developing country delegates and nongovernmental organizations from affected countries.[7]

The organizational setup of the secretariat is to some extent defined by the importance that is attributed to the Regional Annexes of the convention, with distinct divisions for Africa, Asia, Latin America, and the Caribbean, and the Northern Mediterranean.[8] Regional action facilitators at the helm of these divisions maintain close links to national focal points and Regional Coordination Units. The regional divisions are supervised by the office of the Principal Coordinator for the Facilitation of Implementation of the Convention, which links the secretariat's regional activities to the executive secretary and its deputy. The secretariat is complemented by three functional units: one to manage the services for the conference of the parties and its subsidiary bodies, one for external relations and public information, and one for administration and finance.

The material output of the desertification secretariat is small. As a crucial service to the parties it maintains a Web site from which official documents can be downloaded, including all formal decisions in all UN languages. In terms of public outreach, the brochure "Down to Earth" serves as the secretariat's flagship publication. Free of charge, it provides a "simplified guide to the Convention to Combat Desertification, why it is necessary and what is important and different about it" (UNCCD 1995) in all six UN languages as well as in German (the language of its host country). It is complemented by a "convention kit" with leaflets and fact sheets that provide basic information. Moreover, there is a "Down to Earth" biannual newsletter, a nonperiodic series that presents success stories in implementing the convention at the local level (e.g., UNCCD 2003a), occasional information posters, a teacher's kit with maps and a desertification comic book for children, and other similar materials.

The Influence of the Desertification Secretariat

Cognitive Influence

There is plenty of scientific knowledge on the causes and consequences of land degradation in arid and semi-arid environments (see Herrmann and Hutchinson 2006 for an overview and further references). The 1977 UN Conference on Desertification was lauded as one of the scientifically best-prepared intergovernmental gatherings of its time (McCormick 1989, 119). The continuous generation, discussion, and refinement of expert knowledge on dryland degradation has shaped international debates on desertification, although scientific experts were marginalized once negotiations for an international convention begun (Corell 1999; Martello 2004).

The desertification secretariat acts as a relay that compiles and distributes knowledge on desertification within and beyond the convention regime. It indirectly contributes to monitoring global desertification by collecting and documenting the reports submitted by the parties, although these activities amount merely to background documentation for the conference of the parties and its subsidiary bodies. The secretariat also maintains a roster of independent experts on which governments may call upon on an ad hoc basis. Hence, though the secretariat does not have its own research or assessment capacity, its institutional knowledge positions it at the hub of the political discourse on desertification. The secretariat thus helps to maintain an institutional setting that reproduces the concept of desertification, but is hardly conducive to meaningful exchange between scientists and policy makers (Bauer and Stringer 2008).

The very framing of desertification, as opposed to land degradation, has been of particular prominence in institutionalizing the international desertification regime and subsequently bears strong implications for the implementation of the convention. Scientists generally agree that "desertification" is a rather misleading term for the environmental phenomenon of dryland degradation (Thomas 1997; Herrmann and Hutchinson 2006). Yet, the desertification secretariat purposively maintains the usage of the term "desertification," even as most intergovernmental agencies that are involved with the implementation of the convention (e.g., the FAO, the UN Development Programme, the World Bank, and the GEF) prefer to use the term (dry)land degradation. Strikingly, UNEP—which has effectively introduced the term "desertification" to international politics and which has long promoted it, not least by its acclaimed "World Atlas on Desertification" (Middleton and Thomas 1992)—has shifted its parlance to "land degradation."[9]

The desertification secretariat, however, insists that "Desertification has a political appeal that land degradation does not have" (Executive Secretary Diallo, cited in Corell 1999, 65). Desertification thus remains an essential catchword "that conveys an urgent need for action, and has been used to market desertification on the international stage to attract the attention of donors" (Corell 2003, 5). Not only is it vouchsafed by the title of the convention, but the secretariat ensures that it is spread by public outreach activities. These activities capitalize on occasions such as the World Day to Combat Desertification, which commemorates the ratification of the convention on 17 June, the International Year of Deserts and Desertification in 2006, or the UN Decade of Deserts and the Fight against Desertification (2010–2020).

In a similar vein, the desertification secretariat has actively promoted the transformation of desertification from a problem of affected regions into a global commons problem. A senior secretariat officer claimed that making "desertification a global issue [although] it really is a local problem" would be a personal achievement of Executive Secretary Diallo.[10] According to Diallo, once desertification was identified as an issue of the "global village," it was only just to claim that it be addressed not only by the "villagers" immediately affected by desertification, but by all the inhabitants of the village.[11]

Such paradigmatic shift is a striking example for the power of discourse. Acknowledging that desertification is a global issue, at least politically, projects that relate to the implementation of the convention have eventually become eligible for funding through the Global Environment Facility (see GEF operational program 15 on land degradation). This reflects a major concession of donor countries vis-à-vis affected countries. Led by African countries, developing countries pushed for this ever since the establishment of the facility, increasingly so after the fourth conference of the parties of the desertification convention.[12]

Although it is hard to determine the specific impact of the desertification secretariat in achieving this concession, it helped keep the issue on the agenda of the GEF Council and continuously backed developing countries' efforts to tap the facility as a financial mechanism for the fight against desertification (e.g., IISD 2003).[13] In fact, secretariat officials were glad to underscore the pivotal role of the secretariat toward this end. Interviewees claimed that the secretariat helped affected countries to lobby in the runup to the 2002 World Summit on Sustainable Development, and that it had deliberately "orchestrated a number of events to raise the awareness of the issue," notably through personal interventions of Executive Secretary Diallo: "You can clearly see that in this case the executive secretary has played his role . . . to raise the political profile of the convention. He has played his cards in a proactive manner and he has definitely obtained results."[14]

It was thus argued that the gradual facilitation of access for affected country parties to the GEF would be a major achievement of the desertification secretariat and a prime example for its strong influence on a contentious intergovernmental process.

Officers also expressed their satisfaction at the inclusion of land degradation to the GEF portfolio as an overdue step in the absence of a genuine financing mechanism for the desertification convention. Though the enthusiasm for expanding the facility's mandate to include land degradation is not necessarily shared among donor countries, it is conceded nonetheless that the secretariat was a central driver in bringing this about.[15]

Normative Influence

In addition, the desertification secretariat had considerable normative influence in the convention process. I will highlight four examples to illustrate the secretariat's impact on the institutionalization of the convention.

First, the desertification secretariat was pivotal in the establishment of the Committee for the Review of the Implementation of the Convention at the fifth conference of the parties in Geneva in 2001.[16] The creation of such an additional permanent subsidiary body to the conference of the parties was initially seen to be at odds with the interests of donor country parties. Yet after the first meeting of the committee had convened in Rome in November 2002, it was lauded as highly constructive. Subsequently, the acceptance of the Committee for the Review of the Implementation of the Convention increased across parties, and it was acknowledged to be a potentially useful instrument that might work along the lines of the Subsidiary Body for Implementation under the climate convention.[17] The committee's second meeting was held back-to-back with the sixth conference of the parties at Havana in 2003 and suffered from the highly politicized general atmosphere of that particular gathering. Arguably a result of donor countries' revived skepticism vis-à-vis the Committee for the Review of the Implementation of the Convention, its third session had to be rescheduled, because the necessary funds failed to materialize in time.[18]

After a review of the committee's performance at the seventh conference of the parties, which was held in Nairobi in October 2005, there remains a mixed picture (IISD 2005a). In general, industrialized countries remain unconvinced about the added value that is claimed by affected countries and the desertification secretariat. Although it seems unlikely that the Committee for the Review of the Implementation of the Convention will be discarded soon, its work may well be restricted by budgetary constraints. Notwithstanding this likelihood, the desertification secretariat has succeeded in first initiating and then guiding developing countries' haul to establish a regular body for the review of the implementation of the convention and thereby shaped the institutional structure of the desertification convention.

As a second example, a similar pattern can be observed in the development of Regional Coordination Units, which are promoted by the secretariat to strengthen the convention's institutional framework. Although these units are welcomed in affected regions, donor countries are wary of institutional duplication and question the necessity of such units (Bauer 2006, 80).

A third example refers to the cooperation between various international bureaucracies that is seconded by the parties to further the implementation of the convention. For instance, once projects on land degradation were added to the portfolio of the GEF, the desertification secretariat was mandated to negotiate a memorandum of understanding with the secretariat of the facility in order to define the policy measures for interaction between its own conference of the parties and the GEF. The officers of the desertification secretariat have thus been empowered to determine jointly with their counterparts how the facility's operational program on land degradation is implemented. In the process, the desertification secretariat also consults with the Global Mechanism and thereby further expands interagency cooperation on the implementation of the convention.[19] The responsibility for these processes rests with the desertification secretariat, although, as one officer cautioned, the conference of the parties retains the ultimate authority to endorse any memorandum between the secretariat and other agencies.[20]

A fourth and particularly illustrative example refers to the initiative of the desertification secretariat to raise the political profile of the convention by organizing a High Level Segment at the sixth conference of the parties in Havana in 2003. This High Level Segment, which included a "Round Table of Heads of State and Government," had been pursued by the secretariat to elevate the event to a more authoritative political level and to increase media attention. Donor countries showed little enthusiasm. Yet Executive Secretary Diallo insisted that this was an appropriate step to mark the passage of the convention from institutionalization to implementation, which was expected to be the main outcome of the Havana meeting.[21]

Twelve heads of state and government attended the conference of the parties and gathered for a high-level roundtable discussion as envisaged by the secretariat. Yet while the roundtable included a number of politically controversial leaders from the South—such as Fidel Castro Ruz of host country Cuba, Hugo Chávez Frías of Venezuela, and Robert Mugabe of Zimbabwe—no head of state or government of an industrialized country participated. Hence, the High Level Segment was lopsided, and the "Havana Declaration of the Heads of State and Government on the Implementation of the United Nations Convention to Combat Desertification" (UNCCD 2003b) perceived as a confrontation by the North. The event drew harsh criticism even from affected countries that were anxious to deteriorate relations with donor countries. Indirectly, secretariat officials conceded that some criticism was justified and acknowledged that the way the High Level Segment turned out was "humiliating" for industrialized countries.[22]

Still, the desertification secretariat claims credit for successfully raising the profile of the convention by having brought a dozen heads of state and government along with some eighty ministers to attend an ordinary conference of the parties: "the climate change [conferences of the parties], would never manage that! On the other hand we cannot ignore that there were almost no ministers of the North."[23]

Well-intended as the High Level Segment may have been, it was a politically delicate maneuver that may have raised attention, but at a high political cost. Ultimately, it turned out to be a disservice for the cooperative climate among the parties of the convention (e.g., IISD 2003).[24] As a consequence, the reputation of the desertification secretariat has suffered, in particular among industrialized countries, as can be seen from a formal démarche of the EU and the decision to subject the secretariat to a review by the United Nations Joint Inspection Unit.[25]

Executive Influence

Although it is not an executive agency, there is a limited role in capacity building for the desertification secretariat, which is inherent in its mandate to facilitate the development of National Action Programmes by affected country parties. It is thus required to lend administrative support to national-level institution building in affected countries. To this end, the secretariat essentially focuses on empowering national focal points in affected countries, which are often found to operate at "a minimum level of institutional preparedness" to maintain relationships with stakeholders at the international level.[26]

In a similar vein, the desertification secretariat seeks to reinforce national institution building by promoting regional institutions through its Regional Action Facilitators. The secretariat thus advocates the strengthening of existing Regional Coordination Units as well as the creation of additional ones, although the actual value of such units is disputed between parties. Though many developing countries commend proposals to strengthen existing Regional Coordination Units—for instance, by financing them through the secretariat's core budget, as opposed to less predictable supplementary funds—industrialized countries remain concerned about a duplication of inefficient bureaucratic structures and increasing costs (see IISD 2003, 2005a).

In its day-to-day work, the secretariat assists national focal points in preparing and meeting their reporting requirements vis-à-vis the conference of the parties and its subsidiary bodies. In this respect, the desertification secretariat provides specific guidelines and responds to direct requests from national desk officers.[27] Overall, however, the secretariat's role in capacity building remains limited, because it has neither the human resources nor the mandate. Still, it is occasionally possible for secretariat officers to contribute to regional or local capacity development under extra-budgetary schemes, typically in cooperation with international or bilateral implementing agencies or nongovernmental organizations and research institutes (Bauer 2006, 81).[28]

Likewise, the secretariat may, on an ad hoc basis, liaise between donor-driven activities and the appropriate addressees in affected countries. For instance, when Portugal and Monaco offered in 2003 bilateral capacity-building training on agricultural practices that related to dryland degradation, they called upon the desertification secretariat to identify in consultation with national focal points the people to be invited for these trainings.[29]

Explaining the Influence

Problem Structure
Because of its post-1992 emergence, the desertification convention has been framed as a sustainable development treaty rather than as typical multilateral environmental agreement (Bruyninckx 2005). As a result, it is not focused on a single environmental issue, such as dryland degradation, but addresses various interdependent policy issues related to desertification as specified in the convention. Hence, the problem structure of the issue is defined by a variety of policy challenges that renders the implementation of the convention's objectives more complex than those of most other multilateral environmental agreements.

On the other hand, the achievement of wide-spread scientific consensus on the phenomenon has been fairly straightforward—at least, it has been agreed for several decades that desertification describes a process of severe land degradation that is primarily anthropogenic and that expands into regions where it would climatically not be expected (Bauer 2007, with further references). In the context of the UNCED, however, debates about how to define desertification were politically charged by linking it to ongoing debates on anthropogenic climate change.

Thus, the Intergovernmental Negotiating Committee on Desertification eventually defined desertification as a process of "land degradation in arid, semi-arid and dry sub-humid areas resulting from various factors, including climatic variations and human activities" (UNCCD 2002a, article 1, paragraph a). This enters into international law a deviation from earlier definitions that emphasized adverse human impacts of land management (e.g., UNEP 1991).[30] Notably, the integration of "climatic variations" as one cause of desertification led to controversies between industrialized and developing countries about who is ultimately responsible for the degradation of the world's drylands (also Toulmin 1994).

The politicization of the problem structure is further exacerbated by divergent perceptions in North and South. Opinions on the salience of desertification and the need for a global convention differ accordingly.[31] It is a widely shared view in the North that negotiations for a convention on desertification were not so much driven by the need to create a legal instrument to deal with dryland degradation than by the need to reward Southern cooperation on issues such as biological diversity and climate change.[32] Hence, industrialized countries were more or less indifferent to desertification, which enabled developing countries to incorporate their major concerns into an international legal agreement. This caveat makes the convention unique in its comprehensive sustainable development approach, and at the same time elusive in terms of concrete policy objectives. Consequently, it is easy for the desertification secretariat to relate its activities to the broad objectives of the convention and assert these activities as legitimate, even if they are not explicitly mandated by the conference of the parties. At the same time, however, the secretariat needs to be alert to the discrepancies in priorities that parties attribute to the convention: "There are of course positive aspects for a proactive secretariat, but it also entails some risks. You may move in the right direction and it is fine, but if you move, you also take some risks."[33]

Again, the political debate about the Havana conference of the parties is illustrative. The desertification secretariat emphatically refers to the politicization of the convention process to account for the criticism that it faced after the controversial High Level Segment in Havana. Although industrialized countries perceived the High Level Segment as an outright affront, the desertification secretariat argues that it is scapegoated for the own failure of industrialized countries to be adequately represented in the event. And though senior officials acknowledged that the secretariat might not have handled this conference of the parties in the best possible manner, they also complained about the hypocrisy of European governments, which they perceived as pursuing bilateral foreign policy at the expense of the multilateral process. In particular, it was mooted that President Chirac of France and Chancellor Schröder of Germany had initially suggested to attend the High Level Segment, but withdrew in the immediate runup to the conference of the parties because of a sudden backlash in diplomatic relations between Cuba and the EU, as well as to avoid fuelling further transatlantic tensions stemming from French and German opposition to the U.S.–led war on Iraq.[34] The turmoil surrounding the Havana Roundtable of Heads of State and Government thus illustrates the level of politicization of the desertification convention's problem structure and the significance of North–South tensions with a view to its implementation. At the same time, it illustrates that industrialized countries are hardly concerned with the fight against desertification, despite their formal commitment to the global dimension of the problem.

This quandary furthermore indicates an institutional "problem of fit" (Young 2002, 2003), inasmuch as concerns of developing countries with the overarching development implications of global desertification as captured by the convention do not really match the low saliency that industrialized countries attribute to the problem of dryland degradation.

Polity

As a UN convention, the desertification secretariat has a higher status than most environmental treaty secretariats. This status is underscored by the explicit provision that the secretariat "should not be fully integrated in the work program and management structure of any particular department or program of the United Nations" (UNCCD 1997, 28). In political practice, however, the desertification secretariat is answerable to the conference of the parties similar to other secretariats that are subordinate to UNEP, such as the secretariats of the biodiversity convention or the Montreal Protocol. As the level of control through the conference of the parties is not stricter or lower than with other conventions, the difference in status comes down to a more prestigious standing in terms of UN protocol (for instance, through the status of the executive secretary as assistant secretary-general to the UN).

Yet secretariat officials appreciated this as a comparative advantage over other environmental treaty secretariats in the UN system (with the exception of the climate secretariat), because it would bring "a great deal of autonomy," not in the least by reducing "bureaucratic length": "We don't have to go through different layers of administrative processes to get things done. . . . We do not have to go through UNEP or anybody else."[35]

The desertification secretariat is thus fairly autonomous in the structuring of its internal management, the acquisition of external expertise, and, crucially, the hiring and firing of staff, which is an exclusive prerogative of the executive secretary. Financially, the desertification secretariat is as dependent on the parties as any other international bureaucracy, but it enjoys considerable freedom in how to allocate its budget. It also has a record of acquiring supplementary funds for extra-budgetary activities (article 23.g of the convention). This funding helped raise the secretariat's profile vis-à-vis beneficiaries in affected countries, including nongovernmental organizations.[36]

More importantly, the secretariat's potential to influence the convention process can be explained by its networking with affected regions. It could thus sustain the support of the Group of 77 even when its overall performance had at times been questioned. In particular, the desertification secretariat maintains strong connections at national and regional levels through national focal points and its support for Regional Coordination Units in the affected regions. According to the secretariat, the strong links between its Regional Action Facilitators and the Regional Coordination Units are the key to its good standing at the "field level." Accordingly, the desertification secretariat considers a decentralization of secretariat services, which it finds warranted by the convention's Regional Annexes, a viable strategy to facilitate capacity building in affected countries.[37]

An additional factor regarding the secretariat's links to affected countries is to maintain relations with parliaments, including the European

Parliament. Over the years, a Round Table of Members of Parliament has thus become an established sideshow at conferences of the parties and a means for the secretariat to garner indirectly the support of national delegations through members of parliament of their own domestic constituencies.[38] At the very least, it shows that international bureaucracies are capable of employing innovative ways to promote their agenda.

People and Procedures

Within the overall context of the desertification secretariat as determined by polity and problem structure, its behavior as a political actor is largely shaped by its people and procedures. This behavior pertains in particular to organizational leadership and internal management as represented by the secretariat's senior management. Moreover, questions of leadership and management are interdependent, if not mutually reinforcing, with the secretariat's organizational culture.

Organizational Structure   The organizational structure of the secretariat reflects the importance attributed to the Regional Annexes of the convention, which are represented by distinct divisions. Each is directed by a Regional Action Facilitator, who is part of the senior management. Internal workflows meticulously adhere to the formal hierarchy that reflects the authoritative leadership of Executive Secretary Diallo. Officers of the desertification secretariat have described their bureaucracy as a "small shop" and emphasized that ways are literally short in Bonn, notably when compared to United Nations offices in New York or Geneva. Yet internal procedures are not necessarily efficient when there is an "excessive level of hierarchy," as one officer (who has since left the secretariat) has complained: every single move would need to be justified "all the time, even when [you are] a part of the senior management."[39]

This picture is confirmed by other officers who characterized Diallo as "*the* decision-maker in this secretariat, [including] issues that could be more delegated."[40] Indeed, a number of officers stated that their motivation and morale would suffer from an overly authoritative and inflexible management style. (At the time of writing, the secretariat is being restructured due to changes in leadership and the embracement of a results-based management approach; see IISD 2007, 5).

Organizational Culture   Finally, the organizational culture of the desertification secretariat is characterized by the geocultural composition of its staff, which reflects the concern of the convention with affected regions. Africans, in particular, feature prominently in the secretariat's management and staff. Although this seems adequate in view of the emphasis the convention places on Africa, a sense of skepticism has emerged among those who are not part of the secretariat's inner circle.

In particular, some perceive the secretariat as an instrument to serve the interests of a clique of francophone West Africans and Northern Africans. Such suspicion may be nourished by the fact that countries of both regions feature prominently among the most vocal and consistent sponsors of the convention in international forums such as the UN General Assembly or the Commission on Sustainable Development. Though this prominence is unsurprising given the strong sense of ownership among these countries, occasional allegations of clientelism and misconduct—rarely voiced openly—undermine the legitimate cause of such regional leadership.

Such allegations coincide with complaints about a lack of transparency in the secretariat's operations. Most explicitly, such complaints were voiced in the context of the sixth conference of the parties, where there was confusion regarding the election of officials. This complaining was fuelled by allegations of procedural irregularities and patronage relating to disbursements granted by the secretariat to allegedly hand-picked nongovernmental organizations. Against this background, donor countries have become more restrictive in their budgetary policy and have called for the UN Joint Inspection Unit to review governance of the implementation of the convention and to scrutinize the functions, activities and mandate of the secretariat.[41] The Joint Inspection Unit reported to the seventh conference of the parties, which took place in 2005 in Nairobi, and presented a host of recommendations, among other things, to improve on the secretariat's approach toward results-based management and budgeting (Ortiz and Tang 2005; IISD 2005a). Moreover, parties established an intersessional intergovernmental working group to consider adequate responses to the Joint Inspection Unit's assessment.

To the secretariat's defense, Executive Secretary Diallo has offered political explanations for some controversies surrounding the Havana meeting, but has also requested that critics clarify charges of lacking transparency: "Whatever we do is known to countries. So what do parties want to know that they do not know [yet]? I don't know."[42] Even so, the damage to the secretariat's reputation has been considerable.

Organizational Leadership   The pinnacle of authority in an international bureaucracy is personified in its top executive, which could hardly be more obvious than in the case of Hama Arba Diallo, the desertification secretariat's veteran executive secretary. Diallo was closely involved with international responses to desertification long before the convention came into being. As a leading voice among African representatives in the negotiations, he appeared to be an ideal candidate for the position of the convention's top bureaucrat. He took office with great verve and has been characterized both inside and outside the secretariat as a charismatic and visionary leader and "a very hands-on and active executive secretary."[43]

The results are ambiguous, however, as these characteristics have worked both to the benefit and to the disadvantage of the desertification secretariat and the convention process. Virtually no insider to the desertification convention fails to praise the executive secretary's achievements in pushing the convention ahead. At the same time, criticism regarding Diallo's "reign" over "his" secretariat has also been cumulating.

Aides of the executive secretary routinely downplay any criticism directed at the secretariat leadership. It is generally attributed to delegates from industrialized countries, whose disenchantment is seen as a by-product of the convention's prevalence with affected countries. Secretariat officials have a point when claiming that they serve "the interests of the *majority* of parties."[44] Yet they are aware that this stance is at odds with the UN tradition of consensus. Moreover, they should be alarmed by the frustration about the convention expressed in the corridors of agencies such as UNEP, the climate secretariat, or the World Bank.[45]

On balance, however, the organizational leadership by the desertification secretariat has thus far helped push forward the institutionalization of the desertification regime. As the institutional memory of the conference of the parties and a vocal advocate of affected countries, it has repeatedly shown resolve to proactively interpret equivocal policies.

As one senior officer explained, issues that would typically "rest" in between governmental meetings were allowed to progress largely because of actions by the secretariat: before the parties arrive at a "palpable language," the secretariat will "in the best understanding of its mandate to facilitate the implementation of the convention" take the initiative and "push and pull to make things happen."[46]

The very ability of the secretariat to "push and pull" is helped by the convention's problem structure, notably the limited importance assigned to desertification by industrialized countries. For example, some of the most powerful parties seem to send comparatively junior delegates to desertification convention meetings.[47] The senior officers of the desertification secretariat, on the other hand, are typically veteran diplomats who are highly familiar with the ways of the UN and the international politics of desertification, and who can rely on the support of the Group of 77. Hence, it is less difficult for the desertification secretariat to show organizational leadership than it could be (in comparison, see the case of the climate secretariat [Busch, this volume, chapter 10]).

Conclusion

The desertification secretariat illustrates that even small international bureaucracies can interfere with international processes and influence the outcome of international politics. The desertification secretariat even boasts to have been influential on specific matters. This is a remarkable difference from most other international bureaucracies analyzed in this volume, which generally maintain to scrupulously abide by the instructions of governments.

In particular, this chapter shows that the desertification secretariat influenced the discourse about desertification as a global policy problem as well as the progressive institutionalization of the convention at international and regional levels. By examining the conditions that enabled the secretariat to have this influence, the chapter contributes to our understanding of how these activities were influential, why, and to what effect.

As the analysis shows, the influence of the desertification secretariat can be explained first by the convoluted history of the desertification regime and problem structure in which the convention is subsequently embedded, and second, by the proactive, advocacy-like leadership style of the secretariat.

The case study also shows that the influence of the desertification secretariat was not confined to technical issues. At times, they were distinctively political, as has been exemplified, in particular, by the staging of a High Level Segment at the conference of the parties in Havana. The desertification secretariat has thus shown a propensity to trigger developments that may not be easily anticipated by governments, but which they cannot ignore. In fact, the activities have led governments to question the conduct and performance of the desertification secretariat and to seek closer control. Eventually this activity may diminish the potential of the secretariat to influence the convention process. Indeed, it puts Hama Arba Diallo's successor at the helm of the secretariat—the new executive secretary Luc Gnacadja—in a delicate position. He is expected by many parties to enact major reforms within the desertification secretariat, yet each of his steps will be suspiciously monitored by governments.

This evolution of the desertification regime can hardly be understood without the role played by the international bureaucracy at its center. This is not to say that the desertification secretariat has determined in its own right the success or failure of the desertification convention. Neither can it be inferred that interventions of the desertification secretariat have helped or hindered the implementation of the convention. It seems, however, that the influence of an international bureaucracy can make a difference.

In sum, the case of the desertification secretariat shows that the actions of an international bureaucracy are an autonomous factor in international governance and can lead to policy outcomes that are not necessarily desired or anticipated by governments. The behavior of secretariats thus needs to be studied alongside the behavior of states and other non-state actors in order to arrive at a comprehensive understanding of international processes.

Acknowledgments

I am grateful to Gloria Chemin Kwon and Monica Tarouy for facilitating my research visit at the desertification secretariat in Bonn, Germany, and to all my interviewees. For helpful comments to this study, I am indebted to Elisabeth Corell, Pamela Chasek, Karel Mayrand, Benno Pilardeaux, Dino Renvert, Lindsay Stringer, and the MANUS project team.

Notes

1. Both the climate convention and the biodiversity convention were negotiated in advance of UNCED and were merely opened for signature at the conference.

2. For a useful overview, see the edited volume by Johnson, Mayrand, and Paquin 2006.

3. For a critical assessment of the institutionalization of expert knowledge in the desertification regime, see Martello 2004.

4. The author was not allowed to conduct formal interviews with program officers, which limited the application of the research design.

5. The interim secretariat of the desertification convention was seated at the United Nations' Geneva offices.

6. See UN Doc. ICCD/COP(6)/L.30/Rev.1. The budget was USD 14 million for the biennium 2000–2001 and USD 15.3 million for 2002–2003 (Schram Stokke and Thommessen 2003, 215).

7. In sum, these funds amounted to roughly USD 6 million for the biennium 2002–2003 (Schram Stokke and Thommessen 2003, 215).

8. A fifth regional annex for Central and Eastern Europe (Annex V) has been adopted at the fourth conference of the parties in Bonn (see Decision 7/COP.4, UNCCD 2001, Addendum 1: 22–27). However, this is not yet reflected in the secretariat structure.

9. When seeking interview appointments with the UNEP's "desertification experts," I was repeatedly advised that UNEP does not deal with desertification, but with land degradation, which is also reflected in its revised policy on "land use management and soil conservation" (UNEP 2004).

10. Author's interview at the desertification secretariat (November 2003).

11. Author's interview with the executive secretary, Bonn, 28 November 2003.

12. See Decision 9/COP.4 (UNCCD 2001, Addendum 1: 33).

13. Also author's interviews at the desertification secretariat (November and December 2003) and Germany's Federal Ministry for Development Cooperation (December 2003).

14. Author's interview at the desertification secretariat (November 2003).

15. Author's interview at the Federal Ministry for Development Cooperation, Germany (1 December 2003).

16. See Decisions 1/COP.5 (UNCCD 2002b, Addendum 1: 3–8) for the establishment and terms of reference of the Committee for the Review of the Implementation of the Convention. See IISD 2001, 14 for an account of the debate preceding the decision.

17. Author's interview with a member of the German delegation to the conference of the parties (November 2003).

18. Personal communication, September 2004. Originally scheduled for fall 2004, the third session of the Committee for the Review of the Implementation of the Convention was held in May 2005 (IISD 2005b).

19. The Global Mechanism has been established to assist parties in mobilizing funds from donor agencies for the implementation of projects related to the desertification convention (see Falloux, Tressler, and Mayrand 2006 for details).

20. Author's interview at the desertification secretariat (December 2003).

21. Author's interview with the executive secretary, Bonn, 28 November 2003.

22. Author's interview at the desertification secretariat (November 2003).

23. Author's interview at the desertification secretariat (November 2003).

24. Author's interviews with members of the German delegation to the sixth conference of the parties (November and December 2003).

25. A report of the Joint Inspection Unit was presented to the seventh conference of the parties and substantiated parties' criticism of the secretariat on a number of points (see IISD 2005a).

26. Author's interview at the desertification secretariat (December 2003).

27. Author's interview at the desertification secretariat (December 2003).

28. Author's interview at the desertification secretariat (November 2003).

29. Author's interview at the desertification secretariat (November 2003).

30. For an overview of shifting definitions and further references, see Corell 1999, 53–62.

31. For a comprehensive discussion on the globality of desertification, see Bauer 2007.

32. Author's interviews at the Federal Ministry for Development Cooperation of Germany and the desertification secretariat (November and December 2003); also Najam 2004, 2006.

33. Author's interview at the desertification secretariat (November 2003).

34. Author's interviews at the desertification secretariat, including interview with the executive secretary, Bonn, 28 November 2003.

35. Author's interview at the desertification secretariat (December 2003).

36. Author's interview at the Federal Ministry for Development Cooperation of Germany (December 2003).

37. Author's interviews at the desertification secretariat (November and December 2003).

38. See, for instance, the Declaration of Members of Parliament (UNCCD 2003b, Annex VI).

39. Author's interview at the desertification secretariat (November 2003).

40. Author's interview at the desertification secretariat (November 2003).

41. See IISD (2003, 7–8, 14–15); also author's interviews at UNEP headquarters (September 2003), a member of the German delegation to the sixth conference of the parties (November 2003) and at the Federal Ministry for Development Cooperation of Germany (December 2003).

42. Author's interview with the executive secretary, Bonn, 28 November 2003.

43. Author's interview at the desertification secretariat (November 2003).

44. Author's emphasis; the expression was reiterated in interviews and personal communication with several officials of the desertification secretariat.

45. Personal communication of author with officers from UNEP, the climate secretariat, the desertification secretariat, and the World Bank.

46. Author's interview at the desertification secretariat (November 2003).
47. Author's interview at the desertification secretariat (November 2003).

References

Bauer, Steffen. 2006. "The United Nations and the Fight against Desertification: What Role for the UNCCD Secretariat?" In *Governing Global Desertification. Linking Environmental Degradation, Poverty, and Participation*, edited by Pierre M. Johnson, Karel Mayrand, and Marc Paquin, 73–87. Aldershot, UK: Ashgate.

Bauer, Steffen. 2007. "Desertification." In *Handbook of Globalization and the Environment*, edited by Khi V. Thai, Dianne Rahm, and Jerrell D. Coggburn, 77–94. New York: CRC Press.

Bauer, Steffen, and Lindsay C. Stringer. 2008. *Science and Policy in the Global Governance of Desertification. An Analysis of Institutional Interplay under the United Nations Convention to Combat Desertification*. Global Governance Working Paper No. 35. Amsterdam and others: The Global Governance Project. Available at www.glogov.org (accessed February 2008).

Bruyninckx, Hans. 2005. "Sustainable Development: The Institutionalization of a Contested Policy Concept." In *International Environmental Politics*, edited by Michele M. Betsill, Kathryn Hochstetler, and Dimitris Stevis, 265–298. Basingstoke, UK: Palgrave Macmillan.

Chasek, Pamela S., and Elisabeth Corell. 2002. "Addressing Desertification at the International Level: The Institutional System." In *Global Desertification. Do Humans Cause Deserts?*, edited by J. F. Reynolds, and D. M. S. Smith, 275–294. Berlin: Dahlem University Press.

Corell, Elisabeth. 1999. *The Negotiable Desert. Expert Knowledge in the Negotiations of the Convention to Combat Desertification*. Linköping Studies in Arts and Sciences No. 191. Linköping, Sweden: Linköping University.

Corell, Elisabeth. 2003. "Dryland Degradation—Africa's Main Environmental Challenge: International Activities from the 1970s to the 1990s and the Future of the United Nations Convention to Combat Desertification." In *International Environmental Law and Policy in Africa*, edited by Beatrice Chaytor and Kevin R. Gray, 1–29. Dordrecht, Netherlands: Kluwer.

Corell, Elisabeth, and Michele M. Betsill. 2001. "A Comparative Look at NGO Influence in International Environmental Negotiations: Desertification and Climate Change." *Global Environmental Politics* 1 (4): 86–107.

Falloux, Francois, Susan Tressler, and Karel Mayrand. 2006. "The Global Mechanism and UNCCD Financing: Constraints and Opportunities." In *Governing Global Desertification. Linking Environmental Degradation, Poverty and Participation*, edited by Pierre M. Johnson, Karel Mayrand, and Marc Paquin, 131–145. Aldershot, UK: Ashgate.

Herrmann, Stefanie M., and Charles F. Hutchinson. 2006. "The Scientific Basis: Linkages between Land Degradation, Drought, and Desertification." In *Governing Global Desertification. Linking Environmental Degradation, Poverty and Participation*, edited by Pierre M. Johnson, Karel Mayrand, and Marc Paquin, 11–25. Aldershot, UK: Ashgate.

IISD, International Institute for Sustainable Development. 2001. Summary of the Fifth Conference of the Parties to the Convention to Combat Desertification: 1–13 October 2001. *Earth Negotiations Bulletin*, 15 October.

IISD, International Institute for Sustainable Development. 2003. Summary of the Sixth Conference of the Parties to the Convention to Combat Desertification: 25 August–6 September 2003. *Earth Negotiations Bulletin*, 8 September.

IISD, International Institute for Sustainable Development. 2005a. Summary of the Seventh Conference of the Parties to the Convention to Combat Desertification: 17–28 October 2005. *Earth Negotiations Bulletin*, 31 October.

IISD, International Institute for Sustainable Development. 2005b. Summary of the Third Session of the Committee for the Review of the Implementation of the Convention to Combat Desertification: 2–11 May 2005. *Earth Negotiations Bulletin*, 13 May.

IISD, International Institute for Sustainable Development. 2007. Summary of the Eighth Conference of the Parties to the Convention to Combat Desertification: 3–14 September 2007. *Earth Negotiations Bulletin*, 17 September.

Johnson, Pierre M., Karel Mayrand, and Marc Paquin, editors. 2006. *Governing Global Desertification. Linking Environmental Degradation, Poverty and Participation*. Aldershot, UK: Ashgate.

Knabe, Friederike. 2006. "Civil Society's Role in Negotiating and Implementing the UNCCD." In *Governing Global Desertification. Linking Environmental Degradation, Poverty, and Participation*, edited by Pierre M. Johnson, Karel Mayrand, and Marc Paquin, 89–107. Aldershot, UK: Ashgate.

Martello, Marybeth Long. 2004. "Expert Advice and Desertification Policy: Past Experience and Current Challenges." *Global Environmental Politics* 4 (3): 85–106.

McCormick, John. 1989. *The Global Environmental Movement. Reclaiming Paradise*. Bloomington: Indiana University Press.

Middleton, Nicholas J., and David S. G. Thomas. 1992. *World Atlas of Desertification*. London: Edward Arnold Publishers and UNEP.

Najam, Adil. 2004. "Dynamics of the Southern Collective: Developing Countries in Desertification Negotiations." *Global Environmental Politics* 4 (3): 128–154.

Najam, Adil. 2006. "Negotiating Desertification." In *Governing Global Desertification. Linking Environmental Degradation, Poverty, and Participation*, edited by Pierre M. Johnson, Karel Mayrand, and Marc Paquin, 56–72. Aldershot, UK: Ashgate.

Ortiz, Even F., and Guangting Tang. 2005. *Review of the Management, Administration, and Activities of the Secretariat of the United Nations Convention to Combat Desertification (UNCCD)*. Geneva: United Nations Joint Inspection Unit.

Schram Stokke, Olav, and Øystein B. Thommessen, editors. 2003. *Yearbook of International Co-operation on Environment and Development 2003/2004*. London: Earthscan.

Tarradell, Mireia. 2007. *The Influence of International Bureaucracies in Global Environmental Politics: Results from an Expert Survey*. Global Governance Working Paper 26. Amsterdam and others: The Global Governance Project.

Thomas, David S. G. 1997. "Science and the Desertification Debate." *Journal of Arid Environments* 37 (4): 599–608.

Toulmin, Camilla. 1994. "Combating Desertification: Encouraging Local Action within a Global Framework." In *Green Globe Yearbook of International Co-operation on Environment and Development 1994*, edited by Helge O. Bergesen and Georg Parmann, 79–88. Oxford: Oxford University Press.

Toulmin, Camilla. 1995. "Combating Desertification by Conventional Means." *Global Environmental Change* 5 (5): 455–457.

UNCCD, United Nations Convention to Combat Desertification in Those Countries Experiencing Serious Drought and/or Desertification, Particularly in Africa. 1995. *Down to Earth. A Simplified Guide to the Convention to Combat Desertification, Why It Is Necessary and What Is Important and Different about It*. Bonn: UNCCD.

UNCCD, United Nations Convention to Combat Desertification in those Countries Experiencing Serious Drought and/or Desertification, Particularly in Africa. 1997. *Report of the Conference of the Parties on Its First Session, Held in Rome from 29 September to 10 October 1997. Doc. ICCD/COP (1)/1/11 of 29 December 1997*. Geneva: UNCCD.

UNCCD, United Nations Convention to Combat Desertification in those Countries Experiencing Serious Drought and/or Desertification, Particularly in Africa. 2001. *Report of the Conference of the Parties on Its Fourth Session, Held in Bonn from 11 to 22 December 2000. Doc. ICCD/COP (4)/11 of 4 September 2001*. Bonn: UNCCD.

UNCCD, United Nations Convention to Combat Desertification in those Countries Experiencing Serious Drought and/or Desertification, Particularly in Africa. 2002a. *United Nations Convention to Combat Desertification in those Countries Experiencing Serious Drought and/or Desertification, Particularly in Africa*. Bonn: UNCCD.

UNCCD, United Nations Convention to Combat Desertification in those Countries Experiencing Serious Drought and/or Desertification, Particularly in Africa. 2002b. *Report of the Conference of the Parties on Its Fifth Session, Held in Geneva from 1 to 12 October 2001. Doc. ICCD/COP (5)/11 of 5 April 2002*. Bonn: UNCCD.

UNCCD, United Nations Convention to Combat Desertification in those Countries Experiencing Serious Drought and/or Desertification, Particularly in Africa. 2003a. *Making a Difference*. 2nd edition. Bonn: UNCCD.

UNCCD, United Nations Convention to Combat Desertification in those Countries Experiencing Serious Drought and/or Desertification, Particularly in Africa. 2003b. *Report of the Conference of the Parties on Its Sixth Session, Held in Havana from 25 August to 5 September 2003*. Doc. ICCD/COP (6)/11 of 3 November 2003. Bonn: UNCCD.

UNEP. 1991. *External Evaluation of the Plan of Action to Combat Desertification. Report of the Executive Director, Prepared for the 16th Session of the Governing Council*. Nairobi: UNEP.

UNEP. 2004. *UNEP's Strategy on Land Use Management and Soil Conservation. A Strengthened Functional Approach*, edited by UNEP Division of Policy Development and Law. Policy Series 4. Nairobi: UNEP.

Young, Oran R. 2002. *The Institutional Dimensions of Environmental Change. Fit, Interplay, and Scale*. Cambridge, MA: MIT Press.

Young, Oran R. 2003. "Environmental Governance: The Role of Institutions in Causing and Confronting Environmental Problems." *International Environmental Agreements: Politics, Law and Economics* 3 (4): 377–393.

13

The Influence of International Bureaucracies in World Politics: Findings from the MANUS Research Program

Frank Biermann and Bernd Siebenhüner

The research presented in this book revealed two central insights regarding the influence of international bureaucracies in world politics. First, bureaucracies have a sizeable autonomous influence as actors in global environmental policy that goes at times beyond expectations. All case studies have shown that bureaucracies act as knowledge brokers, negotiation facilitators, and capacity builders in international politics: they influence global agendas, they shape international negotiation processes, and they make international cooperation work by assisting in national implementation. Second, this autonomous influence varies considerably in both degree and type. The next three sections focus on this variation in the influence of the nine bureaucracies that we studied in this project. The remaining part of this chapter will then present an explanatory model that can largely account, we argue, for this variation.

Setting the Global Agenda

In all nine case studies, we found that international bureaucracies influence the behavior of political actors by altering their knowledge and belief systems. Most international bureaucracies analyzed in this project have influence through synthesizing scientific findings and distributing knowledge to stakeholders, from national governments to scientific audiences and citizens. The environment division of the IMO, for example, participates in the Joint Group of Experts on the Scientific Aspects of Marine Environmental Protection, which is responsible for a large number of reports that have been cited 1,436 times in scholarly publications since 1967 (Campe, this volume, chapter 6). Some international bureaucracies are also directly involved in the funding and administration of original research, such as the World Bank, with a strong emphasis on quantitative economic research. Every year, the World Bank publishes about 4,000 reports, notes, newsletters, and research articles—one tenth of which are related to environmental policy. From 1995 through 2004, World Bank researchers published 2000 articles in peer-reviewed academic journals, 10 percent of which dealt with environmental issues. On average, each article was cited nearly five times in other scientific publications. The Web site of the World Bank lists 1661 documents on environmental issues (Marschinski and Behrle, this volume, chapter 5). Likewise, the OECD secretariat published 363 books between 1997 and 2005 on environmental issues, and OECD publications have been cited in more than 2700 academic articles on environmental issues between 1995 and 2005 (Busch, this volume, chapter 4). Quite often, bureaucracies are active in all three stages of knowledge generation, knowledge synthesizing, and knowledge dissemination—at the same time.

Mostly, this type of activity has a sizeable autonomous influence on discourses and debates in environmental policy that goes beyond the initial positions and policies of governments. The international response to global warming is an example. In the late 1980s, uncertainty about the reality of global warming prevented governments from acting. Knowledge was either nonexistent, or it was disputed among experts and laypersons alike. In this situation, it was the bureaucrats of the WMO and the UNEP that initiated and organized the Intergovernmental Panel on Climate Change, a network of several thousand leading climate experts, to offer a series of consensus documents on the state of knowledge and on possible political response strategies (Bauer, this volume, chapter 7; Biermann 2002; Siebenhüner 2002a, 2002b). This panel did not generate new knowledge, but helped make existing knowledge accessible for policy makers and external stakeholders. Through its system of peer review and later of geographic balancing in this peer review, the necessary credibility and legitimacy for the existing knowledge were maintained—a task that was beyond the scope of individual governments that would inevitably have been seen as partisan in their assessment. It was then again international bureaucracies (the UNEP and the climate secretariat) that took the lead in disseminating this knowledge through Web sites, brochures, information packages, and workshops, especially in developing countries (Bauer, this volume, chapter 7, Busch, this volume, chapter 10).

Other examples are the many reporting and monitoring schemes that international bureaucracies have implemented, or the outreach activities of their staff through commissioned studies and conference diplomacy.

The OECD environment directorate, with its national environmental policy reports, for instance, was highly influential in many domestic policy debates, where governments referred to the reports when formulating and defending national policies such as ecotaxation and emissions standards for greenhouse gases (Busch, this volume, chapter 4). Likewise, all treaty secretariats require members to report on environmental data and implementation efforts. The desertification secretariat, for instance, monitors worldwide desertification by collecting and documenting the reports submitted by parties. By integrating these data in its publications, the secretariat shaped a particular interpretation of desertification that gained currency among many stakeholders in a way that would not have been likely to emerge without the autonomous activity of the secretariat (Bauer, this volume, chapter 12).

This autonomous cognitive influence of international bureaucracies in the field of global environmental governance, however, differs regarding both degree and type. Regarding the degree of influence, the cognitive influence of the World Bank, the environment directorate of the OECD, and the UNEP secretariat are particularly strong. Especially the UNEP secretariat has launched significant assessment processes to study global and transboundary environmental problems such as climate change, biodiversity loss, water scarcity, and others. Moreover, the UNEP secretariat successfully communicated the results of these assessments to the policy world where political initiatives such as international negotiations or partnership initiatives were triggered. Likewise, the OECD environment directorate has operationalized and promoted several core principles of environmental policy, such as the "polluter-pays principle" that is today widely accepted in most countries as a basis for environmental policy (Busch, this volume, chapter 4). By contrast, the cognitive influence of smaller bureaucracies is more limited.

More interestingly, the *types* of cognitive influence vary among different perspectives, which we describe as technocratic, activist, and environmentalist. A typical example of technocratic cognitive influence is the environment department of the IMO, which restricts itself to informing governments and private actors on the technical details of shipping that is safe and pollutes less. A similar case is the secretariat of the climate convention, which tries to cleanse its information input from any political or policy-sensitive implications. Quite different, however, is the desertification secretariat, which has a mandate comparable to the climate secretariat and even shares the same building, but has evolved into the prototype of what we term an activist bureaucracy with an explicit political agenda. The secretariats of UNEP and of the biodiversity convention for their part developed a more environmentalist type of cognitive influence, going beyond the technocratic restriction of the climate secretariat, but also avoiding the more activist type of influence that the desertification secretariat revealed.

Within these larger categories of technocratic, activist, and environmentalist cognitive influence, we identified further distinctions in the type that range from the economistic discourses promoted by the World Bank to the industry-supportive approach of the environment department of the IMO. Among the environmentalist types, the secretariat of UNEP is known to directly influence domestic and international debates on the basis of a global perspective, and the biodiversity secretariat largely focuses on nature conservation programs.

Shaping Global Cooperation

In addition, we found that international bureaucracies have an autonomous influence in global environmental governance through the creation, support, and shaping of rule-building processes for issue-specific international cooperation. Bureaucracies influence international rule-setting both in its early stages—for example, through the initiation of diplomatic conferences at which international regimes are negotiated—and in the later phase of regime implementation and revision. As one member of the biodiversity secretariat states: "As a national delegate it was my highest ambition to change at least one word in the text of the decision, as part of the secretariat I can influence the whole text."[1]

It was the UNEP secretariat, for example, that initiated the first conferences on negotiating a treaty to phase out ozone-depleting chemicals at a time when the issue was not recognized by most governments (Bauer, this volume, chapter 9). The staff of the World Bank developed the basis for the environmental parts of what later became the "Equator Principles" that twenty-seven major private lending agencies adopted for defining the social and environmental impact of their activities (Marschinski and Behrle, this volume, chapter 5). Likewise, the UNEP secretariat has helped create the Global Reporting Initiative, another major new mechanism of transnational environmental governance (Pattberg 2006).

International bureaucracies were also crucial in the later phase of dynamic implementation and revision of regimes—in particular, the role of the staff of treaty secretariats, who organize meetings, set agendas, and write reports to the conferences of the parties. Secretariats remain accountable to governments that are the final masters of treaty evolution. And yet they are hardly passive to governmental initiative, but are fairly autonomous in their influence. Through their initiative, policy issues have entered or remained on the agenda of multilateral negotiations. In several incidences, negotiators relied heavily on the information provided by treaty secretariats, and many suggestions for treaty language have been taken over by negotiators from the bureaucracies, especially in negotiations under the biodiversity convention (Siebenhüner, this volume, chapter 11), the ozone treaties (Bauer, this volume, chapter 9) and, to a lesser degree, the desertification convention (Bauer, this volume, chapter 12). Also the GEF secretariat had some normative influence, even though not directly comparable to other bureaucracies. The GEF secretariat influences the facilitation of the modalities of the GEF mechanism itself, rather than actual negotiations. For instance, the GEF secretariat develops strategies and operational policies on how to manage and implement the scarce GEF resources. These policies then influence the subsequent reallocation of resources and competences among the different organizations involved in the implementation of GEF projects (Andler, this volume, chapter 8).

Also important is the role of international bureaucracies in the codification and development of international law, including the "soft law" that often precedes legally binding agreements (Abbott and Snidal 2000). International civil servants emphasize the development of international law and soft law agreements as a key area of their work (Töpfer 1998, 11; Tolba and Rummel-Bulska 1998, 11–24; Bauer, this volume, chapter 7). One example of global legalization and regime-creation driven by international bureaucracies is the Regional Seas Programme that the UNEP secretariat has been promoting since 1974. Initially conceptualized to address marine pollution in the Mediterranean Sea, the program has led to a series of international agreements on most regional seas worldwide, now covering more than 130 states and some 50 international agencies. The Regional Seas Programme thus shows the catalytic role that even relatively small bureaucracies can play in the promotion of international cooperation (Bauer, this volume, chapter 7).

Our project also revealed substantial variation in the normative influence of international bureaucracies. The most striking difference is among the four treaty secretariats studied. Though all four secretariats are similar in mandate and setup, they vary considerably in the degree in which they were able to have autonomous influence on negotiations. The climate secretariat limits itself strictly to mere neutral support of international negotiations, which makes it a more technocratic executor of what governments intend (Busch, this volume, chapter 10). The biodiversity secretariat, on its part, followed an environmentalist approach and showed a sizeable autonomous influence on negotiations through drafting decisions and promoting compromises (Siebenhüner, this volume, chapter 11). To a somewhat lesser extent, this could also be observed in the case of the ozone secretariat that actively promotes the participation of countries in the amendments to the regime (Bauer, this volume, chapter 9; also Benedick 1998; Wettestad 2001).

In particular, the desertification secretariat has pushed discourses and decision making in a direction that went against the intentions of a number of governments, notably within the donor community of the rich industrialized countries. Whereas the climate secretariat can thus be seen as the prototype of a technocratic bureaucracy that tries to stay away from any autonomous political influence, the desertification secretariat—with its legally and politically almost identical mandate—evolved into the prototype of an "activist bureaucracy" that promoted its own agenda, in this case the support of the poorer developing countries, especially in Africa (Bauer, this volume, chapter 12).

The variation is similarly strong among the group of larger intergovernmental agencies and their environmental departments. It did come as no surprise that the UNEP secretariat has had some autonomous influence on negotiations, as this is part and parcel of its mandate as the environmental "conscience" and "catalyst" within the UN system. More surprising is a notable influence on rule-setting processes also from the environmental department of the OECD and from the World Bank, even though this influence is empirically difficult to assess, as civil servants—in particular of the World Bank—usually deny any such influence when on record (Busch, this volume, chapter 4; Marschinski and Behrle, this volume, chapter 5). The environmental department of the IMO secretariat, however—even though similar in setup and mandate to the environmental departments in other larger bureaucracies—lacked almost any traceable autonomous influence on negotiations and thus resembled the "technocratic" bureaucracy of the climate secretariat (Campe, this volume, chapter 6).

Making International Cooperation Work

In addition, international bureaucracies show a sizable autonomous influence on global environmental governance through the direct assistance to countries in their effort to implement international agreements. In the ozone regime, for example, three international bureaucracies—the World Bank, the UN Development Programme and UNEP, later joined by the UN Industrial Development Organization organized an international campaign to install in each capital in the developing world a so-called Ozone Unit (Bauer, this volume, chapter 9; for more details, see Biermann 1997). These were small administrative offices linked to the national environment ministry with staff trained and financed by these international bureaucracies to draft and implement national programs on the phaseout of ozone-depleting substances. Even though states paid for these programs, it was the staff of the international bureaucracies that developed and shaped the programs, setting the stage for the emission-control programs in more than one hundred countries. Without the substantive input of these bureaucracies, the overall effectiveness of the ozone regime in the developing countries would hardly be conceivable. Similar programs are now in place for other environmental problems through the GEF, a financial mechanism implemented through the World Bank, the UN Development Programme and the UNEP (Andler, this volume, chapter 8). The initiation and management of capacity building is not restricted to major international agencies, such as the World Bank. It is also an undertaking of the four smaller international bureaucracies even when capacity building is formally not their main function. One example is the influence of the desertification secretariat in setting up coordination units in affected countries and its operations under various extrabudgetary schemes (Bauer, this volume, chapter 12).

Capacity building is more than a technical endeavor, but part of largely autonomous policy development by the international bureaucracies involved. We found repeatedly that international bureaucracies shape through their outreach programs in the capitals of member states the policies of their host countries, for example, through training programs for mid-level civil servants that are influenced by ideas, concepts, and policies that international bureaucracies propagate. Bureaucracies are also agents of diffusion for national policies or technologies that are identified by their staff as particularly promising or useful and are then spread to other countries through targeted programs of the bureaucracy

(Busch and Jörgens 2005). Much of the work of the World Bank and the OECD falls in this category (Busch, this volume, chapter 4; Marschinski and Behrle, this volume, chapter 5).

One key finding of the MANUS project in this area is that not only did most bureaucracies have autonomous executive influence, but that there appears to be a general tendency for all bureaucracies to develop operational activities and capacities, even when their original mandate and function did not provide for it. The UNEP secretariat, for example, is striving for operational capacities, that is, to run programs and projects on the ground parallel to—and to some extent then in competition with—the UN Development Programme. Likewise, most treaty secretariats are assuming some executive functions, partially in line with the overall political development in their policy arenas that shift from norm development to norm implementation (e.g., see the case study on the biodiversity secretariat [Siebenhüner, this volume, chapter 11]).

Yet despite these similarities and the general trend toward the acquisition of more executive competences, the MANUS project also revealed substantial variation in the influence of international bureaucracies. This variation is most striking between the World Bank, whose core mandate is the implementation of projects on the ground, and most secretariats and the environment directorate of the OECD, which have much smaller executive influence. Yet differences also existed among the other cases, for example, between the IMO secretariat, which has a long-standing tradition in implementing programs, and UNEP, which is just developing such programs.

In sum, all international bureaucracies analyzed in this study have autonomous cognitive, normative, and executive influence in their policy domain (see table 13.1).

Yet both degree and type of this influence differ. Some bureaucracies are more influential on all three dimensions, and others are particularly influential in either the cognitive, normative, or executive dimensions. The type of this influence also differs, ranging from rather technocratic approaches to a more activist perspective. Also, all the dimensions of influence are interrelated. For example, the UNEP secretariat influenced negotiations by promoting specific interpretations of international environmental law (normative influence), which led to an increase of legal capacities in developing countries, where UNEP lawyers trained university lecturers, supported capacity building for environmental legislation, or advised parliaments and policy makers (executive influence). The basis for this is the UNEP secretariat's worldwide networking programs in monitoring and assessing global environmental policy (cognitive influence; see Bauer, this volume, chapter 7).

Finally, in most cases we could observe a shift in bureaucratic responsibilities over time that went along with the general policy development in the respective issue areas. In the early development of an issue, the influence of international bureaucracies is most crucial through information and the provision of authoritative knowledge. Later on, international bureaucracies are key in bringing together governments and in facilitating norm-setting processes. Eventually, bureaucracies adopt a role in the implementation of environmental accords, while keeping their part in the continuous development of new knowledge and adjusted norms within the regime.

Explaining Variation in the Influence of International Bureaucracies

How can one explain this variation in the influence of international bureaucracies? In this section, we develop an empirically grounded theoretical model that can account for a large extent of the difference in influence between the bureaucracies that we studied in this project. The model builds on our empirical data and includes explanatory factors at three levels of analysis: the macro level, where the structure of the *problems* addressed by a bureaucracy predetermine its overall autonomy vis-à-vis states; the meso level, with factors such as the competences, resources, and institutional embedding, what we describe as the *polity* of an international bureaucracy; and the micro level, that is, the *people* working in a bureaucracy and the *procedures*, cultures, and leadership styles that they develop over time. We found that these four p's—problems, polity, people, and procedures—can explain a substantial degree of the variation that we observed in the autonomous influence of international bureaucracies (see table 13.2).

Problem Structure
We found that the type of problem that international bureaucracies are mandated to address and the type of policy domain in which they operate considerably affects the degree and type of their autonomous influence. This problem structure emerged as a key factor to explain when and why international bureaucracies could manage to gain some degree of autonomy from governments. The case studies reveal that similar

Table 13.1
Influence of international environmental bureaucracies

	OECD environment directorate	World Bank	IMO secretariat	UNEP secretariat
Cognitive influence	Has influenced scientific and public discourse through neutral expertise	High influence through scientific expertise and specific role as lending institution	Relatively low autonomous influence	High influence in many areas through scientific and policy expertise and active information management
Normative influence	Has influenced several norm-setting processes through expertise Promotion of economic frames and solutions	Has influenced several norm-setting processes through expertise and proactive initiatives (e.g., Prototype Carbon Fund) Promotion of economic frames and solutions	Limited to few instances in negotiations Technocratic orientation	Has initiated and promoted a variety of negotiation processes Promoted several intergovernmental agreements Environmentalist orientation
Executive influence	Limited influence	Major influence as core part of the mandate	Influence through capacity-building and training programs in the South	Limited executive influence Increasing trend in this direction

GEF secretariat	Ozone secretariat	Climate secretariat	Biodiversity secretariat	Desertification secretariat
Low autonomous influence within network of implementing agencies	Significant influence through high issue-specific institutional knowledge	Low autonomous influence through limited outward orientation	Has influenced debates through substantial institutional expertise	Has left marked influence on "desertification" discourse and promoted specific policy interpretations
Sizeable influence on norm development within GEF mechanism	Has promoted ozone agreements and influenced negotiations Environmentalist orientation	Limited influence on actual negotiation Hesitant to develop policy initiates Nonactivist technocratic orientation	Has influenced biodiversity-related negotiations and has brought in ideas, concepts, and policy proposals Environmentalist orientation	Has influenced negotiations through taking active positions, but also raised substantial resistance by major donor countries Advocacy orientation
Limited influence, mainly in connection with the implementing agencies	Influence on capacity building in developing countries, such as through setting up of ozone units	Limited executive influence	Limited yet growing executive influence	Limited executive influence, with increasing tendency

Table 13.2
Schematic overview of explanatory factors

	OECD environment directorate	World Bank	IMO secretariat	UNEP secretariat
Problem Structure	Multi-issue bureaucracy	Multi-issue bureaucracy	High cost of regulation and high saliency of issue for lead countries in IMO decision-making system (shipping nations)	Multi-issue environmental bureaucracy
Polity: Competence	Little autonomous competences	High degree of competences vis-à-vis developing countries; comparatively high degree of independence from member states	Comparatively low degree of independence from member states	As a program, limited autonomous mandate compared to the major agencies
Polity: Resources	Substantial resources for information generation and dissemination	Very large resources available for information generation and dissemination, and for development projects	Substantial resources for information dissemination and conference servicing	Small core budget based on unreliable voluntary contributions, yet access to a variety of resources for designated activities (e.g. GEF projects)

GEF secretariat	Ozone secretariat	Climate secretariat	Biodiversity secretariat	Desertification secretariat
Multi-issue environmental bureaucracy	Decreasing cost of regulation and saliency since early 1990s	Extremely high potential cost of regulation; high saliency in many countries	Different potential costs of regulation depending on country; medium saliency in most countries	Cost of regulation and saliency very low in industrialized countries
Limited autonomous competences	Limited autonomous competences	Limited autonomous competences	Limited autonomous competences	Limited autonomous competences
Limited resources, but influence on GEF grants through decision rights on smaller projects	Small secretariat with little resources	Substantial resources for information dissemination and conference servicing	Limited resources for information dissemination and substantial resources for conference servicing	Medium resources for information dissemination and conference servicing

Table 13.2
(continued)

	OECD environment directorate	World Bank	IMO secretariat	UNEP secretariat
Polity: Embeddedness	Influenced by geographically selected membership Embedded as directorate in larger economic bureaucracy	Environment department and other activities within lending institution	Environment division embedded in shipping-oriented bureaucracy	Embedded in UN system as program of UN Organization
People and procedures	High expertise Economistic culture Leadership less prominent	High expertise Economistic professional culture Many internal evaluation mechanisms, and "pockets of environmental excellence" Domination by economic, quantitative and evidence-based culture Strong external leadership	Technical expertise on shipping, little expertise on environmental problems Structures with limited evaluation or learning structures Seafaring and naval engineering background dominating Leadership less prominent	High expertise Relatively flexible structures with regular reform Staff with mixed backgrounds and environmentalist culture Strong external leadership most of the time

GEF secretariat	Ozone secretariat	Climate secretariat	Biodiversity secretariat	Desertification secretariat
Complex embedding in multi-bureaucracy setting	Part of the UN Environment Programme	Part of the UN Organization, yet relatively independent	Part of the UN Environment Programme, yet relatively independent	Part of the UN Organization, yet relatively independent
Some expertise in relevant issue areas Structures have some evaluation mechanisms, but problems with implementing change Sizable external leadership	High institutional expertise Structures flexible also because of small size Environmentalist culture Relatively strong leadership	Expertise in institutional issues Relatively hierarchical, controlled structures Mixed academic backgrounds with no dominant culture Leadership often strong, yet in neutral role	High expertise on legal and institutional issues Structures open to change with some evaluation mechanisms Mixed staff with overall environmentalist orientation Pronounced leadership	High expertise Structures rather hierarchical, with little evaluation and learning mechanisms No dominant professional culture but distinct regional bias (Sahel region) Strong outspoken leadership

bureaucracies with similar design features and policies show different degrees and types of influence when faced with different problem structures. The relevance of problem structures in international environmental institutions[2] can be confirmed also for the study of international bureaucracies. To some extent, it was already part of the seminal study of Cox and Jacobson's in the 1970s. They concluded that decision making in organizations whose work had little salience for powerful states tends to be driven by "participant subsystems"—delegates, international officials, and associated independent experts, yet other organizations are dominated by "representative subsystems," that is, by member states and, in some cases, private associations (Cox and Jacobson 1973, 425–428).

The MANUS project analyzed variation of problem structures both within different issue domains of environmental policy and over time. We found that two determinants make a problem less conducive for the autonomous influence of an international bureaucracy: the cost of public action and regulation, and the international and national salience of a problem.

First, the higher the costs of international regulation, the more governments try to retain control over the political process and to prevent autonomous influence of international bureaucracies. The cost of regulation is determined by a wide range of factors that include both the political, economic, and social costs of addressing and solving the problem and the political, economic, and social costs of inaction. In view of all these factors, for example, the regulation of the emission of ozone-depleting substances turned out to be less costly than of the emission of greenhouse gases, and the autonomous influence of international bureaucracies was significantly larger when comparatively less costly problems were at stake. The costs also change over time. Scientific discourse and technological innovation, for example, can dramatically increase options and mold actor strategies, as was the case with the technological breakthrough in substituting chlorofluorocarbons that altered the political context in the negotiation of amendments of the treaty for the protection of the ozone layer by lowering the costs of regulation (Parson 2003). We therefore found that international bureaucracies have the more independent influence in the making and implementation of policies, the lesser the costs that governments anticipate for the effective regulation of the problem at stake.

Second, the higher the international and national salience of an environmental problem, the more governments try to retain control and to withhold autonomous authority from international bureaucracies. Salience is determined by a range of factors. These include, among other things, the time span between causes and effects of a problem. If there is a significant delay between cause and effect, as for instance between the gradual loss of biodiversity and the breakdown of an affected eco-system, the problem is unlikely to receive high priority from national decision makers. Clearly visible effects of global environmental problems—such as extreme weather events, in the case of climate change—increase political salience. Geographic differences in the effects of global environmental problems also explain their overall salience. Desertification, for instance, is hardly salient in most rich industrialized countries. Overall, we found that the less urgent the problem is perceived to be by most or by the most powerful governments at the national level, the more likely it is for international bureaucracies to develop their own independent influence in the making and implementation of policies. We speak here of "environmental high politics," marked by high costs of regulation and high salience among governments in larger and more powerful countries, and "environmental low politics," characterized through relatively low costs of regulation and a low political salience among the larger and more powerful countries.

The most costly and salient issue in this study has been climate change. This environmental problem knows no substitutes for the pollutants and no easy technical fix, and it affects core areas of economic activity, notably the energy and transportation sector. It pits against each other the largest countries, with the industrialized nations divided between Australia (until 2007) and the United States against the rest, and the developing countries divided between the large growing economies such as India and China, the critically affected countries such as the low-lying island nations, and finally the oil-producing countries. Negotiations on legally binding emission reduction targets, which took merely three years in the case of ozone-depleting substances, have been dragged out in the case of the climate since 1990. A first set of rules has been agreed in the 1997 Kyoto Protocol, but applies only to some industrialized countries (not to the United States) and is widely seen as insufficient to address the problem in a meaningful way. Climate change was at the center of the Group of Eight meetings in 2005 and in 2007, is a regular issue of transatlantic debate at the highest level, and in several business circles is the most threatening environmental regulatory issue worldwide (Busch, this volume, chapter 10).

Such a politically loaded environment left the climate secretariat, created to assist governments in implementing the 1992 climate convention, not unaffected (Busch, this volume, chapter 10). The climate secretariat clearly differs from the other, otherwise quite similar secretariats in its highly technocratic, politically highly neutral approach to almost all its activities—including the quite wary and vigilant reaction to the visiting field research team of the MANUS project. Consequently, the climate secretariat had been of helpful assistance to governments and thus a source of support in this issue area—yet all this influence was reactive and driven by the wishes and aspirations of governments represented in the conference of the parties and the various committees and commissions. The climate secretariat has truly been first and foremost the servant of governments.

The desertification secretariat, on the other hand, has evolved over time in a completely different direction (Bauer, this volume, chapter 12). We believe that one key factor to explain this evolution—in line with additional factors that we will elaborate further shortly—is the specific problem structure in this area: desertification is a key concern for only a few countries and of peripheral relevance for almost all industrialized countries and most major developing countries. The potential regulatory impact of the desertification regime on these countries is low and related only to the financial mechanism under the desertification convention, which remains to be controlled by consensus procedures. Therefore, in this policy area of minor relevance for most (industrialized) countries, a treaty secretariat could emerge that played a substantially autonomous role and became essentially what could be referred to as an "activist bureaucracy," with more characteristics of a nongovernmental lobbyist organization than of a traditional intergovernmental bureaucracy.

The secretariats under the ozone and biodiversity conventions are largely in the middle between the extremes of the technocratic climate secretariat and the activist desertification secretariat. Biodiversity loss and ozone depletion are less prominent issues than climate change, but still more salient and potentially also costly than desertification. Ozone depletion was a salient issue in the 1980s and early 1990s, but lost this relevance later when the secretariat became operative. Biodiversity depletion is a problem hardly visible and salient. At the same time, it is highly complex and costly to regulate, as interests are difficult to be defined and many problems regulated elsewhere, for example under the FAO, the Convention on International Trade in Endangered Species of Wild Fauna and Flora, or even the World Trade Organization. Therefore, both the ozone and the biodiversity secretariats could assert some maneuvering space to develop an autonomous influence in their respective issue areas.

Similar comparisons between problem structures are more difficult for the larger agencies that address more than one problem, such as the World Bank and the secretariats of the OECD and UNEP. Even here, interview data consistently indicated that the autonomous influence of a multi-issue bureaucracy in negotiations, discourses, or the implementation of policies is more likely when "environmental low politics" are concerned.

A special case is the environmental division of the secretariat of the IMO (Campe, this volume, chapter 6). Although the regulation of shipping through standards for safety and environmental protection is not one of the most salient and most costly political controversies in world politics, the specific structure of shipping governance of the IMO creates a political context in which governments and other political actors most active in shipping have the strongest formal and informal influence on decision making. This includes both the major shipping nations (such as Panama or Liberia) and representatives from all shipping and trading nations that are more favorable to shipping as opposed to environmental interests, notably representatives from transport and trade ministries, national maritime agencies, industry, and semi-public shipping agencies. For these actors, the protection of low-cost free maritime transport and the threat of costly environmental regulation have high priority, and consequently, the room for maneuver of the environmental department within the IMO secretariat was small. Additional factors—such as the particular type of professional culture, leadership, and procedural setting within the IMO secretariat—have further limited the autonomous influence of the IMO secretariat (Campe, this volume, chapter 6).

Polity

In addition to the structure of the particular policy area in which they operate, the autonomous influence of international bureaucracies is affected by their legal, institutional, and financial framework, that is, the overall "polity" within which the staff of bureaucracies is forced to act. The project has analyzed in all nine case studies in what ways this polity affected the autonomous influence of international bureaucracies. The focus was on legal and institutional frameworks, including the mandate of the bureaucracy; on financial and material resources; and on the organizational embedding of the bureaucracy in larger settings.

Most strikingly, the project revealed several instances in which the formal legal and institutional setting of international bureaucracies was quite similar, yet with no noteworthy explanatory power regarding the autonomous influence of the bureaucracy. The comparison of the four secretariats with their similar legal, institutional, and financial framework (in particular, between the climate and the desertification secretariat) illustrates this best. Also the formal competences of the environmental departments of the OECD and the IMO are comparable, yet with surprisingly different degrees and types of influence. The World Bank is here outlier in the MANUS study program, as it has much larger formal competencies vis-à-vis recipient governments and thus naturally a much larger influence in these countries (Marschinski and Behrle, this volume, chapter 5). In such extreme cases, a stronger mandate naturally allows for a much larger influence on countries.

The finding is similar to the limited relevance of financial and material resources of international bureaucracies. Public discourse often maintains that organizational influence increases with more resources. The MANUS project refutes this claim: more or less financial and material resources are not necessarily a strong predictor for the degree and type of autonomous influence of an international bureaucracy in global environmental governance except for extreme varying cases. Material and personnel resources of three of the four treaty secretariats studied here, for example, are comparable, but the kind and degree of their influence seems unrelated to this fact. The observed variation among the secretariats thus requires other explanatory factors. In the other comparable cases analyzed in this study, where the difference in financial and material resources was sizeable yet not overwhelming, money has also not been a strong predictor.

An unsurprising exception is again the World Bank, with its enormous financial resources and staff that includes academic research divisions and a wide global dissemination network (Marschinski and Behrle, this volume, chapter 5). The World Bank has thus a much larger autonomous influence than all other bureaucracies studied here, and in a sense, its autonomy even stems from its size that makes interference from single governments more difficult. Overall, however, this project concludes that there is no clear link between the availability of funds and the autonomous influence of bureaucracies.

Interestingly, the polity of an international bureaucracy seems to shape the type of its influence with respect to the overall embedding in larger organizational structures.[3] Single-issue bureaucracies are in this respect less problematic, such as the climate or ozone secretariats that operate exclusively in a more or less clear-cut political arena. Yet the problem of fit becomes more important for multi-issue organizations and their secretariats. A striking example in this study has been the environmental department of the IMO secretariat (Campe, this volume, chapter 6). For a variety of historical and functional reasons, the regulation of environmental pollution from maritime transport falls under the IMO, which was originally set up for the negotiation and implementation of maritime safety standards. Historically and institutionally, environmental regulation has been an add-on in the IMO secretariat, which remains dominated by a staff with technical backgrounds in shipping. This institutional embedding of marine environmental policy in a larger technical, nonenvironmental bureaucracy has resulted in a domination of environmental interests through nonenvironmental interests, or in other words, in a framing of environmental concerns and problems in an industry-oriented way. Environmental policy in the IMO secretariat thus remains an uphill struggle, and even the civil servants working in the environment department have usually backgrounds in nonenvironmental fields, such as engineering or maritime law. One could speak here of a form of organizational "policy capture" of the smaller environmental concern in the larger technocratic IMO secretariat and organization.

The case of the environmental department of the World Bank is similar to the IMO case, with environmental concerns here being integrated in and dominated by the overarching organizational and discourse context of development economics and the bank's core function of project financing (Marschinski and Behrle, this volume, chapter 5). The environment directorate of the OECD secretariat in this respect likens the environmental department of the World Bank (Busch, this volume, chapter 4). The biodiversity secretariat is a counterexample: here the environmental problem is not clear-cut, but covers also core concerns of other actors— notably, the FAO, the World Intellectual Property Organization, or, as a crosscutting concern, the overarching United Nations organization. Linking the biodiversity secretariat to UNEP[4] has in this case guaranteed that the secretariat evolved into an essentially environmental actor with an organizational paradigm and staff that places central emphasis on environmental protection as its core business (Rosendal and Andresen

2004; Siebenhüner, this volume, chapter 11). This situation is similar to that of the ozone secretariat, which has been closely integrated into UNEP, making it essentially an environmentally oriented small bureaucracy. Here, one piece of counterevidence is that the issue of phasing-out industrially manufactured ozone-depleting substances could have been integrated into the work program of the UN Industrial Development Organization. It is most likely that the type of bureaucracy would have evolved differently than through integration in UNEP. Likewise, it can be shown that the particular organizational embedding of the GEF between significantly larger and more influential agencies gave its secretariat little room for maneuver and the development of autonomous policies and positions.[5]

People and Procedures

In addition to the factors of our theoretical model described previously, we found that a large part of variation in the degree and type of influence of international bureaucracies can be explained by internal factors of bureaucracies, the "people" and "procedures." The relevance of these internal factors has been overlooked or neglected by much previous research that often treated international bureaucracies as black boxes. A focus on the peoples and procedures—and, at the theoretical level, on organizational theories of management studies—allows explaining variation in the influence of bureaucracies that are otherwise largely comparable in their mandate, function, and resources. With the overall problem structure and the institutional polity of a bureaucracy, it is its leadership and staff that shape its policies, programs, and activities, and eventually its autonomous influence. We distinguish four factors: organizational expertise, organizational structure, organizational culture, and leadership.

Organizational Expertise   First, the function of international bureaucracies as knowledge brokers requires a knowledge base within the bureaucracy itself. All bureaucracies studied in this project have effective systems of generating, collecting, selecting, processing, and distributing knowledge. These systems included in most cases analytical expertise in the scientific fields related to the bureaucracy's policy problems, for example, on scientific questions of biodiversity loss; technical expertise to understand existing technologies that cause or might solve the problems; institutional expertise on how to combat the problem effectively, including knowledge on processes and suitable institutional arrangements; and often also legal expertise, for example, on options for designing international treaties or domestic regulation that often go beyond the expertise of government representatives. Overall, the comparison of all nine bureaucracies studied in this project reveals that the more expertise a bureaucracy could build up over time, the larger its cognitive influence eventually became.

Though the general relation between expertise and cognitive influence holds for all cases, the MANUS project also revealed additional conditions for the bureaucratic expertise to influence and shape discourses and debates. Technocratic and environmentalist bureaucracies of our sample predominantly excel through the neutrality of their expertise. When they accomplish the integration of almost all relevant opinions and pieces of knowledge, governments and other stakeholders are more willing to draw on their work. This integration is ensured in most cases through a broad representation of stakeholders. In the case of the Intergovernmental Panel on Climate Change that was initiated by UNEP and the WMO, the inclusion of numerous researchers from the South was pivotal for many of them to accept its results (Busch, this volume, chapter 10; Biermann 2002). Likewise, the World Bank–initiated World Commission on Dams ensured the representation of most relevant stakeholder groups. Its results influenced World Bank decisions on dam projects and its capacity-building efforts in this field (Marschinski and Behrle, this volume, chapter 5; Dingwerth 2005, 2007). By contrast, the desertification secretariat acted more as a partisan actor than as a neutral facilitator: through communication that was often perceived as partisan by Northern governments, and through the organization of a controversial high-level segment of a conference of the parties in Cuba, this bureaucracy lost significant support from rich donor countries in particular (Bauer, this volume, chapter 12).

Organizational Structure   In addition, our research revealed that certain features of organizational structures within international bureaucracies increase their influence. In particular, we found that flexible internal hierarchies—as opposed to rigid and highly formalized hierarchies—facilitated the autonomous influence of an international bureaucracy. Flexible hierarchies have a high degree of delegation where decisions are taken at the lowest possible level, and they can quickly adapt to external challenges. The UNEP secretariat is an example. The secretariat was completely reorganized within a year from a structure that focused on environmental issues (e.g., water, air pollution, or waste) to a structure that focused on functions, such as assessment, policy development, or implementation. Similar flexible hierarchies exist in the World Bank, the biodiversity secretariat, the climate secretariat, the ozone secretariat, the environment directorate of the OECD, and the GEF secretariat. By contrast, rigid and formalized hierarchies preclude rapid adaptation to novel external demands. They are marked by decision-making processes that require consent by people high in the hierarchy with long and formal information and delegation processes. For instance, the environment department of the IMO sticks to traditional and rigid hierarchical structures. Here, even day-to-day decisions require extended hierarchical processes, where officers from several hierarchical levels need to be involved. Likewise, employees in the desertification secretariat must follow strict hierarchical procedures where most decisions and external communication require the consent of the executive level. Limited external influence of the IMO—and to some extent of the desertification secretariat—relate to these rigid and formalized internal hierarchies.

Moreover, we found that bureaucracies differ regarding their internal structures for learning and review. These mechanisms can be internal and rely on internal bodies of knowledge, or external, with the inclusion of individuals and expertise outside the bureaucracy (Siebenhüner 2002a, 2002b). We found this to be a problem particular in the case of the desertification secretariat, which lacked mobilization of independent and external knowledge and deliberately organized its learning processes in a closed manner that led to the sealing off against criticism and outside knowledge. All other influential bureaucracies employ learning mechanisms, such as regular evaluation procedures in the case of the World Bank, high-level task forces in the case of UNEP secretariat, or external reviews in the case of the GEF secretariat (Siebenhüner 2008).

Organizational Culture   The case studies also revealed that organizational culture—quite often rather neglected in political science and international relations research—plays a powerful role in determining the type and also to some extent the degree of autonomous influence of international bureaucracies. We defined organizational culture as the set of commonly shared basic assumptions in an international bureaucracy that result from previous learning and that include professional cultures and backgrounds of staff. We found that although some bureaucracies have a high diversity of staff and professional cultures, others were more homogeneous. This situation has partially shaped the particular direction of the cognitive and normative influence of the respective bureaucracies.

For instance, the World Bank is the prototype of a rather homogeneous staff and professional culture that is dominated by economists. This makeup gave the World Bank a high influence in those communities, yet might also have limited the overall cognitive and normative influence of the Bank, as it became so closely associated with one perspective on problems and solutions (Marschinski and Behrle, this volume, chapter 5). The OECD environment directorate resembles the World Bank, in the sense of a strong emphasis on environmental economics in hiring policies, yet to a lesser degree, because it also has many former members of national agencies and ministries with backgrounds in law, science, or public policy in its ranks (Busch, this volume, chapter 4). The secretariat of the IMO is also dominated by one particular culture and staff composition; in this case, a culture of professionals with a seafaring and naval background. This makeup led to an industry-oriented technocratic perspective on both problems and solutions (Campe, this volume, chapter 6).

By contrast, the UNEP secretariat and most treaty secretariats are marked by high diversity of their workforce, with natural scientists, lawyers, social scientists, and administrators combined. This design prevented these bureaucracies from developing a particular professional culture associated with a particular discipline or perspective. Yet it is notable that the UNEP secretariat and most treaty secretariats have staff who are experts on and are interested in *environmental* issues, which makes environmental protection one key common theme in the overall professional cultures of these bureaucracies. The desertification secretariat is different again, because here, the autonomy granted by principals given the low priority of the issue allowed for the autonomous development of a particular *political* professional culture that made this bureaucracy evolve into an activist bureaucracy with a clear South-oriented political agenda—quite different from the more technocratic, restrained climate secretariat.

Organizational Leadership   Finally, the MANUS project revealed that the particular type of leadership of a bureaucracy leaves its marks on its autonomous influence. Even though governments as principals eventually select the chief civil servant at the helm of most bureaucracies studied,[6] this person can evolve—if charisma, vision, and leadership skills allow for it—into a powerful autonomous factor in the governance of the issue area. This evolution is all the more likely because the leader at the helm of a bureaucracy shapes the other internal factors that have been discussed previously, namely organizational expertise, procedures, and cultures.

The key distinction that we make—based on management theory—is between a "strong" and "weak" leader of international bureaucracies. We defined strong leadership as a style that is charismatic, visionary, and popular, as well as flexible and reflexive. The empirical data of this project shows that such a form of strong leadership matters and correlates with stronger autonomous external influence of the bureaucracy. For instance, both UNEP and the World Bank have been led by rather strong leaders in the past five to ten years. Both leaders initiated structural reforms in their bureaucracies and gained at the same time international reputation in pursuing environmental policies. Strong leadership also explains parts of the influence of the secretariats of the GEF and of the desertification, biodiversity and ozone treaties. By contrast, in the case of the OECD environment directorate, leadership is less pronounced, while the bureaucracy shows significant influence. We believe that in the OECD case, more subdued leadership is compensated by its deep-seated neutral and science-based expertise and effective internal procedures (Busch, this volume, chapter 4). The inverse situation characterizes the climate secretariat, where a well-respected leader is unable to develop significant autonomous external influence beyond the formal mandate. However, as debated previously, the extremely costly and salient problem structure in this field prevents other otherwise conducive factors from developing an autonomous influence of the bureaucracy.

Conclusion

Political realism and a substantial part of the institutionalist tradition in international relations research have effectively neglected the role of international bureaucracies in world politics. For realists, any autonomous agency apart from the most powerful states is theoretically not possible. International bureaucracies, in this perspective, can be only passive instruments of the powerful nations. Institutionalists have been less fundamentally opposed to the assumption of an autonomous role of international bureaucracies. Yet they too have effectively neglected the role of international bureaucracies by grounding their research in statist ontology and by focusing on intergovernmental institutions created by states. Our research—along with other recent work—has shown that both realism and traditional institutionalism are insufficient. International bureaucracies are autonomous actors in world politics that create and disseminate knowledge, shape powerful discourses and narratives on how problems are to be structured and understood, influence negotiations through ideas and expertise, and implement the standards that have been agreed to in day-to-day practices in many countries. International bureaucracies are, indeed, autonomous actors of world politics. This is one core contribution to the theory of international relations, along with other recent work.

In addition, our research has shown that international bureaucracies with similar mandates, resources, and functions vary in both degree and type of their influence. Our second core contribution to the theory of international relations thus is that institutional arrangements and designs matter less than was expected. We explain this difference in this chapter through proposing a theoretical model that combines explanatory factors at the macro level (the *problem structure*) and at the micro level: the *peoples* and *procedures* of a given bureaucracy. The core outcome of this project is that the macro level and the micro level are more relevant for explaining variation in autonomous influence than the level of the polity, that is, the legal, institutional, and organizational framework.

This proposition does not go so far as to argue that the institutional context is completely irrelevant. Once bureaucracies differ in their institutional and financial framework in fundamental aspects, institutional frameworks might well be a core explanatory factor in explaining variation in influence. Extremely large bureaucracies with a very far-reaching mandate will in absolute terms always be more influential than small bureaucracies such as treaty secretariats. The World Bank, for instance, turned out to be highly influential in this study also because of its mandate vis-à-vis grant recipient countries and its vast resources in both knowledge and money. Yet once the polity is more comparable, it becomes much less of a relevant factor in explaining variation in influence. An important exception is the organizational embedding of a bureaucracy in a larger organizational context.

Therefore, one key result of this research for the theory of international relations is the relevance of the people and procedures within the bureaucracies. It is not only the "international organizations" that have autonomous influence, as many recent studies on international relations propose. It is the *bureaucracies* within these international organizations—their staff and leaders and the way they structure their work—that matter. On a theoretical level, therefore, additional progress in understanding the role of international bureaucracies in world politics requires a stronger focus on those academic disciplines that analyze organizational behavior—namely management studies and organizational theory—but also anthropology and cultural studies. This is one core finding of the MANUS project.

The contribution of the findings to the general theory of international relations naturally depends on the degree to which they are generalizable to areas beyond international environmental cooperation. Though there are surely many factors that distinguish different policy areas, we do not see any a priori factors that would let us assume that our basic explanatory model is invalid in other areas. Naturally, the analysis of problem structure—which we have defined as a combination of cost of regulation and salience of problem—needs to be adjusted for the analysis of different policy areas. Also, the organizational cultures that we described will differ in type.

Many policy areas in international relations are also institutionally more centralized than environmental policy, with one larger bureaucracy at the center. For example, the international treaties on labor policy are administered through only one international bureaucracy—the International Labour Office—which makes this field quite different from the many treaty secretariats in the more fragmented arena of environmental policy. The situation is similar in the areas of trade, health, education, and intellectual property. This difference makes empirical cases scarcer than in environmental governance, but is not per se an indication that the overall results of a comparative research program based on our approach would be different from our study. In sum, we assume that our approach would also be useful, and possibly yield similar results, if one were to analyze a sample of bureaucracies from nonenvironmental areas. This holds true in particular, we argue, for our focus on the internal organizational elements of an international bureaucracy, where we would expect similar findings also for bureaucracies in other policy areas. One useful avenue to test this proposition, therefore, would be larger comparative programs that systematically include bureaucracies from different policy areas, and that carefully control for the influence of these differences in policy areas.

Even though our book is exclusively concerned with intergovernmental bureaucracies, we also assume that much of its methodology, as well as many of its conclusions, can be generalized to bureaucracies that have been set up by public actors that are not governments or that include private actors as members. Examples of such hybrid bureaucracies are the Arab States Broadcasting Union, the International Organization for Standardization, and the International Union for Conservation of Nature, all of which have been set up and include among their members governments as well as subnational and private actors.

With regard to policy reform, we believe that our work offers several valuable insights that could be refined and tested in further analysis. For instance, the relevance of people and procedures within bureaucracies that our research emphasizes makes organizational expertise, procedures, cultures, and leadership potential areas of policy reform. If people within bureaucracies make a substantial difference, as we argue, then the recruitment and selection of these people should become an object of stronger interest in political negotiations. A second point regarding policy reform is our finding that organizational embedding explains some variation in influence. This conclusion might support a case for a more careful discussion of what functions are located with which bureaucracies. For example, one could ask why the environmental regulation of shipping is left exclusively with IMO and not shared with UNEP or even a future "world environment organization" that is advocated by France, Germany, and other countries (Biermann and Bauer 2005). Especially such grand reform designs as have been advanced by some governments and policy consultants often lack a solid foundation in political science theory. Our approach and selected findings can help address this situation and add analytical methods, research designs, and empirical insights to a politically crucial debate.

Notes

1. Authors' interview with a member of the biodiversity secretariat, October 2003.

2. On problem structures in regime analysis, see, for example, Miles et al. 2001 and Jacobson and Brown Weiss 1998, 6–7.

3. This relates to the debate on the "problem of fit" of multilateral environmental institutions, in which potential mismatches between the structure of environmental problems and institutional and organizational responses are identified

and analyzed. See in particular Oran Young's discussion on how to match ecosystem properties with the attributes of international institutions (2002, 55–82). See also the contributions in Young, King, and Schroeder 2008.

4. The biodiversity secretariat is headquartered in Montreal, but institutionally linked—like the ozone secretariat—to the UN Environment Programme in Nairobi, notwithstanding a sizeable degree of autonomy. The climate secretariat and the desertification secretariat are linked to the overall UN organization, not to UNEP.

5. Because project implementation remains under the responsibility of UNDP, the World Bank, and UNEP, the GEF secretariat is mainly restricted to moderating and facilitating functions. See Andler, this volume, chapter 8.

6. In the case of the environmental departments of the IMO, the World Bank, and the OECD, the heads of these groups are selected through the overall director of the secretariats of IMO, the World Bank, and OECD, who again is selected by governments.

References

Abbott, Kenneth, and Duncan Snidal. 2000. "Hard and Soft Law in International Governance." *International Organization* 54 (3): 421–456.

Benedick, Richard E. 1998. *Ozone Diplomacy: New Directions in Safeguarding the Planet*. Enlarged edition. Cambridge, MA: Harvard University Press.

Biermann, Frank. 1997. "Financing Environmental Policies in the South: Experiences from the Multilateral Ozone Fund." *International Environmental Affairs* 9 (3): 179–219.

Biermann, Frank. 2002. "Institutions for Scientific Advice: Global Environmental Assessments and their Influence in Developing Countries." *Global Governance* 8 (2): 195–219.

Biermann, Frank, and Steffen Bauer, editors. 2005. *A World Environment Organization: Solution or Threat for Effective International Environmental Governance?* Aldershot, UK: Ashgate.

Busch, Per-Olof, and Helge Jörgens. 2005. "International Patterns of Environmental Policy Change and Convergence." *European Environment* 15 (2): 80–101.

Cox, Robert W., and Harold K. Jacobson, editors. 1973. *The Anatomy of Influence: Decision Making in International Organization*. New Haven: Yale University Press.

Dingwerth, Klaus. 2005. "The Democratic Legitimacy of Public-Private Rule-Making: What Can We Learn from the World Commission on Dams?" *Global Governance* 11 (1): 65–83.

Dingwerth, Klaus. 2007. *The New Transnationalism: Transnational Governance and Democratic Legitimacy*. Basingstoke, UK: Palgrave Macmillan.

Jacobson, Harold K., and Edith Brown Weiss. 1998. "A Framework for Analysis." In *Engaging Countries: Strengthening Compliance with International Environmental Accords*, edited by Edith Brown Weiss and Harald K. Jacobson, 1–18. Cambridge, MA: MIT Press.

Miles, Edward L., Arild Underdal, Steinar Andresen, Jørgen Wettestad, Jon Birger Skjærseth, and Elaine M. Carlin, editors. 2001. *Environmental Regime Effectiveness: Confronting Theory with Evidence*. Cambridge, MA: MIT Press.

Parson, Edward A. 2003. *Protecting the Ozone Layer: Science and Strategy*. Oxford: Oxford University Press.

Pattberg, Philipp. 2006. "The Influence of Global Business Regulation. Beyond Good Corporate Conduct." *Business and Society Review* 111 (3): 241–268.

Rosendal, G. Kristin, and Steinar Andresen. 2004. *UNEP's Role in Enhancing Problem-Solving Capacity in Multilateral Environmental Agreements: Coordination and Assistance in the Biodiversity Conservation Cluster*. FNI Report 10/2003. Lysaker: Fridtjof Nansen Institute.

Siebenhüner, Bernd. 2002a. "How do Scientific Assessments Learn? Part 1. Conceptual Framework and Case Study of the IPCC." *Environmental Science and Policy* 248: 1–11.

Siebenhüner, Bernd. 2002b. "How do Scientific Assessments Learn? Part 2. Case Study of the LRTAP Assessments and Comparative Conclusions." *Environmental Science and Policy* 5: 421–427.

Siebenhüner, Bernd. 2008. "Learning in International Organizations in Global Environmental Governance." *Global Environmental Governance* 8 (4): 92–116.

Tolba, Mostafa K., and Iwona Rummel-Bulska. 1998. *Global Environmental Diplomacy. Negotiating Environmental Agreements for the World, 1973–1992*. Cambridge, MA: MIT Press.

Töpfer, Klaus. 1998. *United Nations Task Force on Environment and Human Settlements*. Nairobi: United Nations Offices at Nairobi.

Wettestad, Jørgen. 2001. "The Vienna Convention and Montreal Protocol on Ozone-Layer Depletion." In *Environmental Regime Effectiveness. Confronting Theory with Evidence*, edited by Edward L. Miles, Arild Underdal, Steinar Andresen, Jørgen Wettestad, Jon Birger Skjærseth, and Elaine M. Carlin, 149–170. Cambridge, MA: MIT Press.

Young, Oran R. 2002. *The Institutional Dimensions of Environmental Change: Fit, Interplay, and Scale*. Cambridge, MA: MIT Press.

Young, Oran R., Leslie A. King and Heike Schroeder, editors. 2008. *Institutions and Environmental Change: Principal Findings, Applications, and Research Frontiers*. Cambridge, MA: MIT Press.

Contributors

Lydia Andler is a project manager with the German development bank "KfW Bankengruppe," where she specializes in the financial sector and economic infrastructure of Latin America and the Caribbean. She holds the German equivalent of a Master of Arts degree (*Diplom*) in Public Policy from the University of Potsdam, and a Master of Arts degree in Development Economics from the University of Sussex, Brighton, UK.

Steffen Bauer is a senior researcher at the German Development Institute (DIE) in Bonn, Germany, and a research analyst with the Advisory Council on Global Change (WBGU) of the Federal Government of Germany. He is a founding member of the Global Governance Project (http://www.glogov.org), where he has coordinated the research group "Managers of Global Change" (MANUS). He specializes in international organization and global environmental governance, with a focus on the United Nations, and has published widely on international bureaucracies, sustainable development, the global governance of desertification, and the security and development implications of global climate change. He is co-editor (with Frank Biermann) of *A World Environment Organization: Solution or Threat for Effective International Environmental Governance?* (Aldershot, UK: Ashgate, 2005).

Frank Biermann is a professor of Political Science and professor of Environmental Policy Sciences at the Vrije Universiteit Amsterdam, The Netherlands. He specializes in global environmental governance, with emphasis on climate negotiations, UN reform, global adaptation governance, public-private governance mechanisms, the role of science, North–South relations, and trade and environment conflicts. Biermann holds a number of research management positions, including head of the Department of Environmental Policy Analysis of the Institute for Environmental Studies (IVM) at the Vrije Universiteit and director-general of the Netherlands Research School for the Socioeconomic and Natural Sciences of the Environment (SENSE), a national research network of nine research institutes with 150 scientists and 350 PhD students. Biermann is also the founding chair of the annual series of Berlin Conferences on the Human Dimensions of Global Environmental Change; the founding director of the Global Governance Project (http://www.glogov.org); and the chair of the Earth

System Governance Scientific Planning Committee, a group of international experts appointed by the International Human Dimensions Programme on Global Environmental Change to draft a new ten-year international research program on governance and institutions (www.earthsystemgovernance.org).

Steffen Behrle   is an associate expert for energy policy and management in the Division for Sustainable Development at the United Nations Department of Economic and Social Affairs in New York. He works on both analytical and operational aspects of access to energy, energy efficiency, cleaner energy technologies, and renewable energy. He regularly works with the United Nations Commission on Sustainable Develolpment. He holds the German equivalent of a Master of Arts degree (*Diplom*) in Political Science from the Freie Universität Berlin, Germany, and has also studied international relations, development policy, and environment policy at the Graduate School of Duke University, NC.

Per-Olof Busch   is a researcher with the Environmental Policy Research Center of the Freie Universität Berlin, Germany. He is a member of the board of the Center, and coordinator of its working groups on "Global Environmental Governance" and on "Environmental Pioneers and the Diffusion of Environmental Policy Innovations." Busch specializes in environmental policy analysis from the perspective of both Comparative Politics and International Relations. He has analyzed the impact of international institutions and trade on the convergence of national environmental policies, the effectiveness of international organizations in global environmental governance, the impact of international processes of learning and emulation on the international spread of environmental policies, and the determinants of environmental pioneering behavior of states. He is a member of the board of the Environmental Policy and Global Change section of the German Political Science Association.

Sabine Campe   is a research associate with the Collaborative Research Center "Governance in Areas of Limited Statehood" at the Freie Universität Berlin, Germany. She was previously a research fellow with the Potsdam Institute for Climate Impact Research, Germany, and a visiting fellow with the Vrije Universiteit Amsterdam, The Netherlands. She holds the German equivalent of a Master of Arts degree (*Diplom*) in International Relations from the Freie Universität Berlin, Germany. She specializes in global environmental governance, business actors in international relations, and transnational public-private partnerships, and has authored several publications in these fields.

Klaus Dingwerth   is assistant professor of International Relations at the Institute for Intercultural and International Studies at the University of Bremen, Germany, and coordinator of the research group "MecGlo—New Mechanisms of Global Governance" of the international Global Governance Project (http://www.glogov.org). He specializes in transnational environmental governance and is the author of *The New Transnationalism: Transnational Governance and Democratic Legitimacy* (Basingstoke, UK: Palgrave Macmillan, 2007).

Torsten Grothmann   is a researcher and project manager at the Potsdam Institute for Climate Impact Research (PIK) and at the University of Oldenburg,

Germany. He is a methodology expert for stakeholder dialogue, research interviews, and questionnaire design and analysis, and specializes in strategies for promoting behaviorial change, mainly related to proactive adaptation to climate change and natural hazards. In this context, he has advised several insurance companies and governmental institutions of the European Union and at the national level. He holds a PhD and the German equivalent of a Master of Arts degree (*Diplom*) in Psychology. He has authored several publications in the fields of natural hazard management, adaptation to climate change, and environmental psychology.

Robert Marschinski is a researcher at the Potsdam Institute for Climate Impact Research (PIK), Germany, where he specializes in economic and policy issues related to climate change. He holds a Master of Science degree in Physics from the University of Bologna, Italy, and is now finalizing his thesis for a PhD in Economics. He has been a visiting researcher at The Energy and Resource Institute (TERI) in New Delhi and a short-term consultant with the Development Economics Research Group of the World Bank. He has authored several publications in the fields of physics and economics.

Bernd Siebenhüner is professor of Ecological Economics at the Oldenburg Center for Sustainability Economics and Management (CENTOS) at Carl von Ossietzky University of Oldenburg, Germany. He is also a faculty member of the Global Governance Project (http://www.glogov.org). He holds a PhD in Economics and master's degrees in Economics and Political Science. He has conducted numerous research projects in the fields of international organizations, global environmental governance, social learning, corporate sustainability strategies, climate and biodiversity governance, and the role of science in global environmental governance.

Mireia Tarradell is a PhD candidate in international relations at the Freie Universität Berlin, Germany, and a research fellow with the Global Governance Project. Mireia's research focuses on the intersection of global environmental change and international organization, with particular emphasis on questions of scientific expertise and of equity and efficiency in transnational sustainability governance. Currently, she is researching the role of intergovernmental organizations in partnerships for sustainability in Mesoamerica. Previously, she has worked for Local Governments for Sustainability (ICLEI), a non-profit international association of local governments and national and regional local government organizations based in Freiburg, Germany. She has published on national strategies for sustainability governance and expert perceptions of the effectiveness of intergovernmental environmental organizations. She holds a degree in environmental sciences from the Autonomous University of Barcelona, Spain.

Index